SARACENIC HERALDRY

SARACENIC HERALDRY

A SURVEY *by* L. A. MAYER, PH.D.

OXFORD

OXFORD
UNIVERSITY PRESS

Great Clarendon Street, Oxford OX2 6DP

Oxford University Press is a department of the University of Oxford.
It furthers the University's objective of excellence in research, scholarship,
and education by publishing worldwide in

Oxford New York

Athens Auckland Bangkok Bogotá Buenos Aires Calcutta
Cape Town Chennai Dar es Salaam Delhi Florence Hong Kong Istanbul
Karachi Kuala Lumpur Madrid Melbourne Mexico City Mumbai
Nairobi Paris São Paulo Singapore Taipei Tokyo Toronto Warsaw

with associated companies in Berlin Ibadan

Published in the United States
by Oxford University Press Inc., New York

Special edition for Sandpiper Books Ltd., 1999

British Library Cataloguing in Publication Data
Data available

ISBN 0-19-817120-X

1 3 5 7 9 10 8 6 4 2

Printed in Great Britain
on acid-free paper by
Bookcraft (Bath) Ltd,
Midsomer Norton

PREFACE

THE object of this book is to provide a fully documented armorial roll of Saracenic sultans, princes, and knights, designed to meet the frequently expressed wish of students of Muslim archaeology for a work of this description. If the list of holders of Ayyubid and Mamluk blazons given in the relevant chapters comes any nearer to being complete than any hitherto published, and if the inscriptions are correctly read, and the knights, so far as identified, properly identified, then the book will have served its purpose. On the other hand, it was not considered necessary to register every single variant of a blazon on potsherds and other objects not accompanied by historical inscriptions.

Since the owners and custodians of Muslim objects with blazons, as well as European heraldists who are interested in Saracenic heraldry, by far outnumber the small group of Muslim archaeologists, the following pages have been written chiefly for their guidance. It is for their convenience, too, that translations and explanations have been added which would be superfluous in a work intended for Arabists.

In transliterating personal names I have been guided by the spelling used by Arab authors, i.e. verbal descriptions of vowels and consonants, or failing this by vowel-signs indicated by scribes. In cases where neither was available, the transcription has been based upon analogy or upon traditional spelling. The object of this system was to convey to the reader an accurate graphic rendering of these names as expressed through the medium of fully vocalized Arabic script and not the phonetical values as pronounced by Turkish tongues therefore Ulmās instead of Ölmäs, Qurqumās instead of Qorqmäs, &c.

Once a transcription had been adopted it was adhered to throughout the book, except in cases in which the Arabic text reproduced here made a different one necessary. Then the latter was used in the translation of the relevant inscription, and in the translation only, e.g. always Māridīnī, but on p. 56: Māridānī; always Naurūzī, but on p. 255: Nayrūzī.

Abbreviations will be found either on p. xvi or at the head of the Bibliography. The latter includes books and articles in European languages only, in which blazons are discussed, mentioned or reproduced. Oriental texts will be found in the footnotes; they have been excluded from the Bibliography except in the case of Quatremère's translation of the Sulūk, which figures there for the sake of its commentary.

In the course of collecting the material and the writing of this book, I fear I must have sorely tried the patience of all those to whose care Saracenic blazons are entrusted or who happen to possess any knowledge of the objects described or the subject-matter dealt with. Yet with one exception, all the doors at which I knocked were opened to me, so that I deem it a pleasant duty to thank the various institutions and private collectors, too numerous to be mentioned individually (but whose names appear as owners in the description of the respective objects), for allowing me to make a study of their treasures and to publish a description of them. I should like to express my grateful thanks to Mr. E.T. Richmond, Director of Antiquities, Jerusalem, for constant support; to Mr. R. A. Harari, of London, for his unfailing help; to Prof. Gaston Wiet, under whose enlightened directorship the treasures of the National Museum of Arab Art, Cairo, were made available for research; to Captain K. A. C. Creswell, F.S.A., in whose collection of photographs I found several with blazons that I am now glad to publish; to Prof. Ernst Herzfeld, Berlin; Prof. Karl Wulzinger, Karlsruhe; Prof. R. M. Riefstahl, New York; Mr. Cyrill Wallis, Edinburgh; Dr. C. J. Lamm, Roslags-Näsby; Prof. L. Rosenthal, Lyon; Mr. A. H. Christie, Cromer, and Monsieur J. Sauvaget, of the Institut Français de Damas, for sketches or photographs of various blazons and for permission to publish them; to Prof. M. Sobernheim and Prof. E. Kühnel, both of Berlin, for photographs and descriptive notes and for their valuable suggestions when we discussed Muslim heraldry together; to Minister-Resident Max Freiherr v. Oppenheim, Berlin, who expressly unpacked a portion of his rich collection of Oriental objects for my benefit; and to Mme Max van Berchem, Geneva, who kindly allowed me to study the collection of squeezes, photographs, and travel notes left by her late husband. In all the cases in which the above-mentioned scholars had the kindness to supply me with texts of inscriptions, their names are given, in brackets, at the end of the relevant texts.

I wish to record my deep gratitude to the late Prof. J. Horovitz of the University of Frankfurt o/M, Visiting Director of the Oriental Institute of the Hebrew University, Jerusalem, for having read and given me the benefit of his valuable remarks on the manuscript of the Introduction and twelve items of the Armorial Roll, and to tender my warmest thanks to the Rev. H. Danby, D.D., Canon of St. George's, Jerusalem, for going over approximately two-thirds of the Introduction, as well as to Mr. St. H. Stephan and

Mr. M. Avi-Yona of the Department of Antiquities, Jerusalem, for their share in reading the proofs, to the latter quite especially for his checking of the index.

All the drawings have been prepared by Mr. N. Reiss, Assistant of Dr. E. L. Sukenik, Archaeological Department of the Hebrew University, partly from drawings made by Miss G. R. Levy, London, and partly from photographs and squeezes.

My special thanks are due to the Government of Palestine, without whose generous assistance the book would never have been published in its present form.

Last but not least it is a pleasant duty to thank the officers of the Clarendon Press for their untiring courtesy, and the readers of the Press for their interest and attention in producing this volume.

The reader is asked to make allowance for any shortcomings in the present study since, although the collecting of the material was started in 1923, the book itself was actually compiled during four short periods of leave abroad.

The terminology usual in descriptions of European coats of arms has—so far as possible—purposely been dispensed with.

In conclusion, I cannot refrain from making a similar appeal to that with which Rogers Bey, some fifty years ago, closed his paper on Muslim Heraldry: that all those who own, or who know of any Muslim objects with blazons should send me rubbings of them and thereby assist me in the pursuit of heraldic studies.

L. A. M.

CONTENTS

LIST OF AND NOTES ON THE ILLUSTRATIONS

PICTURES marked with a proper name only illustrate objects mentioned in the Armorial Roll, where additional information will be found under that name. To facilitate the search occasionally either the number of the object or the page on which it is discussed has been added. The name of the photographer appears in square brackets. Where his name is not given the photographs were supplied either by the owner (whether Museum or private collector) or taken by the present writer.

PLATE I. POTSHERDS. 1, 3, Kaiser-Friedrich-Museum, Berlin. 4, MZERIB, bridge [*Creswell*]. GLASS-SHERDS. 5, 6, Kaiser-Friedrich-Museum. 7, Perfume-sprinkler, Coll. Paravicini, Cairo-Zeitun. 8, Ghāzī b. Abī Bakr [*Creswell*].

PLATE II. POTSHERDS. 1, Max-Freiherr-von-Oppenheim-Stiftung, Berlin. 2, Metropolitan Museum of Art, New York. 3, Victoria and Albert Museum, London. 4, National Museum of Arab Art, Cairo. 5, Hunting bowl, Livrustkammaren, Stockholm.

PLATE III. POTSHERDS. 1, Kaiser-Freidrich-Museum. 2–4, 6, 7, 8 (Inscription on breast: *al-Malik aṣ-Ṣāliḥ*), 9–13, National Museum of Arab Art. 5, Victoria and Albert Museum.

PLATE IV. POTSHERDS. 1, 2, 4, 6, Musée des Arts Décoratifs, Paris. 7, Metropolitan Museum of Art. 9, 10, National Museum of Arab Art. 5, Kaiser-Friedrich-Museum. 3, Victoria and Albert Museum. GLASS-SHERD. 8, Kaiser-Friedrich-Museum.

PLATE V. POTSHERDS. 1, Institut de Damas, Damascus [*de Lorey*]. 3, 4, Metropolitan Museum of Art. 6, 13, Victoria and Albert Museum. 7–11, 15, National Museum of Arab Art. 12, 16, 17, Musée des Arts Décoratifs. 14, British Museum, London. ARCHITECTURE. 2, Madrasa, Damascus [*de Lorey*]. COMB. 5, National Museum of Arab Art.

PLATE VI. POTSHERDS. 1, Musée des Arts Décoratifs. 2, 8, Victoria and Albert Museum, London (*. . . al-aʿazz al-akhaṣṣ Saʿd ad-dīn*). 3, Fitzwilliam Museum, Cambridge. 4, Alṭunbughā al-Māridīnī. 5, National Museum of Arab Art. 6, 7, 9, 10, 12, Kaiser-Friedrich-Museum, Berlin. 11, Khālid. TEXTILES. 13, National Museum of Arab Art.

PLATE VII. POTSHERDS. 1, 4, 6, 16, National Museum of Arab Art. 5, 7, 11, 15, Metropolitan Museum of Art. 8, Max-Freiherr-von-Oppenheim-Stiftung. 3, 10, 17, Victoria and Albert Museum. 2, Kaiser-Friedrich-Museum. GLASS-SHERDS. 12, 13, Kaiser-Friedrich-Museum.

PLATE VIII. Restored BOWL and POTSHERDS. 1, 8, British Museum. 2, Fitzwilliam Museum. 3, 7, 9, Kaiser-Friedrich-Museum. 4, Kunstgewerbe-Museum, Leipzig. 5, 10, National Museum of Arab Art. 6, Max-Freiherr-von-Oppenheim-Stiftung.

PLATE IX. POTSHERDS. 1, 3, 6 (*al-maulawi ash-Shihābi Aḥ[mad]*), 11, 13, 14, 15, National Museum of Arab Art. 2, 5, 7, 8, 16, Max-Freiherr-von-Oppenheim-Stiftung. 4, 12, Kaiser-Friedrich-Museum. 9, (*mimmā ʿumila bi-rasm al- . . . al-muḥtaramī as-saifī Saif ad-dīn dāma ʿizzuhu wa-naṣruhu*, text partly read by Wiet), Victoria and Albert Museum.

PLATE X. POTSHERDS. 1, 5, Max-Freiherr-von-Oppenheim-Stiftung. 2, Metropolitan Museum of Art. 4, 6, 8–12, 14, 16, National Museum of Arab Art. 13, Victoria and Albert Museum. 15, Augsburg. GLASS-SHERD. 3, Kaiser-Friedrich-Museum.

PLATE XI. POTSHERDS. 1, 3, Max-Freiherr-von-Oppenheim-Stiftung. 2, 5–7, 10, 11, 13, 15–17, 19, National Museum of Arab Art. 4, 8, 12, 14, Kaiser-Friedrich-Museum. 9, Victoria and Albert Museum. GLASS-SHERD. 18, Kaiser-Friedrich-Museum.

PLATE XII. POTSHERDS. 1, Shihāb ad-dīn b. Farajī. 2, Max-Freiherr-von-Oppenheim-Stiftung. 3–5, Metropolitan Museum of Art. 7–10, National Museum of Arab Art. 11, Kaiser-Friedrich-Museum. GLASS-SHERD. 6, Kaiser-Friedrich-Museum.

PLATE XII*a*. GLASS-SHERD. 1, Kaiser-Friedrich-Museum. POTSHERDS. 2, 3, Palestine Archaeological Museum, Jerusalem. 4, Victoria and Albert Museum. 5, Kunstgewerbe-Museum, Leipzig. 6–8, National Museum of Arab Art. 9, Victoria and Albert Museum.

PLATE XII*b*. POTSHERDS. 1, Kaiser-Friedrich-Museum. 2, 3, 5, 6, 9, 10, 11, National Museum of Arab Art. 4, 7, Fitzwilliam Museum. 8, Max-Freiherr-von-Oppenheim-Stiftung. 12, Metropolitan Museum of Art.

PLATE XIII. POTSHERDS. 1, Musée des Arts Décoratifs, Paris. 2, 14, 20, British Museum. 3, 4, 5, 8, 13, National Museum of Arab Art. 6, Fitzwilliam Museum, Cambridge. 7, 9, 10, 18, Kaiser-Friedrich-Museum. 11, Kunstgewerbe-Museum, Leipzig. 12, 15, 16, Victoria and Albert Museum. 17, Musée du Cinquantenaire, Bruxelles. 19, Rijksmuseum, Amsterdam.

PLATE XIV. Mūsā b. ʿAlī b. Qalāūn.

PLATE XV. Āqūsh, Governor of Kerak.

PLATE XVI. Ṭuquztamur [*Lehnert and Landrock*, Cairo].

PLATE XVII. Bahādur al-Ḥamawī [*Cipriani*, Florence].

PLATE XVIII. Maḥmūd b. Shirwīn.

PLATE XIX. 1, 3, Maḥmūd b. Zankī (Nuradin) [*Creswell*]. 2, Ḥaidar b. al-ʿAskarī [*Aroichan*, Damascus]. 4, Aḥmad b. Ismaʿīl al-Kujukī [*Creswell*].

PLATE XX. 1, Nūr ad-dīn [ʿAlī], son of ʿImād ad-dīn (p. 54). 2, 4, Kitbughā. 3, copper coins of al-Malik al-Manṣūr, Palestine Archaeological Museum; 5, of al-Malik an-Nāṣir, Ashmolean Museum, Oxford; 6, struck at Hama, Palestine Archaeological Museum.

PLATE XXI. Alṭunbughā al-Māridīnī.

PLATE XXII. 1, 2, Ṭurjī. 3, Muḥammad b. Kitbughā.

PLATE XXIII. Muḥammad al-khāzindār.

PLATE XXIV. 1, Aljāy [*Creswell*]. 2, Shaikhū (No. 12) [*Creswell*]. 3, Mubārak b. Sāliḥ. 4, Palace of Ṭāz, Cairo [*Creswell*].

PLATE XXV. 1, 2, Khudābirdī aẓ-Ẓāhirī.

PLATE XXVI. 1, Almalik (No. 5). 2, Qumārī. 3, Qāzān.

PLATE XXVII. Qarāsunqur.

PLATE XXVIII. 1, Mubārak. 2, Bashtāk (No 2).

PLATE XXIX. Mankuwīrish [*Schweig*].

PLATE XXX. 1, Aydamur. 2, 3, Āqbughā min 'Abd al-Wāḥid.

PLATE XXXI. 1, 'Azīz al-'Alāwī. 2, Ṣirghitmish, No. 3.

PLATE XXXII. Baktūt al-Qaramānī.

PLATE XXXIII. 1, 2, Ishiqtamur al-Māridīnī. 3, Copper dish tinned over (*mimmā 'umila bi-rasm al-janāb al-'ālī al-maulawī al-amīrī Shādbak*), N. Ohan & Sons, Jerusalem. 4, Bahādur aẓ-Ẓāhirī. 5, 6, Abū Bakr b. 'Abd al-Bārr.

PLATE XXXIV. 1, Quṭlūbughā. 2, Mūsā b. Yaghmūr [*Lehnert and Landrock*].

PLATE XXXV. 1, Aynāl al-Yūsufī [*Creswell*]. 2, Sanjar al-Jāwlī (No. 3). 3, Qauṣūn (No. 4) [*Creswell*].

PLATE XXXVI. 1, Bahādur Āṣ. 2, Sīdī Muḥammad (p. 157 f.). 3, Asandamur. 4, Ṭughaydamur.

PLATE XXXVII. Asandamur [*Aroichan*].

PLATE XXXVIII. Bahādur al-Badrī.

PLATE XXXIX. 1, Barqūq (p. 103, second item). 2, Kunjak al-Khwārizmī (*Van Berchem's notes*].

PLATE XL. 1, Aydakīn [*Creswell*]. 2, Muḥammad b. Aḥmad. 3, Bahādur Āṣ. 4, Salmā, wife of 'Alī [*Creswell*].

PLATE XLI. GLASS LAMPS. 1, Metropolitan Museum of Art. 2, Aydakīn. 3, Aḥmad al-mihmandār. 4, Tankiz (No. 5).

PLATE XLII. COPPER VESSELS tinned over. 1, 2, 4 samples of non-heraldic rosettes. 1, *'izz li-maulānā as-sulṭān al-malik al-'ālim al-'āmil* [*a*]*l-ma.* 2, *'izz li-maulānā as-sulṭān al-malik al-kāmil al-'ālim al-'ādil Saif ad-dunyā wa-d-dīn Sha'bān* (British Museum). 3, Ibrāhīm b. 'Aqīl. 4, *al-'ādil al-ghāzī Saif ad-dunyā wa-d-dīn Sha'bān.* 5, 'Alī b. Hilāl ad-daula. 6, Qushtumur.

PLATE XLIII. 1, Khalīl. 2, 'Alī b. Muḥammad (p. 56, middle).

PLATE XLIV. 1, Kujkun [*Creswell*]. 2, Almalik (No. 4) [*Schweig*]. 3, 'Alā' ad-dīn ['Alī] al-Barīdī.

PLATE XLV. Ibrāhīm b. Baktamur al-Ḥusāmī.

PLATE XLVI. Arghūn an-Nāṣirī (p. 77; *Van Berchem's notes*).

PLATE XLVII. 1, Aḥmad b. Buraq. 2, Ibrāhīm b. 'Aqīl.

PLATE XLVIII. Muḥammad al-'Alawī.

PLATE XLIX. Abu-l-Fidā'.

PLATES L and LI. MS. Leiden, Or. 419 W. (p. 18).

PLATE LII. 1, Ṣalāḥ ad-dīn b. Samrī. 2, Bowl, Kaiser-Friedrich-Museum (p. 17 bottom).

PLATE LIII. 1, Duqmāq [*Derounian*]. 2, Yūsuf aẓ-Ẓāhirī [*Creswell*].

PLATE LIV. 1, 2, Shaikh [*Aroichan*]. 3, Naurūz al-Ḥāfiẓī. 4, Damurdāsh al-Muḥammadī.

PLATE LV. Yūnus ad-Dawādār [1, *Creswell*].

PLATE LVI. 1, Aytmish al-Bajāsī. 2, 3, Muḥammad al-Malaṭī. 4, 'Alī b. Shāhīn.

PLATE LVII. 1–4, Ibrāhīm b. Muḥammad b. Yāsīn (the sequence of the text is 1, 4, 2, 3). 5, Muḥyī ad-dīn al-Qādirī. 6, Aḥmad b. Muḥammad b. Idrīs.

PLATE LVIII. 1, 2, Uzdamur. 3, 4, Ulmās. 5, 7, Nāniq al-Ashrafī. 6, 8, Jānībak (p. 130).

PLATE LIX. 1, Timrāz al-Mu'ayyadī. 2, 3, Fāṭima bint Sūdūn al-Mu'ayyadī. 4, 5, Sūdūn al-Yashbakī.

PLATE LX. Muqbil ar-Rūmī.

PLATE LXI. 1, Khushqadam. 2, Ṭashtamur al-'Alā'ī. 3, Maḥmūd al-'Ainī [all *Creswell*].

PLATE LXII. 1, Āqbirdī b. 'Alībāy. 2, 4, Khāirbak min Aynāl (and not Jānibak, p. 129). 3, Sībāy b. Bukht Jukhā. 5, 9, Timrāz. 6, Jauhar al-Mu'īnī 7, 'Allān al-Mu'izzī. 8, Ḥalīma bint an-Nāniq. 10, 11, Tānībak. 14, 15, Timurbāy al-Yaḥyāwī (now in the National Museum of Arab Art). 12, 13, Taghrīwirmish.

PLATE LXIII. Qajmās al-Isḥāqī.

PLATE LXIV. Piece of armour, Musée de la Ville, Lyon.

PLATE LXV. 1, Damurdāsh al-Ashrafī. 2, Bāyazīd. 3, Yashbak al-Ḥamzāwī.

PLATE LXVI. 1, Yashbak ash-Sha'bānī [*Sobernheim*]. 2, Sūdūn b. Jānibak [*Creswell*]. 3, Khān aṣ-Sābūn, Aleppo [*Derounian*]. 4, Qānṣūh al-Yaḥyāwī (No. 4) [*Derounian*].

PLATE LXVII. 1, Fountain in the Marqas Street, Damascus known as the Sabīl Sayyid Aḥmad al-Badawī [1] *ansha'a hadhā as-sabīl al-mubārak al-maqarr al-ashraf*... [3] ...*al-Ashrafī maulānā* (blazon) *malik al-umarā' kāfil al-mamlak*[2]*a ash-sha'miyya a'azza Allāh anṣārahu fī shuhūr sanat thalath* (? *īn*?) [4] *wa-thamanimi'a*. [*Aroichan*]. 2, Aynāl al-'Alā'ī. 3, Aynāl al-Ashrafī [*Creswell*].

PLATE LXVIII. 1, Uzbak al-Yūsufī. 2, 3, Timur min Maḥmūdshāh. 4, 6, Copper dishes tinned over, Max-Freiherr-von-Oppenheim-Stiftung. 5. Damurdāsh al-Ashrafī. 7, 8, Bowl made for the Treasurer of Barqūq, Royal Scottish Museum, Edinburgh. 9, 10, Khushqadam.

PLATE LXIX. 1, Anonymous inscription above the lintel of a portal of a palace in Siūfiyya (p. 228 f.). 2, Uzbak al-Yūsufī [both *Creswell*].

PLATES LXX and LXXI. Typical forgeries.

ABBREVIATIONS

b.	= bottom of page, from bottom	Na.	= Nāṣir ad-dīn
m.	= middle of page	Najm.	= Najm ad-dīn
t.	= from top	R.	= Rukn ad-dīn
A.	= ʿAlāʾ ad-dīn	S.	= Saif ad-dīn
Al.	= ʿAlam ad-dīn	Sa.	= Saʿd ad-dīn
B.	= Badr ad-dīn	Ṣal.	= Ṣalāḥ ad-dīn
Ba.	= Bahāʾ ad-dīn	Ṣār.	= Ṣārim ad-dīn
Bu.	= Burhān ad-dīn	Sh.	= Shams ad-dīn
Gh.	= Ghars ad-dīn	Sha.	= Sharaf ad-dīn
H.	= Ḥusām ad-dīn	Shi.	= Shihāb ad-dīn
I.	= ʿIzz ad-dīn	Shibl.	= Shibl ad-daula
J.	= Jamāl ad-dīn	T.	= Taqī ad-dīn
M.	= Muḥibb ad-dīn	Taj	= Tāj ad-dīn
N.	= Nūr ad-dīn	Z.	= Zain ad-dīn

INTRODUCTION

DEFINITIONS

IN considering the emblems which form the subject of this book, and which scholars have been accustomed to term heraldic,[1] it should be borne in mind that some have been in doubt as to whether 'coat of arms' was the proper description for such emblems.[2] It is only natural, therefore, that certain scholars should have suggested other terms, such as episema[3] or badge.[4] Taking as our starting-point the definition of a blazon considered by Fox-Davies[5] to be one of the best, namely that a coat of arms 'requires the twofold qualification that the design must be hereditary and must be connected with armour', Saracenic blazons are blazons in the full sense of the word, and we shall therefore call them so in the following pages.

To describe the blazons we are dealing with as 'Arabic' or 'Muslim' would be equally inaccurate, because the term 'Arabic' would exclude the vast majority of Ayyubid and Mamluk amirs who were of Kurdish, Turkish, or Circassian origin, while 'Muslim' would include Rasūlids, Naṣrids, Urtuqids, Saljūqs, and others, whose heraldry is not dealt with in this volume. Thus, despite the fact that the exact meaning of the term 'Saracenic' is still open to discussion, it has been chosen as conveying to most readers the idea of 'Muslim in Syria, Palestine, and Egypt, during the period which followed the Crusades and preceded the Ottoman conquest'—which is exactly the compass, geographical as well as historical, of the section of Oriental heraldry which forms the subject of this book.

SOURCES

Literary sources for our knowledge of Saracenic heraldry are very scanty indeed. Eliminating mere quotations and repetitions, the number of passages in Arabic literature in which the word 'blazon' occurs is well under fifty,[6] and of these a fair proportion contains no information of value. In the absence of 'Colleges of Arms', armorial rolls and technical texts are non-existent, and with but a single exception[7] the description of blazons is verbal, and without

[1] Prisse d'Avennes, Karabacek, Rogers, Artin, Ströhl, van Berchem, Lane-Poole, Sarre, Kühnel, Mittwoch. [2] Prinet, H. Devonshire.

[3] A. de B. (Adalbert de Beaumont?), *Bulletin Critique*, XXIV. 527. [4] Gayet, *L'Art Arabe*, p. 280.

[5] *Complete Guide to Heraldry*, London 1925, p. 14. [6] The most interesting ones quoted on p. 28, nn. 1, 2.

[7] Dhahabī, *al-Muntaqā*, MS. in the library of Zeki Pasha, Cairo, s.a. 694 A.H.

any pictorial record to help identification and attribution. Saracenic coats of arms are sometimes mentioned in the chronicles of the Crusaders,[1] but the descriptions given are generally lacking in the very details that would be of assistance in reconstructing and establishing blazons of which no originals have so far been discovered.

European travellers and pilgrims in the later Middle Ages have often misinterpreted the blazons they came across in the East and attributed them to the wrong persons, especially if they resembled European coats of arms.[2] All the greater, therefore, is the importance to be attached to the original blazons and to the inscriptions accompanying them. These were shown on every possible object and made in every possible material, and we actually find them everywhere: in architecture, on the façades of houses of every description, on window-grilles, doors, on capitals of columns, wall-paintings, coats of mail, weapons, coins, lamps, combs, horse-armour, textiles, manuscripts, water-bottles, plates and dishes of all kinds, on figures of shadow-plays, and on perfume sprays. It goes without saying that where the blazon went with a document of an official character or was made of precious material, it was more carefully and reliably depicted than in the case of a cheap piece of crockery; for that reason we have always taken coins, architectural monuments, and glass objects into first consideration, although even here the difference is very small indeed. It is a great pity, in this connexion, that one of the most reliable and informative sources of knowledge of the heraldry of other countries, namely the seals, bear no heraldic devices in Saracenic countries. In illuminated manuscripts blazons as a rule are very carefully painted, but the number of such manuscripts extant is too small to be of any consequence.

[1] e.g. *Itinerarium Ricardi*, ed. Stubbs, p. 272, or *Joinville*, ed. de Wailly, p. 108.

[2] Bertrandon de la Broquière, *Le Voyage d'Outremer* (ed. Schefer, p. 37), attributed a fleur-de-lis on the walls of Damascus to Sultan Barqūq; Ludovico di Varthema, *Itinerary* (ed. Sir Richard Carnac Temple, London, The Argonaut Press, 1928, p. 8), and Jean Thenaud, *Le Voyage d'Outremer* (ed. Schefer, p. 114), considered the same blazon to be the emblem of a Florentine mamluk who, according to an historical legend widely disseminated in the Middle Ages, built the fortress of Damascus; Felix Fabri (ed. Hassler, III. 93) misinterpreted a simple blazon in Jerusalem as Sultan Qāytbāy's. Some information perhaps still lies hidden in the legends about the Oriental origin of certain European coats of arms, as in the case of the arms of the Visconti (Pierre Palliot, *La Vraye et Parfaite Science des Armoiries . . . de Lowan Geliot*, Paris 1660, anastatically reprinted, Paris 1895, p. 355 f., s.v. Givre; H. Nützel, *Embleme und Wappen auf muhammedanischen Münzen*, p. 4), which could be well compared with the dragons on the Bāb aṭ-Ṭalism, Baghdad, or with a relievo on a marble slab in the Arabic Museum, Cairo (Artin, *Contribution*, p. 74, no. 21; Max van Berchem, *CIA. Égypte*, I. 686 ff.; Karabacek, *Sarazenische Wappen*, pp. 1 ff.), or with Urtuqid coins (Lane-Poole, *Catalogue of Oriental Coins in the British Museum*, III, pl. VII, no. 329; Karabacek, l.c., p. 3).

THE STATUS OF A SARACENIC BLAZON

The blazon was one of the many prerogatives of the amir, or military dignitary, in Ayyubid and Mamluk society. Apart from the sultan, amirs, and amirs only, are known from literature to have used it,[1] and none but a sultan or an amir ever figures as the main person in an historical inscription accompanying a blazon. In accordance with the practice of that most bureaucratic chancery of the Mamluks, one would expect endless rules and regulations fixing the status of the blazon and giving infinite minutiae of the circumstances in which it should be worn; but the fact is that in the fourteen volumes of Qalqashandī's *Ṣubḥ al-Aʿshā* there are fewer lines devoted to the blazon than pages to such questions as who should bear the title *sāmīy* with a *yā* and who *sāmī* without a *yā*, or how the *basmalah* should be written. And the fact that the same author did not deem it worth while even to mention the blazon in the corresponding chapter of his abridgement of the above-mentioned work shows that the use of coats of arms was left to the discretion of amirs, and that—in his day, at any rate—it was not one of the privileges controlled by the government.

This was most probably not the original situation. Abu-l-Maḥāsin b. Taghrībirdī, referring to an event in the middle of the thirteenth century, tells us: '. . . Therefore, when he (i.e. al-Malik aṣ-Ṣāliḥ Najm ad-dīn) dubbed him (i.e. Aybak, the later Sultan al-Malik al-Muʿizz) an amir, he gave him the figure of a table (*khānjā*) as blazon.' Qalqashandī, who finished the *Ṣubḥ* in 1412,[2] says: 'It is the custom that every amir . . . have a special blazon . . . according to his choice or preference.'[3] Without unduly pressing these two statements it would appear to be safe to infer that originally the blazon was granted by the sultan. But whether it was granted as a special distinction conferred upon individuals or upon noblemen as a class, we do not know. Later, with the increasing number of amirs entitled as such to arms, the choice of the emblem was apparently left to the discretion of the amir himself. But it should be noted that whether granted or chosen, the emblems, so far as we can understand them, with very few exceptions represented the office held by the amir at the time of his being

[1] In all cases in which holders of ecclesiastic or administrative posts are known to have had blazons, they are also known to have occupied positions reserved for amirs. We can assume, therefore, until further evidence that they wore their badges in their capacity of military dignitaries.

[2] Björkman, *Beiträge zur Geschichte der Staatskanzlei im islamischen Ägypten*, Hamburg 1928, p. 73.

[3] IV. 61 f. It is possible that this passage was copied from the *Masālik al-Abṣār* which Qalqashandī so copiously made use of. At all events, the passage reflects the situation of the early fourteenth century.

made amir,[1] until in the fifteenth century it became a collective badge of military groups.[2]

The reason why the Saracenic blazon never came to be more than one of the many attributes of amirial dignity would seem to be that there was no great personal importance attached to it. The two great stimuli for the development of the coats of arms in Europe, viz. the helmet with the vizier that made the face invisible in tournament and warfare, and hereditary land tenure involving obligatory military service, did not exist in the East. Although the Saracenic blazon was hereditary among amirs, yet those of their sons who, as so many did, chose an ecclesiastic or administrative career, apparently had no right to arms. The blazon could thus never reach the importance it attained in the West; an importance which subsequently led to registration, to 'Colleges of Arms', and to legal protection.

THE MEANING

From the time of Prisse d'Avennes in 1877,[3] Saracenic blazons have been regarded as signs of office on the basis of Ibn Taghrībirdī's statement[4] that al-Malik aṣ-Ṣāliḥ Najm ad-dīn gave Aybak a *khānjā* as blazon when, as his taster, he made him amir. This explanation of Muslim heraldic emblems as signs of office was so self-evident that its correctness was never questioned, although it seemed to stand quite alone, and although, as van Berchem says in his last work with regard to the cup as a symbol of office, this view was never based on any definite fact.[5] But there is another passage extant to corroborate it. Abu-l-Fidā', in his *History*,[6] says that amirs holding certain offices had special emblems. These he described in the following words: 'And the emblem of secretary (*dawādār*) is the pen-box, and of the armour-bearer (*silaḥdār*) the bow, and of the superintendent of stores (*ṭishtdār*) the ewer, and of the master of the robes (*jamdār*) the napkin, and the emblem of the marshal (*amīr akhūr*) is the horseshoe, and the emblem of the *jāwīsh* is a golden *qubbah*.' But despite this

[1] See Chapter 'Signs of Office', p. 10 f.

[2] See Chapter 'Composite Blazons', p. 29.

[3] *L'Art Arabe d'après les monuments du Kaire*, p. 66.

[4] *Nujūm*, MS. Paris, fo. 157ᵛ, quoted by Quatremère, *Sultans Mamlouks*, I a, p. 2, n. 4. The corresponding passage in the *Manhal* has also the very significant words ولهذا رنكه صورة خونجا, and *therefore*, namely, because he was a taster, the emblem of his blazon was a table.

[5] *CIA. Jérusalem, Ville*, p. 288.

[6] Ed. Reiske, IV. 380, ed. Constantinople, III. 156. Although this passage deals with Khwārizmshāh Muḥammad b. Takash, it reproduces so closely the conditions at the Ayyubid and Mamluk courts that it can be quoted as a case in point.

description, it might not be wrong to assume that these emblems were the actual objects used, perhaps for ceremonial purposes, especially as the word used for 'emblem' is *'alāma* and not the usual *rank* or *shi'ār*. But a careful comparison of the emblems with the text of the inscriptions accompanying them and the biographies of their respective holders (see Armorial Roll) proves that the symbols of the duties and the devices on the shields correspond, and that seven blazons at least can without doubt be considered as signs of office: the cup of the cup-bearer (*sāqī*), the napkin of the master of the robes (*jamdār*), the polo-sticks of the polo-master (*jūkandār*), the round table of the taster (*jāshnigīr*), the pen-box of the secretary (*dawādār*), the sword (probably including the dagger and the scimitar) of the armour-bearer (*silaḥdār*), the bow of the bowman (*bunduqdār*) or of the armour-bearer. Among the emblems mentioned by Abu-l-Fidā' and accompanied by historical inscriptions are two concerning which I have not been able to determine whether their holders ever held the posts implied by their blazons, viz. the historian al-'Ainī the post of a *ṭishtdār*, and the *ḥājibs* Sharaf ad-dīn Mūsā and Baktamur (or his son 'Alī) the post of a *jāwīsh*. With a fair degree of certainty we can attribute several blazons which are not accompanied by inscriptions, e.g. the pair of banners to the standard-bearer (*'alamdār*), the drum and sticks to the drummer (*ṭabldār*), the trumpet to another member of the musical corps, the round three-fielded shield to the postman (*barīdī*), the shoe (if it is a shoe) depicted by Artin in his *Contribution*, No. 156 to the shoe-bearer (*bashmaqdār*).

Van Berchem[1] has already pointed out that the offices symbolized by the blazons are not offices of great importance. We do, however, sometimes find higher offices also (*grand dawādār, amīr akhūr, amīr silāḥ*), but they invariably have corresponding designations in the ranks, e.g. the junior dawādār (*dawādār ṣaghīr*), the junior marshal (*amīr akhūr ṣaghīr*), the *silāḥdār*. On the other hand, there are some emblems that would represent only small offices, such as that of the taster, the polo-master or the master of the robes, which, so far as the evidence of the chronicles goes, were never held by any high amir. Yet it would not be unlikely for an amir to perpetuate the memory of his achievements as a page or as one of the rank and file (*jundī*), achievements that had secured for him the distinction of the amirate, just as bezants are displayed on shields of knighted European bankers, and arms on those of soldiers of renown. That amirs were proud of their lowly origin and never sought to hide their humble station in life in the days of their youth is a familiar enough fact.

[1] *CIA. Jérusalem, Ville*, p. 290.

Many dignitaries are known to posterity by the nicknames they earned in their early years, and in cases where such nicknames referred to offices held and did not detract from the good character of their bearers, the amirs were accustomed to mention them in their official inscriptions.

Did the amirs change their blazons when changing their offices? Gayet[1] and Artin[2] took it for granted that they did, without giving any reason for such assumption. Van Berchem[3] held the same view, basing his theory on the difference of blazon on two objects made at different times for the amir Āqbughā min ʿAbd al-Wāḥid. The blazon of one of these objects, namely, of a lamp, shows a white napkin on the red middle field of a white three-fielded shield, whereas the blazon of the other, a hemisphere in bronze, consists of a red cup on the large lower field of a two-fielded shield. The titles of Āqbughā as given on the lamp being of a lower rank than those on the hemisphere, and the identity of the amir being established beyond doubt, van Berchem concluded that with the change of his position Āqbughā changed his blazon as well. Nevertheless the conclusion was wrong. When examining the hemisphere in the Victoria and Albert Museum, I could see traces of the original blazon—outlines of the napkin on the middle field—in two places (see Roll, s.v. Āqbughā m. ʿAbd al-Wāḥid), which makes it quite clear that the blazon of Āqbughā was in both cases the same. However, when at a later date the object changed hands, its new proprietor contented himself with changing the blazon, without changing the text of the inscription.

Another case in point is the blazon of Bahādur Āṣ,[4] on a copper basin, now in the Arab Museum, Cairo. The original emblem, a six-petalled rosette, has been effaced and replaced by two swords, these in turn also having been effaced and replaced by a cup. This example is rather more involved, as Bahādur was for some time an armour-bearer, and therefore should have ordinarily been the holder of a shield with a sword or swords as emblem. But on his mausoleum in Damascus, erected towards the end of his life, there is again the six-petalled rosette as his only blazon. Kitbughā's blazon remained unchanged during his amirate and sultanate, and so did those of Qarāsunqur,[4] Yūnus ad-Dawādār,[4] Manjak,[4] and Ishiqtamur,[4] all of whom left specimens of their arms which can be confidently ascribed to different points in their respective careers and yet in

[1] *L'Art Arabe*, p. 280.

[2] *Contribution*, pp. 43, 181, n. 4, 227; 'Trois différentes armoiries de Kaït Bay' (in *Bulletin de l'Institut Égyptien*, 2e série, no. 9, 1888), p. 74.

[3] *Notes d'archéologie arabe*, III. 78, n. 2; Kahle, 'Islamische Schattenspielfiguren aus Egypten' (in *Islam*, II. 191).

[4] See Roll, s.vv.

no case show the slightest change in the presentment of the emblem.[1] This seems to be conclusive proof that the amirs retained the blazons, once chosen or granted to them, for the whole of their lives.

ARMES PARLANTES

It is generally assumed that many Saracenic coats of arms were armes parlantes, pointing to the names of the bearers. Prisse d'Avennes was the first to use the term,[2] and several writers have since repeated it.[3] Four examples have been quoted: the felines of Baybars and Barsbāy, the duck of Qalāūn, the falcon of Āqsunqur. As to the last three, there is to my knowledge not a single object with an historical inscription mentioning the name of Barsbāy or Qalāūn or Āqsunqur which shows any one of the devices mentioned. There is a bottle of blue glass with a white 'lion' passant attributed to Barsbāy,[4] probably because of the feline and the title al-Malik al-Ashraf, but there were several al-Ashrafs among the Mamluk sultans and there are upwards of a dozen 'lions' in different colours on glass fragments to be found in the museums of Europe and Cairo. There remains only Baybars. Max van Berchem has pointed out[5] that apparently it did not occur to Maqrīzī that Baybars' blazon was a canting coat, as he would otherwise probably have translated it as *fahd* (panther) and not as *sab'* (lion).[6] To this may be added the statement of Ibn Iyās that these lions were 'an indication of his courage'.[7] Without pressing the last argument too far, we may safely assume that at least two Muslim writers living under the Mamluks and well acquainted with their ways of thinking would not consider this blazon to be an arme parlante.

The only piece of evidence in favour of this theory is the hitherto

[1] The various examples of the armorial bearings of Bashtāk, Uzbak, Tankiz, Ṭughāytamur an-Najmī, Ṭuquztamur cannot be quoted in this connexion, as the titles of these amirs prove that the blazons date from one particular period of their lives, during which they did not change their offices.

[2] *L'Art Arabe d'après les monuments du Kaire*, p. 66.

[3] Lane-Poole, *The Art of the Saracens*, p. 270 ('Kalaūn bore a canting coat, the representation of his own name, a duck'); Gayet, *L'Art Arabe*, p. 281; Karabacek, *Papyrus Erzherzog Rainer. Führer durch die Ausstellung*, p. 272, no. 1323 ('redende Personen- oder Staatswappen'); Artin Pasha, *Contribution*, p. 96, &c.; Karabacek, *Sarazenische Wappen*, p. 11; Max van Berchem used this word in a more general sense for symbols of office as well, *CIA. Jérusalem, Ville*, p. 287, and so did Artin Pasha, 'Trois différentes armoiries de Kaït Bay' (in *Bulletin de l'Institut Égyptien*, 2ᵉ série, no. 9, 1888, p. 74); *Quatre lampes*, pp. 78, 81.

[4] I am indebted to Mr. C. J. Lamm for the information that the bottle, formerly in the collection of Baron Alphonse de Rothschild, is now in the possession of Baron Édouard de Rothschild, Paris.

[5] *Amida*, p. 100, n. 2.

[6] This translation of the word *bars* is given also in Houtsma's *Ein türkisch-arabisches Glossar*, pp. 11, 29 (of the Arabic text).

[7] I, p. 110, ll. 4–5.

SIMPLE CHARGES

unpublished plate of Jamāl ad-dīn Āqūsh, Governor of Kerak, whose name means what the shield implies, viz. a white bird. But whether it is a case in point, or a mere coincidence, and his badge is no more an arme parlante than the birds of prey of Ṭuquztamur, al-Baysarī, Bahādur al-Ḥamawī, or the lion of Yashbak the dawādār and perhaps of other powerful Baḥrī amirs, I do not venture to decide; the chances are against it.

ANIMALS

Contrary to European heraldic usage, the lion—or rather the feline animal which was meant to represent a lion and which was accordingly so called in literature—is comparatively rare in Saracenic armoury. If we mention it first among the three heraldic animals, it is only because it is one of the best-known blazons, being the emblem of Baybars. The lion of Baybars is by no means the oldest example known, the earliest datable example being that on the Ḥarrān gate at Urfa, built by al-Malik al-Muẓaffar Shihāb ad-dīn Ghāzī, son of al-Malik al-ʿĀdil Abū Bakr, who ruled over Urfa between 608 and 617 A.H. (1211/12–1220/1). The Saracenic heraldic lion is invariably represented in the act of walking, usually with his right forepaw raised (and in cases where he is seen walking to the left, with his left forepaw raised) and with his tail curled back. Very frequently the lion is depicted as playing with either an animal or a ball (the exact meaning of which has yet to be established), or accompanied by a figure. The lion appears on simple blazons only, with the exception of two coats of arms[1] consisting of two-fielded shields, of which the bottom one is bendy of 10 and 8 pieces respectively.

Among birds the eagle alone seems to be represented, although one would have expected the falcon to occur at least as often as the eagle.[2] The eagle is known in two varieties, the one-headed and the two-headed. Both varieties frequently show a lanceolate patch on their breasts which at times has the appearance of a gash; hence the description 'aigle éventré'. But more often it looks like a pear-shaped shield, and is probably meant to be an ornament only. The claws of the eagles are usually shown grasping the tips of the wings, thus

[1] Both on perfume sprays: one in the Museum of Fine Arts, Boston, published in its *Bulletin*, Dec. 1910, p. 51, the other one in the possession of M. E. Paravicini, Zeitoun, near Cairo, cf. pl. I. 7.

[2] Cf. Quatremère, *Sultans Mamlouks*, I a, p. 91, n. In the opinion of Dr. F. S. Bodenheimer, Research Fellow in Zoology at the Hebrew University, Jerusalem, who was kind enough to look through my relevant photos, all these birds are eagles with the exception of pl. III, 6 (Potsherd no. 3854–4 of the Arabic Museum, Cairo), and pl. XV. (Āqūsh). Assuming that there are no mistakes of perspective, the short and broad head in conjunction with the short beak of the first bird would indicate a falcon rather than an eagle; as to the second, it might represent a griffin-vulture (*Gypaetus barbatus*).

forming a horizontal—or almost horizontal—line strongly contrasting with the vertical axis formed by the eagle's head and tail. The eagle is either displayed with wings inverted, the head turned to the left or to the right, or as rising, with wings inverted and so addorsed that only one wing is visible. The eagle appears both on one, and on two-fielded shields, and at times without a shield; it is never found in conjunction with another animal, but is often depicted standing on some inanimate charge, such as a sword, cup, or napkin. In one case (pl. III, fig. 5) the sword is to the right of the eagle. The peculiar head-ornament on the head of the eagle of Muẓaffar ad-dīn Mūsā b. al-Malik aṣ-Ṣāliḥ (pl. XIV) should be noted.

I have not included in this chapter the horse encountered on Muslim heraldic shields, because to my mind the horse is only the supporter of the parade-saddle which, from a heraldic point of view, is all that matters.

As to Qalāūn's duck, Muḥammad b. Qalāūn's fishes, and the so-called antelope (on a large plate in the Victoria and Albert Museum), there is no reason whatever to believe that these animals ever had heraldic character.

SIGNS OF OFFICE

The Cup

In ascribing certain blazons to certain classes of court officers as definite signs of office, an attempt is made, in the following pages, to establish (*a*) that there were objects used as distinctive symbols to mark the office of some of the court officers,[1] (*b*) that these objects were identical with the charges found on blazons, (*c*) that the holders of these blazons actually were also holders of such offices, the evidence of which was found either in the corresponding titles mentioned in inscriptions accompanying the blazons, or in details gathered from biographical dictionaries and other historic literature. Such combined evidence is not always available, however, so that in some cases I had to be content with one or two points of evidence only. It seemed advisable, therefore, to summarize at the end of each chapter opinions differing from mine, and to bring forward other evidence obviously at variance with the theories here put forward. By this means the reader will be the better able to form an independent opinion.

When the theory explaining the Mamluk blazon as a symbol of office was first advanced,[2] the cup was one of the cases quoted. There was more of intuition

[1] This can be considered proved for six emblems by the passage from Abu-l-Fidā' quoted on p. 4, and for a seventh by *Manhal*, s.v. Aybak, quoted on pp. 3, 4.

[2] Prisse d'Avennes, *L'Art Arabe*, p. 66; Rogers, p. 102; Lane-Poole, *The Art of the Saracens*, p. 271.

than of knowledge in this suggestion, as the inscriptions accompanying the actual examples did not contain any reference to the office of a cup-bearer, nor was any one of the holders of these blazons called 'cup-bearer' in the extracts quoted by the different Arab authors.[1] Yet despite this inadequate foundation the theory is right, and as the number of cup-bearers was greater than that of any other group of pages with special functions, the cup became one of the most frequently occurring blazons. Each of the following holders of simple blazons with a cup is styled 'cup-bearer' (*sāqī*) in the relevant inscriptions: Alṭunbughā al-Māridīnī,[2] Baighudamur as-Sāqī, Qauṣūn an-Nāṣirī, Ṭanbughā (Ṭaybughā) Ḥājjī, Ṭurjī an-Nāṣirī, Ṭashtamur al-Badrī, Ṭughāytamur an-Nāṣirī, Ṭuquztamur, Yalbughā al-Yaḥyāwī.

About Aḥmad b. Baktamur as-Sāqī, Muḥammad b. Kitbughā, Ḥusain b. Qauṣūn, cf. chapter on Heredity, p. 40.

The following is known to have been a cup-bearer: Shaikh (later al-Malik al-Mu'ayyad); Tankizbughā was Superintendent of the Cellar; Kitbughā (later al-Malik al-ʿĀdil), Ṭāz an-Nāṣirī, Yalbughā al-ʿUmarī, and Tankiz an-Nāṣirī served in the corps of the pages (*khāṣṣakī*), from among the ranks of which the cup-bearers were occasionally recruited.

Of the following I know nothing: ʿAlī b. Aḥmad, Aljāy, Arghūnshāh, Aydamur al-Ānūkī, Baktūmān, Ishiqtamur al-Māridīnī, Khālid, Mubārak aṣ-Ṣāliḥī, Muḥammad al-Khāzindār, Shaikhū, Ṭānyaraq, Jamāl ad-dīn al-Muẓaffarī.

Karabacek's theory that the cup is not a mark of office but a chalice of knighthood (*ka's al-futuwwa*) and together with the trousers of knighthood (*sarāwīl al-futuwwa*) forms a general symbol of nobility,[3] should not be altogether ignored. The flaw in this hypothesis is obvious: Karabacek assumed that for heraldic purposes there is no difference between a cup-bearer (*sāqī*) and a taster (*jāshnigīr*), whereas the inscriptions and biographies prove that there was a difference, and that the two emblems were never interchanged. To support his theory, Karabacek promised to describe the ceremony of the investiture on the basis of literary sources and unknown contemporary pictorial material, a promise he never kept.

[1] Rogers, pp. 123–4, gives only one—very unhappily chosen—instance, viz. Alṭunbughā al-Māridīnī, who was a cup-bearer. But the blazon referred to belonged, as the accompanying inscription proves, to ʿAlī al-Māridīnī, who was a master of the robes (*jamdār*).

[2] For the biographies of the amirs enumerated here and in the following chapters, and for the description of their shields and the inscriptions accompanying them, see The Roll, s.vv.

[3] *Geschichte der Mazjaditen*, p. 5; *Ein damascenischer Leuchter*, p. 276, n. 27; *Sarazenische Wappen*, p. 24.

Pen-Box

Abu-l-Fidā' 's list of emblems used by various officers begins with the pen-box of the pen-box holder (*dawādār*), a secretary of lower rank at court. Although the ceremonial pen-box was probably subject to less variation of style than the ordinary one, we have a number of shapes preserved. The typical pen-box consists of four elements: the first, containing the ink-pot, the second the sand-pot and the starch paste-pot, the third a receptacle for thread (for cleaning pens), the fourth two or three receptacles for reeds. The main types are as follows:

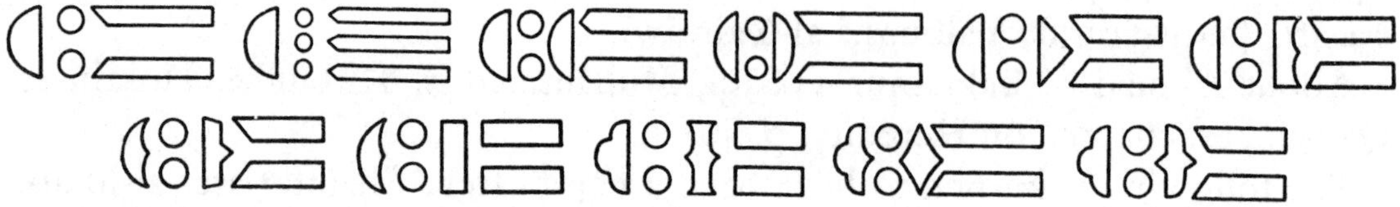

In inscriptions accompanying simple blazons with this device, the holders were usually called dawādārs, e.g. Quṭlūbughā, Sīdī Aḥmad, Ṭashtamur al-'Alā'ī, or else they are known to have been dawādārs, e.g. Jurjī an-Nāṣirī. The holders of composite blazons consisting of pen-box and cup only, were with few exceptions known as dawādārs, although it is doubtful whether they have served as *junior* dawādārs: Jaqmaq, Muqbil, Ṭughāytamur, Yūnus.

The pen-box was the main component of two very common types of composite blazons, one of which consisted of a napkin on the upper and lower fields and a pen-box on the middle field, and the other of a napkin on the upper, of a cup placed between a pair of 'trousers of nobility' and charged with a pen-box on the middle, and of a cup on the lower field.

The pen-box was regarded in the past as the hieroglyphic sign 'Ra neb teta', translated as 'Sun, master of the two horizons' by Rogers,[1] Artin,[2] Lane-Poole,[3] Karabacek.[4] Gayet[5] and Herz[6] accepted this theory, although neither could see

[1] *Le Blason*, p. 102 f.

[2] 'Trois différentes armoiries de Kaït Bay', p. 70 f. Later, Artin Pasha consulted G. Maspero, who read the sign as 'Ra-nib-taoui' and translated it as 'Soleil maître des deux terres', *Contribution*, p. 112. In 1906, Artin Pasha described the pen-box as 'les signes dits hiéroglyphiques', 'Les Armes de l'Égypte aux XVe et XVIe siècles' (in *BIE.*, 4e série, No. 7, 1906, p. 87).

[3] *The Art of the Saracens in Egypt*, p. 233.

[4] *Abendländische Künstler zu Konstantinopel*, p. 88 f. On the advice of Prof. Junker, Karabacek considered this emblem as an erroneous combination of two groups of hieroglyphic signs meaning 'Son of Re, Lord of the two Lands'.

[5] *L'Art Arabe*, p. 280 f.

[6] 'Deux lampes en verre émaillé de l'Émir Toghaitimor' (in *BIE.*, 5e série, t. 1, 1907 (publ. June 1908), pp. 181–7).

how the Mamluks could have understood the meaning of these signs. Other scholars, such as van Berchem,[1] Watzinger and Wulzinger,[2] hesitated to accept this explanation, but were unable themselves to suggest a more plausible theory. It was only in November, 1918, that the late ʿAbdal-Ḥamīd Muṣṭafā Pasha proved in a lecture delivered at the Institut d'Égypte that this emblem represents the pen-box. His paper having been lost was never published. Fortunately, Mrs. H. Devonshire wrote an abstract of the lecture for the *Burlington Magazine*,[3] thus saving for archaeology one of the soundest theories yet put forward on the subject of Saracenic heraldry.

Sword

The second item in Abu-l-Fidā' 's list is the cross-bow, the emblem of the armour-bearer (*silaḥdār*). This statement presents a difficulty of its own. In making a list of all the armour-bearers whose blazons are known to us, we find that—with two exceptions[4]—all those who had simple blazons, invariably displayed on their shields a scimitar, a sword or a pair of swords instead of a cross-bow. The list is as follows:[5] *Āqūsh al-Afram, Asandamur, *Aṣlam, *Bahādur al-Badrī, Malaktimur as-Silaḥdār, *Manjak al-Yūsufī as-Silāḥdār, *Qijlīs an-Nāṣirī, Ṭughāydamur as-Silaḥdār. This excludes amirs who displayed swords on their shields, but whose biographies, so far as I have been able to trace them, contain no reference to their early career, and thus leave it doubtful if they were ever armour-bearers.

In the light of this list it would seem as though Abu-l-Fidā' 's statement must be explained as meaning that the emblem of armour-bearers in general was a weapon, as an example of which—for unknown reasons—he cites the cross-bow only, though the sword and the dagger could equally well be used as emblems.

Bow

According to Abu-l-Fidā', the bow was the device of the armour-bearer; but the evidence of the inscription shows that one bow at least belonged to

[1] *CIA. Jérusalem, Ville*, p. 288, n. 1.

[2] Cf. their description of this emblem in *Damaskus, die islamische Stadt*, pp. 51, 66, and *passim*.

[3] *Sultan Salâh ed-Dîn's Writing-Box in the National Museum of Arab Art, Cairo*, XXXV (December, 1919), 241–5.

[4] Lājīn for a time *silaḥdār* had a three-fielded shield as blazon and Bahādur Āṣ a rosette.

[5] Those known from literature to have been armour-bearers are marked with an asterisk; the others are styled so in the accompanying inscription.

the bowman (*bunduqdār*) who was of the same rank as the armour-bearer (*silaḥdār*). The emblem referred to appears on the lamp of ʿAlā' ad-dīn Aydakīn al-Bunduqdār and consists of two bows addorsed. In the only other case in which this blazon is accompanied by an inscription, it appears in a modified form as a bow with two arrows. The name of its holder, Baktamur, without any indication of his office, provenance, or nickname, does not give us any clue. There were several amirs of this name, and although one of them was armour-bearer,[1] I do not think it advisable, in the absence of any other indication, to identify him, without reservation, with the holder of our blazon.

Napkin

The fourth in Abu-l-Fidā''s list is the napkin (*buqja*)[2] worn by the master of the robes (*jamdār*). A *buqja*, according to native dictionaries, was a piece of cloth[3] in which clothes, chancery deeds, &c., were wrapped up. The normal shape of such a napkin being either square or oblong,[4] there was only one blazon which seemed to answer the description, viz. the rhomb, which appears on a good many heraldic shields. The question whether the rhomb is identical with the *buqja* worn by the *jamdārs* may be answered in the affirmative in view of the following list of amirs whose simple blazon consisted of this emblem only; those known from literature to have been jamdārs are again marked with an asterisk: *Ṣirghitmish *al-jamdār*, *Āqbughā min ʿAbd al-Wāḥid *al-jamdār*, Arghūn al-ʿAlā'ī *ra's naubat al-jamdāriyyah*, Aydamur al-Qaimarī *al-jamdār*, Mankuwīrish al-Fāruqānī *al-jamdār*.

It should be noted that Bahādur al-Ḥamawī, whose blazon consisted of an eagle above a *buqja*, is styled in the accompanying inscription *ra's naubat al-jamdāriyyah*.

In the past the *buqja* was misunderstood by Rogers,[5] who called it in European fashion, 'losange'; by Artin Pasha, who, for no apparent reason at all,

[1] Cf. Ibn Iyās, index; Ibn Ḥabīb, pp. 294–5, 298; Ibn Taghrībirdī, *Manhal*, s.v. (MS. Paris, Ar. 2069, fo. 88ᵛ) and Armorial Roll, s.v.

[2] Reiske had it in his edition as نفجة and consequently could not understand it; and the same form was repeated in the Constantinople edition. The correct text was given by Gaudefroy-Demombynes in *La Syrie*, p. xcii, n. 2.

[3] Quatremère was the first European author to establish this meaning, *Sultans Mamlouks*, I b, p. 204.

[4] Mrs. H. Devonshire had the kindness to call my attention to a square piece of cloth in the Arabic Museum, Cairo, called in the registers 'buqja', which shows that the original meaning of the word was not yet obsolete some fifty years ago.

[5] *Le Blason*, p. 115 and *passim*; also by Lavoix, *Collection Albert Goupil*, p. 303.

called it successively 'losange',[1] 'dé',[2] and 'cachet';[3] by Cordier who called it 'étoile';[4] by Herz, who saw in it the *khānjā*, 'la petite table de sommelier',[5] 'la tablette',[6] by Wulzinger and Watzinger who described it as 'Raute';[7] by the present writer who called it 'rhomb',[8] and by others who accepted one or the other of these appellations.

Table

Apart from the passage from Abu-l-Fidā', our knowledge is derived from still another source and one which dealing, as it does, directly with a Syro-Egyptian amir states even more clearly that the Saracenic blazon pointed to the office held by its owner, namely the very frequently quoted statement that when al-Malik aṣ-Ṣāliḥ Najm ad-dīn dubbed Aybak an amir, he gave him the figure of a *ḵhānjā* as heraldic emblem. The question to be determined is what was a *ḵhānjā* and what did it look like? The passages collected by Quatremère, *Sultans Mamlouks*, I a, p. 2, n. 4, and Dozy, *Supplément*, s.v.,[9] which can easily be augmented by others, clearly indicate that the *ḵhānjā* was a small table, and this translation was almost universally accepted.[10] Most writers refrained from saying anything about its form, and of those who did express an opinion, no two are in accord. Taking as a starting-point medieval miniatures depicting Saracenic tables,[11] we find that the tables consist of large round plates, sometimes with, sometimes without, a support. We have to look, therefore, for round disks as a proper representation of the *ḵhānjā*. To this may be added the evidence of a passage in Maqrīzī's *Khiṭaṭ* (II. 72 l. ult., 2nd ed., III. 117, l. 5 b),[12] where plates (*aṭbāq*) and tables (*ḵhānjāt*) are mentioned together and appear almost synonymous.

Martin[13] attributed a bowl (formerly in the possession of Prof. Sarre and now

[1] 'Trois différentes armoiries de Kaït Bay' (in *BIE.*, 2e série, No. 9, 1888, p. 73); 'Un Sabre de l'Émir Ezbek el Yussufi el Zahery' (in *BIE.*, 3e série, No. 9, 1898, pp. 249, 253). In the latter article, p. 249, Artin Pasha described a carelessly drawn napkin as 'une sorte de vase fermé'.

[2] *Contribution*, p. 104 f.

[3] 'Les Armes de l'Égypte aux XVe et XVIe siècles' (*BIE.* 1906, p. 87); 'Nouvelles preuves concernant la signification du meuble "cachet" dans les armoiries orientales' (in *BIE.*, 4e série, No. 7, 1906, pp. 101 ff.).

[4] 'La Collection Charles Schefer' (in *GBA*, 3e pér., t. xx, 1898, p. 254).

[5] 'Le bain de l'Émir Bechtak' (*BIE.* 1904, p. 33), although no Muslim author called Bashtāk a taster.

[6] *CR.* 1909 (1910), p. 162; *CR.* 1911 (1912), p. 121.

[7] *Damaskus, die islamische Stadt*, p. 101.

[8] 'Arabic Inscriptions of Gaza II' (in *Journal of the Palestine Oriental Society*, V, 1925, p. 68).

[9] Cf. particularly Ibn Baṭṭūṭa, IV. 69: مائدة نحاس يسمّونها خَوَنجة ويجعل عليها طبق نحاس يسمّونه الطالم

[10] With apparently the sole exception of Gaudefroy-Demombynes, who thought it was a chalice, *La Syrie*, p. lxi, n. 1.

[11] e.g. Arnold, *Painting in Islam*, pl. XVIII a.

[12] I am much obliged to Prof. Wiet, who called my attention to this passage.

[13] *Ältere Kupferarbeiten*, pl. II and III.

in the Kaiser Friedrich Museum, Berlin) to Aybak, obviously by identifying its blazon (see pl. LII. 2) with the *khānjā*. For the same reason Herz Bey called the napkin 'la petite table de sommelier'[1] and 'tablette',[2] and Artin Pasha[3] took an otherwise unique emblem, which in his design looks like the section of a stand for a tray, to be a *khānjā*.

Disks appear only on two simple blazons, namely on those of Aybak al-Mauṣilī and Baktūt al-Qaramānī. Unfortunately, no details concerning Aybak's early career are to be found in any of his biographies,[4] but Baktūt al-Qaramānī, in an inscription in Cairo, is called a taster (*jāshnigīr*),[5] the very office we should expect him to have held.

Artin Pasha, who knew this blazon only from potsherds, described it as a target ('cible').[6]

Polo-sticks

Not all the known charges have been mentioned by Muslim historians. Among those not mentioned is the polo-stick (*jūkān*)[7] of the polo-master (*jūkandār*), a well-known officer at court. The blazon was recognized as such by Rogers (pp. 102, 124) and never disputed. There are five simple blazons with polo-sticks and historical texts. They belonged to the following persons: Almalik, Qarāsunqur, Alṭunbughā, Aydamur, Qāzān, Qumarī, and Quṭlū Khātūn. The first two are called *jūkandār* in the relevant texts. Quṭlū Khātūn was the daughter of Bahādur, the polo-master, and may have been the wife of Ṭurunṭāy, the polo-master,[8] both known to have been such from inscriptions and historical texts. Qumarī is one of the several of that name whose biography cannot be established because of the lack of distinguishing detail in the inscriptions. Only Qāzān is called *jamdār* and Aydamur *zardkash*. But, as we have seen, the *jamdār* had a different blazon altogether, so that Qāzān represents, in any case, an exception to the rule.

It was suggested by van Berchem[9] that the badge of Muḥammad b. Aḥmad, an emblem of peculiar shape on the window of the mausoleum of Baraka

[1] *BIE*. 1904, p. 33.

[2] *CR*. 1909 (1910), p. 162; *CR*. 1911 (1912), p. 121.

[3] *Contribution*, p. 180 f., fig. 309.

[4] Cf. Armorial Roll s.v. Aybak of Mosul and literature there quoted.

[5] *CR*. 1910, p. 80.

[6] *Contribution*, p. 134, Nos. 212–19, 242–7.

[7] On the point of whether the *jūkān* is a polo-stick or a racket see *CIA. Jérusalem, Ville*, p. 268. It seems to me that the pictorial evidence is decidedly in favour of its being called polo-stick. In the fifteenth century there was no difference between the two, cf. Qalqashandī, *Ṣubḥ*, V, p. 458, l. 3.

[8] L. A. Mayer, 'Inscriptions of Gaza I' (in *JPOS*. III, 1923, p. 78).

[9] *CIA. Jérusalem, Ville*, p. 195.

Khān, at Jerusalem (pl. XL. 2), also represents polo-sticks. In the absence of any biographical data concerning the holder of this blazon, it is impossible to decide the point. Van Berchem's view is mentioned, however, as a possible hypothesis, although the emblem might, with equal justification, be considered not as a variant of the polo-sticks, but as one standing in a class by itself, the pear-shaped object in the middle possibly representing a drum (cf. Emblem No. 22).

Fesse

A three-fielded shield without any emblem occurs several times as blazon of the Baḥri mamluks, especially of some of those who in the second half of the thirteenth century were elevated to the rank of amir. It was worn by the Sultan Lājīn and the amirs Salār, ʿAlā' ad-dīn al-Barīdī, Arghūn an-Nāṣirī, Kujkun, Baktamur al-Ḥusāmī, and Ibrahīm b. Baktamur al-Ḥusāmī.

In view of the early date of this blazon it seems obvious that the disk divided into three horizontal bands is in itself the emblem displayed, as it were, on an undivided round shield, and the question to be decided is what object it was meant to represent. Among the insignia of officers of low rank the emblem of the dispatch-rider (*barīdī*) suggests itself at once, consisting, as it does, of a small plate of copper or silver inscribed on one side with the creed formula and a verse from the Qur'ān (IX. 33) and on the other with the name and titles of the sultan.[1] The text is almost identical with those found on the inscribed shields, which, as we shall see later (cf. p. 34f.), consisted of round shields divided into three horizontal bars. Of the seven persons mentioned above, ʿAlā' ad-dīn was styled *barīdī* in the accompanying inscription and Salār in a literary text.[2] The early offices of the others are not known.

Ceremonial Saddle

The last among the devices mentioned by Abu-l-Fidā' as having been used as emblems by amirs is a 'dome' (*qubbah*) in connexion with which several Mamluk blazons may be interpreted. There is the one called 'target' which might be mistaken for the outlines of a dome, there is the blazon on a bowl, pl. LII, No. 2, which could be interpreted as the entrance to a tent,[3] and there is a sort of

[1] Quatremère, *Sultans Mamlouks*, II b, 88; *Ṣubḥ al-Aʿshā*, XIV, p. 371; Gaudefroy-Demombynes, *La Syrie*, pp. 239 ff.

[2] Quatremère, l.c. II b, p. 41.

[3] One might be induced to assume this from M. Gaudefroy-Demombynes' translation of *qubbah* as tente ronde', *La Syrie*, p. xcii, n. 2.

palanquin or state saddle on a horse which we meet with on seven occasions:[1]

1. On a basin in the possession of Sir Ronald Storrs, Governor of Cyprus.
2. On two medallions sculptured over the entrance gate of the Khān al-ʿAsal near Aleppo.
3. On a glass lamp once in the possession of the late Baron G. de Rothschild, Paris (Brocart's replica of it is now in the British Museum).
4. On a coin in the Government Museum, Jerusalem, pl. XX, 3.
5. On a stone basin in the Municipal Museum of Beyrouth.
6. On a potsherd in the Arabic Museum, Cairo.
7. On a potsherd in the Musée des Arts Décoratifs, Paris.

As none of these represents a *qubbah* in the ordinary sense of the word, we have to assume it to be a dome-shaped palanquin (Dozy, *Supplément*, s.v.). The only help towards identifying the blazon is the statement by Abu-l-Fidā' that it was the emblem of a *jāwīsh*. The so-called target is not a sign of office, but either the head of a banner or a tamgha. The function of the amir for whom Sarre's bowl was made is not ascertainable, and the last four objects of the third group are anonymous. Therefore the only indications are the inscriptions accompanying 1, 2, and 3. The first of these, which gives the title of al-Manṣūrī al-Malikī al-Ashrafī is for all practical purposes anonymous; the second and third give names of the *ḥājibs* Sharaf ad-dīn Mūsā, and Baktamur (or his son ʿAlī) whose previous career is unknown.

TAMGHA

Several blazons which are neither armes parlantes nor signs of office nor animalic symbols can be identified with Mongolian tamghas. In his *Contribution*[2] Artin Pasha devoted a chapter to tamghas, mistaking cups,[3] trumpets,[4] and napkins[5] for tamghas, confusing the tamghas with a wasm and unable to identify either of them with the heraldic emblems discussed in his book. Among the tamghas of princes depicted in the MS. Leiden Or. 419 W.[6] (*Cat. Cod. Orient.* III. 24 sq., No. 942, fo. 15 b ff.) several show a striking resemblance to some otherwise unexplainable Mamluk blazons, thus 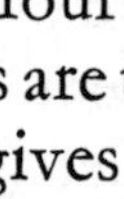 (fo. 15 b, 16 b) to the so-called target[7] (Embl. 26), the 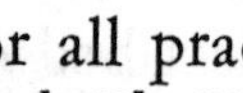 (fo. 17 b) to the 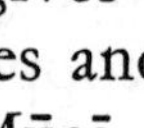 (Embl. 24), the

[1] So far as my knowledge goes these seven objects are here discussed for the first time. Thus there is no previous interpretation of them to be considered.

[2] *Le Wesm*, pp. 182–220.

[3] Ib., p. 198, No. 310.

[4] Ib., p. 198, No. 312.

[5] Ib., p. 121, No. 92.

[6] Pls. L, LI.

[7] But cf. previous chapter p. 18, l. 15.

 (fo. 16 a),  (fo. 17 a),  (fo. 16 a), and  (fo. 18 a) to  (Embl. 43), the  (fo. 17 a) to the  (Embl. 27), the  (fo. 16 a) and  (fo. 18 a) to the  (Embl. 32), and the  to a particular form of the fleur-de-lis (Embl. 25). In view of an explicit passage in Abu-l-Fidā' bow and arrows (fo. 17 b) found among tamghas had better be considered as signs of office only. This suggestion may seem merely to transpose the unknown quantities of the equation, the meaning of the various tamghas being just as obscure as that of those Mamluk blazons to which some of the tamghas show such a striking resemblance.

Among the forty-seven heraldic emblems (p. 8), whose existence we have been able to establish there are some that cannot be scientifically classed in any of the groups dealt with in the previous pages, being neither animals nor marks of office, nor yet tamghas. Although some of them may be, and probably actually are, marks of office, it would be futile, in the absence of inscriptions with sufficiently clear indications and other literary evidence, to try to guess at their exact meaning, and I propose, therefore, to register them here without comment. They are: the fleur-de-lis, the crescent, the rosette, the bend, the 'horns' or 'trousers of nobility', the battle-axe, the cross, the 'gate', the chess-board, the bars, the key, and twelve other emblems that are more easily drawn than described: Nos. 33, 34, 36, 38–42, 44–7.

Horns or Trousers of Nobility

For the consideration of this emblem we have no reliable guides in either Abu-l-Fidā' or any other Mamluk historian. The figure does not recall any of the devices mentioned in Arabic literature and is the first of a series of badges which have to be interpreted without the aid of any contemporary literature. We are forced to guess both at the objects they represent and at their meaning. This method, so frequently employed by previous writers, is the origin of most of the mistakes made in the past.

Since the emblem vaguely resembles the classical and Byzantine cornucopiae, it has been so identified by the majority of writers,[1] notwithstanding

[1] Rogers, l.c. No. 13, p. 119 ('corne d'abondance'); Artin, *Trois différentes armoiries de Kaït Bay*, p. 71 ('cornes'), p. 73 ('cornets'); Kay, 'Arabic Inscriptions in Egypt' (in *JRAS*, 1896, p. 147) ('cornucopiae (?) '). According to Artin Pasha, 'Un Sabre de l'Émir Ezbek El Yussufi El Zahery', *BIE*. 1898, p. 259, the cornucopiae 'indiqueraient en langage héraldique oriental la souveraineté'. I have vainly

the fact that cornucopiae appear nowhere else in Muḥammadan symbolism.[1] Herzfeld was the first to reject the identification. In his description of the blazon of Khāirbak he called it ostrich feathers.[2] It is difficult to adopt his theory, since the barbs of ostrich feathers are almost of the same width till they end abruptly, leaving the quill only, whereas our emblem is invariably designed with wide top which, in a more or less graceful curve, gradually narrows down to a point.

In discussing this problem four facts should be borne in mind:

(1) that the emblem always appears paired;

(2) that the object represented is hollow;[3]

tried to find the source of this statement. As an heraldic emblem they appear only on shields of amirs, never on shields of sultans.

[1] Excluding, of course, works of artists belonging to other civilizations, such as the mosaics of the Dome of the Rock.

[2] Ahmed Djemal Pacha, *Alte Denkmäler aus Syrien, Palästina und Westarabien*, Berlin 1918, Mausoleum of Khāirbak in Aleppo, pl. XLVI.

Prof. Herzfeld, whom I asked for his reasons for calling the emblem under discussion ostrich feathers, very kindly sent me the following note in a letter dated 14th December 1928:

'From its form alone, the object in question is difficult to place. The manner of application of the two leaf-like designs to the base of the vases or cups is the same as that found in the vine and acanthus decorations used in the bases of vases in eastern Hellenistic, Sassanian, and Islamic ornamentation. Cf. e.g., the pillars of Akka, the capital of Bisutun (Sam. Malereien, fig. 9), the silver object published by Smirnoff, &c.

'It seems, therefore, that the object is partly ornamental, and that it is a highly conventionalized and not a true representation of the original. One thing is certain: as some of these coats of arms are of Egyptian origin, I have taken the object under discussion to be also of Egyptian origin and I identify it as the ostrich feathers so commonly met with in ancient Egyptian decorations. Thus, for instance, they were used in crowns, in some cases in side view, in others in front view, but always in pairs (figure). Feathers, moreover, both ostrich and peacock, eventually also came to be used in occidental heraldry. There is a theory or a tradition in western heraldry that peacock feathers in old armorial bearings indicate participation in the crusades. One of my own friends, a Herr v. Behr, whom I used to know in the days of my childhood, had such feathers in his coat of arms.

'I believe, therefore, that feathers—especially ostrich feathers—should be found in Mamluk arms. I am unable to trace a sufficiently clear resemblance to cornucopiae to warrant this explanation being given preference.'

In support of Prof. Herzfeld's theory, the blazon of Khāirbak, painted on the iron gate of his caravanserai in Aleppo, could be quoted. It shows a herring-bone pattern, very similar to a crude design of the feathers of a quill. But it is by no means likely that the painting is contemporary with the construction of the khan. If it were an Ottoman addition, it would have no value at all.

Another point in favour of Prof. Herzfeld's theory is that ostrich feathers on helmets, at least as depicted on some miniatures, do sometimes curve, cf. Blochet, *Les Enluminures des Manuscrits Orientaux —turcs, arabes, persans—de la Bibliothèque Nationale*, Paris 1926, pls. XXI a, XLIII, and elsewhere.

[3] That the artist's intention was to depict a hollow object becomes evident when comparing it with Roman and Byzantine representations of hollow objects. We find there the same disks of different colours at the openings of horns, pipes, &c., which characterize both components of our emblem, which often look like balls.

(3) that it appears for the first time on composite blazons of the second half of the fifteenth century;

(4) that it does not resemble any badge described in Arabic literature as symbol of office.

Although the first of these facts does not exclude such explanations as horns or feathers, it makes them rather improbable; the second excludes feathers, and the last two make it more than probable that it is not a symbol of office.

I venture to suggest that we have here the *sarāwīl al-futuwwa*, the trousers of nobility. It is not the first time that a Muslim badge has been identified as a pair of trousers. Since the author of the *Itinerarium Regis Ricardi* saw on the banner of Taqī ad-dīn ʿUmar, Saladin's nephew, a pair of breeches (*baneriam insignitam miro genere distinctionis, scilicet incisarum schemate braccarum*), his statement has been accepted by many writers on the subject.[1] Among modern orientalists Karabacek in particular believed that 'the trousers of nobility' were a common badge and that Saracenic knights were entitled to display them on their shields together with the cup which, according to Karabacek, was another symbol of nobility.[2] It is difficult to say what particular emblem Karabacek had in mind when writing these statements; he described only one blazon consisting of 'trousers, above them a chalice, with the personal badge, a ram en face, underneath', and all that on a helmet of the twelfth century! It is unfortunate that the collection of Count Alexander von Warsberg, to whom the helmet belonged, has been dispersed and that there is no trace of it in any other museum known to me.

But whatever this enigmatic blazon with the two unknown quantities may have been, the suggested solution has in its favour that the 'sarāwīl' are not a symbol of office, that they appear in the time of the Circassian Mamluks when so many other emblems originally royal or meaningless as symbols of office enter into the composite blazons, that they appear naturally in pairs[3] and,

[1] *Itinerarium peregrinorum et gesta Regis Ricardi*, ed. William Stubbs, London 1864, p. 272 f.; Wilken, *Geschichte der Kreuzzüge*, Leipzig 1826, IV. 416, n. 85; Lane-Poole, *Saladin*, p. 320.

[2] *Ein damascenischer Leuchter*, p. 276, n. 27; *Beiträge zur Geschichte der Mazjaditen*, p. 5. This statement has been accepted by Dozy, *Supplément*, s.v. futuwwa, very cautiously reproduced by Thorning, *Beiträge zur Kenntnis des islamischen Vereinswesens*, p. 217, and lastly by Björkman, s.v. sirwāl, in *The Encyclopaedia of Islām* (Engl. ed. fasc. H, p. 452).

[3] It may be objected that on the blazon of Qānṣūh al-Yaḥyāwī there is only one-half of the pair of trousers; but it seems to me much more probable that we have to deal in this case with another device, namely the one visible on both sides of the chalice on the middle field of Uzbak's blazon, which cannot be identical with the 'trousers of nobility', as the latter are represented in a very different way on the upper field of his badge.

finally, that they have more resemblance to a pair of oriental trousers than to anything else to be taken into consideration.

Fleur-de-lis

The fleur-de-lis appears for the first time in Muslim heraldry as the blazon of Nūr ad-dīn Maḥmūd b. Zankī, the atābak. We find it on two monuments closely connected with Nūr ad-dīn: over the miḥrāb of his madrasah in Damascus (pl. XIX. 1), built between 549 and 569 (1154–1173),[1] and on two columns of the minbar of the Main Mosque at Hims, here alternating with a rosette (pl. XIX. 3). Other datable examples of the fleur-de-lis are a copper coin of the Ayyubid al-Malik aẓ-Ẓāhir Ghiyāth ad-dīn Ghāzī b. al-Malik an-Nāṣir Yūsuf,[2] without indication of mint or date, but struck some time between 582 and 613 (1186–1216), probably in Aleppo, and a dirham of al-Malik al-ʿĀdil Saif ad-dīn Abū Bakr b. Ayyūb[3] struck in Damascus between 605 and 610 (1208/9—1213/14). The frequent occurrence of the fleur-de-lis on Ayyubid coins, although by no means always of heraldic character, shows that it must have meant more to them than any other ordinary emblem. It continued to appear on some of the Mamluk coins, e.g. on copper coins of al-Malik al-Muẓaffar Ḥājjī, struck in Aleppo,[4] al-Malik al-Ashraf Shaʿbān (764 A.H. Hama),[5] al-Manṣūr ʿAlī (Tripoli,[6] Damascus),[7] and al-Malik aṣ-Ṣāliḥ Ḥājjī (Tripoli).[8] The fleur-de-lis appears also on coins of Barqūq[9] (Tripoli,[10] 797 A.H. Damascus),[11] al-Malik aẓ-Ẓāhir Khushqadam[12] and al-Ashraf Qāytbāy,[13] but as other

[1] Creswell, 'The Origin of the Cruciform Plan of Cairine Madrasas' (in *BIFAO.* t. XXI, 1923, p. 27).

[2] *BM.* IV. 86, No. 321.

[3] Ib., p. 99, No. 364 (n.d.); cf. also p. 97, No. 358 (605 A.H.). In both cases below the inscriptions and not heraldic. Lavoix, *Catalogue des monnaies musulmanes de la Bibliothèque Nationale*, vol. Égypte et Syrie, Paris 1896, p. 225 f., No. 590 (610 A.H.).

[4] Lavoix, l.c., p. 356 f., Nos. 870, 871, and in an uncertain mint Nos. 873–5 (pl. VII), all of these without date.

[5] Lane-Poole, l.c. *Additions*, I–IV, p. 362, No. 606 q, pl. XIX ; Lavoix, l.c., p. 375, No. 908.

[6] Lavoix, p. 387 f., Nos. 930–4 (pl. VIII), without dates.

[7] Date much obliterated, obviously [78]3, in the Palestine Archaeological Museum, Jerusalem. Probably identical with Lavoix, p. 385, No. 927, pl. VIII.

[8] Without date, in the Palestine Archaeological Museum.

[9] Without mint or date, in the Palestine Archaeological Museum, Jerusalem, another type Lavoix, p. 409 f., Nos. 967–9, pl. IX.

[10] Without date, in the Palestine Archaeological Museum.

[11] *BM.* IV, p. 196 f., Nos. 633–4 ('ornament resembling fleur-de-lis').

[12] The following references are given with all reservations; on the coin Lavoix, No. 1070, p. 462, reproduced on pl. X, there is no trace of a fleur-de-lis despite the author's assertion to the contrary. Dinars struck in Cairo, Lavoix, p. 463 f., Nos. 1072–4. On others, most probably not heraldic, without mints, one of which was struck in 866 (1461/2), Lavoix, p. 466 f., Nos. 1077, 1078, and on a dirham ib., p. 467, No. 1079, struck in Cairo in 866.

[13] Dirham struck in Cairo, Lavoix, p. 471, No. 1084.

coins of the last-named sultans show a number of other emblems, it is very doubtful whether these are blazons at all. About the middle of the eighth century of the Hijra, the fleur-de-lis appears also as an amirial device. We find it for the first time on the lamp of the wazir Maḥmūd b. ʿAlī b. Shirwīn, now at Edinburgh, probably made in 747 (1346/7). In a waqf text dated second decade of Rabīʿ II 784 (24th June–3rd July 1382) built into the walls of a ruined mosque in Damascus, there is a fleur-de-lis on the lower section of a two-fielded shield worn by Shihāb ad-dīn Ḥaidar al-ʿAskarī, a dignitary of the *janāb* class. Two generations later we find it again on either side of an inscription over the Zāwiya Mawlawiyya in Hims[1] dated Muḥarram 841 (5th July–3rd August 1437). The last dated example, an ornament and not a coat of arms, is the one on a door-knocker of the Madrasa Khiḍriyya, made in 878 (1473) by the Chief Qāḍī Quṭb ad-dīn b. al-Khiḍrī.[2]

In composite blazons we find it always on the lowest fields: on the blazon of Saif ad-dīn Aynāl al-ʿAlāʾī, later Sultan al-Malik al-Ashraf, on an inscription in the Kātib al-Wilāyah mosque in Gaza, dated 835 (1431/2), on a bowl made for Barsbāy ash-Sharafī, on two dishes, one of Jānībak, the second with the name obliterated,[3] all three of them probably dating from the third quarter of the ninth (fifteenth) century.

'Few figures have puzzled the antiquary so much as the fleur-de-lis. Countless origins have been suggested for it', says Fox-Davies, who concludes that 'to France and the arms of France one must turn for the origin of the heraldic use of the fleur-de-lis'.[4] This conclusion, however, will hardly withstand criticism, and that for the following reason: Although the fleur-de-lis, presumably as a mere meaningless form of decoration, is found in use long before the days of armoury in Europe or in Asia, the essential difference is that in the pre-heraldic form of the Western fleur-de-lis the three elements are connected, growing as it were from one stem, whereas the definitely established heraldic form, as seen in the arms of Louis VII, consists of three separate leaves held together in the middle by a band. In the East, all early forms of the fleur-de-

[1] Cf. Armorial Roll, s.v. Aḥmad b. Ismaʿīl al-Kūjukī.

[2] E. de Lorey, 'Quelques monuments arabes de Damas' (in *Actes du Congrès d'Histoire de l'Art*, Paris, 26 Septembre—5 Octobre 1921, I, troisième section, p. 314, pl. 16, fig. 2), Paris 1923.

[3] Louis Massignon, 'Six plats de bronze de style mamelouk', *BIFAO*. t. X, No. 3, p. 10, pl. III. The drawing gives the impression of the emblem being a kind of serpent, but on close examination of the plate itself, which its owner, Professor Massignon, very kindly placed at my disposal, I was able to ascertain that it was originally a fleur-de-lis.

[4] *A Complete Guide to Heraldry*, 2nd ed., London 1925, p. 272 f.

lis, whether merely decorative or heraldic, are of the latter type, namely, with three separate leaves. Thus we find it on an Egyptian seal cylinder of Rameses III,[1] discovered at Baisan, in Samarra, as a wall decoration,[2] and on fragments of Fusṭāṭ pottery. The early European type of the fleur-de-lis (with connected leaves) appears in the East only during the second half of the fourteenth century, the first datable example being on coins of Barqūq. There is not a single case, either on Mamluk coins or on any objects of art, where an early specimen of this form of the fleur-de-lis is of an indisputably heraldic character. The only permissible conclusion, therefore, would seem to be that the true heraldic form of the fleur-de-lis is of Saracenic origin.

Bend

An undivided shield, bendy of seven pieces, occurs once, superimposed on the shield of Ibrāhīm b. Baktamur al-Ḥusāmī, and cannot, therefore, be of earlier date than 700 A.H. (1300). But bends usually appear only on the lower field of two-fielded shields and as such seem to have been a family emblem of the Hama branch of the Ayyubids. Abu-l-Fidā' 's round shield was two-fielded, with the upper field either self-coloured[3] or of unknown colour and the lower bendy of a varying number of pieces. That of Nūr ad-dīn b. 'Imād ad-dīn[4] (who, it would appear, was a great-grandson of Abu-l-Fidā') is very similar, except that the shield, as shown on an inscription in Abu-l-Fidā' 's mosque at Hama, is pointed and the lower field is bendy of five pieces. On two perfume-sprays, one in the possession of M. E. Paravacini,[5] Zeitoun-Cairo, the other in the possession of the Museum of Fine Arts, Boston,[6] the upper field of the blazon shows a lion passant and the lower is bendy of eight and ten pieces respectively.

Rosette

The fourth place among the emblems that are neither symbols nor marks of office is occupied by the rosette. It was one of the oldest devices used under the Ayyubids, and became the badge of the Rasūlid and Rāsid dynasties, and, to judge from its frequent occurrence on pottery, must have been very popular with the early Mamluks. The Ayyubid and Mamluk rosette is usually six-petalled (Mūsā b. Yaghmūr's is eight-petalled), and the Rasūlid five-petalled.

[1] Rowe, 'The Palestine Expedition, Report of the 1928 Season' (in *Museum Journal*, 1929, p. 55).

[2] Herzfeld, *Der Wandschmuck der Bauten von Samarra und seine Ornamentik*, Berlin 1923, Ornament No. 260, p. 200, fig. 285, pl. XCI.

[3] Cf. Armorial Roll, s.v. [4] Cf. pl. XX. 1. [5] Cf. pl. I. 7.

[6] *Bulletin of the Museum of Fine Arts, Boston*, December 1910, p. 51.

The whirling rosette is not a blazon. In the fourteenth century it often formed part of blazons with several emblems, but under the Circassians it went out of fashion and appeared only once, in 1449 (al-ʿAinī).

The list of its holders, in chronological order, is as follows: Mūsā b. Yaghmūr, Kāfūr ar-Rūmī, Bahādur Āṣ, Alṭunbughā b. Yūsuf, Muḥammad b. Qalāūn, Baybughā, Shaʿbān, al-ʿAinī.

Bars

Although bars, as a device, are merely a multiplied fesse, it seems advisable to class them separately, since what in Saracenic heraldry looks like a fesse is in reality an office-mark, whereas no such meaning can be attributed to the bars. This device was borne by three amirs: Bahādur al-Manjakī, Qushtamur, *shādd ad-dawāwīn* in Egypt, and Ṭurunṭay aṭ-Ṭabbākhī, whose biographies afford no clue to the meaning of this blazon.

Crescent

The crescent, although quite common on heraldic potsherds, appears only in two historical blazons: that of ʿAlī b. Hilāl ad-daula, without a shield, and on the lower field of the shield of Ṣārim ad-dīn Ibrāhīm b. ʿAqīl ash-Shihābī. In the first of these cases one might be induced to think of a canting coat, *hilāl* in Arabic meaning 'crescent'. In the second, there are neither biographical indications nor hints in the inscription to help us. Nevertheless, I venture to suggest that the possibility be considered of this emblem being in reality not a crescent, but a horseshoe (according to Abu-l-Fidā' the emblem of the master of the stable, *amīr akhūr*). The oriental horseshoe, even in these days, is very different from the European.[1] It looked—and still looks—like a circle with a small hole inside. Drawn with a pair of compasses it would look just like the device on Ibrāhīm's shield, and still more so on potsherds. But of course, before forming any definite opinion, we shall have to wait until a case with conclusive literary evidence is available.

This emblem often appears in combination with other charges, either displayed on them, e.g. on napkins, or placed alongside or between, e.g. with swords. With the introduction of the composite blazon on three-fielded shields it disappears entirely.

Hitherto certain pictures have been regarded as blazons even though there

[1] To give one instance out of many, cf. the fifteenth-century miniature in Schulz, *Die persisch-islamische Miniaturmalerei*, Volume of Plates, No. 47.

was no evidence for their heraldic character. They are: trees,[1] fishes,[2] the so-called 'Seal of Solomon',[3] the dagger,[4] the flower,[5] the duck,[6] and the antelope.[7]

GRAMMAR OF HERALDRY

TERMINI TECHNICI

In the strict sense of the word there is only one technical term in Arabic heraldic language, and that is the word *rank*. It has already been pointed out that this word meant originally 'colour', and then 'came to mean, like our own expression, the "colours" of a regiment, and hence any distinguishing "badge" or "bearing", "coat of arms"'.[8] The exact meaning of the word is difficult to establish; in some instances it is used in the sense of 'achievement', to signify the whole of the emblazonment; in others it evidently denotes only the devices upon the shield, the exclusive word for the latter being *shiʿār* (emblem, distinctive sign). The shield is called *ad-dāʾira* (the circle), obviously because of the shape of most blazons,[9] the field is called *arḍ* (ground), and its divisions *shaṭfa* or *shaṭab* (the latter once used for fesse). The names of the emblems are given in the paragraphs dealing with them.

THE SHIELD

'The shield is the most important part of the achievement.' FOX-DAVIES, p. 60.

In Muslim Heraldry the use of arms did not necessitate the use of a shield. Arms could be displayed on shields of every conceivable shape, or they could be depicted on an object directly without the medium of a shield. Some of the earliest blazons appear without a shield, e.g. the lion of Baybars on coins, walls, and in the metal-work on doors; or they may appear at one time with,

1 Prisse d'Avennes, *L'Art Arabe*, p. 68; Gayet, *L'Art Arabe*, p. 282.

2 Artin, *Contribution*, p. 76 ff.

3 Artin, ib., pp. 174f.

4 Of the type published by Artin, ib., p. 179, No. 308. A glance at the original, a potsherd in the British Museum, shows that this dagger owes its origin merely to the unskilled hand of Artin Pasha's draftsman. In reality it is a plain and unmistakable sword.

5 Artin, ib., p. 173, No. 302.

6 Prisse d'Avennes, l.c., p. 66; Lane-Poole, *Art of the Saracens*, p. 270.

7 Printed label of the tray 420—1854, in the Victoria and Albert Museum ('... an escutcheon... an antelope within a fence'). Pictures, such as the owl, Karabacek, *Sarazenische Wappen*, pp. 22 ff., Gayet, l.c., p. 282, &c., not having been attributed to Saracens—within the meaning of our definition—are not enumerated here.

8 Lane-Poole, *The Art of the Saracens*, p. 269.

9 I do not remember reading an Arabic term for any other kind of heraldic shield.

and another time without, a shield, e.g. with a shield, Tankiz in his madrasah in Jerusalem and in Damascus, without it on his khan at Qalqīlieh, or again once on a round shield and then on a pointed one, e.g. Qarāsunqur's round shield over the window of his madrasah in Cairo or on the public fountain in Aleppo-Firdaus, and the pointed one on a metal ring on the western column of the prayer-niche in the same madrasah; or Muḥammad b. Kitbughā's round shield on a candle-stick in the Arabic Museum, Cairo, and his pointed one on a plate in the possession of Mr. R. A. Harari, London.

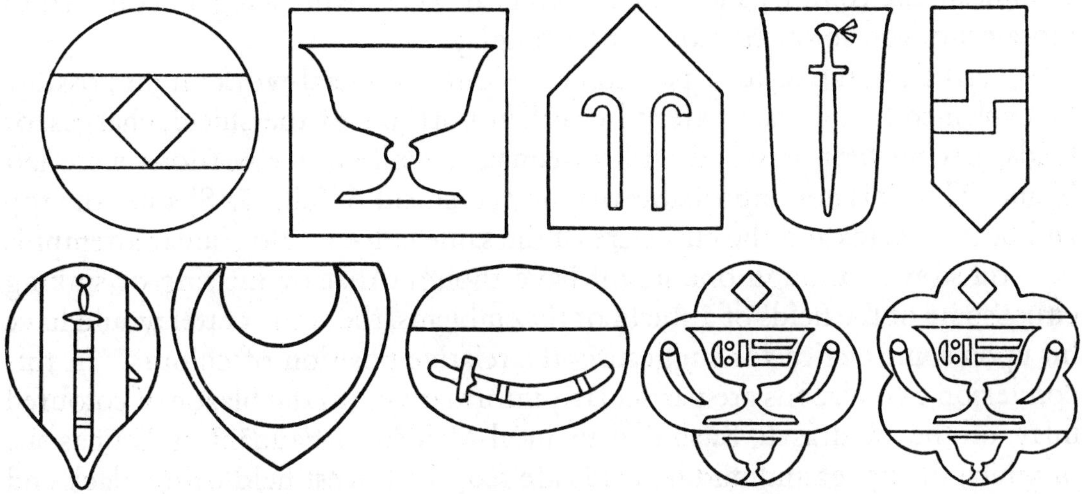

It would not appear that any specific shape of shield was reserved for any particular rank of knights, or for women, or for special classes of blazons.

One of the earliest fields on which Muslim blazons were displayed seems to have been the banner, and this probably accounts for the fact that the original arms had no shield at all. When blazons came to be depicted on shields, the heraldic shields were usually round, and naturally so, because the Saracenic shield, as a piece of armour, was also round. Whether the Ayyubids and Mamluks at some time adopted the pointed shield for warfare under the influence of Frankish armour one cannot say, but in heraldry, pointed, rectangular, and pentagonal shields do appear, although very rarely. The types of shields mentioned in this volume are grouped together on this page.

COLOURS

Since the word used in medieval Arabic for 'blazon' means colour, we should naturally expect all Saracenic blazons to display great variety of colour. Saracenic authors sometimes speak of colours[1] in their descriptions of heraldic shields, but not when the device only is mentioned without description of the shield.[2] The colouring of the objects themselves, however, is very disappointing. The full range of colours appears only on glass, ceramics, in mosaic work and wall paintings; the blazons on pottery are as a rule so unreliable both as to design and colour that neither the shades nor the main colours are to be trusted. On metal objects colours are very rare and where they do appear they are confined to white and red.[3] In architecture generally no attempt was made to indicate the colours, such few attempts as were made being all confined to mosaic work in coloured stone or paste-inlay.

Nevertheless, the relative position of colours on metal-work might possibly be explained to a certain extent by certain portions of the shield, charges, or fields, having been covered with ornaments, while other portions were left blank. Thus it is not improbable that on the shield of Timrāz Shamsī the top and bottom fields and the cup were of the same colour. No similar attempt is seen on stone, although one might have thought that by incising or sinking either some of the fields of a shield or the emblems, the stone cutter would have hit upon some device for suggesting the relative position of colours. In this connexion two blazons are particularly informative: (*a*) the blazon of coloured inlay of the Madrasah Rāshidiyyah in al-Maidān al-Fauqānī at Damascus, of which the upper and middle fields are red, the lowest field being black and the cup on the middle field white, whereas the achromatic shield on the corner of the façade, which shows the same blazon but without inlay, has the cup as well as the upper and lower fields of the shield raised, i.e. brought on a level with the surface of the stone and the middle field sunk; (*b*) three achromatic blazons of Yūnus ad-Dawādār, of which the one on his mausoleum in Cairo has its upper and lower fields raised, i.e. level with the surface of the stone, and the relevant charges sunk, whereas the middle field is sunk and its emblem raised; that on his khan at Khān Yūnis near Gaza has its upper and lower fields sunk and the relevant emblems raised, whereas the middle field is raised

[1] Qalqashandī, *Ṣubḥ al-Aʿshā*, IV. 61 l. ult., V. 34, l. 14, 301, l. 13; Ibn Iyās, II, p. 137, l. 20; Ibn Taghrībirdī, *al-Manhal aṣ-Ṣāfī*, s.v. Āqūsh al-Afram (MS. Paris, Ar. 2069, fo. 3^r); *an-Nujūm az-zāhira* (MS. Paris, Ar. 1783, fo. 77^v, l. 6 f.).

[2] Abu-l-Fidā', ed. Constantinople, IV. 132; Ibn Iyās, II, p. 127, l. 9; Maqrīzī, *an-Nuqūd al-qadīmah*, Constantinople, 1298, p. 15; Ibn Taghrībirdī, *al-Manhal aṣ-Ṣāfī*, s.v. Aybak; Maqrīzī, *Khiṭaṭ*, II. 146, l. 7 b (2nd ed., i.e. Cairo, 1324, vol. III. 238, l. 12).

[3] With the very welcome exception of the pen-box of Abu-l-Fidā', in the possession of Mr. R. A. Harari, London, where black and gold inlay appears as well.

and the emblem sunk, that on his mosque in Damascus has the upper field sunk and the emblem raised, while both middle and lower fields are sunk and the relevant emblems raised. It would be hard to find better examples than these for proving that there was no question of any indication of colour on monochrome stone.

The colours used, making due allowance for changes owing to natural decay or the influence of soil or atmosphere, are: white (silver on metal), yellow (gold on metal and glass), red, green, blue, brown, black, and self-colour.[1] Cream, so often seen on pottery, probably stood for white. All the colours appear in a range of shades, two different shades of the same colour sometimes being used on the same shield.

Simple Charges

The simple charges[2] have been dealt with on pp. 10–26 of the Introduction, so that there is no need to discuss them here. It will be recalled, however, that so far as we are in a position to interpret them, they are either marks of office or symbols, both animate or inanimate, either personal or tribal.

Composite Blazons

Matters are more difficult when we come to deal with composite blazons. These again can be subdivided under two heads: blazons containing one symbol two or three times repeated, and blazons consisting of several devices. The only emblem used in the first subdivision is the cup. So far as my knowledge goes, there is no pair of polo-sticks or swords, or pen-box, napkin, round table, or any other charge repeated on two fields of the same shield without other emblems appearing as well. It must be borne in mind that we are only dealing with blazons accompanied by inscriptions.[3] Some of the holders of these blazons with double or treble cups were cup-bearers, e.g. Shaikh al-Khāṣṣakī, but by no means all of them. We know, for example, that the Atābak Damurdāsh aẓ-Ẓāhirī,[4] Governor of Aleppo and Tripoli in 812, was an armour-bearer (*silaḥdār*) when in the page corps at the court of Sultan

[1] By 'self-colour' I mean cases like the shield of Ṭuquztamur, the upper field of which is of colourless transparency on his glass lamps and yellowish on his copper and brass vases.

[2] To facilitate the survey, all these emblems have been arranged on p. 8 and given numbers to which reference is made in the text.

[3] But cf. p. 79, l. 5 f.

[4] Serving Barqūq's son, al-Malik an-Nāṣir Faraj, he used to be called an-Nāṣirī.

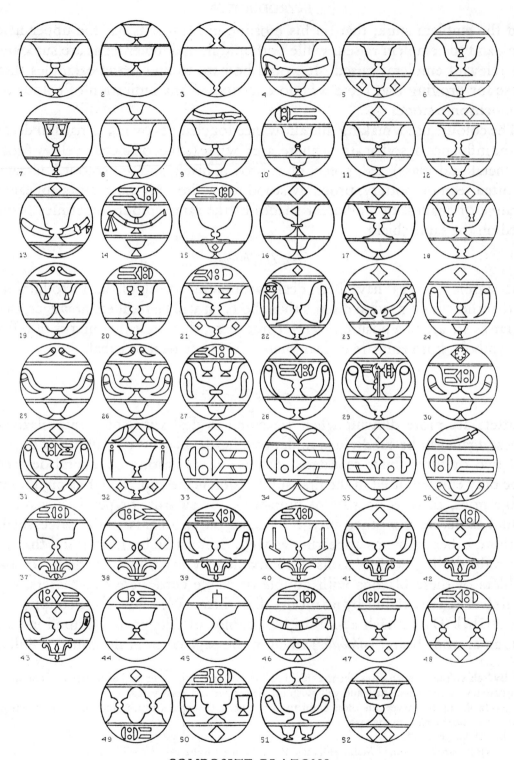

COMPOSITE BLAZONS

Barqūq, Aytmish being jamdār. We have detailed biographies of these men, but there is no record that they ever served as cup-bearers.

These are comparatively simple cases; but the more composite the blazon, the less can the emblem be regarded as a mark of office.

In the first dated fully composite blazon, that of Jamāl ad-dīn al-Ustādār, we have an example of a combination of two marks of office: the pen-box, together with the sword and the emblem No. 26, which would imply that the holder served simultaneously in two different sections of the page corps. Later on we find coats of arms with still more charges: the typical blazon of the end of the fifteenth century contained six figures, and that of Uzbak al-Yūsufī nine, representing three different marks of office. This accumulation of subaltern page offices might be explicable in the rare case of a specially gifted page at court, but as an every day occurrence, as the usual *cursus honorum* of the average cadet, who later on became an average amir, it seems highly improbable, not to say impossible, especially as there is no record of such a *cursus honorum* to be found in contemporary sources. This is an argument *ex silentio*; the positive proof is that biographies of Mamluk amirs of the fifteenth century show in all cases known to us a series of court offices very different from those which we should have to reconstruct on the basis of the charges displayed on their coat of arms.[1]

As we have already noted, the theory which satisfactorily explains the simple blazon does not explain the composite blazon at all, and we must look elsewhere for an explanation.

Similar phenomena are also conspicuous in European heraldry. The very simple charges of the early centuries of our millenium become more and more multiplex as time goes on and long before there is any question of overcrowding shields by quartering or by augmentation of honour, we find from five to six devices on a blazon used merely for the sake of variety. To a certain degree the same may be said to apply to Muslim heraldry. At a time when there was one cup-bearer at court, a shield with a cup was informative enough; when, in the fifteenth century, the number of khāṣṣakīs was increased (under Barsbāy there were about 1,000 of them),[2] the small range of colours used in Muslim heraldry did not afford sufficient differentiation, so that recourse was had to other means, namely, to a variety of emblems. There is also a very marked inconsistency to be taken into account. If we consider in chronologi-

[1] Cf. the biographies of the relevant amirs in 'The Armorial Roll'.

[2] *CIA. Égypte*, I. 287, n. 2.

cal order the blazons of the fifteenth century, which start with two devices and end with nine, we find a constantly growing diversity. But in examining them closer we discover that about four-fifths belong to one or the other of the following three groups:

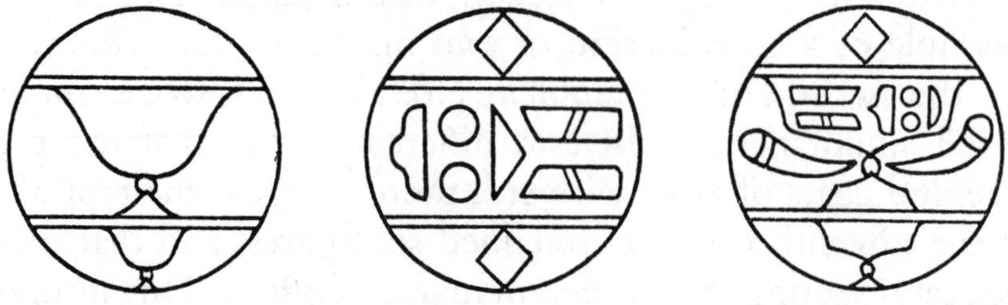

It is as though this incongruity, namely multiplicity of figures, with paucity of types of badges, made a proper explanation of the composite blazon impossible.

It would seem that under the late Ayyubids and early Mamluks, amirs were granted their blazons,[1] whereas under the Circassians they were allowed free choice.[2] And fashion was undoubtedly largely responsible for the choice of the devices, except that it cannot be considered as the only, perhaps not even as the main, determining factor.

Let us consider two examples of larger classes of composite blazons, the *early* fifteenth-century blazon with two cups, and the *late* fifteenth-century blazon having a napkin in the upper field, a big cup charged with a pen-box and placed between two figures representing, perhaps, a pair of trousers in the middle field and a small cup in the lower one. We shall not deal with the middle group, since either by accident or for unknown reasons, the number of historical and identifiable persons among the holders of this blazon is too small to admit of any conclusions being drawn.

The following blazons of the first group are known: Aytmish, Barakab, Damurdāsh, Duqmāq, Kumushbughā, Taghrībirmish, Yashbak ash-Sha'bānī.

Of the second: Āqbirdī, Bilbāy, Jānbalāṭ, Jauhar, Khairbak, Khairbak min Aynāl, Khudābirdī, Muḥammad b. an-Nashāshībī, Muḥsin, Qānībāy, Qajmās, Qānṣūh, Sībāy, Sūdūn, Tanam, Tānībak.

The list is not a very long one; it could, of course, be considerably extended by adding all the instances of inscriptions that make mention either of an 'al-

[1] Quatremère, *Sultans Mamlouks*, I a, p. 2, n. 4; Reinaud, 'Observations générales sur les médailles musulmanes à figures' (in *Journal Asiatique*, 18e cahier, 1823, p. 353).

[2] Qalqashandī, *Ṣubḥ al-a'shā*, IV. 62, l. 1.

Malikī aẓ-Ẓāhirī' or an 'al-Malikī al-Ashrafī', enabling us to identify the amir, although we could not prove in these cases that al-Malik aẓ-Ẓāhir refers to Barqūq, and al-Malik al-Ashraf to Qāytbāy. In a few instances, especially on small objects, space did not allow the craftsman to finish the protocol, so that he had to drop the 'relatif d'appartenance'.

But even as the list stands it contains a fair number of all the blazons extant, and so may serve to suggest, if not, perhaps, to prove, that most of the Ẓāhirīs Barqūq and Ashrafīs Qāytbāy had a blazon of the same design, although evidently different in point of colours.

This being so, we may venture on the general statement that, during the fifteenth century, the Mamluks of each powerful sultan, who, in history, always appear as united groups bound together by a strong *esprit de corps*, had a common badge irrespective of the office held by the individual Mamluk when the amirate was conferred upon him.

This would be the simplest explanation of the apparent inconsistency that in the very period characterized by the tendency to make blazons more and more complicated, big groups of identical blazons should have been formed.

In a class by itself are the two composite blazons showing emblems charged with complete shields, one of Ghars ad-dīn Khalīl on the minbar of the mosque at Qūṣ, consisting of a three-fielded shield, the middle field of which is charged with the emblem No. 26 displayed on an undivided shield, the other of 'Alā' ad-dīn 'Alī b. Nāṣir ad-dīn Muḥammad on the southern wall of the Madrasa Ṣubaibiyya, Jerusalem, consisting of a three-fielded shield, upper field blank, on the middle field a cup charged with a napkin displayed on the middle field of a three-fielded shield, on the lower field a cup.

Hybrid Compositions

We should classify as hybrid compositions all blazons depicting either animals or tamghas together with signs of office. As we have seen in previous chapters, in all cases in which sufficient details about the lives of their holders are known, it is the sign of office that is the essential component of the blazon, the other charge being—it would seem—a meaningless addition; e.g. Ṭuquztamur, the *sāqī*, had a cup placed underneath an eagle, Bahādur al-Ḥamawī, Chief of the corps of *jamdārs*, had a napkin underneath an eagle. Cf. also pls. I. 7, III. 5, 9, 11, 12.

Various Blazons on the Same Object

The third group consists of objects each of which has two different blazons, in most cases one in the centre of a dish or bowl and the other repeated on the inner sides. It is most probable that these are blazons of officers and their masters, but since, with the exception of Aydamur al-Qaimarī,[1] none of them is accompanied by an historical inscription, I am contenting myself with reproducing those that have come to my notice, instead of risking a more or less hypothetical explanation.[2]

THE INSCRIBED SHIELD

We have already seen[3] that some scholars have doubted as to whether the Saracenic blazon could properly be called a blazon in the European sense of the word. These doubts were multiplied in the case of shields which, in the place of emblems, merely showed script.[4] The first of these inscribed shields to attract the attention of Orientalists was the shield of the Naṣrid princes of Granada which bears the motto ولا غالب الا الله هـ ('There is no victor but God'). But whereas in the Saracenic provinces we frequently meet with this type of shield and can trace there its evolution from the first tentative examples in the eleventh century down to its decay in the sixteenth, in Spain it remained an isolated phenomenon.

The first datable examples out of which this shield evolves go back to the end of the thirteenth and beginning of the fourteenth century. They are to be found on lamps, bowls, and similar objects which, to judge from the accompanying inscriptions, are attributable to the later Baḥri Mamluk sultans like Muḥammad, the son, and Ḥasan, the grandson, of Qalāūn. About this time, the three-fielded shield of the amirial blazon had already been in use. In like manner, too, the shield comprising inscriptions only was divided into

[1] Cf. Roll, s.v. [2] Cf. pl. XIII. [3] P. 1.

[4] *CIA. Égypte* I, p. 45. The latest instance is v. Zambaur's review of my *Guide to the Exhibition of Moslem Heraldry*, in the *Wiener Zeitschrift f. Kunde d. Morgenlandes*, XXXIII. 288. It was, therefore, not without some reluctance that I dealt with this matter in my 'Das Schriftwappen der Mamlukensultane' (in the *Jahrbuch der asiatischen Kunst*, 1925, pp. 183 ff.), more especially as the term 'rank' is in no authentically verifiable case applied to an inscribed shield. Nevertheless these shields, in the days of the Circassian mamluks, would seem to have taken the place of blazons, and it is for this reason that they have been included—though again with the greatest reserve and without their being called blazons—in this survey. On the other hand it must not be overlooked that, besides the mottoes, there are in European heraldry more instances than one usually remembers of both city arms and family blazons with shields on which nothing more than letters or words are displayed.

three fields,[1] of which the middle one bore the inscription, whilst the upper and lower fields were left blank.

The texts of the inscriptions on shields of this early period occur in the following versions: ' 'izz li-maulānā', ' 'izz li-maulānā as-sulṭān', ' 'izz li-maulānā as-sulṭān al-malik', ' 'izz li-maulānā as-sulṭān 'azza naṣruhu'.[2] The motto is sometimes distributed over several shields, so that only by reading them together is it possible to get the whole of the text.[3] Who the 'Lord' referred to stood for was clear to the user of the vessel, because in most cases his name or titles were mentioned in the accompanying inscriptions. It is only about the middle of the fourteenth century that the sultanian epithet appears on the shields.

A step towards the transition to the Circassian type is seen in a shield of Muḥammad b. Qalāūn[4] in two lines:

(*a*) Muḥammad
(*b*) 'izz li-maulānā as-sulṭān al-malik an-nāṣir
(*c*) ornament

and in the shields on the Mosque of Sultan Ḥasan in Cairo, with the inscriptions, ' 'izz li-maulānā as-sulṭān al-malik an-nāṣir Ḥasan' and ' 'izz li-maulānā as-sulṭān al-malik an-nāṣir Ḥasan b. Muḥammad'. It is curious to note that Ḥasan's formula, though later in date, occupies but a single line, whereas his father's shield, in two lines, more nearly approaches the later and final type. At all events these inscriptions contain two-thirds of the full text of the later shield.

This final stage of the inscribed shield is reached under Barqūq. In his inscriptions, lamps, &c., we meet with round medallions with a three-line text in the following variants:

1. (*a*) aẓ-ẓāhir
(*b*) 'izz li-maulānā as-sulṭān al-malik
(*c*) 'azza naṣruhu

[1] It is just possible, of course, that there are inscribed shields with an undivided field. Compare the illustration of a lamp formerly in the collection of J. Pierpont Morgan and now in the Metropolitan Museum of Art, New York.

[2] The words *'azza naṣruhu* on the last-mentioned sherd are at the end of the line, and placed in a position vertical to that of the rest of the text.

[3] *CIA. Jérusalem, Ville*, p. 242, pl. LVII. For other examples of this and other kinds of inscribed shields see my 'Das Schriftwappen der Mamlukensultane' (*Jahrbuch der asiatischen Kunst*, 1925, p. 184, n. 8).

[4] Bourgoin, *Précis de l'Art Arabe*, I, p. 6, pl. XXXII: Maison de l'émir Bardak près Sultan Hasan.

2. (*a*) al-malik
(*b*) ʿizz li-maulānā as-sulṭān
(*c*) aẓ-ẓāhir[1]

3. (*a*) Barqūq
(*b*) ʿizz li-maulānā as-sulṭān al-malik aẓ-ẓāhir
(*c*) ʿazza naṣruhu[2]

4. (*a*) aẓ-ẓāhir
(*b*) ʿizz li-maulānā as-sulṭān
(*c*) al-malik.[3]

The fact that the three-fielded inscribed shield had originally only one, a middle line of text, to which at a later stage the first line containing the name was added, shows without need of further explanation that these rows of text must be read in the order of *b*, *a*, *c*, and why they must be so read in most cases.

Of these three forms, No. 3 has become typical, though it took some little time to establish itself. Thus the shield of Faraj, son of Barqūq, reads as follows:

(*a*) Faraj
(*b*) ʿizz li-maulānā as-sulṭān al-malik an-nāṣir
(*c*) b. Barqūq.[4]

Of Faraj's successor, the Caliph al-Mustaʿīn bi-llāh, we possess but a single shield. During the half year of his reign he had little time or occasion to create works of art and to decorate them with blazons. But in the principal mosque at Gaza he did have an inscription[5] engraved to mark the abolition of the unfair taxes (*maẓālim*) imposed by Faraj. In the middle of the slab there is a pear-shaped shield with the following inscription:

(*a*) al-ʿAbbās
(*b*) amīr ul-mu'minīn
(*c*) ʿazza naṣruhu.

The most striking feature about this text, however, apart from its being couched in the terms of a caliphial instead of a sultanian shield, is the absence of the characteristic introduction *ʿizz li-maulānā*.[6]

[1] Wiet, *Lampes*, pl. LXXIX.
[2] Schumacher, 'Researches' (in Q. St. 1886, p. 181).
[3] Wiet, l.c., pls. LXXVIII, LXXX, LXXXIV. The rare forms (2 and 4) represent an exception.
[4] *CIA. Égypte*, I. 318.
[5] The full text of this inscription is to be published in the last instalment of my 'Arabic Inscriptions of Gaza', appearing in the *Journal of the Palestine Oriental Society*.
[6] But the shields of the Sultans Muḥammad b. Qāytbāy (No. 2) and Qānṣūh al-Ghaurī (No. 4) should also be compared.

It is only at this stage, i.e. from the time of the Caliph al-Mustaʿīn bi-llāh, that the inscribed shield takes on a more schematic form and that the expression of the 'formule habituelle des cartouches' becomes justified. The preceding examples have clearly shown that this form was only arrived at after a struggle, to lose it again—as will be seen later—from the time of al-Malik al-ʿĀdil Ṭūmānbāy. But between these two reigns, as evidenced by the following examples, the formula, with two exceptions, was the accepted one. It is chiefly characterized by the upper field consisting of *kunya* and *ism*:

1. (*a*) abu-n-naṣr Shaikh
   (*b*) ʿizz li-maulānā as-sulṭān al-malik al-mu'ayyad
   (*c*) ʿazza naṣruhu [1, 2]

2. (*a*) abu-n-naṣr Barsbāy
   (*b*) ʿizz li-maulānā as-sulṭān al-malik al-ashraf
   (*c*) ʿazza naṣruhu [3]

3. (*a*) abu-n-naṣr Aynāl
   (*b*) ʿizz li-maulānā as-sulṭān al-malik al-ashraf
   (*c*) ʿazza naṣruhu [4]

4. (*a*) [Shihāb ad-dīn?] A[ḥmad]
   (*b*) ʿizz li-maulānā as-sulṭā[n al-malik] al-mu'ayyad
   (*c*) ʿazza naṣruhu [5]

5. (*a*) abu-n-naṣr Qāytbāy
   (*b*) ʿizz li-maulānā as-sulṭān al-malik al-ashraf
   (*c*) ʿazza naṣruhu.[6]

To this period belongs the second caliphial shield that we know. This shield dates from the third quarter of the fifteenth century, and, though its bearer was no sultan, it retained the style of the Mamluk shields. It is the shield of the Caliph Abu-l-Maḥāsin Yūsuf al-Mustanjid bi-llāh, and appears in several

[1] On another shield of Shaikh the words *ʿazza naṣruhu* are omitted:
(*a*) an-naṣr Shaikh
(*b*) ʿizz li-maulānā as-sulṭān al-malik
(*c*) al-mu'ayyad abu.

[2] Van Berchem, *Inschriften Oppenheim*, p. 47.

[3] *CIA. Égypte*, I. 376.

[4] Ib., 401.

[5] *CR.* Exercise 1909, p. 162 f. The next example, on a slab of marble from a house in the Armenian quarter, Jerusalem, now in the Palestine Archaeological Museum, Jerusalem, is an exception to the rule:
(*a*) al-malik aẓ-ẓāhir
(*b*) ʿizz li-maulānā as-sulṭān
(*c*) Abū Saʿīd Khushqadam.

[6] *CIA. Égypte*, I. 431.

medallions on a basin published by Sobernheim.[1] The inscription reads:

'ʿizz li-maulānā amīr al-mu'minīn ʿazza qudsuhu'.

The fact that it is anonymous and occupies only one line gives it the character of a shield dating from the period of the Qalāūn dynasty rather than from the time of Qāytbāy. However, as there can be no doubt about its attribution, the date, too, must be correct.

The first deviation from the form occurs under Muḥammad, the son of Qāytbāy, and consists of the dropping of the *kunya*:

1. (*a*) Muḥammad
(*b*) ʿizz li-maulānā as-sulṭān al-malik an-nāṣir
(*c*) ʿazza naṣruhu[2]

or of the inclusion of the father's name in the top field, and the transposition of the *kunya* to the middle field, to read:

1. (*a*) Muḥammad[3] b. Qāytbāy
(*b*) as-sulṭān al-malik an-nāṣir abu-s-saʿādāt
(*c*) ʿazza naṣruhu.[4]

In the shield of aẓ-Ẓāhir Qānṣūh the old form is again reverted to, thus:

(*a*) Abū Saʿīd Qānṣūh
(*b*) ʿizz li-maulānā as-sulṭān al-malik aẓ-ẓāhir
(*c*) ʿazza naṣruhu.[5]

Under Qānsūh al-Ghaurī practically all the forms up to then in use again recur:

1. (*a*) abu-n-naṣr Qānṣūh
(*b*) ʿizz li-maulānā as-sulṭān al-malik al-ashraf
(*c*) ʿazza naṣruhu[6]

2. (*a*) Qānṣūh al-Ghaurī
(*b*) ʿizz li-maulānā as-sulṭān al-malik al-ashraf
(*c*) ʿazza naṣruhu[7]

3. (*a*) abu-n-naṣr Qānṣūh al-Ghaurī
(*b*) ʿizz li-maulānā as-sulṭān al-malik al-ashraf
(*c*) ʿazza naṣruhu[8]

[1] 'Arabische Gefässinschriften von der Ausstellung islamischer Kunst in Paris ⟨1903⟩' (in *ZDPV*. XXVIII, 1905, p. 184).
[2] *CIA. Égypte*, I. 457.
[3] Erroneously written *m ḥ d.*
[4] Van Berchem, *Arabische Inschriften* (*Exhibition Munich*), p. 18.
[5] *CIA. Égypte*, I. 556.
[6] Ib., 580, n. 1.
[7] Ib., 577, pl. XXXVII, 4.
[8] *CIA. Égypte*, I. 565.

4. (*a*) Qānṣūh
(*b*) al-mālik al-malik al-ashraf abu-n-naṣr al-Ghaurī
(*c*) ʿazza naṣruhu [1]

5. (*a*) Qānṣūh
(*b*) ʿizz li-maulānā as-sulṭān al-malik al-ashraf abu-n-naṣr Qānṣūh al-Ghaurī
(*c*) ʿazza naṣruhu [2]

and, strangest of all, in that it again reverts to the very earliest forms of inscribed shields:

6. ʿizz li-maulānā as-sulṭān al-malik al-ashraf [3]

with blank upper and lower field.

It is this epoch of the complete decay of the inscribed shield from which dates the shield of the Amir Dawlātbāy (the amir whom van Berchem was probably correct in assuming to have been the governor of Gaza), and which reads:

(*a*) Dawlātbāy
(*b*) al-maqarr al-ashraf al-ʿālī as-saifī
(*c*) ʿazza naṣruhu.[4]

It would here seem to have been a case of an insolent amir who, conscious of his own power and the weakness of his sovereign, arrogated to himself one of the prerogatives of the sultan.

Contrary to the amirial blazons, the inscribed shields did not disappear immediately after the Ottoman conquest. In the Citadel at Jerusalem we come across medallions[5] bearing the name of Sultan Sulaimān I. In form these medallions are very similar to the Mamluk type, reading:

(*a*) ʿazza Allāhu	(*a*) abu-n-naṣr Sulaimān shāh
(*b*) as-sulṭān Sulaimān	(*b*) ʿizz li-maulānā as-sulṭān al-malik al-muẓaffar
(*c*) naṣrahu	(*c*) ibn ʿUthmān ʿazza naṣruhu

whilst their date may be taken to be 1531/2. But then these last offshoots of the inscribed shield are already outside the purview of our subject.

The common shape of the inscribed shield was round or pear-shaped, tapering towards the bottom. There are cases, however, of bi-cuspid shields (round shields that bulge at the centre and grow narrower at the top and

[1] Sobernheim, *Zitadelle*, p. 26. [2] Ib., p. 26, pl. IV, fig. 1. [3] *CIA. Égypte*, I. 682.
[4] Van Berchem, *Arabische Inschriften* (*Exhibition Munich*), p. 18.
[5] *CIA. Jérusalem*, *Ville*, p. 149 f., fig. 19. A fine photograph of the second medallion was published in *Jerusalem*, ed. C. R. Ashbee, I, fig. 79.

bottom),[1] and shields with a rounded top field, square centre, and triangular lower field.[2] Other types of shields known to us from the arms of amirs do not, to my knowledge, occur in the inscribed shield.

THE PROBLEM OF HEREDITY

The question as to whether armorial bearings of the Ayyubids and Mamluks were transmitted from father to son is one of the many problems of Muslim heraldry which previous writers have answered partly in the affirmative and partly in the negative.

Rogers[3] was convinced that the blazon was not hereditary. Although he knew that Ānūk carried the blazon of his grandfather Qalāūn,[4] and that two grandsons and a great grandson of Muḥammad b. Qalāūn had the same blazon, viz. the fleur-de-lis,[5] when describing the blazon of Baraka Khān,[6] who carried the same emblem as his father Baybars, he wrote: 'je n'ai vu qu'un seul cas où le fils ait pris les mêmes armoiries que son père' which shows that he considered this to be an exception.

The same view was held by Lavoix,[7] Prisse d'Avennes,[8] and Lane-Poole.[9] Artin Pasha[10] repeated it: 'les armoiries n'étaient pas héréditaires dans une famille', but he changed his opinion fourteen years later.[11]

Karabacek[12] stated several times that the Saracens had family blazons (*Hauswappen*), although he never attempted to prove it.

The difficulty of seeing clearly in this matter lies in the scantiness of the material. There were few sons and still fewer grandsons of amirs who held high rank in the military class of Mamluk society. The children of amirs used to receive a religious and general education fitting them rather for religious

[1] Sobernheim, 'Arabische Gefässinschriften von der Ausstellung in Paris' (in *ZDPV*. XXVIII, 1905, pl. VI).

[2] G. Schumacher, 'Researches in Southern Palestine' (in *Quarterly Statements of the Palestine Exploration Fund*, 1886, p. 181).

[3] *Le Blason*, p. 94. [4] Ib., p. 98. [5] Ib., p. 105. [6] Ib., p. 86.

[7] *GBA*. t. XXXII, 1885, p. 300: n'étaient pas héréditaires.

[8] *L'Art Arabe*, p. 67: chaque émir adoptait ou recevait un signe, que son fils n'était pas tenu de conserver et changeait à volonté.

[9] *The Art of the Saracens*, p. 270: they were not hereditary.

[10] 'Trois différentes armoiries' (in *BIE*., 2e série, No. 9, 1888, p. 74).

[11] *Contribution*, p. 227: nous ne pouvons affirmer avec certitude, et d'une manière générale, que pour tous les chevaliers blasonnés, l'hérédité des armoiries existait ou a pu exister à une certaine époque en Orient.

[12] *Geschichte der Mazjaditen*, p. 5, n.; *Papyri Erzherzog Rainer. Führer durch die Ausstellung*, No. 1323, p. 272 ('erbliche Familienwappen').

and administrative posts (*al-waẓā'if ad-dīniyya* and *al-waẓā'if ad-dīwāniyya*), the holders of which not being military dignitaries most likely had no badges. Of the tens of thousands of blazons which were painted, engraved, or sculptured in the Mamluk realm, perhaps not more than three thousand have so far been discovered, and only a fraction of these is accompanied by inscriptions. Of the latter there are fewer than three hundred and fifty historical texts upon which an identification of their respective bearers could be based. In these circumstances it is hardly to be expected that the small remnant left should contain many blazons of sons and grandsons of amirs, and especially of several sons of the same amir, the evidence we would require to make sure that it is not a case of mere coincidence but a regular system. To make matters worse, in some of the few cases in which blazons of sons of amirs are known to us, neither the blazons nor the offices of their respective fathers are known at all, so that no comparison can be made. Nevertheless, I venture to submit the hypothesis that the blazon was hereditary in the case of sons of amirial rank, not only because of the identity of the blazon in *all* instances in which the blazons of both father and son are known (Baybars and Baraka Khān, Kitbughā and Muḥammad b. Kitbughā, Qauṣūn and Ḥusain b. Qauṣūn, Sha'bān and Ḥājjī, Sha'bān and 'Alī),[1] but also because in a case in which the blazon of the son only is known, it shows the very emblem we should expect on the shield of his father.[2]

THE ARMORIAL BEARINGS OF WOMEN

Although Muslim women of those times enjoyed a great deal of freedom, with the exception of the foundress of the Mamluk Sultanate in Egypt none of them had ever occupied official posts, failing which they could not show any symbols of such posts in their own rights. Nevertheless, we find on four occasions inscriptions to the memory of women or made by their order and ornamented with blazons: on the tomb of Quṭlū Khātūn in Ṭurunṭāy's madrasah (now the Zāwiyat Sayyid Aḥmad al-Badawī) in Gaza,[3] on a plaque in the at-Turkumānī Mosque in Cairo,[4] on a bowl in the Victoria and Albert Museum in London (557—'78)[5] and on a flat copper dish in the collection of

[1] I am quoting only instances of simple blazons, as identical composite blazons can be explained differently, see p. 29 ff.

[2] Aḥmad b. Baktamur as-sāqī, whose blazon was a cup, although he himself never held the post of cup-bearer. Cf. also Mūsā b. Aruqṭāy, p. 170.

[3] Armorial Roll, s.v.

[4] Cf. Armorial Roll, s.v. Salmā.

[5] Cf. Armorial Roll, s.v. Fāṭima.

M. Eustache de Lorey, formerly Director of the Institut Français d'Archéologie et d'Art Musulmans, Damascus.[1]

In the first case it is difficult to say whether the blazon (two polo-sticks with balls) represents the coats of arms of Bahādur, her father, or of Ṭurunṭāy, the founder of the Madrasah, possibly her husband. Both are called polo-masters in their inscriptions left in the Zāwiyah, but the odds are in favour of Ṭuruntāy, as Bahādur's death occurred prior to his daughter's;[2] it is most likely, therefore, that Ṭurunṭāy put his own blazon on the tomb. The second case is clearer: Salmā was the wife of amir ʿAlā' ad-dīn ʿAlī b. at-Turkumānī, and although we do not know the proper meaning of his blazon and do not know what relation—if any—there is between the enigmatic device on his shield and the office he occupied, there is little doubt that the blazon belongs to him and not to his otherwise quite unknown wife. The third example is that of Lady Fāṭima, daughter of Sūdūn al-Mu'ayyadī, Governor of Hama, an amir, whose blazon is not ascertainable from other sources, so that it is impossible to state whether Fāṭima's coat of arms was his or some other Amir's. The copper dish in M. de Lorey's collection was made by order of a certain Ḥalīma bint an-Nāniq (?), a person whom I am unable to trace in the texts at my disposal; the blazon is not identical with that of the only namesake of her father I have come across.[3]

To sum up: If on the basis of the scanty material available any conclusion could be drawn at all, it would be to the effect that on a Mamluk lady's object her father's or—what is more likely in the case of a married woman—her husband's blazon would appear without any impalement or difference marks.

FORGERIES

The collector of Muslim heraldic objects bound to make diligent search for good pieces is in one respect better off than collectors in other fields because forgeries are rare and very easily detected. The main indications pointing to such forgeries are: (*a*) the workmanship in what may be termed Damascus style of the nineteenth century, mainly in the case of metal and pottery; (*b*) the pseudo-historical inscriptions, invariably very clumsy in their wording without regard to the right character and sequence of the titles,

[1] Cf. Armorial Roll, s.v. Ḥalīma. There was one other blazon of a woman in the collection of M. de Lorey on an object which disappeared during the looting of the Palais Azem in 1925.

[2] On the funerary slab he is spoken of as 'deceased' (*marḥūm*).

[3] Cf. Armorial Roll, s.v. Nāniq al-Ashrafī.

usually anonymous; (*c*) the bizarre form of emblems and hybrid combinations. Moreover, it is questionable whether these objects are forgeries in the proper sense of the word since they may quite possibly have been meant and made to represent modern articles inspired by old models without any intention to deceive the buyer. With the exception of a few lamps there are probably no objects of Muslim art with heraldic emblems that have been faithfully copied from old originals and there are certainly none that would have been copied for the sake of the blazon alone. On the contrary (apart from the general description 'ẓāhirī' by which dealers in Muslim antiquities, especially in Syria, qualify everything that is in their eyes old and Arabic no matter whether it is Umayyad or Ottoman), authentic Mamluk objects, including some with historical inscriptions from the fourteenth century, have often been described to me in shops as being a hundred years old more or less. A few examples shown on pls. LXX and LXXI will illustrate those types which most nearly approach genuine objects.

THE ARMORIAL ROLL

ʿABD AL-QĀDIR

BLAZON: *On upper and lower fields device No. 38, on middle field a pen-box.*

BASIN. Collection R. A. Harari, Esq., London.
Four shields and twice-repeated inscription on the outside of the basin.

ممّا عمل برسم الزيني عبد القادر ○ ابن الكاتب الترجمان عظم شأنه ○

This is one of the objects made for Zain ad-dīn ʿAbd al-Qādir, son of the Scribe and Translator, may his dignity increase.

BIBLIOGRAPHY: Unpublished.

ABŪ BAKR B. ʿABD AL-BĀRR

Possibly identical with T. Abū Bakr b. ʿAbd al-Bārr b. Muḥammad b. al-Ḥusain,[1] originally of Hims, died 795 (1392/3). Grandson of a famous judge in Egypt.

BLAZON: *Upper and lower fields blank, on white middle field a pen-box.*[2]

CANDLESTICK, Louvre, Paris. Formerly collection Piet-Latauderie. Pl. XXXIII. 5, 6. Inscriptions, intersected by shields, on top and sides of the neck, and on top and sides of the body. The last of these inscriptions being the fullest, I am copying it here.

ممّا عمل برسم المقرّ الأشرف الكريم العالى المولوى ○ السيّدى المالكى المخدومى

العضدى الذخرى ○ التقوى أبو [ب]كر [ا]جل المرحوم القاضى عبد البارّ عظم شأنه

This is one of the objects made for His Most Noble and Honourable and High Excellency, our Lord, the Master, the Royal, the Well-Served, the Supporter, the Treasure, Taqī ad-dīn Abū Bakr, son of the late Judge ʿAbd al-Bārr, may his dignity increase.

[1] Ibn Ḥajar, *Durar*, s.v. (MS. Br. Mus., Or. 3043, fo. 83v), where he is called Saif ad-dīn, son of Ṣadr ad-dīn, son of Taqī ad-dīn, the Chief Judge.

[2] The upper and lower fields and the pen-box on the middle field are roughened so as to take an inlay, but all traces of the latter are gone.

BIBLIOGRAPHY: Unpublished.
Reproduced, with short descriptions: Migeon, 'Collection de M. Piet-Latauderie' (in *Les Arts*, August 1909, pp. 24 and 25); Migeon, *Exposition des Arts Musulmans au Musée des Arts Décoratifs*, pl. 24; Migeon, *L'Orient Musulman, Armes, Sculpture, &c.*, p. 27, No. 111, pl. 31; Devonshire, 'Some Mihrâb Candlesticks' (in *The Burlington Magazine*, December 1923), fig. D, to which belongs the text under fig. B, where it is ascribed to Abū Bakr b. Muzhir.

ABŪ BAKR MUḤAMMAD B. MUZHIR [1]

Z. Abū Bakr Muḥammad b. Muzhir ad-Dimishqī al-Anṣārī, born 832 (1428/9), became on the 20th Dhu-l-Qaʿda 866 (16th August 1462) Privy Secretary (*kātib as-sirr*), Inspector of Stables (*nāẓir al-iṣṭabl*), then Inspector of the Army (*nāẓir al-jaish*), in 876 appointed Superintendent of the Chancery (*nāẓir dīwān al-inshā'*), an office he held till his death the 3rd [2] Ramaḍān 893 (11th August 1488).

BLAZON: *Pen-box on the middle field of a three-fielded shield.*

MADRASA of Abū Bakr, Cairo.
Inset in the pulpit and the doors in the main hall of the building many shields of wood inlaid with ivory.

BIBLIOGRAPHY: Reproduced: *CR.* fasc. 8, pl. III, Devonshire, *Sultan Salâh ed-Dîn's Writing-box in the National Museum of Arab Art, Cairo*, p. 243, fig. E.
Mentioned: *CR.* Exerc. 1897, fasc. 14, p. vi.

ABU-L-FIDĀ' [3]

ʿImād ad-dīn Abu-l-Fidā' Ismāʿīl b. ʿAlī al-Ayyūbī, born in Jumādā I 672 (which began 13th November 1273); saw military service under his cousin al-Malik al-Muẓaffar Maḥmūd, prince (*ṣāḥib*) of Hama, in 690 (1291) as Amir

[1] *Nujūm*, VII, pp. 696, l. 9, 711, l. 9, 746, l. 6, 749, l. 4; Ibn Iyās, cf. Index, especially II, p. 253, l. 7 ff.; Mujīr ad-dīn, *al-Uns al-jalīl*, p. 389, l. 4 ff.; *CR.* fasc. 8, p. 94; ʿAlī Pasha, V. 114; *CIA. Égypte*, I. 506, n. 4 and 6; Wiet, 'Les Secrétaires de la Chancellerie' (*Mélanges René Basset*), p. 37 f.

[2] Mujīr ad-dīn, l.c.: the 6th.

[3] Abu-l-Fidā', ed. Constantinople, IV, pp. 31, l. 4, 43, l. 4 b, penult., 63, l. 1 ff., 64, l. 12, 70–2, 74–5, 81, l. 4 b, 89–90, 108, ll. 3 ff. (=Ibn al-Wardī, II, p. 297, ll. 11 b–5 b). Autobiography (in *Recueil des Historiens des Croisades, Hist. orient.* I. 166–86). Zetterstéen, *Beiträge*, pp. 153, ll. 14, 15, 169, l. 20, 184, l. 16; al-Kutubī, *Fawāt*, s.v. I. 16–19. Ibn Ḥabīb, pp. 314, 331–2, 354; Qalqashandī, *Ṣubḥ* X, p. 182, ll. 10, 11 (where the word حسن is to be crossed out), 12; Maqrīzī, *Sulūk* (in *Recueil des Historiens des Croisades, Hist. orient.* I. 745–6); Ibn Ḥajar, *Durar*, s.v. (MS. Br. Mus., Or. 3043, fo. 69^v–70^r); Ibn Taghrībirdī, *Manhal*, s.v. (MS. Paris, Ar. 2068, fo. 180^v–184^r); M. Reinaud, *Géographie d'Aboulféda*,

of Ten, from 692 onward as Amir of Forty. After Maḥmūd's death served under Muḥammad b. Qalāūn and Muẓaffar Baybars; appointed Governor of Hama on the 18th Jumādā I 710 (13th October 1310); received the provinces of Hama, al-Ma'arra, and Bārīn, with the rank of prince and the title of al-Malik aṣ-Ṣāliḥ on the 25th Rabī' II 712 (30th August 1312); lost al-Ma'arra on the 19th Muḥarram 713 (6th May 1313); regained it in Jumādā I 716 (which began 22nd July 1316); received on the 17th Muḥarram 720 (28th February 1320) the title of al-Malik al-Mu'ayyad and the hereditary[1] rank of Sultan. Died on the 28th[2] Muḥarram 732 (31st October 1331).

BLAZON: *Two-fielded shield. Upper field of indeterminable colour (perhaps self-coloured), lower field (united middle and lower fields) bendy of a varying number of pieces (10–12) in following sequence of colours: gold, red copper, gold, black resin, gold, red copper, gold, &c.*

PEN-BOX, in possession of R. A. Harari, Esq., London. Pl. XLIX.
Seventeen shields on the sides of the lid and on the body of the pen-box.
Inscription:

عزّ لمولانا السلطان الملك المؤيّد عماد الدنيا والدين أبى الفداء إسماعيل عزّ أنصاره

Glory to our Lord the Sultan al-Malik al-Mu'ayyad 'Imād ad-dunyā wa-d-dīn Abu-l-Fidā' Ismā'īl, may his victories be glorious.

BIBLIOGRAPHY: Unpublished.

SHIHĀB AD-DĪN [AḤMAD (?)]

BLAZON: *Pen-box on the middle field of a three-fielded shield.*

BASIN. Present owner unknown.
Inscription:

ممّا عمل برسم العبد الفقير الراجى عفو ربّه الـ[قدير ?] شهاب الدين المستوفى

عفـ [Sauvaget]

This is one of the objects made for the poor servant hoping for the forgiveness of his Mighty Lord Shihāb ad-dīn the Overseer, [may God] pard[on him].

BIBLIOGRAPHY: Unpublished.

t. I, pp. ii–xxxviii. Weil, cf. Index, particularly IV. 400–1; Brockelmann, *The Encyclopaedia of Islām*, s.v. (Engl. ed. I. 85 f.), quoting other European literature; *Majānī al-adab*, V. 294.

[1] Qalqashandī, *Ṣubḥ* X, p. 184, l. penult.

[2] With regard to this date cf. Weil, IV. 400, n. 2.

AḤMAD[1]

BLAZON: *Napkin on the middle field of a three-fielded shield.*

BOX, brass inlaid with silver, British Museum, London. Formerly collection of the Duc de Blacas.
On the lid an inscription surrounding a shield. Other shields below the rim of the lid.

ممّا عمل برسم العبد الفقير الرجى الغفران من الربّ المنّان المهتار أحمد مهتار

الأمير محمّد بن ساطلمش الجلالى

This is one of the objects made for the poor servant, hoping for forgiveness from the benevolent Lord, the Overseer Aḥmad, Overseer to the Amir Muḥammad b. Sāṭilmish al-Jalālī.

BIBLIOGRAPHY: Lane-Poole, *The Art of the Saracens*, p. 230.

AḤMAD B. BAKTAMUR[2]

Shi. Aḥmad, son of Baktamur, the cup-bearer, a favourite of Muḥammad b. Qalāūn, became Amir of a Hundred and Commander of a Thousand, apparently without having gone through the usual preliminary stages, died on his return from the pilgrimage in Muḥarram 733, about twenty years old.

BLAZON: *Upper and lower fields red, on a middle field of unknown colour a red cup.*

BRONZE BASIN, Louvre, Paris, No. 3370. Originally in the possession of the Marchioness Arconati Visconti.
Three shields on the neck, one in the centre inside the basin.

المقرّ الكريم العالى المولوى الأميرى الكبير الغازى المجا ○ هدى المرابطى المثاغرى

العونى الذخرى الهمامى الكفيلى ○ الشهابى ولد المقرّ السيفى بكتمر الساقى الملكى

الناصرى ○

His Honourable and High Excellency, our Lord, the Great Amir, the Vanquisher, the Defender of the Faith, the Warrior at the Frontiers, the Warden of the Marches, the Helper, the Treasure, the Shelter, the Viceroyal, Shihāb ad-dīn, son of His Excellency Saif ad-dīn Baktamur, the cup-bearer, (officer) of al-Malik an-Nāṣir.

[1] It is doubtful whether this blazon belonged to Aḥmad or to his master Muḥammad b. Sāṭilmish.

[2] Zetterstéen, *Beiträge*, p. 186, l. 6; Ṣafadī, *Wāfī*, s.v. (MS. Oxford, Seld. Arch. A. 20, fo. 125$^{r, v}$); Ibn Ḥajar, *Durar*, s.v. (MS. Br. Mus., Or. 3043, fo. 21^{r}); Ibn Iyās, I. 166–7; Weil, IV. 378.

BIBLIOGRAPHY: Unpublished.
Mentioned: Migeon, *Musée du Louvre, L'Orient Musulman, Armes, &c.*, p. 26, No. 100.

AḤMAD B. BURAQ[1]

BLAZON: ***Pointed shield with close diaper pattern.***

COPPER BASIN, Arabic Museum, Cairo, No. 3400. Pl. XLVII. 1.
Inscription intersected by four shields.

المقر الكريم العالى المولوى الأميرى الكبيرى ا 0 لمالكى العالمى العاملى الكافلى

الغازى 0 المجاهدى المرابطى المثاغرى المؤيّدى العضدى ا 0 الذخرى المهدّى الشهابى

أحمد بن بر[ا]ق الملكى الناصرى 0

His Honourable and High Excellency, our Lord, the Great Amir, the Royal, the Learned, the Governing, the Viceroy, the Vanquisher, the Defender of the Faith, the Warrior at the Frontiers, the Warden of the Marches, the Helped by God, the Supporter, the Treasure, the Administrator, Shihāb ad-dīn Aḥmad b. Buraq[?], *(officer) of al-Malik an-Nāṣir.*

BIBLIOGRAPHY: Unpublished.

AḤMAD B. ISMA'ĪL AL-KUJUKĪ

BLAZON: ***Fleur-de-lis on undivided shield.***

MAUSOLEUM, now occupied by Mawlawī Derwishes, Hims, to the north of the Serail. Pl. XIX. 4.
Inscription over the lintel, flanked by two shields.

(1) أنشأ هذه التربة المباركة العبد الفقير الحقير الذليل الراجي عفو ربّه القدير

احمد بن إسمعيل الكوجكي

(2) غفر الله له ولوالديه ولجميع المسلمين ولمن ترحّم عنه ودعا [له ب]المغفرة امين

بتأريخ شهر الله المحرّم سنة احد وأربعين وثمان مائة

Built this blessed mausoleum, the poor abject, submissive servant hoping for the pardon of his Mighty

[1] The name of Aḥmad's father admits of three different readings, viz. برق , يرق and بيرق, and in the case of an *involutio* also of براق and يراق.

Lord Aḥmad b. Isma'īl al-Kujukī, may God pardon him and his parents and all Muslims and whoever has mercy upon him and prays that his sins may be forgiven, Amen. In the month of Muḥarram of the year 841 (began 5th July 1437).

BIBLIOGRAPHY: Unpublished.
Blazon mentioned and depicted in Uspenski, *Archeologičeski pamyatniki Siryi*, p. 140, fig. 31, where it is attributed to Crusaders.

AḤMAD IBN AL-MAGHRIBĪ

BLAZON: *On upper field a napkin, on middle field a cup (possibly charged with a pen-box), on lower field a cup.*

BRONZE DISH, in possession of Prof. Louis Massignon, Paris.
One shield in the centre of the plate.
Inscription on the rim.

(١) ممّا عمل برسم [المقرّ الأشرف][1] (2) العالى المولوى الأميرى الكبيرى

(3) المخدومى الشهابى سيّدى (4) أحمد ابن المغربى عزّ أنصاره

This is one of the objects made for His [Most Noble? and] High Excellency, our Lord, the Great Amir, the Well-Served, Shihāb ad-dīn Sīdī Aḥmad b. al-Maghribī, may his victories be glorious.

BIBLIOGRAPHY: Louis Massignon, 'Six plats de bronze de style mamelouk' (in *Bulletin de l'Institut Français d'Archéologie orientale*, t. X), No. 6, p. 11 f. (of the offprint), pl. IV.

AḤMAD AL-MIHMANDĀR [2]

Shi. Aḥmad b. Āqūsh al-'Azīzī, Commander of the Army (*naqīb al-jaish*) from the 29th Rabī' I 719 till 5th Rabī' II 727 (25th May 1319–28th February 1327), leader of the Mecca caravan (*amīr ar-rakb*) in Shawwāl 728 (began 9th August 1328), died on the 3rd Rajab 732 (31st March 1332). Built a *khānqāh*, a madrasah, a bazaar-street, and a private house in Cairo, near his mausoleum, outside Bāb Zuwaila.

BLAZON: *Upper and lower fields white, on a red middle field a white disk charged with a golden pointed shield.*

[1] Restored by Massignon.

[2] Zetterstéen, *Beiträge*, pp. 149, l. 19, 169, l. 2, 178, l. 5 f., 179, l. penult., 185, l. 3, 227, l. 18; Maqrīzī, *Khiṭaṭ*, II, pp. 399, l. 11 f., 418 b.

GLASS LAMP, Metropolitan Museum, New York. Previously in the collection Schefer, afterwards in that of Moore. Pl. XLI. 3.
Six shields, three on neck, three on the lower part of the body of the lamp.
Inscription on body (so far as it is visible on the photograph):

هذا ما [. . . أحمـ]ـد المهندار غفر الله له

This is what [founded as a waqf . . . Aḥma]d, the mihmandār, *may God forgive him.*
DATE: The date of Aḥmad's madrasa in Cairo,[1] most probably 725 (1324/5).

BIBLIOGRAPHY: Lamm, *Mittelalterliche Gläser*, p. 437, No. 37, pl. 197, fig. 4.
Blazon depicted and described: Rogers, *Le Blason*, No. 27, p. 129, fig. 47. Lamp reproduced: Pier, *Saracenic Glass*, pl. XXXVIII, fig. 8; *Bulletin of the Metropolitan Museum*, II. 105; Kühnel, *Islamische Kunst*, p. 466, fig. 484.
Mentioned: Lavoix, 'Galerie orientale du Trocadéro' (in *GBA*. t. XVIII, 1878), p. 780; Wiet, *Lampes et bouteilles*, p. 158, No. 23.

AHMAD B. MUHAMMAD B. IDRĪS

BLAZON: ***On the upper field a napkin, on the middle field a pen-box, on the lower field a napkin.***

LUNCH-BOX (*maṭbaqiyya*) in the collection of F. T. Dallin, Esq., Chieveley, Newbury, Berks. Pl. LVII. 6.
On each of the three sections of the box, shields and medallions with inscriptions, the historical portion of which runs as follows:

صاحبه أحمد بن محمّد بن إدريس

Its owner is Aḥmad, son of Muḥammad, son of Idrīs.

BIBLIOGRAPHY: Unpublished.

AHMAD B. SHAIKH[2]

Al-Malik al-Muẓaffar Abu-s-Sa'ādāt b. al-Malik al-Mu'ayyad Abī an-Naṣr Shaikh, succeeded his father to the throne the 9th Muḥarram 824 (15th January 1421) at the age of one year, eight months and seven days, deposed by Ṭaṭar, who ascended the throne the 29th Sha'bān of the same year (29th August 1421), and put Aḥmad into prison. Died of the plague the last day of Jumādā I 833 (24th February 1430).

[1] *Khiṭaṭ*, II, p. 399, l. 12; *CIA. Égypte*, I. 171–6; Creswell, *Brief Chronology*, p. 95.
[2] *Manhal*, s.v. (MS. Paris, 2068, fo. 61ᵛ, 62ʳ); Ibn Iyās, II. 10–13; Weil, V. 150, 157, 160, 161.

BLAZON: *Lion passant.*

COPPER COIN (*fils*), once in the possession of Prince E. Windischgraetz, Vienna.

Obv. السلطان الملك الـ . . . الدين أبو السعادات [1]

Within a circle: أحمد

Rev. ضرب

Lion passant

[بدمشـ]ق

BIBLIOGRAPHY: Karabacek, 'Zur orientalischen Münzkunde' (in *Wiener Numismatische Monatshefte*, 1867), No. 10, p. 7 (of the offprint).

ʿALĀ' AD-DĪN [ʿALĪ] AL-BARĪDĪ[2]

BLAZON: *Three-fielded shield.*

PUBLIC FOUNTAIN, locally known as the *Sabīl al-Barīdī*, Damascus, Rue el-Beridi, between Nos. 76 and 88, near the Jāmiʿ al-Barīdī. Pl. XLIV. 3.
The historical portion of the inscription, in the niche of the Sabīl, flanked by two shields, runs as follows:

[one word broken off] القناة المباركة العبد الفقير الى الله تعالى علاء الدين

[modern plaque] البريدى

[Perhaps: *Ordered to construct this*] *blessed aqueduct, the servant yearning for God the Exalted, ʿAlā' ad-dīn . . . the dispatch-rider.*

BIBLIOGRAPHY: Unpublished.

ʿALĪ B. AHMAD

BLAZON: *Cup on middle field of a three-fielded shield.*

COPPER BASIN. Sometime on offer in the Paris art market.
Six shields.

[1] The Arabic is only a re-translation from the German version given by Karabacek.

[2] On the cloth covering the cenotaph in the Jāmiʿ al-Barīdī and dated 1332 A.H. (1913/14), his name is given as 'ash-shaikh ʿAlī al-Barīdī'. ʿAlā' ad-dīn, together with Nūr ad-dīn being the most common surnames of ʿAlī, this name presumably is based on a reliable tradition. Besides, in 1913/14, the modern slab was probably not yet in existence and the name ʿAlī may have been visible in the inscription.

(1) ممّا عمل برسم المولا الأجلّ و (2) الكهف الاضل (*sic*) نور الدين علىّ

(3) ابن العبد الـ[فقير؟] الى الله أحمد الربرى [Van Berchem]

This is one of the objects made for the Most Magnificent . . . Lord Nūr ad-dīn 'Alī, son of the servant yearning for God, Aḥmad of Tabrīz (?).

BIBLIOGRAPHY: Unpublished.

'ALĪ B. BISHĀRA

BLAZON: *Tamgha, emblem No. 24 facing to the left on undivided shield.*

MARBLE COLUMN, Gaza, small cemetery, locally known as 'al-'Awamīd'. Two shields above first line of text, emblems pointing in the same direction.

(1) بسمله

(2) كُلُّ نَفْسٍ ذَائِقَةُ ٱلْمَوتِ هذا قبر الفقير الى

(3) رحمة الله الراجى عفو الله

(4) الشهيد الحاجّ نور الدين علىّ ابن الأمير

(5) الأجلّ شهاب الدين بشارة ابن خرمشاه [?] ابن

(6) [ ]صر السلورى التركمانى توفّاً الى رحمة

(7) الله تعالى فى الخامس من شهر

(8) شعبان المبارك سنة أربعة

(9) وتسعين وستّمائة رحمه الله

(10) وارحم من ترحم عليه وعلى

(11) جميع المسلمين

In the name of the most merciful God. Every soul shall taste death (Qur'ān XXI. 36 or XXIX. 57). *This is the tomb of the one yearning for God's mercy, hoping for forgiveness from God, the martyr, the Mecca pilgrim Nūr ad-dīn 'Alī, son of the most magnificent amir Shihāb ad-dīn Bishāra b. Khurramshāh (?) b. [ ]ṣr[1] as-Salūrī[2] the Turcoman. Passed into the mercy of God the Exalted on the fifth of the blessed month of Sha'bān of the year* 694 (20th June 1295), *may God have mercy upon him, etc.*

As indicated above, my reading of the name of 'Alī's grandfather is doubtful. Above the first syllable حر there is a stroke which could be interpreted either as ر or as سر. If it really represents a letter, there are too many strokes for Khurramshāh; in any case there are not enough of them to make the word read خوارزمشاه.

BIBLIOGRAPHY: Unpublished.

'ALĪ B. HILĀL AD-DAULA[3]

Perhaps identical with A. 'Alī b. Hilāl ad-daula, a native of Shaizar, Inspector of Monuments (*shādd al-'imāra*), supervised the repairs to the Haram in Mecca, in Shawwāl 727 (began 20th August 1327). On his return, appointed Superintendent of Chanceries (*shādd ad-dawāwīn*), which post he held up to the 5th Rajab 734 (12th March 1334), when his property was confiscated and he himself imprisoned in Alexandria. Released, on the intercession of Tankiz, died in his native town, the 23rd Rabī' II 739 (8th November 1338).

BLAZON: *Crescent without shield.*

LARGE PLATE. Collection R. A. Harari, Esq., London. Pl. XLII. 5.
The inscription, and the two emblems flanking it are a later addition. The original text is anonymous.

برسم العبد الفقير الى عفو مولاه علىّ ابن هلال الدولة

For the servant yearning for the forgiveness of his Lord 'Alī b. Hilāl ad-daula.

BIBLIOGRAPHY: Unpublished.

NŪR AD-DĪN ['ALĪ] SON OF 'IMĀD AD-DĪN

BLAZON: *Upper field blank (perhaps self-coloured), the united middle and lower fields bendy of six pieces. Pointed shield.*

[1] Or: [ ]ḍr.

[2] For Salghurī? Cf. Kāshgarī, p. 56.

[3] Zetterstéen, *Beiträge*, pp. 188, l. 8, 199, l. 10 b; Ibn Baṭṭūṭa, II. 149; Ibn Ḥajar, *Durar*, s.v. (MS. Br. Mus., Or. 3044, fo. 18r).

MOSQUE of ABU-L-FIDĀ', Hama, locally known as 'Jāmiʿ al-Ḥayāya'. Pl. XX. 1. Inscription between two arches of the façade. First line flanked by two shields, the left one with bends sinister.

(1) ⬯ جدّد هذه الأقباء المباركة المقرّ العالى الملكى النورى ⬯

(2) ولد المرحوم العمادى تغمّده الله برحمته فى شهور سنة ستّة وسبعين وسبعمائة

Renewed these blessed arches His High Excellency, the Royal, Nūr ad-dīn, son of the late ʿImād ad-dīn, may God cover him with his mercy, in the months of the year 776 (1374/5).

BIBLIOGRAPHY: Unpublished.

The Nūr ad-dīn of this inscription is probably the son of ʿImād ad-dīn Ismaʿīl b. al-Malik al-Afḍal Muḥammad b. al-Malik al-Mu'ayyad Ismaʿīl (the famous historian Abu-l-Fidā'). Nūr ad-dīn being the most common complement of the name ʿAlī, I venture to assume that this is the way the name should be supplemented in our case. Ismaʿīl having died during the last ten days of Dhu-l-Ḥijja 758 (4th–13th December 1357),[1] Nūr ad-dīn was, in 776, surely of an age to carry out structural repairs in the mosque of his ancestors.[2]

'ALĪ AL-MĀRIDĪNĪ[3]

ʿA. ʿAlī al-Māridīnī, a mamluk of Muḥammad b. Qalāūn, came to Cairo in 728 (1327/8), was appointed Viceroy of Syria in 753 (began 6th February 1352), Governor of Aleppo in 759 (began 14th December 1357), Viceroy of Syria in 762 (1360/1), on al-Malik al-Ashraf Shaʿbān's accession in 764 recalled to Egypt, Viceroy of Egypt in 770[4] (1368/9). Died in Cairo in 772 (1370/1).

BLAZON: *Upper and lower fields red, on white middle field red napkin.*

[1] For his biography cf. Zetterstéen, *Beiträge*, p. 169, l. 4 b; Ṣafadī, *Aʿyān*, s.v. (MS. Berlin, fo. 27ʳ); Ibn Ḥabīb, p. 404; Ibn Ḥajar, *Durar*, s.v. (MS. Br. Mus., Or. 3043, fo. 70ᵛ); Weil, IV. 402, n. 2.

[2] Ṣāliḥ b. Yaḥyā states that Abu-l-Fidā' 's successor was Nūr ad-dīn ʿAlī فلمّا توفّى الملك المؤيّد قام موضعه فى سلطنة حماة ولده الملك الأفضل نور الدين علىّ ابن الملك المؤيّد, (ed. Cheikho, Beyrouth, 1902) p. 147, ll. 2 ff., and then again الملك المؤيّد إسماعيل وامّا ولده الملك الأفضل علىّ, p. 148, l. 5 b, but this seems to be only a *lapsus calami* for al-Malik al-Afḍal Muḥammad.

[3] Ibn Ḥabīb, pp. 397, 404, 409, 421, 429; *Manhal*, s.v. (MS. Paris, Ar. 2071, fo. 162ʳ); Ibn Iyās, I. 211, l. 22, 224–5, 226–7; Weil, IV. 494, 518; *CIA. Égypte*, I. 665.

[4] According to Ibn Ḥabīb, p. 421: in 769.

GLASS LAMP, Arabic Museum, Cairo, No. 294, probably from the Mosque of Alṭunbughā al-Māridīnī, Cairo.
Six shields.
Inscription on body of the lamp:

المقرّ الأشراف العالى | الكافلى | العلائى | المرحوم أميرـر علىّ الماردانى

His Most Noble and High Excellency, the Viceroy, 'Alā' ad-dīn, the late Amir 'Alī al-Māridānī.

BIBLIOGRAPHY: Lavoix, 'La Galerie orientale du Trocadéro' (in *GBA.*2ᵉ pér., t. XVIII, 1878, p. 779f.); Rogers, p. 123, No. 19, fig. 39; Herz, *Catalogue*, Engl. ed., p. 302, fig. 59; *CIA. Égypte*, I, No. 480, p. 665; Herz, 'Le Musée National du Caire' (in *GBA.* 3ᵉ pér., t. XXVIII, 1902), p. 502 f., fig.; Wiet, *Lampes*, p. 42 f., pl. LXII.
Blazon reproduced: Lane-Poole, *Egypt*, p. 314, fig. 70; Artin, *Contribution*, No. 206.
Lamp reproduced: Le Bon, *Civilisation des Arabes*, pl.
Mentioned: Migeon, *Manuel*, 2nd ed., II, p. 135; Schmoranz, pp. 19, n., 69; Lamm, p. 469 f.

'ALĪ B. MUḤAMMAD[1]

A. 'Alī son of Na. Muḥammad, succeeded his father as Governor of the Fortress of Ṣubaibiyya, repeatedly chamberlain (*ḥājib*) in Damascus, at one time Governor of Jerusalem. Died in Damascus, Muḥarram 809 (began 18th June 1406).

BLAZON: *Upper field blank, on middle field a cup charged with a napkin displayed on the middle field of a three-fielded shield, on lower field a cup.*

MADRASA ṢUBAIBIYYA, Jerusalem. Pl. XLIII. 2.
Two shields flanking the lintel of the madrasa facing the Haram.[2]

BIBLIOGRAPHY: *CIA. Jérusalem, Ville*, p. 229 f., fig. 38.

'ALĪ B. MUḤAMMAD

Perhaps the son of Na. Muḥammad b. an-Nashāshībī (q.v.), who appears to be holding the same titles, office and an identical blazon, on an inscription in Jerusalem.

[1] Mujīr ad-dīn, *al-Uns al-jalīl*, pp. 390, l. 6, 609, l. 11 (Sauvaire, pp. 148, 269); *CIA. Jérusalem, Ville*, p. 230 and n. 1.

[2] The identity of this madrasa was established by van Berchem, l.c., pp. 228–230.

BLAZON: *On upper field a napkin, on middle field a cup charged with a pen-box placed between a 'pair of trousers', on lower field a cup.*

COPPER PLATE tinned over. Present owner unknown.

ممّا عمل برسم الجناب العالى | المولوى السيّدى علىّ ولد | المقرّ الناصرى سيّدى

محمّد | أمير خازندار برقوق (?) أعزّه الله [Van Berchem]

This is one of the objects made for His High Excellency (janāb), *our Lord, Sīdī ʿAlī, son of His Excellency Nāṣir ad-dīn Sīdī Muḥammad, Grand Treasurer of Barqūq* (?). *May God give him strength.*

BIBLIOGRAPHY: Unpublished.

ʿALĪ B. MUḤAMMAD B. AS-SADHFIL(?)

BLAZON: *On each of the ornamented upper and lower fields a napkin, on the middle field a pen-box.*

COPPER SAUCER tinned over, Messrs. N. Ohan & Sons, Jerusalem.
Heraldic shield set in an ornamented circle in the middle of the saucer. Round it an inscription intersected by two shields.[1]

ممّا عمل برسم علىّ ابن محمّد ○ ابن السذفل[2] يرجو المغفرة

This is one of the objects made for ʿAlī b. Muḥammad b. as-Sadhfil (?) *who hopes for forgiveness.*

BIBLIOGRAPHY: Unpublished.

ʿALĪ B. SHAʿBĀN[3]

Al-Malik al-Manṣūr ʿAlī, son of al-Malik al-Ashraf Shaʿbān, great-grandson of Muḥammad b. Qalāūn, succeeded his father on the throne the 16th Dhu-l-Qaʿda 778 (15th April 1378) as a child of less than eight. Died of the plague, the 23rd Ṣafar 783 (19th May 1381).

[1] These two shields are so carelessly drawn that the upper and lower fields are reduced to segments 1–2 mm. thick, leaving out the napkins engraved in the central blazon.

[2] The reading of this name, and consequently its transcription, is very doubtful. The *sīn* is established by a differentiating sign and there are two dots over the letters which I have transcribed as ف and ذ. Unfortunately, the resulting name cannot be identified.

[3] Ibn Ḥabīb, pp. 440, 453; Ibn Taghrībirdī, *Nujūm* (MS. Paris, Ar. 1786, fo. 197v ff., 224v), *Manhal*, s.v. (MS. Paris, Ar. 2071, fo. 126v–127v) and s.v. Shaʿbān; Ibn Iyās, cf. Index; Weil, IV. 529, 531 f., 540.

BLAZON: *Fleur-de-lis on undivided field.*

1. COPPER COIN (*fils*), Bibliothèque Nationale, Paris.

Obv.: On the margin: السلطان الملك. In centre: على.

Rev.: Inscription on the margin illegible. In centre: Fleur-de-lis in a circle.

BIBLIOGRAPHY: Lavoix, *Catalogue des Monnaies Musulmanes de la Bibliothèque Nationale*, vol. *Égypte et Syrie*, No. 927, p. 385, pl. VIII.

2. COPPER COIN, struck at Tripoli, Bibliothèque Nationale, Paris.
Obv.: Three-fielded circle:

ضرب بطر
الملك المنصور
ابلس

Rev.: Fleur-de-lis within hexagon inscribed in a circle, annulets in segments.
BIBLIOGRAPHY: Lavoix, l.c., No. 930, p. 387, pl. VIII (and several variants).

ALJĀY[1,2]

S. Aljāy b. ʿAbdallāh al-Yūsufī, Grand Chamberlain (*ḥājib al-ḥujjāb*), *amīr jandār*, from Shawwāl 768 to 10th Ṣafar 769 (June 1367–6th October 1367), in prison, on his release made Amir of a Hundred and appointed *amīr silāḥ barrānī*, made Commander-in-Chief (*atābak al-ʿasākir*) in 774 (1372/3). Owing to quarrels over the property left by his wife, the mother of the Sultan, had several skirmishes with the amirs of the Sultan. Defeated and accidentally drowned in the Nile. Buried the 9th (or 10th) Muḥarram 775 (1st or 2nd July 1373).

BLAZON: *Cup on the middle field of a three-fielded shield.*

MADRASA of Aljāy, Cairo. Pl. XXIV. 1.
Inscription above the entrance gate intersected by an heraldic shield.

[1] Ibn Ḥabīb, p. 435; Maqrīzī, *Khiṭaṭ*, II, p. 399, ll. 18 ff. (2nd ed., IV, p. 249, ll. 6 ff.); Ibn Ḥajar, *Durar*, s.v. (MS. Br. Mus., Or. 3043, fo. 76^{r}); Ibn Taghrībirdī, *Nujūm*, obituaries s.a. 775 (MS. Paris, Ar. 1786, fo. 186$^{r, v}$), *Manhal*, s.v. (MS. Paris, Ar. 2069, fo. 8^{v}–9^{v}); Ibn Iyās, I, pp. 220, ll. 7 b ff., 224, ll. 14, 17, 227, l. 5 b, 228, l. 8 ff.; Weil, IV. 521 f.; *CIA. Égypte*, I. 290 f.

[2] In Zettersteen, *Beiträge*, p. 185, l. 9, and *Nujūm*, s.a. 774 (MS. Paris, Ar. 1786, fo. 182^{r}, l. ult.), vocalized أُلْجَاى.

(١) بسمله . . . امر بانشاء هذا الجامع ○ والمدرسة المبارکة المقر الأشرف الجاى
أ(2)تابك العساكر المنصورة الملکی الأشرفی ○ غفر الله له ولجميع المسلمين بتأريخ شهر
رجب سنة أربع وسبعين وسبعمائة

In the name of the most merciful God. Ordered to construct this Mosque and blessed school His Most Noble Excellency Aljāy, Commander-in-Chief of the victorious armies, (officer) of al-Malik al-Ashraf, may God forgive him and all Muslims. In the month of Rajab 774 (January 1373).

BIBLIOGRAPHY: *CIA. Égypte*, I, No. 188, p. 289 f.

'ALLĀN AL-MU'IZZĪ

BLAZON: *On upper field a napkin, on middle field a cup charged with a pen-box and placed between a 'pair of trousers', on lower field a cup.*

COPPER BOWL with spout, tinned over. Collection R. A. Harari, Esq., London. Pl. LXII. 7.
Inscription and four shields on exterior of bowl.

ممّا عمل برسم الجناب العالی ○ . . . السيفی علّان المعزّی ○

This is one of the objects made for His High Excellency (janāb) . . . *Saif ad-dīn 'Allān al-Mu'izzī* (?).

BIBLIOGRAPHY: Unpublished.

ALMALIK[1]

S. Almalik, a native of Abulustain,[2] bought by Baybars in 676 (1277), passed

[1] Zetterstéen, *Beiträge*, pp. 136, l. 9, 156, l. ult., 222, l. penult., 226, l. 11; Abu-l-Fidā', ed. Constantinople, IV, pp. 141, l. 19, 142, l. 7, 149, l. 8 b; Ibn al-Wardī, II, pp. 334, l. 18, 335, l. 10, 343, l. 12; Ibn Baṭṭūṭa, I. 50, 51, 374; II. 150; Ṣafadī, *A'yān*, s.v. (MS. Berlin, fo. 32v); Ibn Ḥabīb, pp. 379, 384; *Khiṭaṭ*, I. 425 m; II. 310–11 (2nd ed., II. 280–1; IV. 108–9); *SM.* II b, pp. 123, 126, 284; Ibn Ḥajar, *Durar*, s.v. (MS. Br. Mus., Or. 3043, fo. 77r, v); Ibn Taghrībirdī, *Manhal*, s.v. (MS. Paris, Ar. 2069, fo. 18v–19v), and s.v. al-Malik al-Kāmil Sha'bān (MS. Paris, Ar. 2070, fo. 152r, ll. 10 ff.); Mujīr ad-dīn, *al-Uns al-jalīl*, pp. 376, l. 3, 390, l. 12, 393, l. 1; Ibn Iyās, I, pp. 148, l. 10, 181–182, 184 t; Defrémery and Sanguinetti in Ibn Baṭṭūṭa, I. xxix f.; Weil, IV. 408, 422, 432, 434, 441, 456, 462, 463, 465 f.; *CIA. Égypte*, I, No. 115, p. 170 f. and n. 4; *CIA. Jérusalem, Ville*, p. 267 f.

[2] Spelling indicated by Yāqūt, s.v.

into the service of Qalāūn, became polo-master (*jūkandār*) of Muḥammad b. Qalāūn, by 708 at the latest had been dubbed amir.[1] On Aḥmad b. Muḥammad b. Qalāūn's accession to the throne appointed Governor of Hama, vice Sanjar al-Jāwlī, recalled to Egypt by al-Malik aṣ-Ṣāliḥ Isma'īl, in 744 (1343/4)[2] became Viceroy of Egypt, in Rabī' II 746 (August 1345) appointed Viceroy of Syria by al-Malik al-Kāmil Sha'bān, vice Ṭuquztamur, but dismissed from office while on his way to Damascus, and appointed Governor of Safad, recalled to Egypt, arrested in Gaza by Arāq, Governor of that province, towards the close of the year 746 (April 1346) sent to Alexandria. Died as a nonagenarian in 747 (1346).[3]

BLAZON: *White polo-sticks on green field.*

1. GLASS LAMP, Çinili Köşk, Istanbul, once in the Monastery of the Mawlawi Derwishes at Konia.
Two shields on neck.
Inscription on body:

[1] A word should be said with regard to the spelling of the name الملك. Scribes of both literary texts and inscriptions have very often separated the two components of this name, and in a number of cases they have set a *madda* over the *alif* to make it clear that in this case آل was not to be mistaken for the article. Consequently the name has been transcribed Almulk or Al Mulk (Weil, IV. 408, 416, 422 and *passim*, Quatremère, *SM*. II b, 284); Âlmalik or Âl-Malik (Ravaisse, 'Essai sur l'histoire et sur la topographie du Caire', *MMAFC*. III. 77 and *passim*; *CIA*. *Égypte*, I. 170–4; Creswell, *Brief Chronology*, p. 95), and by other European scholars.

In his last work van Berchem (*CIA*. *Jérusalem*, *Ville*, p. 267) adopted the transcription Yl-malak, laying stress on the assertion of Ibn Baṭṭūṭa (ed. Defrémery et Sanguinetti, I. 50–1) that the proper spelling of the name was Yalmalak, and that he was wrongly called Almalik by the plebs (والعامّة تقول فيه الملك فيخطئون). But this cannot be considered the very last word on the subject. Ṣafadī, himself a member of the Mamluk society and well versed in Turkish, a historian who made a point of indicating the orthography of the Turkish names in his biographical dictionaries and who is surely a more reliable guide in point of spelling Mamluk names than the Maghrebin traveller, says *expressis verbis* that the spelling of this name is Almalik (*A'yān*, s.v. (MS. Berlin, fo. 32^v, and MS. Aya Sofia)). Besides, it is by no means established beyond doubt, that these two persons are identical. The amir whom Ibn Baṭṭūṭa met at Mecca was a page in the bodyguard of the Sultan (*khāṣṣakī*), whereas Almalik was a polo-master (*jūkandār*). Despite the fact that both offices were court-offices of the lower grades, and the term *khāṣṣakī* was sometimes used in a more general sense, it is inadmissible to suppose that all the junior court-officers, such as cup-bearers, polo-masters, armour-bearers, secretaries, junior treasurers, &c., were called *khāṣṣakī*. Cf. also p. 87, n. 3.

[2] Ibn al-Wardī, II, p. 335, l. 10: in Muḥarram 743 (began 6th June 1342).

[3] Ibn Ḥabīb, p. 384, speaks of his death under the events of the year 746, according to Ibn Ḥajar Almalik died either by the end of 746 or in 747, according to others on the 19th Jumādā II 747 (7th October 1346).

ممّا عمل برسم المقرّ العالى | المولوى الأميرى ا | الكبيرى المحترمى | المخدومى

السيفى سيف | الدين الملك | الجوكندار الملكى ا[لناصرى]

This is one of the objects made for His High Excellency, our Lord, the Great Amir, the Honoured, the Well-Served, Saif ad-dīn Almalik, the polo-master of al-Malik a[*n-Nāṣir*].

BIBLIOGRAPHY: *CIA. Jérusalem, Ville*, p. 269, nn. 5, 6 and p. 270, fig. 47.

Mentioned: Wiet, *Lampes*, p. 157, No. 18; Lamm, *Gläser*, p. 431 f., No. 18.

2. GLASS LAMP, National Museum of Arab Art, Cairo, No. 312.
Three shields on neck, three others on the lower part of the body.
Inscription on neck:

ممّا عمل برسم المقرّ العالى السيفى الملك الناصرى

This is one of the objects made for His High Excellency, Saif ad-dīn Almalik an-Nāṣirī.

Date: Almalik's mosque in Cairo was founded in 719 (1319).

BIBLIOGRAPHY: Schmoranz, p. 58, pl. xxiv; Herz, *Catalogue*, p. 292, *Musée National*, p. 502, fig.; *CIA. Jérusalem, Ville*, p. 270, n.; Wiet, *Lampes*, p. 67 f., pl. x.
Reproduced: Devonshire, *L'Égypte Musulmane*, pl. XXIII; Lamm, pl. 198.
Blazon reproduced: Artin, *Contribution*, fig. 160, p. 132 (without attribution).
Mentioned: Migeon, *Manuel* (2nd ed.), II, p. 134; Lamm, p. 431, No. 17.

3. MADRASA ALMALIKIYYA, Jerusalem.
Inscription over the middle pillar of the portico, flanked by two shields.
The essential portion runs as follows:

(1) . . . تقرّب بعمارة هذا المكان المبارك العبد الفقير الى الله تعالى الحاجّ ال

ملك (2) الجوكندار الملكى الناصرى . . وكان الفراغ (3) منه فى شهر الله المحرّم

غرّة عام أحد وأربعين وسبع مائة من الهجرة النبويّة . . .

Approached (*God*) *by building this blessed place, the servant yearning for God the Exalted, the pilgrim Almalik, the polo-master,* (*officer*) *of al-Malik an-Nāṣir . . . This was finished during the month of Muḥarram, the beginning of the year* 741 *of the Hijra of the Prophet* (27th June 1340).

BIBLIOGRAPHY: *CIA. Jérusalem, Ville*, p. 266 ff., fig. 46, pl. LXV (left).

4. SAME BUILDING. In each of the four corners of a panel over the entrance door a shield. Pl. XLIV. 2.

BIBLIOGRAPHY: Unpublished.

5. COPPER PLATE tinned over, National Museum of Arab Art, Cairo, No. 3757. Pl. XXVI. 1.
Inscription intersected by four shields.

المقرّ العالى المواْ O لوى الأميرى الكبيرى O السيفى الملك كافل المما O لك
الشريفة الإسلاميّة عزّ نصره O

His High Excellency, our Lord, the Great Amir, Saif ad-dīn Almalik, Viceroy of the noble Islamic provinces, may his victory be glorious.

BIBLIOGRAPHY: Unpublished.

6. SLAB OF MARBLE, badly damaged, now embedded in the façade of the ruined shrine of Sh. Aḥmad al-ʿUrainī at ʿArāq al-Manshiyyeh, Palestine. Obviously not in situ.

(1) بسمله . . . (2) O فَزَعٍ يَوْمَئِذٍ آمِنُونَ . . .
(3) الفقير الى ربّه ال ملك الجوكندا[ر] اا . . .

In the name of the most merciful God. [Whoever shall have wrought righteousness shall receive a reward beyond the desert thereof; and] they shall be secure from the terror of that day (Qur'ān XXVII. 91) . . . *yearning for His Lord, Almalik, the polo-master of al-[Malik an-Nāṣir].*

BIBLIOGRAPHY: Unpublished.

ALṬUNBUGHĀ AL-ʿALĀʾĪ[1]

A. Alṭunbughā, Grand Chamberlain, in Rajab 714 appointed Governor of Aleppo, which he entered early in Shaʿbān (began 10th November 1314), recalled to Egypt in 727[2] (1326/7); returned to Aleppo as Governor early in 731 (1330), on the 13th Jumādā I 739 (27th November 1338), appointed

[1] Zetterstéen, *Beiträge*, pp. 147, ll. 14–16, 162, ll. 4–7, 172, l. 7 f., 176, l. 11, 177, l. 20 f., 183, l. 1 f., 188, l. 22, 199, l. 9, 200, l. 4, 213, l. 10; Ṣafadī, *Aʿyān*, s.v. (MS. Berlin, fo. 30r, v); Ibn Ḥajar, *Durar*, s.v. (MS. Br. Mus., Or. 3043, fo. 76v); Ibn Taghrībirdī, *Manhal*, s.v. (MS. Paris, Ar. 2069, fo. 11v–12r); Weil, IV, cf. Index, especially pp. 382, 421, 428–31, 441, Ṭabbākh, *Aʿlām* II. 369 ff., IV. 573 ff.

[2] According to *Manhal*, l.c. fo. 11v, l. 5, appointed Viceroy of Syria.

Governor of Gaza; succeeded Tankiz as Viceroy of Syria, entered Damascus the 6th Muḥarram 741 (2nd July 1340). Strangled in the prison of Alexandria in Shawwāl or Dhu-l-Qaʿda 742 (March–April 1342). Built a mosque at Aleppo.

BLAZON: *Two polo-sticks.*

وكان رنك المنفصل [i.e. Alṭunbughā] جوكانين

BIBLIOGRAPHY: Abu-l-Fidā', ed. Constantinople, IV. p. 132, l. 18; Ibn al-Wardī, II, p. 324, l. 7b.

ALṬUNBUGHĀ AL-MĀRIDĪNĪ [1]

A. Alṭunbughā b. ʿAbdallāh al-Māridīnī an-Nāṣirī, *khāṣṣakī* and cup-bearer of al-Malik an-Nāṣir, dubbed Amir of Ten, rose in a short time to the rank of Amir of a Hundred and Commander of a Thousand, imprisoned in Ṣafar 742 (began 17th July 1341), released on Kujuk's accession to the throne, in Rabīʿ I 743 appointed Governor of Hama and about two months later, Governor of Aleppo. Died on the 1st Ṣafar 744 (25th June 1343), less than twenty-five years of age.

BLAZON: *Upper field red, on white lower field (united middle and lower fields) red cup.*

1. GLASS LAMP, National Museum of Arab Art, Cairo, Nos. 4065, 5880–2 (built up of four fragments).
Five, originally nine, shields.
Inscription on neck: Qur'ān, XXIV. 35.
Inscription on body:

المقر العالى العلائى الـ طنبغ]ا الساقى الناصرى

His High Excellency ʿAlā' ad-dīn Al[ṭunbugh]ā, cup-bearer of (al-Malik) an-Nāṣir.

BIBLIOGRAPHY: Wiet, *Lampes et Bouteilles*, p. 131 f., pl. IX.

Mentioned: *CR.* 1914, fasc. 31, pp. 70–1; Lamm, *Gläser*, p. 440 f.

2. BRONZE REVETMENT, fragments. Arabic Museum, Cairo, Nos. 3105, 3106, originally from the Mosque of Alṭunbughā in Cairo. Pl. XXI. 1. 2.
Two shields in the centre of convex stars. Cup inlaid in red copper.

[1] Ṣafadī, *Aʿyān*, s.v. (MS. Berlin, fo. 30^v, 31^r); Ibn Ḥabīb, II. 378, 379; *Zubdah*, pp. 29, 31; Maqrīzī, *Khiṭaṭ*, II, p. 308, ll. 25 ff. (2nd ed., IV, p. 105, ll. 12 ff.); Ibn Ḥajar, *Durar*, s.v. (MS. Br. Mus., Or. 3043, fo. 76^v); Ibn Taghrībirdī, *Manhal*, s.v. (MS. Paris, Ar. 2069, fo. 14^v–15^v); Ibn Iyās, I, p. 181, l. 7 b; Weil, IV, cf. Index, especially pp. 453, 460; *CIA. Égypte*, I. 192 and n. 3, 665.

BIBLIOGRAPHY: Mentioned: *CR.* 1905, fasc. 22, p. 124, n. 1; Herz, *Descriptive Catalogue of the objects exhibited in the National Museum of Arab Art*, p. 197, Nos. 23–5, fig. 37.

3. POTSHERD, Arabic Museum, Cairo, No. 5106. Pl. VI. 4.
Inscription to the left of the shield, half of which has been broken off.

. . . العلائى الطنبغا الساقى الملكى الن]اصرى . . .

'Alā' ad-dīn Alṭunbughā, the cup-bearer of al-Malik an-N[āṣir . . .

BIBLIOGRAPHY: Unpublished.

ALṬUNBUGHĀ B. YŪSUF [1]

BLAZON: ***Six-petalled rosette without shield.***

FOUNDATION TEXT, slab of limestone, now abandoned near the bridge at Hama, opposite the Hotel d'Oronte.
Inscription flanked by two blazons:

(1) بسمله . . . أنشأ هذه التربة المباركة العبد الفقير الى الله تعالى الراجى رحمة
ربّه الطنبغا ابن الأمير المرحوم جمال الدين يوسف

(2) ابن عبد الله الصالحي المعينى نائب السلطنة المعظّمة بقلعة البيرة رحمه الله
بتأريخ شهر رجب الفرد سنة ثلاث وعشرين وسبعمائة

In the name of the most merciful God. Founded this blessed mausoleum the servant yearning for God the Exalted, desiring the mercy of his Lord, Alṭunbughā, son of the late amir Jamāl ad-

[1] Rare as it is to find among mamluks a man with a Turkish name, whose father's name was Arabic, the case of Alṭunbughā is not without parallel, cf. Sultan Kujuk b. Muḥammad b. Qalāūn, Ānūk b. Muḥammad, Uzdamur b. 'Alī Bāy, A'uzlū b. Ḥasan aṭ-Ṭawīl, &c. Names such as Tanam b. 'Abd ar-Razzāq or Bukhshbāy b. 'Abd al-Karīm are not cases in point, 'Abd ar-Razzāq and 'Abd al-Karīm being in this instance presumably just as fictitious as the more popular 'Abdallāh. Sometimes one son was given a Turkish name, whilst the others had Arabic ones, cf. e.g. the sons of al-Āqūsh, viz. Saif ad-dīn Kujkun, Nāṣir ad-dīn Muḥammad, Zain ad-dīn Amīr Ḥājj, Ghars ad-dīn Khalīl (*A'yān*, s.v. Muḥammad b. Āqūsh, MS. Berlin, fo. 127^{r}). On the other hand, we know of dignitaries of Arabic origin, who changed their Arabic into Turkish names, e.g. the two brothers Taghrībirmish and Ḥasan-shāh whose original names were Ḥusain b. Aḥmad and Ḥasan b. Aḥmad respectively (*Manhal*, s.v. Taghrībirmish, MS. Paris, Ar. 2069, fo. 130^{r}), cf. also the Circassian Ḥājj Khalīl who changed his name into Qānibāy (*Ḍau'* s.v. Qānibāy al-Yūsufī al-mihmandār).

dīn Yūsuf b. ʿAbdallāh aṣ-Ṣāliḥī al-Muʿīnī (or: *al-Mughīthī*), *Governor of the August Sultanate in the fortress of al-Bīreh, may God have mercy upon him, in the month of Rajab the Unique of the year* 723 (6th July–4th August 1323).

BIBLIOGRAPHY: Unpublished.

ĀNŪK[1]

S. Ānūk, the favourite son of Muḥammad b. Qalāūn, born in Rajab 721 (began 27th July 1321), became Amir of a Hundred and Commander of a Thousand, whereas his brothers ranked as Amirs of Forty only. Died in Rabīʿ I 740 (began 6th September, 1339).

BLAZON: *The arms of his grandfather Qalāūn.*[2]

كان يحمل رنك جدّه المنصور (قلاون)

BIBLIOGRAPHY: Ṣafadī, *Aʿyān*, s.v. (MS. Berlin, fo. 33^v, l. 17) quoted in *Manhal*, s.v. (MS. Paris, Ar. 2069, fo. 24^r); Quatremère, *SM*. II a, p. 15; Rogers, p. 98.

ĀQBIRDĪ B. ʿALĪBĀY[2]

S. Āqbirdī b. ʿAlībāy, originally a mamluk of Qāytbāy, became *amīr silāḥ*, in 886[3] succeeded Yashbak min Mahdī as Grand Dāwādar, in Dhu-l-Qaʿda 891 (November 1486) appointed Vezier, in 897 appointed Major-domo, deposed the 26th Dhu-l-Qaʿda 901 (6th August 1496), in Rajab 902 reinstalled in all the offices he previously held. Two months later headed a civil war; several times defeated, having capitulated in Ramaḍān 904 was appointed Governor of Tripoli. Died the 3rd Dhu-l-Qaʿda 904 (12th June 1499), less than fifty years old.

BOWL. In the possession of Messrs. J. Sassoon, London. Pl. LXII. 1.
Inscription intersected by six shields on the outside of the bowl.

[1] *Aʿyān*, s.v. (MS. Berlin, fo. 33^v–34^r); Ibn Ḥajar, *Durar*, s.v. (MS. Br. Mus. Or. 3043, fo. 78^v); *Manhal*, l.c., Weil, IV. 370, 403–405.

[2] Ibn Iyās, especially II. pp. 202, l. 5 b, 239, l. 3 b, 277, l. 4 b., 319, l. 6 ff., 358, l. 21 ff., 359, l. 4 ff.; Ibn Ṭūlūn, esp. 73 [٧٣], ll. 5, penult., 71 [٧١], l. 26, 64 [٦٤], ll. 14, 18; Weil V. cf. Index; *CIA. Égypte I.* p. 457 f.

[3] Ibn Iyās, II, p. 202, l. 5 b: 4th Muḥarram 886, p. 359, l. 10: 887.

مِمّا عمل برسم المقرّ الأشرف الكريم العالى ا ○

لمولوى الأميرى الكبيرى المالكى العـ○ـالمى العادلى المجاهدى المرابطى المثاغرى ○

السيّدى السندى الذخرى المخدومى ا ○ لسيفى آقبردى أمير دوادار كبير ومدبّر

الممالك ○ الشريفة الإسلاميّة الملكى الأشرفى عزّ نصره ○

This is one of the objects made for His Most Noble and Honourable and High Excellency, our Lord, the Great Amir, the Royal, the Learned, the Just, the Defender of the Faith, the Warrior at the Frontiers, the Warden of the Marches, the Master, the Treasure, the Well-served, Saif ad-dīn Āqbirdī, Grand Amir Dawādār, Regent of the Noble Islamic provinces, (officer) of al-Malik al-Ashraf, may his victory be glorious.

BIBLIOGRAPHY: Unpublished.

2. HEAD OF A STANDARD, Treasury, Istanbul.

Inscription intersected by five shields.

○ المقرّ الأشرف الكريم العالى المولوى الأميرى ○ الكبيرى الأجلّى المحترمى

السيّدى السندى ○ المالكى المخدومى السيفى آقبردى أمير دوادار كبير وما مع

ذلك ○ وقريب المقام الشريف السلطان الملكى الأشرف أبو النصر قايتباى ○

His Most Noble and Honourable and High Excellency, our Lord, the Great Amir, the Most Magnificent, the Honoured, the Master, the Royal, the Well-Served, Saif ad-dīn Āqbirdī, Grand Amir Dawādār, and what goes with it, and a relative of His Majesty the Sultan, (officer) of al-Malik al-Ashraf Abu-n-Naṣr Qāytbāy.

On the shaft, below the head, there is another short inscription, mentioning Āqbirdī's name and title.

BIBLIOGRAPHY: Unpublished.

ĀQBUGHĀ MIN ʿABD AL-WĀḤID[1]

A.[2] Āqbughā b. ʿAbdallāh min ʿAbd al-Wāḥid an-Nāṣirī, originally a mamluk of Muḥammad b. Qalāūn, then his *jamdār*, later appointed Inspector of Buildings (*shādd al-ʿamā'ir*), became Amir of a Hundred and Commander of a Thousand. Appointed major-domo, Tuesday, the 26th Muḥarram 732 (29th October 1331), Chief of the Sultanian Mamluks and *Amīr Manzil*, thus accumulating five offices, all of which he held until al-Malik al-Manṣūr Abū Bakr b. Muḥammad arrested him, the 30th Muḥarram 742 (16th July 1341), put him into prison, and confiscated his possessions. Under Kujuk, Āqbughā was released by Qauṣūn and sent to Damascus. Made Governor of Hims by Aḥmad b. Muḥammad b. Qalāūn,[3] an appointment which he held until Jumādā II 743 (November 1342). He then proceeded as Commander of a Thousand to Damascus, where he remained until Shawwāl 743 (March 1343), when he was again arrested and sent first to Cairo and then to Alexandria. Executed in 744 (1343–4). His house stood in the vicinity of the Jāmiʿ al-Azhar, where he also built his madrasah.

BLAZON: *Upper and lower fields white, on red middle field a white napkin.*

1. LAMP, Victoria and Albert Museum, London, No. 1056–69, formerly collection Meymar.
Six shields.
Inscription on neck: Qur'ān, XXIV. 36, intersected by three shields.
Inscription on body.

مما عمل برسم الجناب | العالى المولوى | الأميرى الكبيرى |
السيفى سيف الدين | آقبغا عبد الواحد | الملكى الناصرى |

This is one of the objects made for His High Excellency (janāb), *our Lord, the Great Amir, Saif ad-dīn Āqbughā ʿAbd al-Wāḥid, (officer) of al-Malik an-Nāṣir.*

BIBLIOGRAPHY: Nesbitt, *A Descriptive Catalogue of the Glass Vessels in the South Kensington*

[1] Zetterstéen, *Beiträge*, pp. 148, l. 9, 224, l. 17; Ṣafadī, *Aʿyān*, s.v. (MS. Berlin, fo. 28ʳ); Maqrīzī, *Khiṭaṭ*, II, pp. 48, l. 8, 116, l. 9, 384, l. 14 b–386 l. 1 (2nd ed., IV, pp. 225, l. 3 b–228, l. 3); Ibn Ḥajar, *Durar*, s.v. (MS. Br. Mus., Or. 3043, fo. 73ʳ); Ibn Taghrībirdī, *Manhal*, s.v. (MS. Paris, Ar. 2068, fo. 203ʳ,ᵛ); Weil, IV. 365 f., 377, 404 f., 414 f.; *CIA. Égypte*, I. 186, 189 and n. 1.

[2] In inscriptions called *Saif* ad-dīn, cf. also *CIA. Égypte*, I. 183, 185–6, 187, 188.

[3] *Durar*, s.v. (l.c., l. penult.): by al-Malik al-Muẓaffar Kujuk.

Museum, p. 36 f., pl. VIII (frontispiece); Lane-Poole, *Art of the Saracens*, pp. 256–58, fig. 93.
Blazon mentioned and reproduced in: Schmoranz, *Old Oriental Gilt and Enamelled Glass Vessels*, fig. 14, pp. 18 n., 19 n., 69; P[ier], *Saracenic Heraldry*, fig. 5, p. 10. Mentioned: Kahle, 'Islamische Schattenspielfiguren' (in: *Islam*, II. 190 f., 192, n. 1); van Berchem, 'Notes d'archéologie arabe' (in: *Journal Asiatique*, 1904, I. 78 f.); Artin, *Contribution*, p. 127, No. 203; Migeon, *Manuel*, 2nd ed., II, p. 134; Wiet, *Lampes et bouteilles en verre émaillé*, p. 160, No. 31; Lamm, *Gläser*, p. 440, No. 47 (both with rich literature).

2. HEMISPHERICAL VASE of bell-metal, Victoria and Albert Museum, London, No. 576–97. Pl. XXX. 2, 3.
Inscription intersected by four shields.

المقرّ العالى المولوى الأميرى الكبيرى (B) الغازى المجاهدى المرابطى المثاغرى

المؤ(AB)يّدى الذخرى العونى الغياثى المخدومى السيفى آقبغا (AB) أستاذ الدار العالية الملكى

الناصرى عزّ نصره (AB)

His High Excellency, our Lord, the Great Amir, the Vanquisher, the Defender of the Faith, the Warrior at the Frontiers, the Warden of the Marches, the Helped (by God), the Treasure, the Helper, the Rescuer, the Well-Served, Saif ad-dīn Āqbughā, Major-domo of al-Malik an-Nāṣir, may his victory be glorious.

On the shields marked (A) traces of the original shield are still left, on the others (B) the superimposed blazon is seen, consisting of a two-fielded shield, upper field white (silver inlay), on lower field (united middle and lower fields) red cup.

BIBLIOGRAPHY: Unpublished.

Mentioned: van Berchem, *Notes d'archéologie arabe*, III. p. 79; Kahle, *Islamische Schattenspielfiguren*, p. 190 f.

Although the belongings of Āqbughā were disposed of by public sale,[1] and the names of the buyers have not been handed down, I venture to suggest that the superimposed blazon is that of Qauṣūn, who, twice having played an important role in the life of Āqbughā—once interceding on his behalf when his property was confiscated, and later on using his influence in obtaining a pardon for him from Sultan Kujuk—might easily have acquired or been presented with a part of Āqbughā's possessions.[2]

[1] Maqrīzī, *Khiṭaṭ*, II, p. 384, l. 8 b (2nd ed., IV, p. 226, ll. 5 ff.).
[2] Maqrīzī, l.c., p. 385 m (2nd ed., IV, p. 227 t).

ĀQBUGHĀ AṬ-ṬŪLŪTUMRĪ[1]

A. Āqbughā b. ʿAbdallāh aṭ-Ṭūlūtumrī aẓ-Ẓāhirī, nicknamed al-Lakkāsh, a mamluk of Barqūq, made by his master Amir of Ten, then Amir of Forty, Ra's naubah, and finally Amir of a Hundred and Commander of a Thousand. On 29th Jumādā I 800 (17th February 1398) nominated *amīr majlis*, in 801 (1398/9) appointed Governor of Kerak, but on his way to Kerak[2] arrested and put into the prison of Qalʿat aṣ-Ṣubaiba. By the end of Dhu-l-Ḥijja of the same year (August 1399), he joined Tanam in his rebellion against Faraj. Kept Gaza from Rabīʿ I till Rajab 802 (November 1399–March 1400). After Tanam's defeat near Jītīn, he was arrested and imprisoned, and executed at Damascus on 14th Shaʿbān 802 (10th April 1400).

BLAZON: *Upper field two napkins, middle field a cup, lower field a cup.*

MOSQUE OF IBN ʿUTHMĀN, Gaza.
Inscription over the lintel of the western entrance door.

(1) بسمله إنّما يَعْمُرُ مَسَاجِدَ ٱللّٰهِ مَنْ آمَنَ

(2) بِٱللّٰهِ وَٱلْيَوْمِ ٱلْآخِرِ أمر بإنشاء هذا الجامع ا (?)

(3) المبارك المقرّ الأشرف ○ العالى المولوى السّيدى

(4) المالكى المخدومى العلائى آقبغا الطولوتمرى الملكى ا (!)

(5) الناصرى أعزّ الله أنصاره بتأريخ شهر رجب الفرد سنة اثنين وثمان مائة

In the name of the most merciful God. He only shall visit the temples of God, who believeth in

[1] Ibn Duqmāq, V, p. 20, l. 13 (A's fief); Ibn Ḥajar, *Ta'rīkh*, s.a. 802 A.H. (MS. Br. Mus. Add. 7321, fo. 115^{v}, 116^{v}); Ibn Taghrībirdī, *an-Nujūm*, VI, pp. 11, l. 15, 20, l. 15, 33, l. 6, 36, l. 10, 37, l. 5, 39, l. 18, 146, ll. 6–11; *Manhal*, s.v. (MS. Paris, Ar. 2068, fo. 203^{v}, 204^{r}); as-Sakhāwī, *aḍ-Ḍau' al-lāmiʿ*, s.v. (MS. Damascus, Ẓāhiriyyah-Library); Ibn Iyās, I, pp. 308, l. 11, 312, ll. 5, 9, 10, penult. and ult., 313, l. 1, 322, ll. 7 b, 3 b, 323, l. 10, 324, l. 14 b. L. A. Mayer, 'Arabic Inscriptions of Gaza. II' (in: *Journal of the Palestine Oriental Society*, V, 1925, p. 64 ff.), and 'Arabic Inscriptions of Gaza. III' (ib., IX, 1929, p. 219, n. 2).

[2] According to as-Sakhāwī, l.c., he was appointed Governor of Gaza and arrested on his way there. According to Ibn Iyās he was imprisoned in aṣ-Ṣalībah. الصليبة and الصبيبة are very similar in Arabic script and the former is probably only a graphic variant.

God and the Last Day (Qur'ān IX. 18). *Ordered to build this blessed Mosque, His most Noble and High Excellency, our Lord, the Master, the Royal, the Well-Served, 'Alā' ad-dīn Āqbughā aṭ-Ṭūlūtumrī, (officer) of al-Malik an-Nāṣir, may God make his victories glorious. In the month of Rajab the Unique of the year* 802 (27th February–27th March 1400).

BIBLIOGRAPHY: L. A. Mayer, *Arabic Inscriptions of Gaza. II*, pp. 64 ff.

ĀQSUNQUR [1]

Sh. Āqsunqur an-Nāṣirī, for a time Muḥammad b. Qalāūn's Master of the Hunt (*amīr shikār*), made Amir of a Hundred and Commander of a Thousand. On al-Malik an-Nāṣir Aḥmad's accession to the throne, offered the post of a Superintendent of the Stables (*amīr akhūr*), which he declined. Sent as Governor to Gaza, where he stayed till al-Malik aṣ-Ṣāliḥ Isma'īl recalled him to Cairo and appointed him Superintendent of the Stables. Early in Shawwāl 744 (began 16th February 1344) became Governor of Tripoli, a post he held till Rabī' II 746 (August 1345). On his return to Cairo lived as one of the most important amirs at court, organized the plot against al-Malik al-Kāmil Sha'bān. Killed in Rabī' II 748 (began 11th July 1347).

BLAZON: *Upper field self-coloured, on red middle field a white cup, lower field white.*

GLASS LAMP, from the Āqsunqur Mosque, now in the Arabic Museum, Cairo, No. 3202/1–3.
Originally six shields, three of them intersecting the inscription on the neck, and three on the lower part of the body.
Inscription on the body, text as restored by Wiet:

ممّا عمل برسم العبد الفقير الى الله تعالى اقسـ[ـنـ]ـقر الـ[ـنـ]ـاصرى الملكـ[ـى المظفّرى

. . . عزّ أنصـ]ـاره.

This is one of the objects made for the servant yearning for God the Exalted, Āqsunqur an-Nāṣirī, (officer) of al-Malik [*al-Muẓaffar . . . may his vict*]*ories* [*be glorious*].

DATE: The mosque having been finished in 748 (1347), the lamp is probably of the same date.

BIBLIOGRAPHY: Herz, *Catalogue*, p. 294, No. 6; Wiet, *Lampes*, p. 124 f., pl. XIV.

Mentioned: *CR.* 1904, fasc. 21, p. 75; Lamm, *Gläser*, p. 448, No. 80.

[1] Ibn Ḥabīb, p. 379; Ṣafadī, *A'yān*, s.v. (MS. Berlin, fo. 28^{v}); *Manhal* s.v. (MS. Paris, Ar. 2068, fos. 207^{v}–208^{r}); Ibn Iyās, I, especially pp. 185, l. 16, 187, ll. 13–19.

ĀQṬURAQ

BLAZON: ***Sword displayed diagonally on a three-fielded shield.***

MOSQUE, locally known as as-Saqraqiyya, Tripoli.
Inscription on both sides of entrance gate, on the lintels of each pair of windows, a heraldic shield.

بسمله . . . وقف الجناب الكريم السيفى آقطرق الحاجب هذا المكان المبارك مسجدًا

لله تعالى وتربةً للدفن الخ

. . . *His Honourable Excellency* (janāb), *Saif ad-dīn Āqṭuraq, the chamberlain* (ḥājib) *piously founded this blessed spot as a mosque for God the Exalted and as a mausoleum for burial, &c.*

BIBLIOGRAPHY: Sobernheim, *CIA. Syrie du Nord*, No. 49, p. 109, pl. XI.

ĀQŪSH GOVERNOR OF KERAK[1]

J. Āqūsh b. ʿAbdallāh al-Ashrafī, an Egyptian amir, nicknamed al-Burnāq, originally a mamlūk of al-Malik al-Ashraf Khalīl b. Qalāūn,[2] Governor of Kerak from 690 to the middle of Shawwāl 708 (4th January–23rd December 1291, to the end of March 1309); Viceroy of Syria from Jumādā I 711[3] to Rabīʿ I 712 (15th September–14th October 1311 to the 9th July 1312). Following the appointment of Tankiz as Viceroy of Syria, Āqūsh was put in prison where he stayed until the 20th Rajab 715 (20th October 1315). On his release he was appointed *ra's al-maimana* and later Inspector of the Māristān. In Rabīʿ I 734 (which began 10th November 1333), he was

[1] Zetterstéen, *Beiträge*, cf. Index, especially p. 81, l. penult., 136, l. 13, 141, l. 15, 156, l. 9, 157, l. ult., 163, l. 18, 187, l. 19, 189, l. 13, 191, l. 8; Ibn al-Wardī, II, pp. 261, ll. 6, 17, 309, l. 1; Ṣafadī, *Tuḥfa* (MS. Paris, Ar. 5827, fo. 198ʳ); Ibn Ḥabīb, 359, 363; Qalqashandī, *Ṣubḥ*, XII. 12–16 (Letter of Appointment as Viceroy of Syria); Maqrīzī, *Khiṭaṭ*, II 55, l. 9 ff. (ed. Cairo 1325 A.H., III. 88 f.); *Sulūk*, *SM.* II a, especially pp. 129, II b. 286; Ibn Ḥajar, *Durar*, s.v. (MS. Br. Mus., Or. 3043, fo. 74ᵛ–75ʳ); Ibn Taghrībirdī, *Manhal*, s.v. (MS. Paris, Ar. 2069, fos. 5ᵛ–6ᵛ); Ibn Iyās, I, p. 151, l. 6 b; Weil, cf. Index; Mrs. R. L. Devonshire, *Some Dated Objects in Mr. Ralph Harari's Collection*, p. 125.

[2] According to Ibn Ḥajar, l.c., he was originally a mamluk of al-Malik al-Manṣūr Qalāūn. Al-Malik al-Ashraf Khalīl appointed him Governor of Kerak.

[3] This is the date given by Qalqashandī. According to Zetterstéen, l.c., p. 156, Āqūsh was given the robe of honour, the distinctive sign of his appointment, on Saturday, 2nd Jumādā II.

appointed Governor of Tripoli. In 735 he was arrested by Tankiz and imprisoned, first in the fortress of Damascus, then in the Tower of Safad, and finally in Alexandria, where he died on the 7th of Jumādā I 736 (23rd December 1335). Built a mosque in the Ḥusainiyya Quarter, Cairo.

BLAZON: *White falcon (? Griffin-vulture) on undivided round shield.*

1. BRASS PLATE. Collection R. A. Harari, Esq., London. Pl. XV.
Inscription intersected by three shields. Falcon (? griffin-vulture) looking to the right.

مما عمل برسم المقرّ العالى العالى العادلى ا ○ المجاهدى المرابطى الثاغرى المظفّرى

المنصورى ○ الجمالى جمال الدين آقش[1] نائب السلطنة بالكرك المحروس

This is one of the objects made for His High Excellency, the Learned, the Just, the Defender of the Faith, the Warrior at the Frontiers, the Warden of the Marches, the Victorious, Jamāl ad-dīn Āqūsh, Governor of the protected Kerak.

BIBLIOGRAPHY: Unpublished.

Mentioned and reproduced: Devonshire, l.c., p. 125, fig. VII.

2. COPPER STAND FOR A TRAY, lower half, collection R. A. Harari, Esq., London. Pl. XV.
Inscription intersected by three shields. Falcon (? griffin-vulture) looking to the left.

مما عمل برسم المقرّ الشريف العالى ○ الجمالى نائب السلطنة ا ○ المعظّمة

بالكرك المحروس

This is one of the objects made for His Noble and High Excellency Jamāl ad-dīn, Governor of the August Sultanate in the protected Kerak.

Although the inscription contains neither name nor date, there cannot be the least doubt with regard to the attribution of this stand, not only because of the identical blazon and surname (Jamāl ad-dīn), but also because Āqūsh was usually called 'Jamāl ad-dīn, Governor of Kerak', or simply 'the Governor of Kerak'.[2]

BIBLIOGRAPHY: Unpublished.

Mentioned: Devonshire, l.c., p. 125.

[1] Same defective spelling in Ibn Ḥajar, *ad-Durar al-kāmina* (MS. British Museum) and in Sobernheim, *CIA. Syrie du Nord*, p. 45, n. 2, in a passage quoted from Nuwairī.

[2] Cf. the literature quoted p. 71, n. 1.

ĀQŪSH AL-BURUNLĪ

BLAZON: *Six-petalled rosette without shield.*

MAUSOLEUM, to the north of Kafr Sīb, near Tul Karm, marked 'Amâd ed-Dîn' on the map of the Palestine Exploration Fund, Sheet XI. K. m..
Inscription embedded in the northern side of the gable-roof of the cenotaph, two shields forming the fifth line of the text.

(١) بسمله . . . (2) يُبَشِّرهم ربّهم بِرَحْمَةٍ مِنْه (3) وَرِضْوانٍ هذا قبر الفقير

(4) الى رحمة الله الأمير الغازى (5) ○ ○ (6) جمال الدين آقوش البرلى

(7) توفّى فى مستهلّ جمادى (8) الأ[و]ل سنة ثمان وستّين وستّمائة رحمه لله

In the name of the most merciful God. Their Lord sendeth them good tidings of mercy from him, and good will (Qur'ān IX. 21). *This is the tomb of the one yearning for God's mercy the Amīr, the Vanquisher, Jamāl ad-dīn Āqūsh al-Burlī.*[1] *Passed away on the 1st Jumādā I of the year* 668 (27th December 1269). *May God have mercy upon him.*

BIBLIOGRAPHY: Unpublished.

ARGHŪN AL-'ALĀ'Ī[2]

S. Arghūn al-'Alā'ī, stepfather of al-Malik aṣ-Ṣāliḥ, Isma'īl and al-Malik al-Kāmil Sha'bān, Chief of the Corps of jamdārs under al-Malik an-Nāṣir Muḥammad, sent by Qauṣūn to Safad, shortly afterwards returned to Egypt, imprisoned in Alexandria by al-Malik al-Muẓaffar Ḥājjī. Died in 748 (1347/8).[3] Built a *kuttāb as-sabīl* at the gate of the Māristān and a khānqāh in Cairo.

BLAZON: *Upper and lower fields golden, on a red middle field a golden napkin.*

[1] The letters, squeezed into the end of the line, seem to allow only for البرى which stands probably for البرلى al-Burlī, cf. the transcription of this name in Abu-l-Fidā', ed. Reiske.

[2] Ṣafadī, *A'yān*, s.v. (MS. Berlin, fo. 22^{v}, 23^{r}); Ibn Ḥabīb, p. 385; Ibn Ḥajar, *Durar*, s.v. (MS. Br. Mus., Or. 3043, fo. 65^{v}); *Manhal* s.v. Arghūnshāh (MS. Paris, Ar. 2068, fo. 159^{r}, l. 5 b); Ibn Iyās, I, pp. 184, l. 9 b, 8 b, 185, ll. 7, 13, 17; Weil, IV, cf. Index, especially pp. 469, 473.

[3] According to Ibn Ḥabīb, l.c., in 747.

GLASS GLOBE, Museum of Fine Arts, Boston, Mass., No. 12–61.
Inscription:

ممّا عمل برسم المقرّ الا ○ شرف العالى المخدومى ○ السيفى أرغون ○ العلائى عزّ

[ا]لله أنصاره ○ [Kühnel]

This is one of the objects made for His Most Noble and High Excellency, the Well-Served Saif ad-dīn Arghūn al-'Alā'ī, may God make his victories glorious.

BIBLIOGRAPHY: *Museum of Fine Arts Bulletin*, X, August 1912, No. 58, p. 29; Martinovitch, 'A Glass Globe of Arghūn' (in *Eastern Art Annual*, vol. II, 1930, p. 245, pl. CXXXVI.)

Reproduced: *Handbook of the Museum of Fine Arts*, Boston, 16th ed., Nov. 1923, p. 98.
Mentioned: Migeon, *Manuel*, 2nd ed., II. 126, 137, 142; Wiet, *Lampes*, p. 165, No. 55.
Mentioned and reproduced: Lamm, *Gläser*, p. 447 f., pl. 196, fig. 3.
Referred to in F.V.P., 'Oriental Glass' (in *Museum of Fine Arts Bulletin*, December 1910, Nos. 50–1) with the following translation of the text: One of those made by the great, the exalted al-Naki, el-Arjawan: the glory be to God.

ARGHŪN AL-KĀMILĪ[1]

S. Arghūn b. 'Abdallāh aṣ-Ṣaghīr ('the small one'), originally mamluk of al-Malik aṣ-Ṣāliḥ Isma'īl, later on of al-Malik al-Kāmil Sha'bān, made Amir of a Hundred by the latter. Tuesday, 15th Rajab 750 (29th September 1349), appointed Governor of Aleppo, thence transferred as Governor to Damascus,[2] which he entered on Monday, 11th Sha'bān 752 (3rd October 1351), and again of Aleppo 752 (1352/3).[3] Deposed in 755 (1354), arrested in Cairo, imprisoned at Alexandria in 756 and exiled to Jerusalem, where, at the age of about thirty, he died on the 28th Shawwāl 758 (14th October 1357).

BLAZON: *Napkin on middle field of a three-fielded shield.*

[1] Ṣafadī, *A'yān*, s.v. (MS. Berlin, fo. 23 v. ff.), *al-Wāfī*, s.v., *Tuḥfa* (MS. Paris, Ar. 5827, fo. 220 v); Ibn Ḥabīb, pp. 391, 395, 397, 399, 404; Ṣāliḥ b. Yaḥyā, p. 177, l. 15; Maqrīzī, *Khiṭaṭ*, II, p. 73, ll. 11–30 (2nd ed., III, p. 118, l. 10–p. 119, l. 4); Ibn Ḥajar, *ad-Durar*, s.v. (MS. Br. Mus., Or. 3043, fo. 65 v–66 r); Ibn Taghrībirdī, *Manhal*, s.v. (MS. Paris, Ar. 2068, p. 160 v f.); Mujīr ad-dīn, *al-Uns al-jalīl*, pp. 383, l. 8, 388–9, 392, l. penult., 559, l. 15, 644, l. 6, 693, l. 8 b. (Sauvaire, pp. 134, 145 f., 154); Ibn Iyās, I, pp. 195, l. 11, 8 b, 201, l. 5 ff.; Weil, IV. 484, 492, 495; *CIA. Egypte*, I, pp. 200, n. 2, 219, 220; van Berchem, *Arabische Inschriften (Oppenheim)*, p. 51; *CIA. Jérusalem, Ville*, pp. 281 ff.

[2] According to Ibn Iyās, I, p. 195, l. 11, appointed Governor of Egypt, a detail not confirmed by any other historian.

[3] According to Ibn Ḥajar, l.c.: in Ramaḍān 753; according to Ibn Iyās I 201, l. 5: in 754.

1. HOSPITAL, Aleppo, near the Qinnasrīn Gate.
Four shields in the bottom row of the stalactites of the portal.
Inscription immediately underneath the stalactites.

بسمله مَنْ جَاءَ بِٱلْحَسَنَةِ فَلَهُ عَشْرُ أَمْثَالِهَا أمر بإنشآء هذا البيمارستان المبارك (?)

فى أيّام مولانا السلطان الملك الصالح ابن السلطان الملك الناصر محمّد بن قلاون

خلّد الله ملكه الفقير إلى ربّه أرغون الكاملى نائب السلطنة المعظّمة بحلب المحروسة

غفر الله له وأثابه الجنّة فى شهور سنة خمس وخمسين وسبعمائة يتولّى أمرها

الفقير الى ربّه سيف الدين طنجا (?) استاذ دار المشار اليه عفى الله عنه

In the name of the most merciful God. He who shall appear with good works shall receive a tenfold recompense for the same (Qur'ān VI. 161). *Ordered to build this blessed hospital during the reign of our Lord the Sultan al-Malik aṣ-Ṣāliḥ, son of the Sultan al-Malik an-Nāṣir Muḥammad b. Qalāūn, may God make his reign eternal, he who yearns for his Lord Arghūn al-Kāmilī, Governor of the August Sultanate in Aleppo the protected, may God forgive him and give him paradise as reward. In the months of the year* 755 (1354). *He who yearns for his Lord Saif ad-dīn Ṭanjā* (?) *major-domo of the* (*Amir*) *referred to was in charge of the work. May God forgive him.*

BIBLIOGRAPHY: van Berchem, *Arabische Inschriften* (*Oppenheim*), No. 59, pp. 49 ff., figs. 6, 7.
Reproduced: Herz, *Az Iszlám Művészete*, fig. 234, p. 204.

Only inscription: Bischoff, *Tuḥaf al-anbā' fī ta'rīkh Ḥalab ash-shahbā'*, p. 140.
Blazon reproduced: Artin, *Contribution*, fig. 200, p. 126 (without attribution).

2. MAUSOLEUM AND MADRASAH, Ṭarīq Bāb al-Ḥadīd, Jerusalem, known locally as Dār al-Khaṭīb.
Two shields intersecting the inscription carved on the lintel of the door.

(1) بسمله ○ أمر بإنشاء هذه التربة والمدرسة المباركة المقرّ الأشرف السيفى

أرغون الكاملى ○ نائب السلطنة الشريفة

(2) بالشأم المحروس كان ○ وتوفّى الى رحمة الله تعالى ثامن عشرين شوّال سنة

ثمان وخمسين وسبع مائة وتولّى شدّها وتكميلها ركن الدين بيبرص السيفى ○

وكملت فى ربيع الآخر سنة تسع وخمسين وسبع مائة

In the name of the most merciful God. Ordered to build this mausoleum and this blessed madrasah His Most Noble Excellency Saif ad-dīn Arghūn al-Kāmilī, late Governor of the Noble Sultanate in the protected Damascus. Passed into the mercy of God the Exalted the 28th Shawwāl 758 (14th October 1357). *Rukn ad-dīn Baybarṣ as-Saifī was charged with the inspection and completion of the building. It was completed in Rabī' II* 759 (13th March–10th April 1358).

BIBLIOGRAPHY: *CIA. Jérusalem, Ville*, p. 281 ff., fig. 50, pl. LXX.

Blazon reproduced: Artin, *Contribution*, fig. 200, p. 126 (without attribution).

ARGHŪN AN-NĀṢIRĪ

BLAZON: *Napkin on the middle field of a three-fielded shield.*

GLASS LAMP, in 1885 in the collection Goupil, destroyed since. A copy kept in the Musée des Arts Décoratifs. Paris. Three shields on the upper part of the body of the lamp. Inscription on the body:

المقرّ الأشرف الكريم العالى المولوى السيّدى المالكى الممهّدى المشيّدى العونى الغياثى

الهما(م)ى السيفى أرغون الناصرى نائب السلطنة المعظّمة

His Most Noble and Honourable and High Excellency, our Lord, the Master, the Royal, the Administrator, the Organizer, the Helper, the Rescuer, the Shelter, Saif ad-dīn Arghūn an-Nāṣirī, Governor of the August Sultanate.

BIBLIOGRAPHY: Lavoix, 'La Collection Albert Goupil, II. L'Art Oriental' (in *GBA*. 2e pér., t. XXXII, 1885), p. 303 f. and pl.; Wiet, *Lampes*, p. 158 f., No. 24.

Mentioned: Schmoranz, pp. 15, n., 27, 69; *CIA. Jérusalem, Ville*, p. 282, n. 3; Devonshire, 'Some Objects' (in: *Apollo*, January 1927), p. 15; Lamm, *Mittelalterliche Gläser* I. p. 436 f., No. 34.

ARGHŪN AN-NĀṢIRĪ [1]

Possibly identical with S. Arghūn, originally a mamluk of Muḥammad b.

1 Zetterstéen, *Beiträge*, especially pp. 146, l. ult. –147, l. 2, 158, l. 14, 177, l. 16 ff., 182 l. ult. f.; Ibn Ḥabīb, pp. 319, 344, 351, *Manhal*, s.v. (MS. Paris, Ar. 2068, fo. 157[r] f.); Ibn Iyās, I, 157, l. penult., 174, l. 4 b, 175, l. 13; Schmoranz, p. 69; Weil cf. Index; Rāghib Ṭabbākh, *A'lām* II, p. 375.

Qalāūn, received a scholarly education, succeeded Baybars as Grand Dawādār; Monday, the 1st Jumādā I 712 (4th September 1312) appointed Viceroy of Egypt; Monday the 12th Muḥarram 727 (8th December 1326) transferred to Aleppo as Governor. Died the 18th Rabīʿ I[1] or Rabīʿ II 731 (30th December 1330 or 29th January 1331). Built a mausoleum in Aleppo and a madrasa for the Hanefites in Mecca.

BLAZON: *Upper and lower fields red, middle field either golden or self-coloured.*

GLASS LAMP. Once in the possession of the late Baron Gustave de Rothschild, present owner unknown. Pl. XLVI.
Inscription on neck, intersected by three shields:

المقرّ الأشرف الكريم العالى المولوى السيّدى المالكى المهّدى ○ المشيّدى العونى

الغياثى الكافلى السيفى أرغون الناصرى ○ نائب السلطنة المعظّمة المقرّ الأشرف الكريم

العالى المولوى ○ [Van Berchem]

His Most Noble and Honourable and High Excellency, our Lord, the Master, the Royal, the Administrator, the Organizer, the Helper, the Rescuer, the Viceroy, Saif ad-dīn Arghūn an-Nāṣirī, Governor of the August Sultanate. His Most Noble and Honourable and High Excellency, our Lord.

BIBLIOGRAPHY: Unpublished.
Mentioned: van Berchem, *Inschriften Oppenheim*, p. 52, n.; *CIA. Jérusalem, Ville*, p. 283, n. 3; Wiet, *Lampes*, p. 156, No. 14; Lamm, p. 430, No. 13.

ARGHŪNSHĀH

BLAZON: *Cup on middle field of a three-fielded shield.*
DRUM. Present owner unknown.
Inscription:

المقرّ العالى المولوى المالكى العالمى العادلى السيفى أرغونشاه المالكى الأشرفى

أعزّ الله أنصاره [Sauvaget]

His High Excellency, our Lord, the Royal, the Learned, the Just, Saif ad-dīn Arghūn Shāh, (officer) of al-Malik al-Ashraf, may God make his victories glorious.

BIBLIOGRAPHY: Unpublished.

[1] According to *Manhal*, l.c., he died on a Friday night, an indication which does not help in this case, as the 18th Rabīʿ I was a Sunday and the 18th Rabīʿ II a Tuesday.

ARUQṬĀY[1,2]

S. Aruqṭāy, known as Ḥājj Aruqṭāy, originally a mamluk of al-Malik al-Ashraf Khalīl b. Qalāūn, made jamdār by al-Malik an-Nāṣir Muḥammad b. Qalāūn, followed Tankiz to Damascus, was sent to Hims as Governor on Sunday, 7th Rajab 716[3] (25th September 1316), appointed Governor of Safad in 718 (1318), remained in office till 736 (1335/6), when he was recalled to Egypt as Commander of a Thousand and appointed Viceroy during occasional periods of absence of the Sultan (*nā'ib al-ghaibah*). After the dismissal of Ṭaynāl appointed Governor of Tripoli. Following upon Alṭunbughā's defeat in Aleppo, imprisoned in Alexandria. Released by al-Malik aṣ-Ṣāliḥ Isma'īl, resided in Cairo as Commander of a Thousand up to aṣ-Ṣāliḥ's death. Under al-Malik al-Kāmil Sha'bān appointed Governor of Aleppo, remained there for about five months from Jumādā I 746 (began 30th August 1345) onwards, recalled to Egypt, became Viceroy during the reign of al-Malik al-Muẓaffar Ḥajjī.[4] After al-Malik an-Nāṣir Ḥasan's accession to the throne appointed at his own request Governor of Aleppo. Following upon the death of Arghūnshāh, appointed Governor of Damascus. Died on his way to Damascus, 5th Jumādā I 750 (22nd July 1349), seventy-eight years old.

BLAZON: *In each of the upper and lower fields of a three-fielded shield a key, middle field blank.*

COPPER VASE, formerly in the possession of A. Baudry, Cairo, present owner unknown.
Inscription:

مما عمل برسم المقرّ العالى المولوى السيفى أرقطاى نائب المملكة الصفديّة عزّ نصره

This is one of the objects made for His High Excellency, our Lord, Saif ad-dīn Aruqṭāy, Governor of the province of Safad, may his victory be glorious.

DATE: Between 1318 and 1335.

[1] Ṣafadī, *A'yān*, s.v. (MS. Berlin, fo. 25v, 26r); Ibn Ḥabīb, pp. 383, 386, 392; Maqrīzī, *Khiṭaṭ*, II, pp. 40, l. 3 b–41, l. 15; Ibn Ḥajar, *Durar*, s.v. (MS. Br. Mus., Or. 3043, fo. 66r); *Manhal* s.v. (MS. Paris, Ar. 2068, fo. 163r); Ibn Iyās, I, pp. 184, l. 4, 189, l. 9, 190, l. 12; Weil, IV. 350 f., 430, 433, 435, 463, 471, 476, 484.

[2] Vowel signs in *A'yān*, s.v.; vulgar pronunciation without 'A' (*Khiṭaṭ*, II. 40, l. 3 b).

[3] According to *Khiṭaṭ*, II, p. 41, l. 2: 710.

[4] According to Ibn Iyās I p. 184, l. 4, under Sha'bān.

BIBLIOGRAPHY: Rogers, *Le Blason*, No. 24, p. 125 f. fig. 44; Artin, *Contribution*, p. 237 (with the wrong reference to No. 164).

Reproduced: Ströhl, *Heraldischer Atlas*, p. 3, fig. 11; P[ier], *Saracenic Heraldry*, fig. 12, p. 10 ; Fox-Davies, *A Complete Guide to Heraldry* (2nd ed.), p. 13, fig. 9.
If blazon and inscription really belong together—a supposition which on the information supplied by Rogers can be neither proved nor disproved—then this blazon would be one of the rare cases in which amirs, despite their having served as jamdārs, wore an emblem other than a napkin on their shields, the others being Baybars (later Sultan), Baybars Jāliq and Qāzān, but cf. the blazon of Mūsā b. Aruqṭāy.

ASANBUGHĀ B. BAKTAMUR[1]

S. Asanbughā b. Baktamur al-Abūbakrī, made Amir of a Hundred and Commander of a Thousand by Muḥammad b. Qalāūn; after the latter's death imprisoned in Alexandria, released under al-Malik aṣ-Ṣāliḥ Isma'īl, in 769 (1367/8) became Governor of Aleppo,[2] which post he occupied for six months; transferred to Cairo as Great Amir. Died in 777 (1375/6), over seventy years of age.
Built the Būbakriyya near the Sūq ar-Raqīq, Cairo.

BLAZON: *Sword with sword-knots placed diagonally on the middle field of a three-fielded shield.*

MADRASA, Cairo.

On the restored wooden railing of the sabil, a modern inscription flanked by two shields, imitating the original blazon on the ceiling.
BIBLIOGRAPHY: Unpublished.
Mentioned: *CR.* Exerc. 1897, fasc. 14, p. 58.

ASANDAMUR

Probably identical with S. Asandamur Kurjī,[3, 4] an amir at Damascus, im-

[1] Ibn Ḥabīb, pp. 424, 439; Ibn Ḥajar, *Durar*, s.v. (MS. Br. Mus., Or. 3043, fo. 72^{r}); Ibn Taghrībirdī, *Nujūm*, obituaries s.a. 777 (MS. Paris, Ar. 1786, fos. 193$^{r, v}$).

[2] According to Ibn Ḥabīb, p. 424, he was appointed in 770.

[3] Abu-l-Fidā' ed. Reiske, V., 176, 222, 228–34, 240–2 (ed. Constantinople, IV. 47, l. 4 b, 60, l. 8 b, 62, ll. 1, 7, 23 ff., 3 b, 63, l. 10, 65, l. 3 ff.); Zetterstéen, *Beiträge*, pp. 110, l. 11, 144, l. 7, 151, l. 6, 152, l. 6, 153, l. 14, 154, l. 11; Ibn Ḥabīb, pp. 304, 313, 314; *Ṣubḥ*, X, 182, l. 9 f.; *SM.* II b, 181, 185; Ibn Ḥajar, *Durar*, s.v. (MS. Br. Mus., Or. 3043, fo. 72^{v}); *Manhal* s.v. (MS. Paris, Ar. 2068, fos. 193^{v}–194^{v}); Ibn Iyās, I, pp. 152, l. 5, 154, l. 9 b; Weil, IV, especially pp. 202, 272, 288, 299, n. 2, 300 f., 305–7.

[4] Spelling based on the vowel signs in Ṣafadī, *A'yān*, s.v. Asandamur al-'Umarī (MS. Berlin, fo. 27^{r}).

prisoned in Muḥarram 696 (November 1296) by Kitbughā, took up office as Governor of Tripoli in 701 (1301/2), appointed Governor of Hama the 18th Dhu-l-Ḥijja 709 (19th May 1310), Governor of Aleppo in Jumādā I 710 (began 26th September 1310). Arrested and executed in 710 or 711 (1310/11). Built a bath in Tripoli.

BLAZON: *Sword on undivided field. Shield either pointed (No. 1) or round (No. 2).*

1. LID OF A CENOTAPH. National Syrian Museum, Damascus. Pl. XXXVII. On each of the long sides of the lid a shield above the inscription:

بسمله . . . هذا قبر الفقيرة الى الله المتوفّاة فى سبيل الله بحى بنت عبد ا | لله

عتيقة الجناب | العالى السيفى أسندمر السلحدار المنصورى الأشرفّى توفيت يوم الأحد

تاسع رجب الفرد سنة تسعين وستّمائة رحمها الله ورحم من ترحّم عليها

In the name of the most merciful God. This is the tomb of the woman yearning for God, who died in the path of God [1 word] *daughter of 'Abdallāh, the freed slave (wife) of His High Excellency* (janāb), *Saif ad-dīn Asandamur, the armour-bearer, (officer) of (al-Malik) al-Manṣūr (and al-Malik) al-Ashraf. Passed away the 9th Rajab the Unique of the year* 690 (8th July 1291), *may God have mercy upon her*, &c.

Despite the diacritical points, the name of Asandamur's wife is very difficult to establish. The rendering of 'Tukhayna' has been suggested by Professor G. Weil, Berlin, and that of 'Bakhtī' by Professor G. Wiet, Cairo. For the convenience of the reader, I am passing on both variants.

BIBLIOGRAPHY: Unpublished.

2. BRASS BOWL. Collection R. A. Harari, Esq., London. Pl. XXXVI. 3. In centre a shield with inscription round it, both completely obliterated. On the outside an inscription intersected by three shields and three eight-petalled whirling rosettes.

المقرّ العالى ا ○ لمولوى المالكى | العالمى العاد ○ لى المجاهدى الذخرى | السيفى

أسندمر السلحدار ○ المنصورى الناصرى

His High Excellency, our Lord, the Royal, the Learned, the Just, the Defender of the Faith, the Treasure, Saif ad-dīn Asandamur, the armour-bearer (officer) of (al-Malik) al-Manṣūr (and) (al-Malik) an-Nāṣir.

DATE: Between 694, al-Malik an-Nāṣir's accession to the throne, and 711.

BIBLIOGRAPHY: Unpublished.

AṢLAM[1]

Ba. Aṣlam b. ʿAbdallāh an-Nāṣirī, a mamluk of Muḥammad b. Qalāūn and his silaḥdār, made by him Amir of a Hundred and Commander of a Thousand. The victim of malicious slander, he was imprisoned for six years and five months.[2] Towards the end of Muḥammad b. Qalāūn's reign he was re-appointed Amir of a Hundred and Commander of a Thousand, and in Ramaḍān 741 (February–March 1341) made Governor of Safad. In 742 sent back to Cairo by Quṭlūbughā, where he remained up to his death, the 10th Shaʿbān 747 (26th November 1346). Built a madrasah near his house at the Bāb al-Maḥrūq, Cairo, as well as a mausoleum, a private house, and a cistern for public use.[3]

BLAZON: *Upper and lower field golden, on a red middle field a golden scimitar.*

LAMP, Kaiser Friedrich Museum, Berlin, formerly collection Sarre.
Six shields, three intersecting the qur'ānic inscription on the neck, three on the lower part of the body.
Inscription on body:

ممّا عمل برسم المقرّ العالى المولوى الأمير[ى] الكبيرى المحترمى المخدومى

بهاء الدين أسلام دامت سعادته

This is one of the objects made for His High Excellency, our Lord, the Great Amir, the Honoured, the Well-Served, Bahā' ad-dīn Aslām, may his happiness last for ever.

BIBLIOGRAPHY: Sarre and Martin, *Die Ausstellung von Meisterwerken Muhammedanischer Kunst in München 1910*, I. 8, pl. 174; Karabacek, 'Muhammedanische Kunststudien' (in: *Zur orientalischen Altertumskunde*, IV), pp. 10 ff.

Reproduced in: Sarre, 'Vergoldete und emaillierte syrische Gläser' (in: *Amtliche Berichte aus den Kgl. Kunstsammlungen*, XXXII (1911), p. 138 f., fig. 81e); Diez, *Die Kunst der islamischen Völker*, p. 205, fig. 287; Kühnel, *Kunst des Orients*, p. 53, fig. 73.
Mentioned: Wiet, *Lampes*, p. 163, No. 47; Lamm, *Gläser*, p. 447, No 73.

1 Zetterstéen, *Beiträge*, pp. 171, l. 6, 187, l. 11 f., 219, ll. 3–6; Ṣafadī, *Aʿyān*, s.v. (MS. Berlin, fo. 27r, v), where the date of his death is given as 746; Maqrīzī, *Khiṭaṭ*, II, p. 309, ll. 2 ff. (2nd ed., IV, p. 106, ll. 3 ff.); Ibn Ḥajar, *Durar*, s.v. (MS. Br. Mus., Or. 3043, fo. 73r); Ibn Taghrībirdī, *Manhal*, s.v. (MS. Paris, Ar. 2068, fo. 196v, 197r); Weil, IV. 425, 455, 457; *CIA. Égypte*, I. 196, 766.

2 Zetterstéen, *Beiträge*, p. 187, l. 11 f.; according to Ibn Taghrībirdī, *Manhal*, l.c., fo. 197r, l. 1, and *Aʿyān*, l.c., five years; according to Ibn Ḥajar, l.c., l. 8, 'about seven years'.

3 *Manhal*, l.c., fo. 197r, l. 12, 'a cistern *and* a public fountain' حوضاً وسبيلاً.

Van Berchem's view[1] that this lamp was made for Aṣlam, in spite of the spelling Aslām, was challenged by Karabacek,[2] who tried to prove (*a*) that neither can the vulgar pronunciation of Cairo be considered as support for the spelling of Aslan, nor can the name be derived from Arslān, (*b*) that different spelling rules out the identity of these two persons,[3] and (*c*) that, therefore, the Aslām mentioned in the inscription on the lamp is a different person from Aṣlam, the builder of the Mosque at Cairo.

The first argument is irrelevant to the solution of our problem, the second is wrong, because there are many known instances showing that the name of an amir was spelt in different ways, even in texts of a more or less official character, and, curiously enough, there is just the one group of names quoted by Karabacek which furnishes the most convincing proof to the contrary, viz. names ending with تمر, e.g. Ṭuquztamur,[4] Tuquzdamur,[5] &c.

The following facts prove that we were justified in dismissing Karabacek's theory:

(*a*) There exists an intermediate form between Aṣlam and Aslām, viz. Aṣlām.[6]

(*b*) The change from s to ṣ is a well-established fact in the spelling of common Turkish names.[7]

(*c*) There is no amir of the name of Aslām, as opposed to Aṣlam.

(*d*) The amir Arslān, quoted by Karabacek, was a *dawādār* and not a *silaḥdār*.[8]

We cannot, therefore, go wrong in assuming that the holder of this blazon is Bahā' ad-dīn Aṣlam, who founded a madrasah in Cairo in 746, and that the lamp was made about the same time.

AYBAK OF MOSUL[9]

I. Aybak b. ʿAbdallāh of Mosul, a mamluk of Qalāūn, Governor of Shaubak, appointed Governor of Kerak in 685 (1286), and of Tripoli in 694 (1294/5). Died there in 698[10] (1298/9).

BLAZON: *Table* (khānjā) *on middle field of three-fielded shield.*

1 *Die Ausstellung von Meisterwerken, &c.*, I. 9.

2 *Muhammedanische Kunststudien*, pp. 10 ff.

3 l.c., p. 13: 'In den Biographien und Nomenklaturen werden derlei Namensschreibungen stets strenge auseinander gehalten, wie z.B. ارسلان und ارصلان, تيمور, تمر und دمر usw.'

4 In inscriptions, cf. the Roll, s.v.

5 In literary texts, cf. *Manhal*, s.v.; Ibn Ḥabīb, cf. Index.

6 Zetterstéen, *Beiträge*, p. 187, l. 11.

7 e.g. Baybarṣ as-Saifī, cf. *CIA. Jérusalem, Ville*, p. 282, n. 1.

8 Karabacek, l.c., p. 12, n. 1.

9 *SM.* II a, p. 83, II b, pp. 25, 81, 135; Ibn Taghrībirdī, *Manhal*, s.v. (MS. Paris, Ar. 2069, fo. 29ʳ); Sobernheim, *CIA. Syrie du Nord*, p. 84 f.

10 Maqrīzī mentions the death of Aybak al-Mauṣilī, Governor of Tripoli, first s.a. 697 (*SM.* II b, p. 81), then s.a. 698 (ib. p. 135).

MAUSOLEUM, locally known as Walī Sīdnā 'Izz ad-dīn, Bāb al-Ḥadīd Quarter, Tripoli.

Inscription over the window, facing the street. Beneath three heraldic shields, partly hidden by the window-frame.

(1) بسمله . . . هذه تربة العبد الفقير الى(2)رحمة الله تعالى ايبك ابن عبد الله الموصلى

نائب السلطنة(3)الشريفة بالفتوحات المحروسة رحمه الله تعالى المتوفّى فى خامس(4)شهر

صفر من سنة ثمان وتسعين وستّمائة من الهجرة النبويّة

In the name of the most merciful God. This is the mausoleum of the servant yearning for the mercy of God the Exalted, Aybak, son of 'Abdallāh of Mosul, Governor of the Noble Sultanate in the protected conquered countries, may God the Exalted have mercy upon him, who passed away the 5th Ṣafar of the year 698 of the Hijra of the Prophet (12th November 1298).

BIBLIOGRAPHY: Sobernheim, *CIA. Syrie du Nord*, No. 37, p. 84, pl. IX (where the blazon is invisible).

AYDAKĪN[1]

A. Aydakīn b. 'Abdallāh, the arquebusier, originally a mamluk of 'Alā' ad-dīn Āqsunqur, the cup-bearer,[2] later of al-Malik aṣ-Ṣāliḥ Najm ad-dīn Ayyūb, became an arquebusier and then Governor of 'Ajlūn. Later on dismissed and his possessions confiscated by the Sultan. In 648 (1250) appointed Governor of Egypt by Aybak for the time of the latter's absence. Became major-domo under Baybars, his former mamluk, was for a time Viceroy of Syria; in 659 (1261), became Governor of Aleppo. Deposed in 677 (1278) by Baraka Khān, became commander of the left wing of the army in 679 (1280). Died in Rabī' II 684 (began 6th June 1285) and was buried in his mausoleum in the ash-Shāri' al-a'ẓam, opposite the Ḥammām al-Fāraqān, outside Cairo.

BLAZON: *Two golden cross-bows addorsed on undivided red shield.*

1. LAMP. Metropolitan Museum of Art, New York, once collection Morgan.

Inscription on neck intersected by three shields.

[1] *SM.* I a, pp. 17, 139, 168, I b, p. 13; Ibn Ḥabīb, 247, 274; *Manhal*, s.v. (MS. Paris, Ar. 2069, fo 34v); Artin Pasha, 'Description de quatre lampes en verre émaillé et armoiriées' (in: *BIE.* 5e sér. t. I, 1907), pp. 78–81; Weil, IV. 23, 30, 31.

[2] According to *Manhal*, s.v., he was originally a mamluk of J. Mūsā b. Yaghmūr.

مما عمل برسم تربة المقرّ العالى العلائى البندقدار قدّس الله روحه

This is one of the objects made for the mausoleum of His High Excellency 'Alā' ad-dīn the arquebusier, may God sanctify his soul.

On body the same inscription intersected by two shields.

BIBLIOGRAPHY: Y. Artin Pacha, *Description de quatre lampes*, pp. 69–81, pl. 1.

Reproduced: Migeon, *Manuel*, 2nd ed., II, p. 133, fig. 294.
Mentioned: *CIA. Jérusalem, Ville*, p. 288, n. 2; Wiet, *Lampes*, p. 154, App. No. 4.
Mentioned and reproduced: Lamm, *Gläser*, p. 427, No. 2, pl. 197, fig. 3.

2. MAUSOLEUM, Cairo, known locally as Zāwiyat al-Abbār. Pl. XL. 1.

Inscription on the façade, with a series of titles suitable for Aydakīn intersected by two shields. The portion containing the name is hidden behind a modern building.

... ○ المالكى الأميرى الكبيرى الإسفهسلارى العضدى ○

... the Royal, the Great Amir, the General, the Supporter ...

BIBLIOGRAPHY: Unpublished.

Mentioned: *CIA. Jérusalem, Ville*, p. 288, n. 2.

AYDAMUR[1]

Most probably identical with I. Aydamur,[2] Governor of Kerak, appointed Viceroy of Syria in 670 (1271/2). Died the 2nd Rabī' I 700 (15th November 1300).[3]

BLAZON: *(a) Napkin on undivided ornamented field; (b) white lion striding to the left, on undivided ornamented field.*

BASIN. Collection R. A. Harari, Esq., London. Pl. XXX. 1.

[1] Spelling indicated in *A'yān* s.vv. *A. al-Marqabī* and *A., Governor of Gaza* (MS. Berlin, fo. 36r).
[2] Zetterstéen, *Beiträge*, p. 95, l. 16; Ibn Ḥabīb, pp. 257, 301; *SM.* I b, p. 93, II b, p. 184.
[3] Ibn Taghrībirdī evidently mixed up the biography of our Aydamur with that of *Saif* ad-dīn Aydamur b. 'Abdallāh aẓ-Ẓāhirī at-Turkī. In his article on the latter (MS. Paris, Ar. 2069, fo. 40r) he makes a mamluk freed by Baybars die in Rabī' I 790.

Inscription intersected by six heraldic shields, three with a napkin and three with a lion passant. The latter marked by circles enclosing the letter L. The napkins are roughened, probably to receive some incrustation, indicating colour.

مـّما عمل برسم المقرّ الكريم العالى المولوى ○ الأُميرى الكبيرى المجاهدى

المرابطى المثاغرى Ⓛ المؤيّدى المظفّرى العالى العاملى العا○دلى الأعزّى الأخصّى الذخرى

النصرى نصرة Ⓛ الغزاة والمجاهدين عمدة الملوك والسلا○طين الأمير عزّ الدين

ايدمر الجمدار القيمرى Ⓛ

This is one of the objects made for His Honourable and High Excellency, our Lord, the Great Amir, the Defender of the Faith, the Warrior at the Frontiers, the Warden of the Marches, the Helped by God, the Victorious, the Learned, the Governing, the Just, the Most Glorious, the Favourite, the Treasure, the Victor, the Pillar of Kings and Sultans, the Amir 'Izz ad-dīn Aydamur, the jamdār, *the Qaimarite.*

BIBLIOGRAPHY: Unpublished.

AYDAMUR AL-ĀNŪKĪ[1]

I. Aydamur b. 'Abdallāh, originally a mamluk of Prince Ānūk, son of Muḥammad b. Qalāūn, held various offices before he came to be *Dawādār* of al-Malik an-Nāṣir Ḥasan; following upon Yalbughā's rebellion, exiled to Syria, then appointed Governor of al-Bīreh, later made Commander of a Thousand in Cairo, then appointed Governor of Tripoli, whence transferred to Aleppo as Governor early in 773 (January 1731). Dismissed from office, returned to Cairo in 774 (1372), again Governor of Tripoli, on Aljāy al-Yūsufī's death in 775, succeeded him as Commander-in-Chief. Died in 776 (1374), over seventy years of age.

BLAZON: *Cup on middle field of three-fielded shield.*

MADRASA, locally known as al-Madrasa al-Khātūniyya, Tripoli.
One shield over the lintel of each of the three windows.

Inscription in the porch over the entrance door:

[1] Ibn Ḥabīb, p. 430; Ibn Taghrībirdī, *Manhal*, s.v. (MS. Paris, Ar. 2069, fo. $39^{r,\ v}$); Ibn Iyās, I, p. 228, l. 4 b; Sobernheim, *CIA. Syrie du Nord*, p. 118 f.

. . . انشأ هذا المكان المبارك مولانا المقرّ الأشرف العالى المولوى المخدومى الكافلى العزّى ايدمر الأشرفى مولانا ملك الأمرآء . . . وكان الفراغ من ذلك فى سنة خمس وسبعين وسبعمائة

Constructed this blessed place our Lord His Most Noble and High Excellency, our Lord, the Well-served, the Viceroy, 'Izz ad-dīn Aydamur al-Ashrafī, our Lord the Governor-General . . . and this (work) was finished in the year 775 (1373/4).

BIBLIOGRAPHY: Sobernheim, l.c., pp. 114 ff., pl. XII.

AYDAMUR AL-ASHRAFĪ

BLAZON: *Upper field blank, on middle field a red cup charged with a napkin, on lower field a red cup.*[1]

CYLINDRICAL BOX, Musée du Louvre, Paris, No. 7438, formerly in the collection Delort de Gléon.

Four shields, one on the lid, two intersecting the inscription on the body, one on the outside bottom of the box.

Inscriptions on body and lid. The latter, being the shortest, is reproduced here:

المقرّ الأشرف العالى المولوى المالكى المخدومى العزّى ايدمر الأشرفى كافل المملكة الشريفة بحلب المحروسة

His Most Noble and High Excellency, our Lord, the Royal, the Well-Served, 'Izz ad-dīn Aydamur al-Ashrafī, Viceroy of the Noble Province of Aleppo, the protected.

BIBLIOGRAPHY: Sobernheim, *Arabische Gefässinschriften*, p. 184 f.
Mentioned: Migeon, *L'Orient Musulman*, vol. *Armes*, p. 26, No. 99.

AYDAMUR AZ-ZARDKĀSH

BLAZON: *Polo-sticks with balls on undivided field.*

BRONZE STAND FOR A TRAY, present owner unknown: once in the collection Schefer, then Duseigneur.

Inscription:[2]

[1] Traces of red incrustation still visible.

[2] The following text is a compilation of what I read on fig. 101 of the sale catalogue of the collection Schefer (*A* and *B*) and on the fragment of a rubbing in the collection van Berchem (*C*).

A ○ ممّا عمل برسم الجناب العالى ا ○ لمولوى . . .

B الذخرى الزعيمى ا ○ لكفيلى الممهّدى ال . . .

C العزّى عزّ ○ الدين ايدمر الزردكاش عزّ نصره

This is one of the objects made for His High Excellency (janāb), *our Lord . . . the Treasure, the Chieftain, the Viceroy, the Administrator, the . . . 'Izz ad-dīn Aydamur, the Armourer, may his victory be glorious.*

BIBLIOGRAPHY: Unpublished.

Reproduced and briefly described: *Catalogue des Objets d'Art . . . composant la collection de M. Ch. Schefer*, No. 101, p. 17 and pl.

AYNĀL AL-'ALĀ'Ī[1]

S. Aynāl[2] b. 'Abdallāh al-'Alā'ī az-Ẓāhirī an-Nāṣirī, nicknamed '*ajrūd*' (i.e. thin-haired, beardless), one of the mamluks of Barqūq, after whose death he was freed and made a Master of the Robes (*jamdār*)[3] by Faraj; then made

[1] Maqrīzī, *Khiṭaṭ*, II, 244, l. 11 f. (2nd ed., III. 396); Sakhāwī, *at-Tibr al-masbūk*, pp. 423–4, ll. 6, 13, 429–31, *aḍ-Ḍau' al-lāmi'*, s.v.; Ibn Taghrībirdī, *Manhal*, s.v. (MS. Paris, Ar. 2069, fo. 46^r); *Nujūm*, VI, cf. Index, especially pp. 510, l. 22, 601, l. 14, 621, l. 17, 634, l. 1, 709–10, 750, l. 22, 826, l. 16; as-Suyūtī, *Ḥusn al-muḥāḍara*, Cairo 1327, II, p. 80, l. 11 f.; Mujīr ad-dīn, *al-Uns al-jalīl*, pp. 444–5; Ibn Iyās, cf. Index s.vv. al-Malik al-Ashraf and Aynāl al-'Alā'ī al-Ajrūd, especially his biography II. 39–40; Weil, V, cf. Index; Sobernheim, *The Encyclopaedia of Islām*, s.v. Īnāl (English ed. II. 477 f.), *CIA. Égypte*, I, cf. Index.

[2] With regard to the spelling of this name, cf. L. A. Mayer, 'Arabic Inscriptions of Gaza IV' (in: *JPOS*. X, 1930, p. 60, n.1), where Ibn Taghrībirdī's statement that the name means 'moon-rays' (*ay-nāl*), and should accordingly be written in two words (*Manhal*, s.v. Aynāl al-Yūsufī, MS. Paris, Ar. 2069, fo. 42^v, ll. 5–3 b) was considered sufficient reason for the adoption of the spelling *Ay*nāl instead of Īnāl. It might be said, of course, that Ibn Taghrībirdī's explanation of this name has only the value of a popular etymology, but it shows that the name was pronounced, at least in his day, with an initial *ay* and not with an *ī*. The same vocalization is to be found in a verse of Aḥmad b. al-'Aṭṭār quoted by Ibn Taghrībirdī, *Nujūm* s.a. 780 (MS. Paris, Ar. 1786, fo. 215^r, l. 9).

[3] Ibn Iyās II, p. 39, l. 8 b وبقى جمداراً, Ibn Taghrībirdī, *Manhal*, s.v. وجعله خاصّكيّاً. It is a mistake to consider the word *khāṣṣakī* as being a general term for the various corps of pages, although passages could be quoted in corroboration of such a statement. In the proper sense of the word, the *khāṣṣakiyyah* were a corps by themselves, obviously of a low grade, from which some of the higher grade pages with special functions, the *arbāb al-waẓā'if*, used to be chosen. This can be proved by the careers of several mamluks, e.g. the later Sultan Shaikh, who was first *jamdār*, then *khāṣṣakī*, and finally *sāqī*, before being dubbed amir. Qānṣūh al-Muḥammadī, a mamluk of Barsbāy, was first *khāṣṣakī*, then *sāqī*, Jānibak aẓ-Ẓarīf was first *khāṣṣakī*, then *khāzindār ṣaghīr*, then *dawādār ṣaghīr*, Jānibak min Ṭuṭukh was first *jamdār*, then *khāṣṣakī* and finally became Amir of Ten (*Ḍau'* s.vv.).

dawādār by Shaikh, and Amir of Ten by Aḥmad b. Shaikh. Under Barsbāy made Amir of Forty and appointed *Third Ra's Naubah*, promoted in 830 (1426/7) to the post of a *Second Ra's Naubah*. On 18th Shawwāl 831 (31st July 1428) appointed Governor of Gaza; in 836 (1432/3) made Commander of a Thousand and Governor of ar-Ruhā' (Edessa). Replaced by Shād Bak al-Jakamī, he lived for some time in Egypt. On the 10th Rajab 840 (18th January 1437), made Governor of Safad, an appointment he held until recalled by Jaqmaq, who made him Amir of a Hundred and Commander of a Thousand in Egypt. On the 13th Jumādā II, 846 (19th October 1442)[1] appointed Grand Dawādār, on Thursday, the 3rd Sha'bān 849 (4th November 1445) Commander-in-Chief in Egypt. On Monday, 8th Rabī' I 857 (19th March 1453) ascended the throne as al-Malik al-Ashraf. Died Thursday, 15th[2] Jumādā I 865 (26th February 1461).

BLAZON: *On upper field pen-box, on middle field cup, on lower field fleur-de-lis.*

MINARET of the Kātib al-Wilāyah-Mosque, Gaza. Pl. LXVII. 2.

(1) بسمله . . . أمر بعمارة هذه المأذنة O مولانا المقرّ الأشرف السيفى اينال العلائى

(2) نائب السلطنة الشريفة بغزّة المحروسة ابتغاء لوجه الله O تعالى فى مستهلّ

ذى الحجّة الحرام سنة خمسة وثلاثين وثمان مائة

In the name of the most merciful God. Ordered to build this minaret our Lord, His Most Noble Excellency Saif-ad-dīn Aynāl al-'Alā'ī, Governor of the Noble Sultanate in the protected Gaza, in his desire to please God the Exalted, on the 1st of Dhu-l-Ḥijja of the year 835 (30th July 1432).

BIBLIOGRAPHY: Unpublished.

Blazon described: L. A. Mayer, *Guide to the Exhibition of Moslem Heraldry in Palestine*, p. 7. Blazon reproduced: Artin, *Contribution*, fig. 96, p. 121 (without identification).

AYNĀL AL-ḤAKĪM[3]

S. Aynāl al-Ibrāhīmī al-Ḥakīm (i.e. the physician) in Muḥarram 876 (began

[1] Ibn Iyās, II 29, l. 15, mentions it under the events of the year 848.
[2] Mujīr ad-dīn gives a slightly different date, viz. the 9th.
[3] Ibn Iyās, II. 128, l. 4 b, 151 b., 159, l. 6, 163, l. penult.

20th June 1471) appointed Governor of Malatia, in 879 or 880 Atābak of Aleppo. Died there in Dhu-l-Ḥijja 880 (began 27th March 1476).

BLAZON: *On upper field a pen-box, on middle field a cup, on lower field a fleur-de-lis.*

COPPER DISH. Present owner unknown.

Inscription:

ممّا عمل برسم المقرّ الأشرف العالى المولوى الأميرى

الكبيرى المخدومى السيفى اينال حكيم أتابك العساكر بحلب

This is one of the objects made for His Most Noble and High Excellency, our Lord, the Great Amir, the Well-Served, Saif ad-dīn Aynāl Ḥakīm, the Commander-in-Chief in Aleppo.

Rogers attributed this blazon to Aynāl al-Yūsufī the *atābak*. It seems to me impossible that a man dubbed amir about 778 should have a three-fielded shield with three different emblems, whereas such a blazon would be quite normal if granted about 860. Another reason which might have induced Rogers to make this attribution was, perhaps, the fact that the Aynāl al-Yūsufī was stationed for a time in Aleppo. But in Aleppo he was *Governor* and not *atābak al-ʿasākir*.

BIBLIOGRAPHY: Rogers, *Le Blason*, p. 117, No. 11, fig. 31.

Reproduced: P[ier], *Saracenic Heraldry*, fig. 22, p. 10.

AYNĀL AL-ASHRAFĪ

Possibly identical with Aynāl al-Ashqar al-Ashrafī,[1] who died of the plague in 897 (1491/2).

BLAZON: *On upper field a napkin, on middle field a cup charged with a pen-box and placed between a 'pair of trousers of nobility', on lower field a small cup between two napkins.*

DECREE, Main Mosque, Hama. Pl. LXVII. 3.

Inscription on the lintel of the window in the courtyard flanked by two shields:

(1) لما كان بتاريخ أربع [و]عشرين شهر شعبان سنة أربع وتسعين وثمان مائة

أمر مولانا المقرّ الأشرف الكريم العالى المولوى الملكى[2] المخدومى

[1] Ibn Iyās, II, p. 275, l. 4. To be distinguished from his more famous namesake Aynāl al-Ashqar az-Ẓāhirī, who at various stages of his career occupied the posts of *ra's naubat kabīr*, *amīr silāḥ*, Governor of Cairo, Malatia, and Aleppo.

[2] Mistake of the stone-cutter for المالكى.

(2) الكافلى السيفى اينال الأشرفى كافل المملكة الحمويّة المحروسة عزّ الله أنصاره

بإبطال ما كان يؤخذ على القطّانين بحماة الخ

On the 24th Sha'bān 894 (23rd July 1489), *our Lord, His Most Noble, Honourable and High Excellency, our Lord, the Royal, the Well-Served, the Viceroy Saif ad-dīn Aynāl al-Ashrafī, Viceroy of the province of Hama, the protected, may God make his victories glorious, ordered to abolish (the taxes) taken from the cotton-merchants in Hama, &c.*

BIBLIOGRAPHY: Unpublished.

AYNĀL AL-YŪSUFĪ[1]

S. Aynāl b. 'Abdallāh al-Yūsufī al-Yalbughāwī, originally a mamluk of Yalbughā al-'Umarī al-Khāṣṣakī, made his career after the death of his master. Under 'Alī b. Sha'bān, came to be one of the Egyptian amirs. In 779 (1377/8) appointed *amīr silāḥ*. Following an unsuccessful attempt at stirring up a rising, on Monday, 14th Sha'bān 781 (25th November 1379), was imprisoned in Alexandria, then set free by Barqūq and appointed Governor of Tripoli. Later (after the dismissal from office of Minklībughā ash-Shamsī) transferred to Aleppo as Governor of that province. When Barqūq ascended the throne Aynāl was sent to Damascus as *atābak*. Again appointed Governor of Aleppo during the rebellion of Yalbughā an-Nāṣirī, he secretly favoured Yalbughā. In 792 appointed Governor of Safad. After Barqūq's second accession to the throne, 14th Ṣafar 792 (1st February 1390) recalled to Cairo as *atābak al-'asākir*. Died the 4th Jumādā II 794 (28th April 1392).

BLAZON: *Upper and lower fields blank, on middle field a scimitar.*

WINDOWS of his madrasah, outside Bāb Zuwailah, Cairo. Pl. XXXV. 1.

On each of the arches of the two windows in the southern wall a heraldic shield.

DATE: The madrasah having been commenced in 794 and finished in 795, after Aynāl's death, the windows are probably of the latter date.

BIBLIOGRAPHY: Unpublished.

[1] Ibn Ḥabīb, pp. 450, 453, 479; *Khiṭaṭ* II p. 401, ll. 19–24; *Durar*, s.v. (MS. Br. Mus., Ar. 3043, fo. 81^{v}); *Manhal*, s.v. (MS. Paris, Ar. 2069, fo. 41^{v}–42^{v}); Ibn Iyās, I, pp. 243, ll. 9, 10, 244, ll. 6 ff., 270, l. 11, 281, ll. 9 b ff., 284, l. 3, 291, l. 4; Weil, IV. 536, 539, 549, 551, 565, 566; Rogers, *Blason*, p. 117 f.

AYTMISH AL-BAJĀSĪ[1]

S. Aytmish[2] b. ʿAbdallāh al-Asandumrī al-Bajāsī, originally a mamluk of Asandamur[3] al-Bajāsī al-Jurjāwī, after the death of his master became amir in Egypt, appointed Marshal (*amīr akhūr*) owing to the help of Barqūq, following whose accession to the throne he became Amir of a Hundred and Commander of a Thousand and *ra's naubat an-nuwwāb*, appointed *atābak al-ʿasākir* some time after the 8th Dhu-l-Qaʿda 785 (2nd January 1384), imprisoned in 791 (1389), released and appointed *ra's naubat al-umarā'* in 792, succeeded Kumushbughā al-Ḥamawī as *atābak al-ʿasākir* in 800 (1397/8), rebelled, defeated near Gaza, imprisoned in the fortress of Damascus, executed 14th Shaʿbān 802 (10th April 1400). Built a madrasah near the Bāb al-Wazīr and a tower in Tripoli.

BLAZON: *On each of the upper and middle fields a cup, lower field blank.*

ROCK INSCRIPTION near the bridge on the Nahr al-Kalb. Pl. LVI. 1.

Two shields at the beginning and at the end of the first two lines, an inscribed shield in the middle marked ①. The inscribed shield contains the name of Barqūq, for its text cf. p. 33, No. 3.

Inscription:

(1) ○ بسمله . . . اصدق الله . . . ① العظيم وصدق رسوله الكريم أمر بعمارة

هذا الجسر المبارك ○

(2) ○ المقرّ الأشرف العالى المولوى المالكى المخدومى السيفى أبو العزائم ①

أيتمش البجاسى الظاهرى أتابك العساكر الإسلاميّة ورأس نوبة النوّاب ○

[1] Ibn Duqmāq, V, p. 29, l. 12; Ibn Taghrībirdī, *Nujūm*, VI, cf. Index, especially p. 143 f.; *Manhal*, s.v. (MS. Paris, 2069, fo. 31^r–33^v); Sakhāwī, *aḍ-Ḍau' al-lāmiʿ*, s.v. Weil, cf. Index, especially IV. 536, 538, 543, V. 62, 73, 75, 78; F. H. Weissbach, 'Die Denkmäler und Inschriften an der Mündung des Nahr el-Kelb' (in *Wissenschaftliche Veröffentlichungen des deutsch-türkischen Denkmalschutzkommandos*, Heft 6), p. 45 f.

[2] Spelling indicated in words by Ṣafadī, *Aʿyān*, s.v. Aytmish an-Nāṣirī, the *jamdār*; Zettersteén, *Beiträge*, p. 188, l. 5 b, vocalizes Aytamush.

[3] Asandamur was originally a mamluk of Bajās, Bajās a mamluk of Jurjī, the Governor of Aleppo.

(3) الجمداريّة الملكيّة الظاهريّة أثابه الله الجنّة . . . مظلمة فمن فعل شيأً فيها من ذلك فعليه لعنة الله والملائكة

(4) والناس أجمعين . . . العبد الفقير الى الله تعالى الحاجّ بهادر

(5) . . . بد[مشق] المحروسة . . . فى الشهر المحرّم . . .

In the name of the most merciful God . . . truthful is Mighty God and truthful is His noble Apostle. Ordered to build this blessed bridge His Most Noble and High Excellency, our Lord, the Royal, and Well-Served Saif ad-dīn Abu-l-'Azā'im Aytmish al-Bajāsī, (officer) of al-Malik az-Zāhir, Chief Commander of the Muslim Troops and Chief of the corps of jamdārs *of al-Malik az-Zāhir, may God give him paradise as reward.* [A few words missing] *wrong, and whosoever does anything of this kind in it, the curse of God and His angels and all men be upon him.* [Several words missing] *the servant yearning for God the Exalted, Ḥājj Bahādur* [1–2 words missing] *in Da[mascus] the protected. In the month Muḥarram . . .*

BIBLIOGRAPHY: van Berchem-Fatio, 'Voyage en Syrie' (in: *MIFAO*, XXXVII), pp. 99 ff., especially p. 100, n. 1; Weissbach, l.c., pp. 43 ff., pl. XIV. On p. 46 Kumushbughā's blazon, *upper field blank, on each of the middle and lower fields a cup*, is depicted (fig. 14) and so discussed as if it were identical with that of Aytmish, and on the basis of this—wrongly assumed—identity attributed to Barqūq. For full bibliographical references see Weissbach, l.c.

'AZĪZ AL-'ALĀWĪ

BLAZON: *Upper field self-coloured, on red middle field a white napkin, lower field white.*

GLASS 'EGG'. Victoria and Albert Museum, London, Nos. 333–1900, formerly collection Myers. Pl. XXXI. 1.

Inscription three times intersected by heraldic shields.

ممّا عمل برسم المقرّ الاشرف العالى O المولوى الكبيرى المحترمى المخدومى O السيفى عزيز العلاوى الملكى الصالحى عزّ نصره O

This is one of the objects made for the most Noble and High Excellency our Lord, the Great

(*Amir*), *the Honoured, the Well-Served, Saif ad-dīn 'Azīz al-'Alāwī,* (*officer*) *of al-Malik aṣ-Ṣāliḥ, may his victory be glorious.*

BIBLIOGRAPHY: Schmoranz, p. 18 f., figs. 15, 17.

Mentioned: Wiet, *Lampes*, p. 163, No. 49; Lamm, *Gläser*, p. 442, No. 57.

BAHĀDUR ĀṢ[1]

S. Bahādur b. 'Abdallāh, called Āṣ (name of a Tatar tribe), originally a mamluk of Qalāūn, one of the amirs of Damascus, where he lived, with the exception of about a year and a half, 711/12 (1311/12), spent at Safad as Governor, and two years, 715/17 (1315/17), during which he was confined in prison. In 715 head of the right wing of the Syrian army. Died in Ṣafar 730 (November–December 1329).

BLAZON: *Six-petalled rosette on undivided round shield.*

1. COPPER BASIN. Arabic Museum, Cairo, No. 3751. Pl. XXXVI. 1.

Twelve shields: six on the outside of the object, six on the inside.

Inscription inside the basin:

ممّا عمل برسم ا○لجناب العالى ○ المولوى الأ○ميرى الكبيرى ا○لسيفى بهادر

ا○لسلاحدار ○

This is one of the objects made for His High Excellency (janāb), *our Lord, the Great Amir*[2] *Saif ad-dīn Bahādur, the armour-bearer.*

Inscription on the outside of the basin:

ممّا عمل برسم الجناب العالى المولوى الأميرى ا○لغازى المجاهدى المرابطى المالكى

○ السيفى بهادر آص السلاحدار الملكى الناصرى ○

This is one of the objects made for His High Excellency (janāb), *our Lord, the Amir, the*

[1] Zetterstéen, *Beiträge*, cf. Index, especially pp. 156, l. 6, 158, l. 17, 163, ll. 8, 9, 166, ll. 13, 14; Ibn al-Wardī, II, p. 293, l. 2; Ṣafadī, *al-Wāfī*, s.v. (MS. Br. Mus., Add. 23, 357, fo. 62v); Ibn Ḥabīb, p. 350, l. 5; *SM.* especially IIa, p. 12; Ibn Ḥajar, *ad-Durar*, s.v. (MS. Br. Mus., Or. 3043, fo. 94r); Ibn Taghrībirdī, *Manhal* (MS. Paris, Ar. 2069, fo. 94v); Ibn Iyās, cf. Index; Weil, IV. 282, 295, 300.

[2] With regard to Bahādur's title 'Great Amir', cf. *Manhal*, s.v.

Vanquisher, the Defender of the Faith, the Warrior at the Frontiers, the Royal, Saif ad-dīn Bahādur Āṣ, the armour-bearer of al-Malik an-Nāṣir.

The rosette was effaced at a later date and two slanting swords engraved in its stead. Still later these were likewise erased and replaced by a cup.

BIBLIOGRAPHY: Unpublished.
Mentioned: *CR.* Exerc. 1911, fasc. 28, p. 13.

2. MAUSOLEUM, corner of Jāddat al-Marqaṣ and Sūq al-Ghanam, Damascus, Mīdān quarter. Known locally as the mausoleum of 'Malik al-Ghōr'. Pl. XL. 3.

Inscription originally in four sections of one line each, each flanked by two shields. Only three sections visible.

(2) المسجد المعمور والتربة المباركة العبد

(3) الفقير الى الله تعالى الراجى عفو ربّه بهادر آص الملكى

(4) الناصرى وذلك في شهور سنة أحد وعشرين وسبعمائة

[Beginning missing. Perhaps: *Ordered to build this*] *prosperous mosque and blessed mausoleum, the servant yearning for God the Exalted, hoping for forgiveness from his Lord, Bahādur Āṣ, (officer) of al-Malik an-Nāṣir. This was made during the months of the year* 721 (= 1321).

BIBLIOGRAPHY: Unpublished.

BAHĀDUR AL-BADRĪ[1]

S. Bahādur al-Badrī, the sword-bearer, appointed Governor of Hims in 719 (1319), Governor of Kerak on the 1st Dhu-l-Ḥijja 725 (8th November 1325), remained in office till Ramaḍān 731 (began 8th June 1331). Imprisoned by Tankiz; on his release appointed Governor of Tripoli; died there in 740 (1339/40).

BLAZON: *On the middle field of a three-fielded shield, a scimitar.*

STAND FOR A TRAY, Metropolitan Museum of Art, New York. Pl. XXXVIII.

Shields on the upper and lower rims and on the embossed collar of the object.
Inscription on the upper half:

[1] Zetterstéen, *Beiträge*, pp. 176, l. 13, 183, ll. 19, 22; Ibn Ḥajar, *Durar*, s.v. (MS. Br. Mus., Or. 3043, fo. 94v); Sauvaire in de Luynes, *Voyage d'exploration à la Mer Morte*, II, p. 206, No. 23; Weil, IV. 396.

برسم المقرّ الكريم العالى المولو[ى] المالكى الأميرى الكبيرى الغازى المجاهدى

المرابطى المثاغرى الأعزّى

Inscription on the lower half:

الأخصّى الذخر[ى] الكفيلى العالى العاملى الهمامى السيفى بهادر البدرى السلحدار

الملكى الناصرى

For His Honourable and High Excellency, our Lord, the Royal, the Great Amir, the Vanquisher, the Defender of the Faith, the Warrior at the Frontiers, the Warden of the Marches, the most Glorious, the Favourite, the Treasure, the Viceroy, the Learned, the Governing, the Shelter, Saif ad-dīn Bahādur al-Badrī, the Sword-bearer, (officer) of al-Malik an-Nāṣir.

BIBLIOGRAPHY: Unpublished.

BAHĀDUR AL-ḤAMAWĪ

BLAZON: *Under an eagle looking to the left, a napkin.*

HANDWARMER, upper part of, R. Museo Nazionale, Florence, Coll. Carrand No. 370. Pl. XVII.

Three shields intersecting the inscription, a fourth in the centre of the object.

ممّا عمل برسم الجناب الكريم العالى المولوى الأ○ميرى الكبيرى المحترمى

المخدومى السيفى سيف الدين ○ بهادر الحموى رأس نو[بة] الجمداريّة الملكى

الناصرى ○

This is one of the objects made for His Honourable and High Excellency (janāb), *our Lord, the Great Amir, the Honoured, the Well-Served, Saif ad-dīn Bahādur al-Ḥamawī, Chief of the Corps of* jamdārs *of al-Malik an-Nāṣir.*

BIBLIOGRAPHY: Unpublished.

The difficulty in the attribution of this blazon centres in the fact that our Bahādur is called an-Nāṣirī, whereas the only Bahādur with whom the holder of this emblem could be identified, namely S. Bahādur *ra's nauba*,[1] was killed 15th Muḥarram 693 (16th December 1293), three days before the first Mamluk Sultan bearing the title of al-Malik an-Nāṣir ascended the throne.[2] Ibn Iyās mentions in his narrative of the events of the year 693 A.H. a certain Bahādur, *ra's naubat an-nuwwāb*,[3] but this date is again prior to Muḥammad b. Qalāūn's accession to the throne, and the title altogether much too high for our Bahādur.

BAHĀDUR AL-MANJAKĪ[4]

S. Bahādur b. ʿAbdallāh al-Manjakī, of Christian origin,[5] a freed mamluk of and major-domo to S. Manjak al-Yūsufī, Viceroy of Syria, became a favourite of Barqūq who made him Amir of a Hundred and Commander of a Thousand, and appointed him major-domo, an office he held up to the time of his death on 1st Jumādā II 790 (Sunday, 7th June 1388).

BLAZON: *Five bars on round shield.*

COPPER BOWL, present owner unknown.

Inscription:

مما عمل برسم الجناب العالي السيفى سيف الدين بهادر استادار مولانا الملك

الأمراء كافل الممالك الشريفة بالشأم المحروس

This is one of the objects made for His High Excellency (janāb), *Saif ad-dīn Bahādur, major-domo to our Lord, the Viceroy of the noble provinces of Syria, the protected.*

DATE: Rogers attributed this blazon to Bahādur al-Muʿizzī. The attribution is obviously wrong as the latter, though he was in the service of Lājīn when Viceroy of Syria, never occupied the post of a major-domo to an amir. The only Bahādur who comes into question is Bahādur al-Manjakī, and the blazon may, therefore, be taken to date either from the very end of the year 759 (1358), or from the years between 771/775 (1369/70–

[1] Zetterstéen, *Beiträge*, p. 28, l. 4 b.

[2] Muḥammad b. Qalāūn, cf. Ibn Iyās, I, p. 129, l. 11 b.

[3] Ibn Iyās, I, p. 127, l. 3.

[4] Ibn Duqmāq, IV, cf. Index (where the page reference is wrongly given); Ṣāliḥ b. Yaḥyā, pp. 215, l. 9, 232, l. 9; Ibn Ḥajar, *Durar*, s.v. (MS. Br. Mus., Or. 3043, fo. 94ᵛ); Ibn Taghrībirdī, *Manhal*, s.v. (MS. Paris, Ar. 2069, fo. 95ᵛ, 96ʳ); Ibn Iyās, I, pp. 262, l. 7 b, 268, l. penult, 269, l. 8, 316, l. 11.

[5] According to al-ʿAinī, quoted by Ibn Taghrībirdī, Bahādur was either an Anatolian or a European; according to Ṣāliḥ b. Yaḥyā (p. 215), he was an Armenian educated in Beyrouth.

1373/4), i.e. the period of Manjak's terms of office as Viceroy of Syria. The latter date is the more probable.

BIBLIOGRAPHY: Rogers, No. 28, p. 129 f., fig. 48.

Reproduced: P[ier], *Saracenic Heraldry*, fig. 8, p. 10.

Mentioned: Lane-Poole, *Art of the Saracens*, p. 272; *CIA. Égypte*, I, p, 767.

BAHĀDUR AẒ-ẒĀHIRĪ[1]

Perhaps identical with S. Bahādur aẓ-Ẓāhirī, called Ḥājj Bahādur, appointed Grand Chamberlain (*ḥājib al-ḥujjāb*) by Kitbughā in 694 (began 21st November 1294), remained in office during the sultanate of Lājīn and the second reign of Muḥammad b. Qalāūn, followed Muḥammad to Kerak, appointed Governor of Tripoli the 8th Muḥarram 709 (18th June 1309). Died the 18th or 20th Rabīʿ II 710 (14–16th September 1310).

BLAZON: *Sword on middle field of three-fielded shield.*

CANDLESTICK, lower part of, Arabic Museum, Cairo, No. 7229, formerly in the possession of M. Vitali Maggiar, Cairo.

Inscription twice intersected by shields.

المقرّ الاشرف العالى المولوى السيّدى المخدومى O السيفى بهادر استادار [ا]لعالية

الملكى الظاهرى O

His Most Noble and High Excellency, our Lord, the Master, the Well-Served, Saif ad-dīn Bahādur, major-domo of al-Malik aẓ-Ẓāhir.

BIBLIOGRAPHY: Unpublished.

BAIGHUDAMUR

BLAZON: *Upper field blank, on united middle and lower fields a cup.*

SMALL CANDLESTICK, once in the collection Duseigneur,[2] present owner unknown.

[1] Abu-l-Fidā', ed. Reiske, V. 230 (ed. Constantinople IV. 62, l. 17); Zettersteen, *Beiträge*, pp. 33, l. 12, 39, l. 14, 43, l. 20, 57, l. 13, 81, l. 19, 108, l. 6, 130, l. 10, 131, l. 13, 133, l. 16, 134, l. 13, 140, l. 2, 143, l. 15 f., 151, l. 6, 153, l. 6; Quatremère, *SM*. II a, 14, II b, 23, 40, 42, 51; Ibn Taghrībirdī, *Manhal*, s.v. (MS. Paris, Ar. 2069, fo. 96$^{r, v}$), Ibn Iyās, I, pp. 133, l. 16, 152, l. 2.

[2] According to a manuscript note of van Berchem, the candlestick passed into the possession of the

مما عمل برسم الجناب العالى المولوى الأميرى السيفى بيغدمر الساقى الملكى الناصرى [Van Berchem]

This is one of the objects made for His High Excellency (janāb), *our Lord, the Amir, Saif ad-dīn Baighudamur,*[1] *the cup-bearer of al-Malik an-Nāṣir.*

BIBLIOGRAPHY: Unpublished.

BAKTAMUR [2]

Possibly identical with S. Baktamur b. ʿAbdallāh, the *silaḥdār*, one of the mamluks of al-Malik aẓ-Ẓāhir Baybars, became amir under Qalāūn, served as *ḥājib* at least during the years 693/6. About the end of 697 or early in 698 appointed Governor of Tripolis. In Rabīʿ II 698 (6th January–3rd February 1299), fled to Ghāzān. On his return he lived as amir in Cairo from the 10th Shaʿbān 699 (1st May 1300) up to the time of his death in Shawwāl 703 (7th May–5th June 1304).

BLAZON: *Bow and two arrows on undivided field.*

POTSHERD, Arabic Museum, Cairo, No. 2537.

Blazon on the outside, inscription on the inside of the sherd.

. . . المخدومى السيفى بكتمر اا . . .

. . . *the Well-Served Saif ad-dīn Baktamur* . . .

BIBLIOGRAPHY: Artin Pasha, Y.: *Description de quatre lampes en verre émaillé et armoiriées*, p. 76 f., pl. II (omitting the ى of السيفى, and the last letter, most probably a *lām* after an *alif*).

Mentioned: Herz, *Catalogue*, p. 233.

BAKTAMUR AL-ḤUSĀMĪ [3]

S. Baktamur al-Ḥusāmī, appointed Governor of Gaza the 5th Muḥarram 710 (4th June 1310), became Great Ḥājib of Damascus on the 3rd Rabīʿ II 711

Musée Diocésain at Angers. The keeper of the Museum informs me that no such candlestick is kept there at present.

[1] In van Berchem's copy the name could be read بيغدم as well; neither variant is satisfactory.

[2] Zetterstéen, *Beiträge*, pp. 2, l. 10, 24, l. 3, 37, l. 6, 43, l. 19 f., 47, ll. 11 ff., 48–9, 55, l. 15 f., 64, l. 20, 79, l. 14, 80, l. 9, 84, l. 4, 129, l. 3; *SM.* II b, p. 41 f.; Ibn Ḥajar, *Durar*, s.v. (MS. Br. Mus., Or. 3043, fo. 91ʳ, ᵛ); Ibn Taghrībirdī, *Manhal*, s.v. (MS. Paris, Ar. 2069, fo. 88ᵛ); Ibn Iyās, I, pp. 127, l. 9, 144, l. 5.

[3] Zetterstéen, *Beiträge*, pp. 147, l. 5 f., 152, l. 9; 173, l. penult., 174, l. penult.; Ibn Ḥajar, *Durar*, s.v. (MS. Br. Mus., Or. 3043, fo. 92ʳ).

(19th August 1311), arrested the 1st Rabīʿ I, 715 (5th June 1315), appointed Governor of Alexandria the 16th Shaʿbān 723 (20th August 1323),[1] died there the 4th Ramaḍān 724 (25th August 1324) as Governor.

BLAZON: *A three-fielded shield.*

PLATE, once in the possession of M. Mailly, Paris.

In the centre of the plate a heraldic shield.

المقرّ العالى المولوى الأميرى الكبيرى | الغازى المجاهدى المرابطى المثاغرى

ا | لسيفى بكتمر العنمى الحسامى الجمقدار الناصرى [Van Berchem]

His High Excellency, our Lord, the Great Amir, the Vanquisher, the Defender of the Faith, the Warrior at the Frontiers, the Warden of the Marches, Saif ad-dīn Baktamur al-ʿAnamī al-Ḥusāmī, jamaqdār *of (al-Malik) an-Nāṣir.*

BIBLIOGRAPHY: Unpublished.

BAKTŪMĀN[2]

BLAZON: *A cup displayed over the middle and lower fields of a three-fielded shield.*

COPPER VASE, at one time in the possession of M. Suarès, Cairo.

Inscription:

مما عمل برسم المقرّ العالى | المولوى الأمير(?) الكبير(?) | العالمى العا | دلى الهمامى

النظامى | المخدومى البدرى بدر الدين | بكتومان(?) القربى(?) الناصرى

This is one of the objects made for His High Excellency, our Lord, the Great Amir, the Learned, the Just, the Shelter, the Regent,[3] *the Well-Served, Badr ad-dīn Baktūmān al-Qirabī, (officer) of (al-Malik) an-Nāṣir.*

BIBLIOGRAPHY: Rogers, *Le Blason*, No. 5, p. 114, fig. 25.

[1] Ibn Ḥajar gives a different date, viz. 716 (1316/17), in both the Damascus and the British Museum MSS.

[2] The rendering of this name, like that of several other words of the inscription, is hardly correct. As no trace of this object could be found, it was deemed useless to speculate on the correct form of the name, so that Rogers's transcription has been accepted, the doubtful words having been indicated by the present writer with a question mark.

[3] These three epithets, placed by Rogers at the end of the text, obviously belong to the middle of the inscription, where the enigmatic دلى is self-explanatory as the second part of the word العادلى.

BAKTŪT AL-QARAMĀNĪ[1]

B. Baktūt al-Qaramānī, a mamluk of Qalāūn, dubbed in 698, in 709 taster in Cairo, in 711 sent by Muḥammad b. Qalāūn to Damascus as Inspector of Chanceries (*shādd ad-dawāwīn*), appointed Governor of Hims, became amir in Damascus, sent by Tankiz to Sīs in 724, arrested in the fortress of Damascus the 27th Jumādā I 726 (1st May 1326), brought to Cairo the 19th Shawwāl (18th September) and imprisoned in the Qal'at al-Jabal. After seven years' imprisonment released on the 1st Muḥarram 734 (12th September 1333), and installed as Amir of Forty; made the pilgrimage in Shawwāl 735 (May–June 1335). Died of the plague in 749 (1348).

BLAZON: *Red table* (khānja) *on silver middle field, the colour of the upper and lower fields now unknown, the inlay having been removed.*

CANDLESTICK, in the possession of Messrs. Stora, Boulevard Haussman, Paris. Pl. XXXII.

Two shields on the body proper, two on the upper part of the body, and three on the neck of the candlestick.

Inscription on body of the candlestick:

ممّا عمل برسم المقرّ العالى المولوى الأميرى الكبيرى ○ المالكى البدرى بدر
الدين بكتو! القرمانى الملكى الناصرى ○

On the upper part of the body:

ممّا عمل برسم المقرّ العالى المولوى الأميرى الكبيرى الما|لكى البدرى بدر
الدين بكتوت القرمانى الملكى الناصرى

On neck:

المقرّ العالى المولوى الأ○ميرى الكبيرى البدرى بدر الدين ○ بكتوت القرمانى[2]
الناصرى ○

This is one of the objects made for His High Excellency, our Lord, the Great Amir, the Royal, Badr ad-dīn Baktūt al-Qaramānī, (officer) of al-Malik an-Nāṣir.

[1] *CR.* 1910, p. 80; Zetterstéen, *Beiträge*, pp. 178, ll. 21 ff., 187, ll. 11 ff., 190, l. 12; *SM.* II b, 128; Ibn Ḥajar, *Durar*, s.v. (MS. Br. Mus., Or. 3043, fo. 92v).

[2] المالكى omitted.

DATE: On a marble slab commemorating the foundation of a mosque, Baktūt is styled in 709 A.H. *janāb*, on the candlestick *al-maqarr al-ʿālī*. The candlestick must, therefore, have been made either between Baktūt's first outstanding promotion after 709 and his death, i.e. between 712 and 749, or, what is more probable, between 735 (his promotion to the rank of an Amir of Forty) and 749.

BIBLIOGRAPHY: Unpublished.

Reproduced on an advertisement sheet of Messrs. Stora, Paris, attached to the portfolio of Les Amis de l'Art Musulman, Alexandria.

BARAKA

Perhaps identical with Z. Baraka al-Jūbānī,[1] *ra's naubat al-Manṣūrī*, appointed *amīr majlis* in 779 (1377/8), built an aqueduct from ʿAin al-Azraq to Mecca in 781 (1379/80), made an attack on his brother, the Great Amir, and, being defeated, was imprisoned in Alexandria and executed in 782 (1380).[2] Buried there outside the Bāb Rashīd.

BLAZON: *Upper field blank, on each of the middle and lower fields a cup.*

MOSQUE in ruins, Kerak.

Inscription above the lintel of the main entrance flanked by two shields.

(1) بسمله . . . جدّد عمارة هذا الباب المبارك والركن (?) المبارك المقرّ

(2) الأشرف الزينى بركة رأس نوبة الملكى المنصورى أعزّ الله أنصاره من ماله

(3) المبارك بسفارة المقرّ السيفى مينكلى الطرخانى نائب الكرك المحروس (?) أثابه الله

(4) وذلك فى سنة اثنين وثمانين وسبعماية[3]

In the name of the most merciful God. Renewed the construction of this blessed door and buttress with his own blessed money His Most Noble Excellency Zain ad-dīn Baraka, Chief of a Corps of

[1] Ibn Ḥabīb, pp. 449, 451; Ibn Iyās, I, pp. 242, ll. 4, 12, 14, 243, ll. 2, 14, 244, l. 5, 245, ll. 3, 12, 16 ff., 248, l. 13, 252, ll. 17 ff.

[2] According to Ibn Iyās, I, p. 252, l. 18, Baraka died in 781.

[3] The fourth line is written in different characters and is, perhaps, not contemporary with the main portion of the text.

pages of al-Malik al-Manṣūr, may God make his victories glorious, with the help of His Excellency Saif ad-dīn Mīnklī[1] *aṭ-Ṭarkhānī,*[2] *Governor of the protected Kerak, may God reward him. In the year* 782 (7th April 1380–27th March 1381).

BIBLIOGRAPHY: Sauvaire in de Luynes, *Voyage d'exploration à la Mer Morte*, II, p. 200, No. 18.

There being no other blazons that could have served for purposes of comparison, I have tentatively attributed these armorial bearings to Baraka and not to Mīnklī, although the chances of the blazon belonging to the latter are almost equal.

BARAKA KHĀN[3]

Na. Muḥammad Baraka Khān,[4] son of al-Malik aẓ-Ẓāhir Baybars, born in Ṣafar 658 (began 17th January 1260), in 663 (1264/5) appointed successor to the throne, which, as al-Malik as-Saʿīd, he ascended on the death of his father in 676. Died at Kerak in Dhu-l-Qaʿda 678 (March 1280).

BLAZON: *Lion passant.*

SILVER COINS (*dirham*), Bibliothèque Nationale, Paris; National Library, Cairo; Ashmolean Museum, Oxford.

Lion beneath the text of the reverse.

Damascus: 676 (1277/8), 677 (1278/9), 678 (1279/80) and others of uncertain date.

Cairo: date uncertain.

BIBLIOGRAPHY: Lavoix, *Catalogue des Monnaies Musulmanes de la Bibliothèque Nationale*, vol. *Égypte et Syrie*, pp. 295–8; Lane-Poole, *Catalogue of the Collection of Arabic Coins preserved in the Khedivial Library at Cairo*, p. 248; id. *Catalogue of the Muhammadan Coins preserved in the Bodleian Library at Oxford*, p. 9.

[1] I have transliterated the name on the basis of Sauvaire's transcription of the Arabic original; Ṣafadī, *Aʿyān*, s.v. Manklībughā (MS. Berlin, fo. 166r), spells the name not only without a *yā* but with a *fatḥa* over the *mīm*.

[2] Ibn Iyās, I, p. 239, l. 26, mentions a certain Minklī*bughā* aṭ-Ṭarkhānī, appointed Amir of Ten by al-Malik al-Manṣūr ʿAlī b. Shaʿbān in 778.

[3] Ibn Ḥabīb, pp. 251, 254, 260, 262, 263, 265–6; Maqrīzī, *Muqaffa* s.v. (MS. Leyden, p. 67 ff.) *SM.* I b, pp. 154, 156 ff. II a, p. 9; Mujīr ad-dīn, *al-Uns al-jalīl*, p. 434, l. 3 b; Ibn Iyās, I, pp. 103–4, 107 b, 109, l. 6, 110, l. 6 b, 111–14; Weil cf. Index; Sobernheim, in *The Encyclopaedia of Islām*, s.v. Baibars I (English ed., I, 589).

[4] Sometimes spelt Qān.

BARQŪQ [1]

Barqūq, originally a mamluk of Jaqmaq, became Superintendent of the Cellar, in Rabīʿ I 873 (began 19th September 1468) promoted to the rank of a Commander of a Thousand, in Dhu-l-Ḥijja of the same year appointed Inspector of the Land (*kāshif at-turāb*) in the Sharqiyya-Province, in Ṣafar 875 (July 1470) appointed Viceroy of Syria. Died in Ramaḍān or Shawwāl 877 (March 1473). Built a mausoleum in the Qarāfa, Cairo, and a shrine over the tomb of Shaikh ʿUmar b. al-Fāriḍ.

BLAZON: *On golden upper field a silver napkin, on golden middle field a black cup charged with a silver pen-box and placed between a pair of black 'trousers of nobility' with silver openings, on black lower field a silver cup.*

HEAD OF A STANDARD, Treasury, Istanbul.

Two shields. The inscription of historical interest runs as follows:

ممّا عمل برسم المقرّ الأشرف برقوق كافل المملكة الشاميّة عزّ نصره

This is one of the objects made for His Most Noble Excellency, Barqūq, Viceroy of Syria, may his victories be glorious.

DATE: Between July 1470 and March 1473.

BIBLIOGRAPHY: Unpublished.

BARQŪQ

BLAZON: *On upper field a napkin, on both the middle and the lower fields a cup.*

COPPER BOX of cylindrical shape. Once in the possession of Ch. Gabeau. Pl. XLIX. 1.

ممّا عمل برسم المقرّ الأشرف العالى المولوى الأميرى الكبيرى السيفى برقوق

عين مقدّمين [2] الألوف الملكى الأشرفى [Van Berchem]

This is one of the objects made for His Most Noble and High Excellency, our Lord, the Great Amir, Saif ad-dīn Barqūq, Commander designate of a Thousand of al-Malik al-Ashraf.

BIBLIOGRAPHY: Unpublished.

[1] *Nujūm*, VII, cf. Index, s.v. Barqūq an-Nāṣirī; Ibn Iyās, II, pp. 102, l. 15, 109, l. 28, 110, ll. 10, 14, 112, l. 9, 122, l. ult., 123, ll. 1, 20, 136, ll. 13 ff., 138, l. 3, 142, ll. 17 ff. (biography); Weil, V. 335 f.; *CIA. Égypte*, I, p. 224.

[2] So in van Berchem's copy and in a reference to it *CIA. Égypte*, I, p. 545, n. 4.

BARSBĀY ASH-SHARAFĪ

Probably identical with Amir Barsbāy al-Ashrafī,[1] in 864 (1459/60) Marshal (*amīr akhūr*) of al-Malik al-Ashraf Aynāl, arrested the following year, leader of the Mecca caravan in 876 and 877. Died as *ustādār aṣ-ṣuḥba* in Jumādā I 878 (began 24th September 1473).

BLAZON: *On upper field a pen-box, on middle field a cup, on lower field a fleur-de-lis.*

BRASS BASIN, in the collection of R. A. Harari, Esq., London.

Inscription on the outside of the basin, intersected by four shields.

مما عمل برسم المقرّ الأشرف الكريم العالى ○ المولوى الأمير[ى] الكبيرى العونى

الغياثى المجاهدى ○ المرابطى الهمامى النظامى الأعزّى الأخصّى ? التقى ○ المخدومى

برسباى الشرفى المالكى الملكى الأشرفى ○

This is one of the objects made for His Most Noble and Honourable and High Excellency, our Lord, the Great Amir, the Helper, the Rescuer, the Defender of the Faith, the Warrior at the Frontiers, the Shelter, the Regent, the Most Glorious, the Favourite, the Well-Served, Barsbāy ash-Sharafī, the Royal, (officer) of al-Malik al-Ashraf.

BIBLIOGRAPHY: Unpublished.

The word المالكى is misplaced and being crossed by another word بسر which means nothing in its present context, shows perhaps that an attempt was made to erase the name of the amir for whom the basin was originally made.

BASHTĀK[2]

S. Bashtāk an-Nāṣirī held a fief, the revenue from which was equal to seventeen times the salary of an Amir of Forty; appointed Viceroy of Syria by Muḥam-

[1] Ibn Taghrībirdī, *Nujūm*, VII, pp. 547, l. 5, 697, l. 3; *Ḍau'* s.v.; Ibn Iyās, II, pp. 129, l. 8 b, 132, ll. 13 b, 11 b, 133, l. 4 b, 139, l. 6 b, 147, ll. 5, 7 b.

[2] Jacob of Verona, ed. Röhricht, *ROL*, t. III. 1895, p. 250, Zettersteén, *Beiträge*, cf. Index; Ṣafadī, *A'yān*, s.v. with indication of spelling (MS. Berlin, fo. 37v); *Wāfī*, s.v. (MS. Br. Mus., Add. 23357, fo. 23v–24v); Khalīl aẓ-Ẓāhirī, *Zubda*, pp. 29, l. 18, 31, l. 4; Maqrīzī, *Khiṭaṭ*, II, pp. 34, 70 (2nd ed., III, pp. 54 ff., 113 f.); Ibn Ḥajar, *Durar*, s.v. (MS. Br. Mus., Or. 3043, fo. 90r, v); Ibn Taghrībirdī, *Manhal* (MS. Paris,

mad b. Qalāūn when the latter was on his death-bed; arrested by Quṭlūbughā al-Fakhrī after the Sultan's death, imprisoned in Alexandria and there executed in Rabīʿ II 742 (began 14th September 1341).

BLAZON: *Upper field self-coloured, on white middle field a red napkin, lower field red.*

1. BATH, Shāriʿ Ḥammām Bashtāk, Cairo.

One shield in the upper part of the porch.

Inscription above the entrance door.

أمر بإنشاء هذه الحمّام المباركة المقرّ الأشرف العالى المولوى الأميرى الكبيرى

السيفى بشتاك الملكى الناصرى دام عزّه

Ordered to build this blessed bath, His Most Noble and High Excellency, our Lord, the Great Amir, Saif ad-dīn Bashtāk, (officer) of al-Malik an-Nāṣir, may his glory last for ever.

BIBLIOGRAPHY: Herz, l.c., pp. 33–6, 1 pl.

Reproduced: Briggs, *Muhammadan Architecture in Egypt and Palestine*, fig. 70; Fago, *Arte Araba*, pl. XXXIV, 2; Devonshire, *Rambles*, pl. 94; Herz, *Iszlám*, fig. 187.

Mentioned: Creswell, *Brief Chronology*, p. 101.

2. GLASS LAMP, Collection of H.H. Prince Yūsuf Kamāl, Cairo. Pl. XXVIII. 2.

Six shields, three on the neck, three on the lower part of the body.

Inscription on body:

المقرّ الشريف العالى المولوى الأميرى الكبيرى المحترمى المخدومى السيفى بشتاك

الناصرى عزّ نصره

His Noble and High Excellency, our Lord, the Great Amir, the Honoured, the Well-Served, Saif ad-dīn Bashtāk an-Nāṣirī, may his victory be glorious.

BIBLIOGRAPHY: Wiet, *Lampes*, p. 160, No. 30.

3. GLASS LAMP, fragment of, Arab Museum, Cairo, No. 4067.

Ar. 2069, fo. 80ᵛ); Weil, IV. 387, 415, 416; *CIA. Égypte*, I, pp. 182, 659, n. 3; Herz, 'Le Bain de l'Émir Bechtak' (in: *BIE*. 4ᵉ sér., No. 5, 1904), pp. 34 ff.

Originally at least three shields, of which only one on the lower part of the body left. Inscription on body:

مما عمل برسم المقر العالى المولوى الأميرى السـ[ـيّـ]ـدى [. . . ب]شتك? الملكى الناصرى

This is one of the objects made for His High Excellency, our Lord, the Amir, the Master . . . Bashtak (?), *(officer) of al-Malik an-Nāṣir.*

BIBLIOGRAPHY: Wiet, *Lampes*, p. 133 f., pl. XIV.

BĀYAZĪD

BLAZON: *On upper field pen-box, on middle field cup flanked by two smaller cups, on lower field napkin.*[1]

BRASS STAND FOR A TRAY, Victoria and Albert Museum, London, No. 934—1884. Pl. LXV. 2.

The same inscription on both halves of the stand, intersected in each case by two shields.

الجناب العالى المولوى ا? ○ السيفى بايزيد أمير دوادار أعزّ أنصاره[2] ○

His High Excellency (janāb), *our Lord, Saif ad-dīn Bāyazīd* Amīr Dawādār, *may his victories be glorious.*

BIBLIOGRAPHY: Lane-Poole, *Art of the Saracens*, p. 233.

BAYBARS[3]

R. Baybars aṣ-Ṣāliḥī, born in 620 (1223), originally a mamluk of al-ʿImād aḍ-Ḍāʾiʿ, then bought by Amir Aydakīn, passed into the service of al-Malik

[1] Similar blazon in colours, but without inscription on a fayence tile in the Victoria and Albert Museum.

[2] In the lower text دواادار is written by mistake with an additional *alif*.

[3] Abu-l-Fidā', ed. Reiske, IV, esp. p. 606 ff., V. 40 ff. (ed. Constantinople, esp. III. p. 216 f., IV. p. 10 f.); Kutubī, *Fawāt*, pp. 85 ff.; Ibn Ḥabīb, cf. Index, s.v.; Quatremère, *SM.* I a, esp. p. 116, I b. esp. 150 f.; Ibn Taghrībirdī, *Manhal*, s.v. (MS. Paris, Ar. 2069, fo. 98v ff.); Mujīr ad-dīn, *al-Uns al-jalīl*, p. 432, ll. 3 b ff.; Ibn Iyās, cf. Index, especially I, pp. 98, 109–12; Weil, cf. Index, especially IV, pp. 19, 21 f., 98; Muir, *The Mameluke or Slave Dynasty of Egypt*, pp. 13 ff.; Sobernheim in *The Encyclopaedia of Islām*, s.v. (English ed., I, 588 f.).

aṣ-Ṣāliḥ Ayyūb, who freed him and made him Chief of the Corps of the *jamdārs*; passed into the service of Aybak, became Commander-in-Chief (*atābak al-ʿasākir*) under al-Malik al-Muẓaffar Quṭuz, elected Sultan on the 15th Dhu-l-Qaʿda 658 (22nd October 1260). Assumed the title al-Malik aẓ-Ẓāhir. Died the 27th Muḥarram 676 (1st July 1277).

BLAZON: *Lion passant.*[1]

1. MADRASA of Baybars, Cairo.[2]

'Pair of panthers in tympanum of relieving work over first window in south-western façade.'

BIBLIOGRAPHY: Creswell, 'The Works of Sultan Bibars al-Bunduqdârî in Egypt' (in *BIFAO*. t. XXVI, 1926), p. 147 and pl. II.

Reproduced: Briggs, *Muhammadan Architecture*, fig. 57; Devonshire, *Rambles*, p. 39.

2. BOSS of brass-plated door from the Madrasa of Baybars, Cairo, now in the Victoria and Albert Museum, London.

BIBLIOGRAPHY: Bourgoin, *Les Arts Arabes*, pl. 74; Lane-Poole, *Art of the Saracens*, p. 223 f., fig. 83; Briggs, *Muhammadan Architecture*, p. 223, fig. 232; Creswell, l.c., pp. 138, 147; Migeon, *Manuel* (2nd ed.) I. p. 388, II. pp. 69, 82.

3. FORTRESS, Kerak.

Inscription flanked by two lions, the latter now embedded on either side of the doorway at the Government Head-quarters, Kerak.

بسمله . . . السلطان المالك! الظاهر السيّد الأجلّ الكبير العالم العادل المجاهد المرابط

المؤيّد المظفّر المنصور ركن الدنيا والدين سلطان الاسلام والمسلمين سيّد الملوك

والسلاطين قاتل الكفرة والمشركين نا[صر]? الحق مغيث الخلق ملك البحرين صاحب

القبلة خادم الحرمين الشريفين محيى الخلافة المعظّمة ظلّ الله فى الأرض قسيم

أمير المؤمنين بيبرس بن عبد الله الصالحى أعزّ الله سلطانه

[1] Maqrīzī, *Nuqūd* (ed. Constantinople 1298 A.H.) p. 15, *Khiṭaṭ* II 146, ll. 7 b, penult. (2nd ed. III p. 238, ll. 12, 18), Ibn Iyās I, p. 110, l. 4.

[2] Only monuments with inscriptions of Baybars appear in the following list. For heraldic lions found in buildings restored or repaired by Baybars, but without his inscriptions, see *CIA. Jérusalem, Ville* p. 435, nn. 1, 2; Creswell, l.c.; Migeon, *Manuel* (2nd ed.) I, p. 262 f.

In the name of the most merciful God. The Sultan al-Malik aẓ-Ẓāhir, the Most Magnificent Lord, the Great, the Learned, the Just, the Defender of the Faith, the Warrior at the Frontiers, the Helped by God, the Victorious, Rukn ad-dunyā wa-d-dīn, Sultan of the Islam and the Muslims, Lord of Kings and Sultans, Killer of unbelievers and polytheists, who makes the truth prevail, rescues the creatures, King of the two Seas, the Lord of the Qiblah, the Servant of the Two Noble Sanctuaries, the Restorer of the August Khalifate, God's shade on earth, the Associate of the Commander of the Faithful, Baybars, son of ʿAbdallāh, aṣ-Ṣāliḥī, may God make his sultanate glorious.

BIBLIOGRAPHY: Sauvaire in de Luynes, *Voyage d'exploration à la Mer Morte*, II. 199.

Mentioned: van Berchem et Fatio, *Voyage en Syrie*, I, p. 144, and n. 1; *CIA. Jérusalem, Ville*, p. 435, n. 2; Creswell, l.c., p. 148 and pl. VIII B; de Saulcy, *Voyage*, I, 364, pl. XX.

4. FORTRESS, Qalʿat al-Ḥuṣn.

Inscription over the entrance; the second line flanked by two lions.

(1) بسمله . . . (2) [Lion] أمر بتجد[يد] هذا الحصن المبارك فى دولة مولانا

السلطان الملك الظاهر العالم [Lion] (3) العادل المجاهد المرابط [المؤيّد] المظفّر

المنصور ركن الدنيا والدين أبو الفتح بيبرس قسيم أمير المؤمنين وذلك بتأريخ

نهار يوم الثلاثاء خامس وعشرين من شعبان سنة تسع وستّين وستّمائة

In the name of the most merciful God. It was ordered to renew this blessed fortress during the reign of our Lord, the Sultan al-Malik aẓ-Ẓāhir, the Learned, the Just, the Defender of the Faith, the Warrior at the Frontiers, the Helped by God, the Victorious, Rukn ad-dunyā wa-d-dīn, Abu-l-Fatḥ Baybars, the Associate of the Commander of the Faithful, on Tuesday, 25th Shaʿbān 669 (8th April 1271).

Two inscriptions on two round towers at the south-western and south-eastern corners of the enclosure, both flanked by panthers. Texts similar to the one quoted above except for the middle portion which mentions in each case Baybars and his heir al-Malik as-Saʿīd; in the inscription at the south-eastern corner the latter is given the title *as-Sulṭān . . . Nāṣir ad-dunyā wa-d-dīn.*

BIBLIOGRAPHY: Rey, *Étude sur l'Architecture militaire des Croisés*, pp. 46, 272; van Berchem, 'Inscriptions Arabes de Syrie' (in *Mémoires de l'Institut d'Égypte*, III), 482 f. and pl. VI. 12, VII. 14; Sobernheim, *CIA. Syrie du Nord*, p. 21 f.

Mentioned and reproduced: van Berchem et Fatio, l.c., I, pp. 141, n. 1, 144, 148, II, pl. XII, XIV.

Mentioned: Creswell, l.c., p. 149.

5. BRIDGE, Lydda, locally known as Jisr Jindās. Two inscriptions with identical texts, each flanked by a pair of lions, facing each other. In front of each lion a mouse (?).

(1) بسمله . . . وصلواته على سيّدنا محمّد وصحبه وآله أجمعين (2) أمر بعمارة هذا

الجسر المبارك مولانا السلطان الأعظم الملك الظاهر ركن الدين بيبرس بن (3) عبد

الله فى أيّام ولده مولانا السلطان الملك السعيد ناصر الدين بركة خان أعزّ الله

أنصارهما وغفر لهما (4) وذلك بولاية العبد الفقير الى رحمة الله علاء الدين علىّ

السوّاق غفر الله له ولوالديه فى شهر رمضان سنة أحد وسبعين وستّما[ئة]

In the name of the most merciful God, whose blessings be on our Lord Muḥammad and all his companions. Ordered to build this blessed bridge our Lord, the most August Sultan al-Malik aẓ-Ẓāhir, Rukn ad-dunyā wa-d-dīn, Baybars son of ʿAbdallāh, in the time of his son, our Lord the Sultan al-Malik as-Saʿīd Nāṣir ad-dīn Baraka Khān, may God make their victories glorious and forgive both of them. This (was done) under the direction of the servant yearning for the mercy of God ʿAlāʾ ad-dīn ʿAlī as-Sawwāq, may God have mercy on him and on his parents, in the month of Ramaḍān 671 (began 22nd March 1273).

BIBLIOGRAPHY: Clermont Ganneau, 'Notes d'épigraphie et d'histoire arabes' (in *Journal Asiatique*, 8e série, t. X, pp. 509–27 and pl., t. XII, pp. 305–10, 2 pl.). Partly reprinted in Cl.–G.'s *Recueil d'Archéologie Orientale*, I, pp. 262–79, and re-edited in his *Archaeological Researches in Palestine*, II, pp. 110–18, 470; *Jerusalemer Warte*, LXIX (1913), pp. 92 f., 100.

Mentioned and reproduced: Creswell, l.c., pp. 146, 149, and pl. X B.

Mentioned: Conder, *Survey of Western Palestine, Memoirs*, vol. II, p. 264 f.

6. FORT, to the west of Alexandria, in 1847 known as Qaṣr al-ʿUmaid, since disappeared.

'Inscription . . . explaining that this castle was built by Ahmad-el-Tahir-el-Yasmuri, under the orders of Bibars, Sultan of Egypt, whose arms appear beneath in the shape of two lions rampant.'

BIBLIOGRAPHY: Bayle St. John, *Adventures in the Libyan Desert*, p. 173, quoted by Creswell, l.c., pp. 152, 192.

7. COINS, in many collections in Europe, Syria, Palestine, and Egypt.

Lion passant to left on gold and silver coins (*dīnār* and *dirham*) beneath the text of the reverse, on copper coins (*fils*) in the middle of the reverse, between the words السلطان and الملك الظاهر.

BIBLIOGRAPHY: Lane-Poole, *Catalogue of Oriental Coins in the British Museum*, IV. 140–5 and pl. VI; id. *Catalogue of the Collection of Arabic Coins preserved in the Khedivial Library at Cairo*, pp. 244–7; id. *Catalogue of the Mohammadan Coins preserved in the Bodleian Library*, p. 9; Lavoix, *Catalogue des Monnaies Musulmanes de la Bibliothèque Nationale*, vol. *Égypte et Syrie*, pp. 277–94.

BAYBARS JĀLIQ[1]

R. Baybars b. ʿAbdallāh aṣ-Ṣāliḥī an-Najmī, called *al-Jāliq* ('a strong and frolicsome horse'), *jamdār* under al-Malik aṣ-Ṣāliḥ Ayyūb, dubbed amir by Baybars, later sent to Damascus. Died in Ramleh the 10th Jumādā I 707 (7th November 1307). Buried in Jerusalem.

BLAZON: *Fleur-de-lis with eleven leaves, instead of three, on an undivided shield.*

MAUSOLEUM, locally known as Dār al-Bāshkātib, Jerusalem, situated at the corner of the Ṭarīq Bāb as-Silsila (David Street) and al-Wād.

Two shields both at the beginning and at the end of the first line of the inscription.

Inscription above the lintel of the window in the south wall.

○ بسمله . . . هذاه تربة الأمير الأجلّ ○ (2) الكبير الغازى المجاهد المرابط فى
سبيل الله تعالى ركن الدين (3) بيبرس الجالق الصالحى توفّا الى رحمة الله تعالى
عاشر (4) جماد(ى) الأوّل سنة سبع وسبعمائة غفر الله له ولمن دعا له بالرحمة

In the name of the most merciful God. This is the mausoleum of the most Magnificent and Great Amir, the Vanquisher, the Defender of the Faith, the Warrior at the Frontiers in the path of God the Exalted, Rukn ad-dīn Baybars al-Jāliq aṣ-Ṣāliḥī. Passed into the mercy of God the Exalted the 10*th Jumādā I of the year* 707 (7th November 1307), *may God forgive him and whosoever asks* (*God's*) *mercy for him.*

BIBLIOGRAPHY: van Berchem, *CIA. Jérusalem, Ville*, No. 72, p. 223 f., pl. LV.

[1] Nuwairī, s.a. 707 (MS. Leyden, fo. 38ʳ b); Ibn Ḥabīb, p. 311; Ṣafadī, *Wāfī*, s.v. (MS. Br. Mus., Add. 23357, fo. 76ᵛ); Quatremère, *SM*. I b, p. 101, II a, p. 11, II b, p. 60, 281; Ibn Ḥajar, *ad-Durar*, s.v. (MS. Br. Mus., Or. 3043, fo. 96ʳ); Ibn Taghrībirdī, *Manhal*, s.v. (MS. Paris, Ar. 2069, fo. 105ᵛ); Mujīr ad-dīn, *al-Uns al-jalīl*, p. 396, ll. 1–4 (Sauvaire, p. 160); Weil, IV. 116, 211; *CIA. Jérusalem, Ville*, p. 224.

BAYBUGHĀ[1]

S. Baybughā al-Qāsimī, known as Baybughārūs,[2] a page (*khāṣṣakī*) of Muḥammad b. Qalāūn, first came to be known under al-Malik aṣ-Ṣāliḥ Isma'īl, was *amīr majlis* under al-Malik al-Muẓaffar Ḥājjī, in 748 (1347) appointed Viceroy of Egypt; arrested the 26th Dhu-l-Qa'da 751 (25th January 1351) while on his pilgrimage, and imprisoned in Kerak. Appointed Governor of Aleppo by al-Malik aṣ-Ṣāliḥ Ṣāliḥ in Sha'bān 752 (began 23rd September 1351). Stirred up a rebellion which proved unsuccessful. Beheaded early in 754 (1353).

BLAZON: *On the middle field of a three-fielded shield a cup placed between two six-petalled rosettes.*

PUBLIC FOUNTAIN, Aleppo, at one time known as the Qasṭal Ḥammām at-Tall, now turned into a shop.

The inscription, intersected by the shield, is illegible, being partly covered with a thick layer of plaster, and for the rest having had paper pasted over it.

Above this, another inscription, without armorial bearings, but most probably by the same amir.

(١) أمر بعمارة هذا السبيل المبارك الجناب العالى العلائى الملكى[3] (2) الصالحى باشارة المقرّ الأشرف الأمير بيبغا كافل المملكة (3) الحلبيّة أعزّ الله أنصاره في شهور سنة ثلاث وخمسين وسبعمائة من الهجرة النبويّة

Ordered to build this blessed public fountain His High Excellency (janāb), *'Alā' ad-dīn (officer) of al-Malik*[3] *aṣ-Ṣāliḥ, under the supervision of His Most Noble Excellency, the Amīr Baybughā, Viceroy of the province of Aleppo, may God make his victories glorious. In the months of the year* 753 *of the Hijra of the Prophet* (1352/3).

BIBLIOGRAPHY: Bischoff, *Tuḥaf al-anbā'*, p. 156 (several mistakes, blazon not mentioned).

[1] Ibn Ḥabīb, pp. 386, 395, 396; Ibn Ḥajar, *Durar*, s.v. (MS. Br. Mus., Or. 3043, fo. 96v–97r); *Manhal*, s.v. (MS. Paris, Ar. 2069, fo. 108v–109v) and s.v. Ḥajji (ib. 2070, fo. 13r, l. 1); Ibn Iyās, I, pp. 185, l. 13 b, 189, ll. 6–11, 190, l. 11, 193, l. 5 b, 195, ll. 10, 11, 10 b, 5 b ff., 196, ll. 4, 7, 9 b ff., 200, l. 9, 201, l. 6. Weil, cf. Index; Ṭabbākh, *A'lām*, II, 431 ff.

[2] More correctly spelt in two words: بيبغا اروس. Urūs is a Tatar tribe (*Manhal*, l. c.).

[3] In Bischoff's text المولوى which, from the position of this word in the series of titles, must have been intended for الملكى. To-day the word is no longer visible, being hidden behind a shelf.

BAYSARĪ[1]

B. Baysarī aṣ-Ṣāliḥī ash-Shamsī, one of the mamluks of al-Malik aṣ-Ṣāliḥ Ayyūb, made Commander of a Thousand by Baybars I on the latter's accession to the throne, in 677 (1278) imprisoned by Baraka Khān, became one of the most powerful amirs under Salāmish, in 681 (1282/3) imprisoned for a second time, released in 690 (1291), imprisoned in 693 (1294), released, and finally put in prison in 697 (1297/8) where he died the following year, over seventy years old.

BLAZON: *Double-headed eagle.*

BRASS HANDWARMER, British Museum.

Two inscriptions, one on each hemisphere, each accompanied by shields.

مما عمل برسم المقرّ الكريم العالى المولوى الأميرى الكبيرى المحترمى المخدومى
الإسفهسلارى المجاهدى المرابطى الثاغرى المؤيّدى المظفّرى المنصورى البدرى بدر
الدين بيسرى الظاهرى السعيدى الشمسى عز نصره

This is one of the objects made for His Honourable and High Excellency, our Lord, the Great Amir, the Honoured, the Well-Served, the Commander, the Defender of the Faith, the Warrior at the Frontiers, the Warden of the Marches, the Helped by God, the Victorious, Badr ad-dīn Baysarī, (officer) of (al-Malik) aẓ-Ẓāhir (and) of (al-Malik) as-Saʿīd, ash-Shamsī, may his victory be glorious.

DATE: Between 1264 and 1279.

BIBLIOGRAPHY: Lane-Poole, l.c., p. 209 ff., fig. 81.
Mentioned and reproduced: Migeon, *Manuel* (2nd ed.) II, p. 70, fig. 249.
Mentioned: van Berchem, *Notes III*, p. 37 and n.

BILBĀY AL-ʿALĀ'Ī[2]

S. Bilbāy al-ʿAlā'ī aẓ-Ẓāhirī, Amir of Ten, in Ṣafar 873 (began 21st August 1468) appointed Governor of Alexandria, in 875 (1470/1) Governor of Safad. Died Rajab 879 (began 11th November 1474), as a sexagenarian.

[1] Mufaḍḍal, especially pp. 139, 290, 323, 385, 435, 467. Ibn Ḥabīb, pp. 294, 297; Ibn Iyās, I, pp. 91, l. 7, 99, l. 3, 112, l. 3 b, 114, l. 12 f., 115, l. 4 b, 124–5, 127, l. 9, 131, l. 4; *Khiṭaṭ*, II, 69, l. 23, *SM.* I a, 57, II b, 135, n., 137 f.; *Manhal*, s.v. (MS. Paris, Ar. 2069, fo. 112r, v). Lane-Poole, *Art of the Saracens*, p. 210 f.; Van Berchem, l.c. pp. 23, 24, n. 1, 35, n. 1; *CIA. Égypte*, I, p. 118 (and further lit.).

[2] Ibn Iyās, II, pp. 100, l. 4 b, 125, l. 5, 154, l. 16.

BLAZON: *On upper field a napkin, on middle field a cup charged with a pen-box placed between a 'pair of trousers', on lower field a cup.*

COPPER PLATE, tinned over, National Museum of Arab Art, Cairo, No. 4121.

Inscription intersected by three shields.

ممّا عمل برسم المقرّ الأشرف العالى المولوى ○ المالكى المخدومى العضدى

الذخرى ○ السيفى بلباى العلائى كافل المملكة الصفديّة عزّ نصره ○

This is one of the objects made for His Most Noble and High Excellency, our Lord, the Royal, the Well-Served, the Supporter, the Treasure, Saif ad-dīn Bilbāy al-'Alā'ī, Viceroy of the province of Safad, may his victory be glorious.

DATE: Between 875 and 879 (1470/1–1474/5).

BIBLIOGRAPHY: Unpublished.

DAMURDĀSH AL-ASHRAFĪ[1]

BLAZON: *On upper field a cup, on middle field a cup placed between a 'pair of trousers', on lower field two cups.*

1. LUNCH-BOX (*maṭbaqiyya*), in the collection of J. Home, Esq., Cairo. Pl. LXV. 1. Four shields and an inscription on lid and the same on the body. The fuller of the two inscriptions, the one on the body, is reproduced here.

ممّا عمل برسم الجناب العالى المولوى السيفى دمرداش الملكى الأشرفى امير

دوادار المقام الشريف بحلب المحروسة عزّ أنصاره

This is one of the objects made for His High Excellency (janāb), *our Lord, Saif ad-dīn Damurdāsh, (officer) of al-Malik al-Ashraf, Amīr Dawādār of His Majesty in Aleppo, the protected, may his victories be glorious.*

BIBLIOGRAPHY: Unpublished.

2. COPPER PLATE, once in the collection of Sulaiman Pasha Abaza, later in that of Rogers Bey, then in that of Mrs. Sheldon Amos, present owner unknown.

[1] Pronunciation indicated in words in *Manhal*, s.v. Damurdāsh al-Yūsufī (MS. Paris, Ar. 2070, fo. 72v, l. 8 b).

مّما عمل برسم الجناب العالى المولوى المالكى المخدومى السيفى دمرداش الملكى

الأشرفى دوادار المقام الشريف [بـ]؟حلب المحروسة عزّ أنصاره

This is one of the objects made for His High Excellency (janāb), *our Lord, the Royal, the Well-Served, Saif ad-dīn Damurdāsh, (officer) of al-Malik al-Ashraf, Dawādār of His Majesty in Aleppo, the protected, may his victories be glorious.*

BIBLIOGRAPHY: Rogers, p. 426, fig. 38 (Germ. ed.); Artin, *Contribution*, No. 91, p. 121.

DAMURDĀSH AL-MUḤAMMADĪ[1]

S. Damurdāsh al-Muḥammadī, a mamluk of Barqūq, served as armour-bearer (*silāḥdār*) during Barqūq's first reign, dubbed amir on Barqūq's second accession to the throne, appointed Governor of Hama, where he remained till he was transferred in 795 (began 17th November 1392) to Tripoli as Governor; the following year arrested, but shortly afterwards released and appointed Commander-in-Chief in Aleppo; succeeded Yūnus Balṭā as Governor of Hama; after the suppression of Tanam's rebellion, in which he took part, appointed Governor of Aleppo, which he entered the 1st Ramaḍān 802 (26th April 1400). Deposed in Muḥarram 804 (August 1401) after an unsuccessful fight with Duqmāq, his successor in office, fled to the Turcomans; returned nearly a year later, in Dhu-l-Ḥijja 804 (July 1402) appointed Governor of Tripoli, the 18th Rajab 806 (31st January 1404), transferred to Aleppo for a third time, remained in office from Ramaḍān 806 to Shaʿbān 807 (13th March 1404/February 1405); dismissed from office, returned to the Turcomans; in 808 returned to Syria, the 24th Rabīʿ I 808 (19th September 1405) appointed Governor of Gaza, made unsuccessful attempts to obtain possession of Aleppo and Hama, became Amir of a Hundred and Commander of a Thousand, in 810 (1407/8) appointed Governor of Safad, after Jakam's death transferred again to Aleppo which was shortly afterwards taken from him by Shaikh. Appointed Commander-in-Chief in Egypt, on the 15th Muḥarram

[1] *Nujūm*, especially VI, pp. 3, l. 13, 39, l. 6, 93, l. 3, 100, l. 14, 131, l. 3, 204, l. 18, 232, l. 15, 244, l. 13, 305, l. 11, 316, l. 6, 333, l. 13, 343, l. 15, 451, l. 14 ff.; *Manhal*, s.v. (MS. Paris, Ar. 2070, fo. 72^{v}–75^{r}); *Ḍau'*, s.v.; Ibn Iyās, cf. Index, especially I, pp. 322, l. 5 b, 324, ll. 9, 11, 334, l. 11, 342, l. 14 f.; Weil, V. 78, 85, 102, 109, 110, 115, 117–19, 121, 123, 131, 132; Cheikho in Ṣāliḥ b. Yaḥyā, p. 56, n. 1; Rāghib Ṭabbākh, *Aʿlām an-nubalā'*, II. 485 f., 504–10.

815 (27th April 1412) appointed Viceroy of Syria, fled the 11th Ṣafar (23rd May 1412), in Ramaḍān of the same year arrested after his return to Cairo, executed in the prison of Alexandria the 18th Muḥarram 818 (30th March 1415). Completed the mosque begun by Aqbughā al-Hadbānī al-Aṭrūsh in Aleppo, and built a monastery (*zāwiya*) in Tripoli.

BLAZON: *Upper field blank, on both the middle and lower field a cup.*

MOSQUE, Aleppo. Pl. LIV. 4.

Inscription over the main entrance door covered over with whitewash and therefore illegible.

Inscription on the lintel of the side door, flanked by two shields.

(1) عمّر هذا الجامع المبرور ابتغا لوجه الله تعالى المقرّ الأشرف العالى المولوى

العالمى العادلى المخدومى الكافلى (2) السيفى دمرداش الناصرى مولانا ملك الأمراء

كافل المملكتين الشريفتين الحلبيّة والطرابلسيّة أعزّ الله أنصاره وضاعف اقتداره

(3) بمحمّد وآله بتولّى العبد الفقير الى الله تعالى يوسف الأشرفى وكان الفراغ

منه سلخ شعبان المكرّم سنة اثنا عشر وثمان ماية

In his desire to please God the Exalted built this pious mosque His Most Noble and High Excellency, our Lord, the Learned, the Just, the Well-Served, the Viceroyal Saif ad-dīn Damurdāsh an-Nāṣirī, our Lord, Governor-General, Viceroy of the two Noble Provinces of Aleppo and Tripoli, may God make his victories glorious and double his power through Muḥammad and his family. Under the supervision of the servant yearning for God the Exalted, Yūsuf al-Ashrafī. It was completed the last day of the honoured Sha'bān of the year 812 (6th January 1410).

BIBLIOGRAPHY: Unpublished.

DUQMĀQ[1]

S. Duqmāq al-Muḥammadī, a freed mamluk and page of Barqūq, on Barqūq's second accession to the throne dubbed Amir of a Hundred, in 796 appointed

[1] *Nujūm*, especially VI, pp. 10, l. 13, 23, l. 17, 42, l. 17, 90, l. 4, 93, l. 2, 109, l. 5; *Manhal*, s.v. (MS.

Governor of Malaṭia; on his dismissal from office returned to Cairo the 9th Dhu-l-Qaʿda 801 (13th July 1399). In Rabīʿ II 802 (December 1399) appointed Second Chamberlain, the 28th Ramaḍān 802 (23rd May 1400) appointed Governor of Hama; imprisoned by Timur in 803, fled to Egypt, in the same year appointed Governor of Safad, on the 22nd Muḥarram 804 (1st September 1401) replaced Damurdāsh as Governor of Aleppo, where he remained till he fled in 806, fearing arrest; after the Saʿīdiyya-event appointed Governor of Hama. Killed by Jakam outside Hama, in Rajab 808 (began 23rd December 1405). Built a mausoleum outside Aleppo.

BLAZON: *Upper field blank, on both the middle and the lower field a cup.*

CITY GATE, Aleppo, called Bāb Anṭākiya. Pl. LIII. 1.

Above the entrance underneath the arch. Inscription set in a tabula ansata-frame, flanked by four shields.

(1) عزّ يد(و)م ونعمة وسعادة لمقام مالكنا المليك! الناصرى! ملك المشارق

(2) والمغارب خادم الحرمين عهد من أبيه الظاهرى أمر (3) بتجديده بعد دثوره

مولانا المقرّ الأشرف السيفى دقماق (4) الملكى الناصرى كافل المملكة الشريفة

الحلبيّة المحروسة أعزّ الله تعالى أنصاره [To the right] بتأريخ شهر شعبان

[To the left] سنة أربع وثمانمائة

Glory may last and grace and happiness for His Majesty, our King, al-Malik an-Nāṣir, King of the East and the West, Servant of both Ḥarams (scl. at Mecca and Madina), inheritor of his father (al-Malik) aẓ-Ẓāhir. Ordered its renewal after its destruction our Lord, His Most Noble Excellency, Saif ad-dīn Duqmāq, (officer) of al-Malik an-Nāṣir, Viceroy of the noble and protected province of Aleppo, may God make his victories glorious. In the month of Shaʿbān of the year 804 (began 6th March 1402).

BIBLIOGRAPHY: Van Berchem, *Inschriften Oppenheim*, No. 52, p. 43.

Paris, Ar. 2070, fo. 71^{v}–72^{v}); *Ḍau'*, s.v.; Ibn Iyās, I, pp. 303, l. 7, 322, l. 5, 324, l. 11, 334, l. 13, 337, l. 2, 342, l. 13; Weil, V. 78, 102, 104, 109; Rāghib Ṭabbākh, *Aʿlām an-nubalā'*, II. 504, V. 149 f.

FĀṬIMA BINT SŪDŪN AL-MU'AYYADĪ

The father of Fāṭima is probably identical with S. Sūdūn al-Abūbakrī,[1] originally a mamluk of al-Malik al-Mu'ayyad Shaikh, in course of time became one of the amirs of Aleppo, in 842 (1438/9) appointed Grand Chamberlain of Aleppo, in 850 Commander-in-Chief of the same province, in 855 succeeded Bayghūt min Ṣafar Khujā as Governor of Hama, before the 15th Sha'bān 856 (31st August 1452) dismissed from office. Later appointed Commander-in-Chief of Aleppo, died in the last days of Ramaḍān 865 (early in July 1461).

BLAZON: *On upper field a napkin, on middle field a cup charged with two small cups, on lower field a cup.*

1. COPPER BOWL tinned over, Victoria and Albert Museum, London, 557–78. Pl. LIX. 2. 3.
Two shields.

(1) ممّا عمل برسم الستّ فاطمة بنت المقرّ الأشرف السيفى سودون المؤيّدى

(2) مولانا ملك الأمراء بحماة المحروسة كان تغمّده الاله! برحمته

This is one of the objects made for Lady Fāṭima, daughter of His Most Noble Excellency Saif ad-dīn Sūdūn al-Mu'ayyadī, formerly Governor-General of Hama, the protected, may God cover him with his mercy.

DATE: After 865 A.H.

BIBLIOGRAPHY: Unpublished.

2. COPPER DISH tinned over, present owner unknown.

ممّا عمل برسم الستّ فاطمة بنت المقرّ المرحوم سودون المؤيّدى [Sauvaget]

This is one of the objects made for Lady Fāṭima, daughter of His late Excellency Sūdūn al-Mu'ayyadī.

BIBLIOGRAPHY: Unpublished.

[1] *Nujūm*, VII, pp. 107, l. 16, 229, l. 7, 252, l. 10, 572, l. 11, 767, l. 4; *Manhal*, s.v. (MS. Paris, Ar. 2070, fo. 133v); *Ḍau'*, s.v.; Rāghib Ṭabbākh, *A'lām*, V. 276.

GHĀZĪ B. ABĪ BAKR[1]

Al-Malik al-Muẓaffar Ghāzī, son of al-Malik al-ʿĀdil Abū Bakr, in 608 (1211/12) received ar-Ruhā' (Edessa) and Sarūj from his father, in 617 recognized as heir of his brother al-Malik al-Ashraf, exchanged these two towns for Khalāṭ and Mayāfāriqīn, in 621 (1224) lost Khalāṭ as result of an unsuccessful revolt against al-Malik al-Ashraf, in 627 (began 20th November 1229) conquered Arzan, near Diarbekr, died in 642 (1244/5).

BLAZON: *A lion facing a man (? or a fish?).*

CITY GATE ('Ḥarrān Gate'), Urfa. Pl. I. 8.

Inscription on the inner face of the gate, above two blazons.

(1) بسمله

(2) امر بعمارته مولانا السلطان الملك المظفّر العالم العادل المؤيّد المنصور شهاب الدنيا والدين أبى الفتح شاه غازى بن السلطان الملك العادل أبو بكر بن أيّوب بولاية الفقير الى رحمة الله كافور العادلى (one word) الدولة

... Ordered the building of this (Gate) our Lord, the Sultan, al-Malik al-Muẓaffar, the Learned, the Just, the Helped (by God), the Victorious, Shihāb ad-dunyā wa-d-dīn Abu-l-Fatḥ Shāh Ghāzī, son of the Sultan al-Malik al-ʿĀdil Abū Bakr b. Ayyūb, under the direction of the one yearning for the mercy of God, Kāfūr al-ʿĀdilī ...

BIBLIOGRAPHY: Unpublished.

ḤAIDAR B. AL-ʿASKARĪ

BLAZON: *Upper field blank, on united middle and lower fields a fleur-de-lis.*

MOSQUE in ruins, corner of az-Zanbīl and Jāddat Sūq al-Maidān Streets, Damascus. Pl. XIX. 2.

One shield in the fourth line of the inscription.

[1] Abu-l-Fidā', ed. Reiske, IV, pp. 246, 292–4, 322, 366, 468, 478, ed. Constantinople, III, pp. 120, l. 12, 133, ll. 13–16, 140 b–141 t, 153, l. 8 b, 178 b, 181, l. 4 b; Weil, III. 469.

The inscription is embedded in the only niche left of the mosque to-day, several words are covered partly or wholly with plaster and therefore illegible, a few words hammered away.

The beginning of the text runs as follows:

(1) بسمله . . . بتأريخ العشر الأوسط من ربيع الآخر سنة أربع وثمانين وسبعمئة (2) امر بنقش جهات الوقف على مصالح المسجد المعمور بذكر الله تعالى بانيه وواقفه الفقير الى الله تعالى (3) الجناب الشهابى حيدر بن العسكرى تقبّل الله منه وجهات الوقف المذكور الخ

In the name of the most merciful God. On the date of the middle third of Rabīʿ II of the year 784 (end of June–beginning of July 1382) *ordered to engrave these particulars of the waqf endowed in favour of the mosque, prosperous by worship of God the Exalted, its builder and founder, the one yearning for God the Exalted, His Excellency* (janāb), *Shihāb ad-dīn Ḥaidar son of al-ʿAskarī, may God accept* (*this offering*) *from him. The particulars of the above-mentioned endowment are* (*as follows*), *&c.*

BIBLIOGRAPHY: Unpublished.

ḤĀJJĪ[1]

Al-Malik al-Muẓaffar S. Ḥājjī b. Muḥammad b. Qalāūn, born 732, arrested in Jumādā I 747, acceded to the throne the 1st Jumādā II 747 (19th September 1346), killed the 12th Ramaḍān 748 (16th December 1347).

BLAZON: *Fleur-de-lis on undivided field.*

1. COPPER COIN (*fils*), Bibliothèque Nationale, Paris.

Obv. In centre: Fleur-de-lis within double circle, plain and dotted.

Rev. الملك المظفّر
———
بحلب

BIBLIOGRAPHY: Lavoix, *Catalogue des Monnaies Musulmanes de la Bibliothèque Nationale*, vol. *Égypte et Syrie*, No. 870, p. 356, pl. VII.

[1] Ibn Ḥabīb, pp. 384, 387; *Durar*, s.v. (Br.Mus., Or. 3043, fo. 103v–104r); Ṣāliḥ b. Yaḥyā, pp. 176–7; *Khiṭaṭ*, II, p. 240, ll. 14 ff. (2nd ed. III, p. 390, ll. 12 ff.); *Manhal*, s.v. (MS. Paris, Ar. 2070, fo. 12r–13v); Ibn Iyās, I, pp. 174, l. 18, 184–9, 210, l. 16; Weil, IV. 469, 470, 475.

2. COPPER COIN (*fils*), Bibliothèque Nationale, Paris; Palestine Archaeological Museum, Jerusalem.

Obv. In centre: Fleur-de-lis within circle.

On margin obliterated inscription:

ضرب . . . سبعمائه

Rev. In centre: جى
حا

On margin obliterated inscription:[1]

السلطان الملك . . . الدين

BIBLIOGRAPHY: Lavoix, l.c., Nos. 873 and 874, p. 357, pl. VII.

ḤALĪMA BINT AN-NĀNIQ (?)

BLAZON: *On upper field a napkin, on middle field a cup charged with a pen-box placed between a 'pair of trousers', on lower field a cup.*

COPPER DISH tinned over. Collection M. Eustache de Lorey,[2] Paris. Pl. LXII. 8, 11.
Inscription intersected by a shield.

برسم حليمة بنت النانق[3]

For Ḥalīma, daughter of an-Nāniq.

BIBLIOGRAPHY: Unpublished.

ḤUSAIN B. QAUṢŪN

BLAZON: *Two-fielded shield, upper field self-coloured, on lower field a red cup.*

STAND FOR A TRAY, Metropolitan Museum of Art, New York.

Inscription on upper half (*a*)

ممّا عمل برسم الجناب العالى المولوى الأميرى الكبيرى الغازى

[1] Text compiled from portions legible on both specimens mentioned in the bibliography.

[2] This dish, together with other objects in the collection of M. de Lorey, will be fully published by Prof. Wiet.

[3] My reading of this name is doubtful, the second part of it being perhaps دىس. A name تنق exists, cf. Ibn Iyās, Index, s.v. تنق باى, but not in composition with الىا. Cf. also the name ذانق (p. 171).

Inscription on lower half (*b*)

المخدومى الحسامى حسين بن المقرّ المرحوم ○ السيفى قوصون الملكى الناصرى

Inscription on the embossed collar (*c*)

○ ممّا عمل برسم الجناب العالى المولوى ○ الأميرى الكبيرى الخ

(a) *This is one of the objects made for His High Excellency* (janāb), *our Lord, the Great Amir, the Vanquisher*, (b) *the Well-Served, Ḥusām ad-dīn Ḥusain, son of His late Excellency Saif ad-dīn Qauṣūn*, (*officer*) *of al-Malik an-Nāṣir*.

(c) So far as is visible on the photograph repetition of (a) up to '*the Great Amir*'.

BIBLIOGRAPHY: Dimand, 'Near Eastern Metalwork' (in *Bulletin of the Metropolitan Museum of Art*, XXI, 1926, p. 199 and fig. 6).

IBRĀHĪM B. 'ABD AR-RAZZĀQ[1]

Sa'd ad-dīn Ibrāhīm b. 'Alam ad-dīn 'Abd ar-Razzāq b. Shams ad-dīn Ghurāb, of a family of Coptic officials,[2] qāḍī, started his career under Jamāl ad-dīn Maḥmūd al-Ustādār, the 19th Dhu-l-Ḥijja 798 (23rd September 1396) became Keeper of the Privy Purse (*nāẓir al-khāṣṣ*) before he was twenty years old, in addition to which he obtained the post of an Inspector of the Army (*nāẓir al-jaish*) under Faraj. On his dismissal the 19th Rabī' II 802 (19th December 1399) his property was confiscated, but shortly afterwards he was reappointed, then repeatedly dismissed from office but reappointed, during which time he obtained and lost the posts of Major-domo, Inspector of the Army, Keeper of the Privy Purse, and Privy Secretary (*kātib as-sirr*). The 7th Jumādā II 808 (30th November 1405) appointed *ra's mashwara*[3] with the rank of a Commander of a Thousand. Died the 19th Ramaḍān 808 (10th March 1406).

[1] *Ṣubḥ*, XI, p. 87; *Ḍau' aṣ-ṣubḥ*, p. 39, l. 2; *Khiṭaṭ*, II. 419f. (2nd ed. IV. 279–82); *Nujūm*, especially VI, pp. 91, l. 8 ff., 107, l. 11, 109, l. 1, 115, l. 6, 126, l. 9, 131, l. 2, 166, l. 10, 167, l. 2, 173, l. 8, 175, l. penult., 276 f.; *Manhal*, s.v. (MS. Paris, Ar. 2068, fo. 18ᵛ–20ʳ); *Ḍau'*, s.v. (MS. Leyden, Cod. Warn. 369 b, fo. 30ᵛ–31ᵛ); Ibn Iyās, I, pp. 304, l. 6 b, 330 l. ult., 339, ll. 13, 18, 6 b, 347, l. penult., 348, ll. 3, 22, 3 b; Weil, V. 99, 105–7; Herz, l.c.; Wiet, *Les Secrétaires de la Chancellerie en Égypte* (Mélanges René Basset) No. VIII, p. 7 f. (of the offprint) with further lit.; Björkman, *Beiträge*, p. 69.

[2] His grandfather Ghurāb was the first of his ancestors to profess Islam.

[3] *Ra's mashwara* or *amīr mashwara* is the old title of the *amīr al-majlis*, cf. *CIA. Égypte*, I, p. 585, n. 3, and compare *Nujūm*, VI, p. 173, l. 8 with p. 277, l. 1. According to Ibn Iyās, I, 347, l. penult., he was appointed *amīr majlis* in 804.

BLAZON: *Pen-box on the middle field of a three-fielded shield.*

ZĀWIYAH, Cairo.

A shield near the miḥrāb.

Badly damaged inscription on both sides of the doorway.
The essential portion of it:

. . ابراهيم بن غراب استاذ دار العالية . . . وناظر الجيوش المنصورة والخواصّ

الشريفة وما مع ذلك . . .

Ibrāhīm b. Ghurāb, the Major-domo . . . and Inspector of the victorious Armies and Keeper of the Privy Purse and what goes with it . . .

DATE: Between 803 and 808 (1400–6).

BIBLIOGRAPHY: Herz, *Zaouyeh Saad el-Dyn ibn Ghorâb à Darb el-Gamamiz, au Caire* (Appendix to *CR*. Exerc. 1911, fasc. 28, p. 126).

IBRĀHĪM B. ʿAQĪL

BLAZON: *Upper field blank, on united middle and lower fields crescent.*

COPPER PLATE, collection R. A. Harari, Esq., London. Pl. XLII. 3, XLVII. 2.

One shield in the centre of the plate, three others intersecting the inscription.

الجناب العالى المولوى الاميرى O الكبيرى الملكى الصارمى صارم O الدين [1]

ابراهيم ابن عقيل الشهابى عزّ انصاره O

His High Excellency (janāb), *our Lord, the Great Amir, the Royal, Ṣārim ad-dīn Ibrāhīm b. ʿAqīl ash-Shihābī, may his victories be glorious.*

BIBLIOGRAPHY: Unpublished.

[1] This word looks as if it had to be read الدار, but in reality the two *alifs* belong to ابراهيم and the *alif* over the *h* of هيم belongs to ابن.

IBRĀHĪM B. BAKTAMUR AL-ḤUSĀMĪ[1]

BLAZON: *A three-fielded round shield.*

CANDLESTICK, in the possession of Mr. A. E. Benachi, Athens, in 1880 in the collection Gaston de St. Maurice. Pl. XLV.

Two shields, both of them now disfigured by 8 diagonal lines, probably cut when the object passed into the hands of a new proprietor.

ممّا عمل برسم الجناب العالى ○ المولوى الأميرى الكبيرى | المخدومى المالكى

الجما○لى جمال [ا]لدين إبرهيم بن بكتمر الحسامى

This is one of the objects made for His High Excellency (janāb), *our Lord, the Great Amir, the Well-Served, the Royal, Jamāl ad-dīn Ibrahīm b. Baktamur al-Ḥusāmī.*

BIBLIOGRAPHY: Rogers, No. 29, p. 130, fig. 49 (omitting the last three words and reading the name Tamim).

Reproduced: P[ier], *Saracenic Heraldry*, fig. 14, p. 10.

IBRĀHĪM B. MUḤAMMAD B. YĀSĪN

BLAZON: *On upper field a napkin, on middle field a pen-box, on lower field a napkin.*

BRASS LANTERN, Kaiser Friedrich Museum, Berlin. Pl. LVII. 1–4.

The lantern has the shape of an octagonal pyramid, its upper part cut away and replaced by a globular crown. Three lines of inscription: (*a*) on the base, (*b*) on the upper portion of the octagon, (*c*) on the globe. In the middle of each side of the pyramid (except the one with the door) a shield.

(*a*) ممّا عمل برسم الجناب ا | العالى سيّدى إبرهيم | ابن المرحوم سيّدى محمّد

ابن الواثق بالملك الحقّ المبين الشيخ | ياسين ? غفر له وللمسلمين آمين [2]

(*b*) ممّا عمل برسم الجناب العالى القاضوى | البرهانى سيّدى إبراهيم ابن المرحوم

[1] Cf. the blazon of his father, p. 99.

[2] Text (*a*) being only an abridged version of (*b*) is not translated.

سيّدى محمّد ابن الواثق بالملك | الحقّ المبين سيّدى الشيخ | ياسين اللهم اغفر له وللمسلمين | آمين يا ربّ العالمين

This is one of the objects made for His High Excellency (janāb), *the Qāḍī Burhān ad-dīn Sīdī Ibrāhīm, son of the late Sīdī Muḥammad, son of the one trusting in the King, the Manifest Truth, Sīdī Shaikh Yāsīn, oh God forgive him and the Muslims, Amen. Oh Lord of the Worlds!*

(*c*) المقرّ الأشرف الكريم | العالى المولوى الا | الأميرى الكبيرى ا |

His Most Noble and Honourable and High Excellency, our Lord, the Great Amir, t[he . . .

BIBLIOGRAPHY: Unpublished.

ILYĀS B. SĀBIQ

BLAZON: *Emblem No. 24 without shield.*

SHRINE, locally known as Shaikh Ilyās, Gaza.

On the lintel of the entrance door inscription flanked by two blazons. The essential portion of it runs as follows:

. . . أمر بإنشاء هذا المسجد المبارك . . . الفقير الى الله تعالى الشيخ إلياس بن سابق بن خضر . . . فى شهر صفر سنة أحد وسبعين وستّمئة . . .

. . . *Ordered the construction of this blessed mosque . . . the servant yearning for God the Exalted, Shaikh Ilyās, son of Sābiq, son of Khiḍr . . . in the month of Ṣafar* 671 (began the 28th August 1272).

BIBLIOGRAPHY: Mayer, *Arabic Inscriptions of Gaza*, I, pp. 70 ff., pl. 1.

ISHIQTAMUR AL-MĀRIDĪNĪ[1]

S. Ishiqtamur al-Māridīnī, called an-Nāṣirī after al-Malik an-Nāṣir Ḥasan, grandson of Qalāūn, by whom he was educated and dubbed amir; was *amīr*

[1] Ibn Ḥabīb, pp. 414, 426, 432, 435, 436, 448, 450, 453, 463; Ibn Ḥajar, *Durar*, s.v. (MS. Br.Mus. Or.

majlis in 764, under al-Malik al-Ashraf Sha'bān became Governor of Aleppo, a post he held five different times, viz.: 765 till Rajab 766 (1363 March–April 1365), 771–3 (1369–71–2), 774–5 (1372–3–4), 775–80, 781–2 (10 months). In 776 he successfully besieged Sīs. Twice Governor of Tripoli, replacing first Qushtamur al-Manṣūrī and then Aydamur ad-Dawādār, three times Viceroy of Syria, viz. for four months in 775 (1373–4), from Rabī' I 782 till Muḥarram 784 (June–July 1380–April–March 1382), for four months in 788 (1386). Died in Aleppo either in Shawwāl 791[1] (September–October 1389), or in Jumādā I 789[2] (May–June 1387).

BLAZON: *Cup on the middle field of a three-fielded round shield.*

1. PUBLIC FOUNTAIN, Shāri' Ḥammām al-'Āshiq, Aleppo, locally known as Qasṭal Sakākīnī, now fallen into disuse.
Inscription in three lines within a bi-cuspid frame. Four shields in the corners.

(1) بسمله إِنَّ ٱلْأَبْرَارَ يَشْرَبُونَ مِنْ كَأْسٍ كَانَ مِزَاجُهَا كَافُورًا

(2) أنشأ هذا السبيل المبارك مولانا المقرّ الأشرف العالى المولوى الكافلى السيفى إشقتمر

(3) الأشرفي كافل الممالك الشريفة الحلبيّة المحروسة عزّ نصره في شهور سنة إحدى وسبعين وسبعمائة

In the name of the most merciful God. The just shall drink of a cup of wine, mixed with the water of Kāfūr (Qur'ān, LXXVI, 5). *Founded this blessed fountain our Lord, His Most Noble and High Excellency, our Lord, the Viceroy, Saif ad-dīn Ishiqtamur al-Ashrafī, Viceroy of the protected and noble provinces of Aleppo, may his victory be glorious. During the months of the year* 771 (began 5th August 1369).

BIBLIOGRAPHY: Unpublished.

3043, fo. 72v); Ibn Taghrībirdī, *Nujūm* (MS. Paris, Ar. 1786, fo. 211v–212r, 213v, 221v, l. 9), *Manhal*, s.v. with indication of vowels (MS. Paris, Ar. 2068, fos. 195v–196v and s.v. Aydamur al-Ānūkī ad-Dawādār); Ibn Iyās (throughout whose History the name is spelt 'Ishiqtamur عشقتمر, in one instance only does it appear as اشقتمر, and in another as طشقتمرى, the latter variant possibly being only a misprint) I, pp. 213, l. 13 b, ult., 226, l. 13 b, 265, l. 9, 266, ll. 4, 5 b, 3 b; Weil, IV. 488 f., 507, 511, 519, 524, 545; Sobernheim, *Arabische Gefässinschriften von der Ausstellung in Paris*, pp. 200–5; Rāghib Ṭabbākh, *A'lām*, II. 441 f., 449–53, V. 104–6.

[1] *Manhal*, l.c.

[2] Ibn Iyās, I, p. 266, l. 5 b.

2. BODY OF A CANDLESTICK, Max Freiherr v. Oppenheim-Stiftung, Berlin. Pl. XXXIII. 1, 2.

Inscription intersected by three shields.

المقرّ الأشرف العالى المولوى ○ المالكى المخدومى السيفى إشقتمر المنصورى ○

كافل الممالك الشريفة الشامية ○

His Most Noble and High Excellency, our Lord, the Royal, the Well-Served, Saif ad-dīn Ishiqtamur al-Manṣūrī, Viceroy of the noble Syrian provinces.

DATE: The appellation 'al-Manṣūrī', i.e. officer of al-Malik al-Manṣūr, enables us to date this object to within less than a year. The sultans who reigned during Ishiqtamur's three terms of office as Viceroy of Syria were al-Malik al-Ashraf Sha'bān, al-Malik al-Manṣūr 'Alī, al-Malik aṣ-Ṣāliḥ Ḥājjī, al-Malik aẓ-Ẓāhir Barqūq. Ishiqtamur could have styled himself both 'al-Manṣūrī' and 'Viceroy of Syria' only from Rabī' I 782, the date of his second appointment to that office, till the 23rd Ṣafar 783, the date of Sultan 'Alī's death or—at the latest—until the end of that month, assuming that at least four days[1] were needed before the news could reach Damascus. The candlestick must, therefore, have been made between the 5th June 1380 and the fourth week of May 1381.

BIBLIOGRAPHY: Unpublished.

ISMA'ĪL[2]

Al-Malik aṣ-Ṣāliḥ 'Imād[3] ad-dunyā wa-d-dīn Abu-l-Fidā' Isma'īl b. Muḥammad b. Qalāūn acceded to the throne the 22nd Muḥarram 743 (27th June 1342), died the 4th Rabī' II 746 (3rd August 1345), twenty years old.

BLAZON: *Six-petalled rosette on undivided field.*

COPPER COIN (*fils*), Bibliothèque Nationale, Paris; British Museum, London; Palestine Archaeological Museum, Jerusalem.

[1] Maqrīzī, *SM.* II a, p. 4, puts on record that in 678 (1279) the amirs Lājīn aṣ-Ṣaghīr and Baybars Jāliq covered the distance Cairo–Damascus in two days and seven hours, a story obviously too good to be true.

[2] Dhahabī, II, p. 193, l. 3 b; Ṣafadī, *A'yān*, s.v. (MS. Berlin, fo. 26^{v}–27^{r}); Ibn Ḥabīb, pp. 377, 383; Ṣāliḥ b. Yaḥyā, pp. 140, l. 10, 176, l. 4 ff.; *Khiṭaṭ*, II, p. 240, l. 7 ff. (2nd ed. III, p. 390, l. 3 ff.); *Manhal*, s.v. (MS. Paris, Ar. 2068, fo. 188^{v}–189^{v}); Ibn Iyās, I. 181 f.; Weil, IV. 452, 459; Cheikho in Ṣāliḥ, p. 146, n. 1.

[3] Ibn Iyās, I, p. 181, l. 13 b, calls him 'Alā' ad-dīn.

Obv. In centre: Six-petalled rosette within circle.

Around: سنة ثلاث وأربعين وسبعمائة

Rev. In centre: Six-petalled rosette within circle.

Around: السلطان الملك الصالح عماد الدنيا والدين

BIBLIOGRAPHY: Lane-Poole, *Catalogue of Oriental Coins*, IV, No. 538, p. 164; IX, No. 538 a, p. 351; Lavoix, *Catalogue des Monnaies Musulmanes*, vol. *Égypte et Syrie*, No. 865, p. 352, pl. VII.

JAMĀL AD-DĪN AL-MUẒAFFARĪ

BLAZON: *Cup on the middle field of a three-fielded shield.*

PUBLIC FOUNTAIN, Baalbek.

Two shields on the frame of the niche.

The historical portion of the inscription runs as follows:

(1) أمر بتجديد هذه السبيل! المبارك (2) العبد الفقير الى الله تعالى الأميرى

(3) الكبيرى المخدومى الجمالى المظفّرى (4) نائب السلطنة [الشريفة] ببعلبكّ

المحروسة

(a) وذلك (b) بتأريخ سنة (c) ثمان وأربعين (d) وسبعماية

Ordered the renewal of this blessed public fountain, the servant yearning for God the Exalted, the Great Amir, the Well-Served, Jamāl ad-dīn, (officer) of al-Malik al-Muẓaffar, Governor of the Noble Sultanate in Baalbek, the protected. This was done in the year 748 (1347).

BIBLIOGRAPHY: Sobernheim, *Baalbek in islamischer Zeit*, No. XXII, p. 26 f.

JĀNBALĀṬ B. YASHBAK[1] [2]

S. Jānbalāṭ, originally a mamluk of Yashbak min Mahdī, given as a present to Qāytbāy, made by the latter successively *jamdār, khāṣṣakī,* junior *dawādār,*

[1] So called in the only original text at my disposal. In view of the fact that he was a mamluk of Yashbak, Jānbalāṭ *min* Yashbak would have been probably more correct.

[2] Ibn Iyās, cf. Index, especially II, pp. 303, l. 6 b, 370, 392, l. 12 ff.; Weil, V. 351, 367, 372, 373–80, 387. Ṭabbākh, *A'lām* III. 107 f.

dubbed amir in 894 (1489), in 896—then Amir of Forty—sent to Constantinople as special envoy, on the 26 Dhu-l-Qaʿda 901 (4th August 1496) Amīr Dawādār, promoted by Qāytbāy to the rank of an Amir of a Hundred and Commander of a Thousand, in Rabīʿ II 903 (began 27th November 1497) appointed Governor of Aleppo, in Rabīʿ I 904 (began 17th October 1498) appointed Viceroy of Syria (after the death of Kurtbāy), and, after Uzbak's death, Commander-in-Chief, elected Sultan on the 2nd Dhu-l-Ḥijja 905 (29th June 1500), acceded to the throne as al-Malik al-Ashraf, deposed and imprisoned in Alexandria, the 5th Rajab 906 (25th January 1501), executed prior to the 4th Shaʿbān (23rd February) of that year.

BLAZON: *On upper field a napkin, on middle field a cup charged with a pen-box placed between a 'pair of trousers', on lower field a cup.*

1. COPPER BASIN, in 1880 in collection of E. T. Rogers Bey, present owner unknown. Inscription:

مـمّا عمل برسم المقرّ الأشرف الكريم العالى المولوى السيّد[ى] ? الملكى ? المخدومى

الأميرى الكبيرى السيفى جان بلاط اشرف ? الأشرافى ? أمير دوادار المقام الشريف

عزّ نصره [1]

This is one of the objects made for His Most Noble and Honourable and High Excellency, our Lord, the Master, the Royal, the Well-Served, the Great Amir, Saif ad-dīn Jānbalāṭ al-Ashrafī, Amīr Dawādār of His Majesty, may his victories be glorious.

DATE: Between Dhu-l-Qaʿda 901 and Rabīʿ II 903.

BIBLIOGRAPHY: Rogers, No. 13, p. 119, fig. 33.

Mentioned: Van Berchem, *Notes*, III. 76, Herz, *Deux lampes*, p. 183, n.

2. COPPER PLATE tinned over. Collection R. A. Harari, Esq., London. Inscription round a central medallion on back of plate. Both shield and inscription almost entirely obliterated.

[1] Not having seen the object I must content myself with indicating by question marks what I think was misread by Rogers.

مما عمل برسم المقرّ الأشرف العالى المولوى السيفى جان بلاط كافل المملكة

الحلبيّة الملكى الأشرفى

This is one of the objects made for His Most Noble and High Excellency, our Lord Saif ad-dīn Jānbalāṭ, Viceroy of the province of Aleppo of al-Malik al-Ashraf.

DATE: Between Rabīʿ II 903 and Rabīʿ I 904.

BIBLIOGRAPHY: Unpublished.

Mentioned: Mrs. R. L. Devonshire, *Some Dated Objects*, p. 122.

JĀNBALĀṬ[1]

BLAZON: *On upper field a napkin, on middle field a cup charged with a pen-box and placed between a 'pair of trousers', on lower field a cup.*

COPPER PLATE tinned over, present owner unknown.

○ مما عمل برسم المقرّ العالى ○ المولوى المخدومى السيفى ○ جان بلاط

الملكى الأشرفى

This is one of the objects made for His High Excellency, our Lord, the Well-Served, Saif ad-dīn Jānbalāṭ, (officer) of al-Malik al-Ashraf.

BIBLIOGRAPHY: Unpublished.

JĀNIBAK

BLAZON: *On upper field a napkin, on both middle and lower fields a cup.*

COPPER DISH tinned over. Collection R. A. Harari, Esq., London. Pl. LXII. 2. Four shields intersecting the inscription, the fifth, engraved in the centre of the dish, is now entirely obliterated.

[1] Perhaps identical with the preceding one.

مما عمل برسم المقرّ الأشرف الكريم ○ العالى المولوى المالكى المخدومى ○

السيفى جانبك [خايربك ?] الظاهرى أمير آخور ○ كبير الملكى الأشرفى عزّ

نصره ○

This is one of the objects made for His Most Noble and Honourable and High Excellency, our Lord, the Royal, the Well-Served, Saif ad-dīn Jānbak (or: Khāirbak) aẓ-Ẓāhirī, Grand Marshal of al-Malik al-Ashraf, may his victory be glorious.

BIBLIOGRAPHY: Unpublished.

JĀNĪBAK[1]

BLAZON: *On upper field a pen-box, on middle field a cup placed between two napkins, on lower field a fleur-de-lis.*

COPPER PLATE tinned over, collection J. W. A. Young, Esq., London. Pl. LVIII. 6, 8.

Inscription on back of plate intersected by heraldic shields. In the centre of the plate an obliterated shield.

مما عمل برسم المقرّ الأشرف الكريم ○ العالى المولوى الأميرى ○ المخدومى

السيفى جانى بك ○

This is one of the objects made for His Most Noble and Honourable and High Excellency, our Lord, the Amir, the Well-Served, Saif ad-dīn Jānībak.

On the rim the name of the maker is engraved: المعلّم صدقة ('the master Ṣadaqah'), and once more repeated صدقة ('Ṣadaqah').

BIBLIOGRAPHY: Unpublished.

[1] In view of the great number of amirs of this name—in the Index to Ibn Iyās 48 Jānībaks and 3 Jānībāys are mentioned—and the total absence of any indications as to the personal status of the holder of this blazon, no attempt is made to identify him.

JĀNĪBAK

BLAZON: *On upper field two napkins, on middle field a cup charged with two small cups, on lower field a cup.*

COPPER CANDLESTICK, present owner unknown.

المقرّ الأشرف العالى المولوى السيفى جانى بك أمير آخور السيفى تنم المؤيّدى

الملكى الظاهرى [Sauvaget]

His Most Noble and High Excellency, our Lord, Saif ad-din Jānībak, Marshal of Saif ad-dīn Tanam al-Mu'ayyadī, (officer) of al-Malik aẓ-Ẓāhir.

DATE: Even though, despite his high rank, Jānībak cannot be identified with any of his better-known namesakes, the candlestick can be dated within a few years. Of the three persons called Tanam al-Mu'ayyadī, viz. (*a*) the cupbearer, under Barsbāy, an Amir of a Hundred in Damascus, who died in 837,[1] (*b*) Tanam al-'Alā'ī al-Mu'ayyadī, the dawādār, a partisan of Aynāl al-Jakamī during his rebellion against Jaqmaq, executed in 842,[2] (*c*) Tanam min 'Abd ar-Razzāq al-Mu'ayyadī,[3] Chief of the Police (*muḥtasib*) under Jaqmaq, Inspector of the Haram at Mecca, later Governor of Alexandria, in 851 Governor of Hama, 851–2 Governor of Aleppo, the 13th Ṣafar 853 appointed *amīr majlis*, in 857 under al-Malik al-Manṣūr 'Uthmān *amīr silāḥ*, in 865 appointed Viceroy of Syria, died there in 868, only the last mentioned should be taken into consideration. In all probability the candlestick was made either between 851 and 852, or between 865 and 868.

BIBLIOGRAPHY: Unpublished.

JĀNĪBAK[4]

S. Jānībak b. 'Abdallāh, originally a mamluk of Asanbughā aṭ-Ṭayyārī, acquired by Jaqmaq, on the latter's accession to the throne, made a page

[1] *Manhal*, s.v. (MS. Paris, Ar. 2069, fo. 163^{v}).

[2] *Manhal*, s.v. (l.c. fo. 163^{v}–164^{r}).

[3] *Manhal*, s.v. (l.c. fo. $164^{r, v}$); *Nujūm*, VII. 788 ff.; Ibn Iyās, II, pp. 40, l. 7, 73, l. 3 f., 83, l. 20; Weil, V. 295; *CIA. Égypte*, I. 538 f.

[4] *Manhal*, s.v. (MS. Paris, Ar. 2069, fo. 182^{v}–184^{r}); Ibn Iyās, cf. Index, especially II, pp. 37, l. 13, 40, l. 14, 44, l. 9, 53, l. 10, 225, l. 7; Weil, V. 250, 260, 285–7, 298 f. This Jānībak should be distinguished from his namesake who in Rabī' II 880 (began 4th August 1475) was Governor of Bireh (Ibn Iyās, II, p. 159, l. 6), in 882 Governor of Jidda (Quṭb ad-dīn, *Chroniken der Stadt Mekka*, III. 226, quoted by van Berchem, *CIA. Égypte*, I, p. 421, n. 4).

(*khāṣṣakī*), dubbed amir, in charge of the harbour of Jidda from 849 (1445/6) to 855 (1451), and again from 856 (began 23rd January 1452) till Jaqmaq made his son ʿUthmān his successor. Appointed Major-domo by ʿUthmān b. Jaqmaq, held this office until Aynāl made him an Amir of Forty and once more Governor of Jidda. In 863 (began 8th November 1458) promoted to the rank of a Commander of a Thousand. On Khushqadam's accession to the throne appointed Grand Dawādār. Killed in Dhu-l-Ḥijja 867[1] (began 17th August 1463).

BLAZON: *On upper field a napkin, on middle field a cup crossed by a sword, on lower field a cup.*

1. MAUSOLEUM of Jānībak, Cairo.

There are two inscriptions to right and left of both the east and north entrance with Jānībak's name and titles, and a badly damaged inscription in the interior of the mausoleum with heraldic shields. The essential portion of the latter text runs as follows:

. . . الأميرى الكبيرى . . . بالديار المصريّة و[نا]ئب [السلطنة] الشريفة . . .

شهر رجب الفرد من سنة تسعة وستّين وثمانمائة . . .

. . . the Great Amir . . . [Grand Dawādār?] in the province of Egypt and Viceroy . . . during the month of Rajab the Unique, of the year 869[2] (March 1465). . . .

BIBLIOGRAPHY: *CIA. Égypte*, I. 412, and fig.

Reproduced: P[ier], *Saracenic Heraldry*, p. 10, fig. 9.

Mentioned: *CR.*, Exerc. 1892, fasc. 9 (2nd ed.), p. 69.

2. LINTEL from Jānībak's Mosque, National Museum of Arab Art, Cairo, No. 3788. One shield, almost obliterated.

BIBLIOGRAPHY: Unpublished.

JAQMAQ[3]

S. Jaqmaq, a freed mamluk of Arghūnshāh, after whose death on the 14th Shaʿbān 802 (10th April 1400) he passed into the service of Shaikh al-Maḥ-

[1] According to Weil, V. 298, on the 1st Dhu-l-Ḥijja 867; according to *Ḍau'*, s.v. J. aṭ-Ṭayyārī aẓ-Ẓāhirī, Director of Customs at Jidda, died in 868.

[2] With regard to this date, cf. Creswell, *Brief Chronology*, p. 136.

[3] *Nujūm*, VI, especially pp. 316, l. 18, 318, l. 19, 324, l. 11, 342, l. 12, 356, l. 6, 406, l. 10, 486, l. 11

mūdī who made him first Chief of the Corps of Jamdārs, then Junior Dawādār. The 9th Rabī' II 815 (19th July 1412) appointed dawādār to the Caliph; after Shaikh's accession Jaqmaq was dubbed amir, served in Syria, became Amir of Forty in Cairo and Second Dawādār, on the 25th Dhu-l-Ḥijja 818 (25th February 1416) succeeded Āqbāy al-Mu'ayyadī as Grand Dawādār, the 3rd Shawwāl 822 (23rd October 1419) appointed Viceroy of Syria. After the death of Sultan Shaikh refused to obey Ṭaṭar; defeated and executed the 26th Sha'bān 824 (26th August 1421). Buried in his madrasa in Damascus.

BLAZON: *On upper field a pen-box, on middle field a cup charged with two small cups, on lower field a cup.*

MADRASA, Damascus, near the North Gate of the Main Mosque. The historical portion of the inscription runs as follows:

... أنشأ هذه الخانقاة والتربة المباركتين المقرّ الأشرف العالى المولوى الأميرى
الكبيرى العالمى العادلى الممهّدى العابدى الحاشمى؟ الناسكى الزعيمى المقدّمى الذخرى
الظهيرى السيفى عزّ الإسلام والمسلمين سيّد الأمراء فى العالمين سيف أمير المؤمنين جقمق
الدوادار المؤيّدى كا[فل المما]لك الشاميّة المحروسة ضاعف الله له الثواب وغفر له
ولوالديه ولأحبابه يوم الحساب بمباشرة الجناب السيفى تغرىورمش فى شهور سنة
أربع وعشرين وثمان مائة

Constructed this blessed monastery and mausoleum His Most Noble and High Excellency, our Lord, the Great Amir, the Learned, the Just, the Administrator, the Worshipper, the Chieftain, the Commander, the Treasure, the Protector, Saif ad-dīn, the Glory of the Islam and the Muslims, the Lord of Amirs in the Worlds, the Sword of the Caliph, Jaqmaq, the Dawādār, al-Mu'ayyadī, Viceroy of the protected Syrian provinces, may God double his reward and forgive him and his parents and his friends on the day of the settling, under the direction of His Excellency (janāb), *Saif ad-dīn Taghrīwirmish during the months of the year* 824 (1421).

BIBLIOGRAPHY: Unpublished.

Inscription partly copied: *CIA Egypte*, I, p. 449, n. 3.

Mentioned and reproduced: Wulzinger und Watzinger, *Damaskus*, p. 63, No. 11, pl. 22a.

492, l. 14, 503, l. 17, 551–3, 829, l. 3; *Manhal*, s.v. (MS. Paris, Ar. 2069, fo. 189^{v}–190^{v}); Ibn Iyās, II, pp. 11, l. 10, 13, l. 17, 16, l. 8; Weil, V. 127, 158, 160.

JAUHAR AL-MUʿĪNĪ[1]

Z. Jauhar the Abyssinian, called al-Muʿīnī after Muʿīn ad-dīn ad-Dimyāṭī, passed into the service of Birdibak al-Ashrafī, under Qāytbāy became cup-bearer, in 902 (1497) succeeded Fīrūz ar-Rūmī as Warden of the Princesses (*zimām*), died either in 905 or 906. In Jumādā II 906 (began 23rd December 1500) replaced by ʿAbd al-Laṭīf, the eunuch.

BLAZON: *On upper field a napkin, on middle field a cup charged with a pen-box and placed between a 'pair of trousers', on lower field a cup.*

EWER, Musée de la Ville, Lyon.
One shield.
Inscription on spout:

المقرّ الزينى جوهر المعينى

His Excellency Zain ad-dīn Jauhar al-Muʿīnī.

Inscription on body:

المقرّ الأشرف الكريم العالى المولوى الأميرى الكبيرى | المخدومى المحترمى

[one word] الزينى جوهر المعينى أمير رأس نوبة الآدر الشريفة دام عزّه

His Most Noble and Honourable and High Excellency, our Lord, the Great Amir, the Well-Served, the Honoured . . . Zain ad-dīn Jauhar al-Muʿīnī, the Warden of the Noble Princesses, may his glory last for ever.

BIBLIOGRAPHY: Unpublished.

JURJĪ AN-NĀṢIRĪ[2]

S. Jurjī, originally a mamluk of Muḥammad b. Qalāūn, Junior Dawādār under al-Malik aṣ-Ṣāliḥ Ismaʿīl, in Jumādā II 748 (began the 8th September 1347) appointed Grand Dawādār by al-Malik al-Muẓaffar Ḥājjī. After Ḥājjī's death, in Ramaḍān of the same year, was sent to Damascus as Amir of Ten, returned

[1] *Ḍau'*, s.v., Ibn Iyās, II, p. 318, l. 7, 352, l. 15, 362, l. 15, 381–2.

[2] Ṣafadī, *Wāfī*, s.v. (MS. Br. Mus., Add. 23357, fo. 125ʳ); Ibn Ḥabīb, pp. 416, 417, 429; Ibn Ḥajar, *Durar*, s.v. (MS. Br. Mus., Or. 3043, fo. 101ᵛ); *Manhal*, s.v. (MS. Paris, Ar. 2069, fo. 188ʳ and ᵛ).

to Cairo as Amir of Forty, became Second Chamberlain, under Ḥasan appointed Treasurer, under al-Malik al-Ashraf Sha'bān Grand Marshal; in 766 made Governor of Aleppo, remained in office for about two years, transferred to Damascus as Commander-in-Chief, died there Ṣafar 772 (began 25th August 1370).

BLAZON: *Upper and lower fields red, a red pen-box on a white middle field.*

GLASS FLAGON, Victoria and Albert Museum, London, 223—'79. Inscription on body:

المقرّ الكريم العالى ا | لمولوى المالكى المخدومى | السيفى جرجى أستادار ا |

العالية بالأبواب الشريفة ا | الملكى الناصرى أعزّ أنصاره و | ضاعف اقتداره

His Honourable and High Excellency, our Lord, the Royal, the Well-Served, Saif ad-dīn Jurjī, Major-domo of the Noble Porte, (officer) of al-Malik an-Nāṣir, may (God) make his victories glorious and double his power.

DATE: Between 748 (al-Malik an-Nāṣir Ḥasan's first accession to the throne) and 762 (the year of Jurjī's death).

BIBLIOGRAPHY: Schmoranz, pp. 25, 59, 68, fig. 56, pl. XXV; Artin, *Contribution*, No. 104, p. 124 f.; Wiet, *Lampes*, p. 162, No. 41.

Mentioned: *CIA. Égypte*, I. 762; Herz, *Deux lampes*, p. 184, n.; Migeon, *Manuel* (2nd ed.), II. 130; Lamm, p. 406 f.

KĀFŪR[1]

Shibl ad-daula Kāfūr aṣ-Ṣafawī, originally a eunuch of al-Malik al-'Ādil (most likely Abū Bakr II), served as *khāzindār* in the fortress of Damascus under Baybars, Baraka Khān, and Qalāūn, for some time also as Governor of the fortress of Damascus. Died there in 684 (began 9th March 1285).

BLAZON: *White six-petalled rosette on undivided red shield.*

GLASS LAMP, Victoria and Albert Museum, London, 6820—1860.
Inscription on neck (1), intersected by three shields, continued on the body (2). Three further shields on the lower part of the body.

[1] *Manhal*, s.v. (MS. Paris, Ar. 2072, fo. 37v).

(1) ممّا عمل برسم الجناب | العالى ا ا | المولوى الشبلى |

(2) كافور الرومى الخزندار الملكى ا ا | الصالحى أعزّ أنصاره |

This is one of the objects made for His High Excellency (janāb), *our Lord, Shibl ad-daula Kāfūr ar-Rūmī, the* khāzindār, (*officer*) *of al-Malik aṣ-Ṣāliḥ, may* (*God*) *make his victories glorious.*

There is some difficulty in the attribution of this lamp. Of the three Kāfūrs, whose biographies are given in the *Manhal*, two bear the honorific surname Shibl ad-daula, and one, K. aṣ-Ṣafawī, is mentioned as having served in the capacity of *khāzindār*. On the other hand, on the lamp K. is called aṣ-Ṣāliḥī, which would seem to fit better K. al-Hindī, who, having died in 786 (24th February 1384–11th February 1385) could have easily served either aṣ-Ṣāliḥ Isma'īl or aṣ-Ṣāliḥ Ṣāliḥ or even aṣ-Ṣāliḥ Ḥājjī, whereas the nearest Ṣāliḥ with whom K. aṣ-Ṣafawī could have been connected is Najm ad-dīn Ayyūb. Seeing, however, that K. al-Hindī is not known to have been a *khāzindār* and that he was not of Anatolian origin, he need not be taken into consideration.

BIBLIOGRAPHY: Nesbitt, *A Descriptive Catalogue of the Glass Vessels in the South Kensington Museum*, p. 35 f.; Lane-Poole, *Art of the Saracens*, p. 255; van Berchem, *Notes*, III. 81 ff.

Mentioned and reproduced: Schmoranz, fig. 46; Artin, *Contribution*, No. 300, p. 172; Lamm, p. 443, pl. 200, fig. 2.

Mentioned: Migeon, *Manuel* (2nd ed.), II. 134; Wiet, *Lampes*, p. 164, No. 51.

KHĀIRBAK B. BILBĀY[1]

S. Khāirbak b. Bilbāy, a mamluk of Qāytbāy, became his *jamdār,* subsequently a page, and eventually Junior Dawādār; in 901, under Muḥammad b. Qāytbāy dubbed Amir of Ten, some time later, under his reign, promoted to the rank of an Amir of Forty, under Jānbalāṭ became Amir of a Hundred. In 906, after Qānṣūh al-Ghaurī's accession, became Grand Chamberlain, in 910 appointed Governor of Aleppo, remained in office till the Ottoman conquest, on the 11th (or 13th) Sha'bān 923 (29th or 31st August 1517) became Governor of Egypt. Died the 14th Dhu-l-Qa'da 928 (5th October 1522).

[1] Ibn Iyās, especially III, pp. 3, l. 17, 62, l. 2, 131, ll. 2, 5 b, 314, l. 18–316, l. 11. In the Index many passages refer to Khāirbak, the 'Sultan of one night', and several others; Ibn Ṭūlūn, esp. 60 [٣٥], l. 4 b, 46 [٣٩], l. 8 b, 36 [٤٩], l. 9; Hammer, *Geschichte des Osmanischen Reiches*, II. 473, 507, III. 34; Weil, V. 412, n. 1, 436; Lane-Poole, *History of Egypt*, p. 355; *CIA. Égypte*, I. 567 f., 602, n. 2; van Berchem, *Inschriften Oppenheim*, p. 53; Ṭabbākh, *A'lām*, III. 113–115, V. 429–34.

BLAZON: *On upper field a napkin, on middle field a cup charged with a pen-box placed between a 'pair of trousers', on lower field a cup.*

1. MAUSOLEUM, near Bāb al-Maqām, Aleppo, locally known as 'Shaikh 'Alī Shātīlā'.

Inscription along the façade of the building, intersected by shields. A few shields on the north and west walls.

بسمله . . . أنشأ هذه التربة المباركة المقرّ الأشرف الكريم العالى المولوى الكافلى

السيفى خايربك الأشرفى كافل المملكة الحلبيّة المحروسة أعزّ الله تعالى أنصاره

بتاريخ شهر ربيع الأوّل عام عشرين وتسعمائة

In the name of the most merciful God. Constructed this blessed mausoleum His Most Noble and Honourable and High Excellency, our Lord, the Viceroy Saif ad-dīn Khāirbak al-Ashrafī, Viceroy of the protected province of Aleppo, may God the Exalted make his victories glorious; on the date of Rabī' I of the year 920 (began 26th April 1514).

BIBLIOGRAPHY: Van Berchem, *Inschriften Oppenheim*, p. 53, No. 61, fig. 8; Bischoff, *Tuḥaf al-anbā'*, p. 149; Tabbākh, l.c., V. 434.

Mentioned and reproduced: Herzfeld in Djemal Pasha, *Alte Denkmäler*, pl. 46 b.; Devonshire, *Cairo Mosques*, p. 110, pl.; Glück-Diez, *Kunst d. Islam*, p. 189.

2. CARAVANSERAI, Aleppo, locally known as 'Khān Khāirabak'.
Inscriptions divided into two halves one on each leaf of the iron door of the khan. Two painted shields on the door, thirteen others in the courtyard. The date of the painting is doubtful.

(1) ممّا عمل برسم المقرّ الأشرف الكريم العالى خايربك الأشرفى (2) كافل

المملكة الحلبيّة المحروسة أعزّ الله أنصاره فى ربيع الأوّل سنة عشرين وتسعمائة

This was made for His Most Noble and Honourable and High Excellency Khāirbak al-Ashrafī, Viceroy of the protected province of Aleppo, may God make his victories glorious; in Rabī' I 920 (began 26th April 1514).

BIBLIOGRAPHY: Unpublished.

KHĀIRBAK[1]

BLAZON: *On upper field a napkin, on middle field a cup charged with a pen-box placed between a 'pair of trousers', on lower field a cup.*

COPPER DISH tinned over. Collection J. W. A. Young, Esq.,London. Inscription intersected by three shields.

ممّا عمل برسم المقرّ الكريم (ا)لعا(لى) ○ المولوى السيفى خايربك عين

مقدّمين ○ الألوف بالديار المصريّة [2] عزّ نصره ○

This is one of the objects made for His Honourable and High Excellency Saif ad-dīn Khāirbak, Commander designate of a Thousand in the province of Egypt, may his victory be glorious.

BIBLIOGRAPHY: Unpublished.

Mentioned: Mayer, *Guide to the Exhibition of Moslem Heraldry*, p. 5.

KHĀIRBAK[3] MIN[4] AYNĀL[5]

S. Khāirbak min Aynāl, originally a mamluk of Aynāl al-Ashqar, served at the head of the army (*bāsh al-ʿaskar*), appointed District Officer of the Gharbiyya province not later than 902 (1496/7), dismissed in Rabīʿ II 905 (began 5th November 1499), lived in exile, after Jānbalāṭ's accession to the throne returned to Cairo, promoted to the rank of Commander of a Thousand, leader of a successful expedition to the Ḥijāz against the Banū Ibrahīm tribe. Died Thursday, 2nd Ṣafar 922 (7th March 1516).

BLAZON: *On upper field a napkin, on middle field a cup charged with a pen-box and placed between a 'pair of trousers', on lower field a small cup. The napkin, the cup on the middle field, the 'trousers', and the lower field are ornamented.*

1 Perhaps identical with the preceding one.

2 The *alif* of المصريّة is out of place and looks more like a *lām*.

3 The spelling of this name varies, both forms, with and without the *alif*, being used, e.g. Ibn Iyās, II, p. 380, l. 6 b.

4 Sometimes called '*ibn* Aynāl', a mistake easily explicable by the similarity of بن and من in Arabic. That *min* is the proper word is proved by the statement of Ibn Iyās that he was the *mamluk* of Aynāl (and not his son), cf. the texts mentioned in the following note.

5 Ibn Iyās, II, pp. 324, l. 1, 336, l. 4 b, 362, ll. 10 b ff., 375, ll. 12 b ff., 380, l. 6 b, 384, l. 9 b (mentioned among Amirs of Twenty), III, p. 3, l. 11, 10–11; Weil, V. 391, n. 3. The references to this amir are scattered in the index to Ibn Iyās over Kh. as-Saifī Aynāl, Kh. al-kāshif, and Kh. kāshif al-Gharbiyya.

COPPER BASIN, in possession of M. Henri Léman, 37 Rue Lafitte, Paris.
Shields on the outside and inside of the basin.
Inscription:

(1) ممّا عمل برسم الجناب العالى المولوى الأمير الكبيرى

(2) السيفى خايربك من اينال ملك الأمرآء بالغربيّة

This is one of the objects made for His High Excellency (janāb), *our Lord, the Great Amir, Saif ad-dīn Khāirbak min Aynāl, Governor-General of the Gharbiyya province.*

BIBLIOGRAPHY: Unpublished.

KHĀLID

BLAZON: *Upper field blank, on the yellow united middle and lower fields a dark brown cup. Pointed shield.*

POTSHERD excavated at Fusṭāṭ, now in the National Museum of Arab Art, Cairo, No. 5109. Pl. VI. 11.

Inscription intersected by one shield.

ممّا ع[مل . . .] المخدومى الشمسى شمس الدين خالد O

This is one of the objects m[ade for . . .] the Well-Served, Shams ad-dīn Khālid.

BIBLIOGRAPHY: Unpublished.

KHALĪL[1]

BLAZON: *Emblem No. 26 displayed on a round shield (or on a table?) placed on the middle field of a three-fielded shield.*

QUR'ĀN PULPIT of the Main Mosque, Qūṣ. Pl. XLIII. 1.
Inscription intersected by three shields.

[1] Perhaps identical with one of the two Khalīls whose letters of appointment to the offices of an Inspector of the Southern District of Syria and of a *mihmandār* respectively, are reproduced in Qalqashandī, *Ṣubḥ*, XII. 296 f., 313 ff.

(A)—Qur. II. 256—القيّوم ○—(B) السموات—حفـ(C)ظهما—العظيم ○ صدق الله العظيم (D) أمر بانشاء هذا المصحف المبارك المقرّ الكريم العالى المولوى الأميرى الأجلّى ○ العررى عرر[1] الدين خليل الملكى الناصرى أعزّ الله أنصاره بمحمّد واله [Wiet]

. . . Ordered the construction of this blessed reading-desk His Noble and High Excellency, our Lord, the Most Magnificent Amir, Ghars (?) *ad-dīn Khalīl,* (*officer*) *of al-Malik an-Nāṣir, may God make his victories glorious . . .*

BIBLIOGRAPHY: Unpublished.

KHUDĀBIRDĪ AL-ASHRAFĪ[2]

S. Khudābirdī, appointed Governor of Alexandria before 922 (began 5th February 1516), in 922 promoted to the rank of a Commander of a Thousand and in Ramaḍān of the same year replaced by Tanam as-Saifī Mughulbāy. Killed in battle near Baisan the 24th Dhu-l-Qaʿda 922 (17th December 1516).

BLAZON: *On upper field a napkin, on middle field a cup charged with a pen-box placed between a 'pair of trousers', on lower field a cup.*

COPPER PLATE tinned over, National Museum of Arab Art, Cairo, No. 4456, originally in the collection of J. Home, Esq., Cairo.

Inscription round the shield in the centre of the plate.

ممّا عمل برسم الجناب العالى المولوى الأميرى السيفى خدابردى عزّ أنصاره

This is one of the objects made for His High Excellency (janāb), *our Lord, the Amir, Saif ad-dīn Khudābirdī, may his victories be glorious.*

On the back of the plate there is another inscription, very clumsily engraved several years later, when Khudābirdī was much more advanced in his career:

برسم المقرّ الأشرف | السيفى خدابردى | الأشرفى كافل الثغر السكندرى | أعزّ الله أنصاره

[1] عرر dût-il être lu غرز pour غرس? [Wiet].

[2] Ibn Iyās, III. pp. 3, l. 14, 26, l. 11, 73, l. 11, 75, l. 8, 80, l. 11.

For His Most Noble Excellency Saif ad-dīn Khudābirdī al-Ashrafī, Viceroy of the March of Alexandria, may God make his victories glorious.

BIBLIOGRAPHY: *CR.* 1915–19, fasc. 32, p. 499 f.

KHUDĀBIRDĪ AẒ-ẒĀHIRĪ[1]

Khudābirdī aẓ-Ẓāhirī died after Muḥarram 954.

BLAZON: *Cup on undivided shield.*

CENOTAPH, National Museum of Arab Art, Cairo, No. 3568. Pl. XXV.

The historical portion of the inscription:

(1) ممّا عمل برسم الأمير خضابردى الظاهرى (2) [معم]ار درب الحاجّ الأمير

خضابردى الظاهرى [3-4 words] (3) الأمير خضابردى الظاهرى (4) ممّا عمل

برسم الأمير خضابردى الظاهرى المعمار بدرب الحجاز غفر الله له وللمسلمين [Wiet]

This is one of the objects made for the Amir Khuḍābirdī aẓ-Ẓāhirī, builder of the Pilgrims' Road, Amir Khuḍābirdī aẓ-Ẓāhirī . . . This is one of the objects made for the Amir Khuḍābirdī aẓ-Ẓāhirī, builder of the Ḥijāẓ Road, may God forgive him and the Muslims.

BIBLIOGRAPHY: Unpublished.

Described: *CR.* Exerc. 1908, p. 103.

KHUSHKILDĪ

BLAZON: ***On upper field a napkin, on middle field a cup charged with a pen-box placed between a 'pair of trousers', on lower field a cup.***

COPPER PLATE tinned over, National Museum of Arab Art, Cairo, No. 5694.

Inscription in the centre of the plate illegible.

Inscription on the borders intersected by four shields.

[1] *CR.* Exerc. 1913, p. 130 f.

ممّا عمل برسم المقرّ الأشرف ○ العالى المولوى الأميرى ○ الكبيرى السيفى

خشكلدى ○ الخازندار الأُشرفى ○

This is one of the objects made for His Most Noble and High Excellency, our Lord, the Great Amir, Saif ad-dīn Khushkildī, the Treasurer of (al-Malik) al-Ashraf.

BIBLIOGRAPHY: Unpublished.

KHUSHQADAM[1]

Z. Khushqadam, the eunuch, called al-Aḥmadī after the merchant of slaves who sold him, in 873 (1468/9) became Chief of the Corps of Cup-bearers (*ra's naubat as-suqāt*), in 879 (1474) replaced Yashbak, the Dawādār, as vizier, in Rabīʿ I 882 (began 13th June 1477) appointed Great Treasurer (*khāzindār*) and Warden (*zimām*) of the Princesses, in 884 (1479/80) leader of the pilgrims' caravan to Mecca, in Rabīʿ II 889 (began 28th April 1484) dismissed from the vizierate, in Ramaḍān 891 (September 1486) exiled to Qūṣ, in Muḥarram 894 (began 5th December 1488) exiled to Suwākin, died there in Shawwāl 894 (began 28th August 1489).

BLAZON: *On red upper field a white napkin, on white middle field a black cup placed between a red 'pair of trousers' with white openings, on black lower field a white cup.*[2]

1. LUNCH-BOX (*maṭbaqiyya*), Victoria and Albert Museum, London, No. 1242—'88. Pl. LXVIII. 9, 10.

Inscription on lid, repeated on body.

ممّا عمل برسم المقرّ الأشرف العالى | المولوى الأميرى الكبيرى الزينى |

خشقدم الصاحب زمام الآدر الشريفة | وأمير خازندار[3] وما مع ذلك الملكى . . .

[1] Ibn Iyās, II, pp. 108, l. ult, 152, l. 5 b, 172, l. 16, 190–1, 193, l. penult., 194, l. 15, 207, l. 13, 215, ll. 11, 17, 222, l. 5, 223, l. 16, 233, l. 6, 238, ll. 5, 12, 256, l. 2, 261, l. 12; Weil, V. 356 (the one mentioned V. 219, n. 1, is not identical with Khushqadam al-Aḥmadī); Herz, *Mosquée Khoshqadam el-Ahmadi, à Darb el-Hosr, au Caire* (in *CR.* 1909, p. 163 f.).

[2] The colours are given according to Herz, l.c., p. 162, n. 2. Artin's drawing, *Contribution*, No. 85, is slightly different, the napkin, the openings of the 'trousers', and the cup on the lower field being golden.

[3] This word is spelt in the inscription on the body: خازندام by mistake of the engraver.

This is one of the objects made for His Most Noble and High Excellency, our Lord, the Great Amir, Zain ad-dīn Khushqadam, the Vizier, Warden of the Noble Princesses, and Amīr Treasurer and what is implied by it, (officer) of al-Malik . . .

BIBLIOGRAPHY: Unpublished.

2. MADRASA,[1] Cairo. Pl. LXI. 1.

On the ceiling of a corridor several painted shields.

BIBLIOGRAPHY: Unpublished.

Blazon described: Herz, l.c., p. 162.

Reproduced: Artin, *Contribution*, p. 118 f., No. 85.

KITBUGHĀ[2]

Z. Kitbughā b. ʿAbdallāh al-Manṣūrī, made prisoner in the first battle of Hims in 659 A.H.,[3] taken by Sultan Qalāūn, who freed and educated him and under whom he became one of the highest amirs. Despite a relatively short time spent in prison, his position remained unchanged under the reign of al-Malik al-Ashraf Khalīl and the first reign of al-Malik an-Nāṣir Muḥammad, whose Viceroy he was. Elevated to the throne on the 11th Muḥarram 694,[4] he assumed the title of al-Malik al-ʿĀdil. After his deposition in 696 by Lājīn fled to the fortress of Damascus where for a while he remained a prisoner. Later in the year appointed Governor of Ṣarkhad, where he remained until Muḥammad b. Qalāūn's second accession to the throne. Made Governor of Hama by the latter, a position Kitbughā held till his death on the 10th Dhu-l-Ḥijja 702 (26th July 1303). Buried in his mausoleum in Damascus, on the slope of Jabal Qāsyūn, to the west of the Ribāṭ an-Nāṣirī.

[1] For the history of this building and the attribution of its various portions to their respective builders cf. Herz, l.c., and Creswell, *Brief Chronology*, p. 111 f.

[2] Zettersteen, *Beiträge*, cf. Index, especially pp. 26, l. 4, 29, l. 9, 31, ll. 9, 10, 33, l. 7, 40–3, 45, l. 15, 81, l. ult., 96, l. 17, 108, l. 11, 130, l. 15, 131, l. 18, 133, l. 20, 223, l. 17; Dhahabī (ed. Hyderabad), II, pp. 151, l. 5 b, 152, l. 7 b, 154–5, 162–3; Ibn al-Wardī, II, especially pp. 238–9, 242, l. 4 ff., 251–2; Mufaḍḍal, pp. 370, 374, 412, 421–3, 432, 439, 445, 507; Kutubī, s.v., II. 138; *Jawāhir as-sulūk* (MS. Br. Mus., Or. 6854, fo. 210), *SM.* II a, 12, 27, 113, 121, II b, 21–39, 43 f., 169, 220, 226; *Khiṭaṭ*, II, p. 239, ll. 15 ff.; Ibn Ḥajar, *Durar*, s.v. (MS. Br. Mus., Or. 3043, fo. 41^{r,v}); *Manhal*, s.v. (MS. Paris, Ar. 2072, fo. 38^{v} ff.), and s.v. Salār (MS. Paris, Ar. 2070, fo. 94^{r}); Ibn Iyās, especially I, pp. 115, l. 1, 129, l. 9 b, 133, 135, l. 12 b ff., 136, l. 1, 174, l. 5 b; Mujīr ad-dīn, p. 436–437; Weil, especially IV. 175, 191, 197, 202, 203, 206, 236; Blochet in Mufaḍḍal, l.c., p. 53 f.

[3] According to Ibn Ḥajar, l.c., in 658.

[4] According to Manhal, l.c.: on the 11th or 9th, Mujīr ad-dīn: on the 9th.

BLAZON: (a) *Cup on undivided shield,*

(b) *Cup on lower part of a two-fielded U-shaped shield.*

1. COPPER COIN (*fils*), Palestine Archaeological Museum, Jerusalem. Pl. XX. 2, 4.

Obv. Within double circle, plain and dotted:

السلطا

ن الملك ا

لعادل

Rev. Chalice within double circle, plain and dotted.

(*a*) 2·241 gr., maximum width 18 mm.
(*b*) 1·713 gr., maximum width 17 mm.

BIBLIOGRAPHY: Unpublished.

Reproduced in William Marsden, 'The Oriental Coins, ancient and modern, of his collection, described and historically illustrated' (in *Numismata Orientalia*, Part 1), London, 1823, No. 301, p. 291 f., pl. XVII. Marsden could neither read the title of the sultan (*al-ʿādil*) nor classify the coin.

2. ILLUSTRATION in adh-Dhahabī, *al-Muntaqā min taʾrīkh al-islām*, VII, manuscript in the library of Ahmed Zeki Pasha, Cairo.

S.a. 694:

. . . وكان رنكه فى أيّام إمرته هكذا  وفى أيّام ملكه الرايات الصفر . . .

'*While amir he* (i.e. Kitbughā) *carried this coat of arms*(fig.), *while king yellow banners.*' The fact that some of his coins displayed the cup clearly shows that the passage quoted should not be understood as if Kitbughā's sultanian banner were plain yellow cloth. Adh-Dhahabī wanted to specify the colour which was obviously different from that which Kitbughā used on his amirial banners, but he could not have meant that the emblem was suppressed.

BIBLIOGRAPHY: Ahmed Zeki Pacha, *Les Couleurs Nationales de l'Égypte Musulmane*, Cairo, 1921, p. 26.

Mentioned: Mayer, *Arabic Inscriptions of Gaza*, I. 72.

KUJKUN[1, 2]

S. Kujkun b. ʿAbdallāh al-Manṣūrī, made Amir of Ten in Damascus by Muḥammad b. Qalāūn, probably during the period of his first reign,[3] proclaimed in Damascus Lājīn's accession to the throne, died in 739 (1338/9) nearly ninety years old.

BLAZON: *Three-fielded shield.*

MAUSOLEUM, Damascus, 55 Shāriʿ as-Sikkeh, Waqf No. 162. Pl. XLIV. 1. Inscription on façade, flanked by two shields.

(1) بسمله . . . هذا ما أنشأه وأوقفه وحبسه على التربة المباركة المقرّ العالى

المولوى الأميرى الكبيرى (2) المخدومى السيفى كجكن بن عبد الله الملكى

الناصرى أعزّه الله جميع ما يذكر وهو جميع الكرم ببلد المعروف بجنينة المسكى

قديمًا وجميع القيساريّة جوار الدار المباركة (3) بدمشق ومن غربها جميع الحديقة

جوار الدار المذكورة ومن شرقها شمالى المدرسة الريحانيّة وجميع الحصّة وهى سبع

قراريط بحارة قصر حجّاج وقفًا بدار وذلك فى سنة اثنتى وعشرين وسبعمائة

In the name of the most merciful God. This was founded and constituted as a waqf for the mausoleum by His High Excellency, our Lord, the Great Amir, the Well-Served, Saif ad-dīn Kujkun b. ʿAbdallāh, (officer) of al-Malik an-Nāṣir, may God give him strength, all that is mentioned (herewith), namely, the whole of the vineyard in the village, formerly known as Junainat al-Musakī, and the whole of the bazaar-street in the vicinity of the blessed house[4] in Damascus, to the west of it the whole of the fruit-garden in the vicinity of the aforementioned house and to the

[1] Zetterstéen, *Beiträge*, pp. 42, l. 19, 47, ll. 17, 18, 48, l. 15, 49, l. 9, 110, l. 12; Dhahabī, *Duwal al-islām*, II (Hyderabad, 1337 A.H.), p. 190, l. 4; *Durar*, s.v. (MS. Br. Mus., Or. 3044, fo. 42ʳ); *Manhal*, s.v. (MS. Paris, Ar. 2072, fo. 41ʳ), and s.v. Kitbughā (ib., fo. 39ᵛ, l. 13); Birzālī, *al-Muntakhab*, s.a. 696 (MS. Berlin, fo. 463ʳ); Kutubī, *Fawāt al-wafayāt*, II, p. 139, l. 6 (biography of Kitbughā) where كجلن is a misprint for كجكن; *SM.* II. b, 45; Weil, IV. 206, 211, 221.

[2] So spelt by Ibn Taghrībirdī, *Manhal*, s.v., and explained as يوم صعب 'a difficult day'.

[3] Zetterstéen, *Beiträge*, p. 42, l. 19, he is mentioned as one of the amirs of Damascus in a passage relating Lājīn's accession to the throne, 696 A.H.

[4] Perhaps a reference to Kujkun's private house.

east of it the north side of the Madrasa Rīḥāniyya and the whole of a share consisting of seven parts (out of twenty-four) *in the quarter Qaṣr Ḥajjāj. . . . In the year* 722 (1322).

BIBLIOGRAPHY: Unpublished.

KUMUSHBUGHĀ[1]

S. Kumushbughā al-Ḥamawī, originally a mamluk of Abu-l-Fidā''s son, who presented him to Sultan Ḥasan. On the death of the latter he passed into the service of Yalbughā al-ʿUmarī, at whose death, the 10th Rabīʿ II 768 (14th December 1366), he was Chief of a Corps of Mamluks (*ra's nauba*). Served under Asandamur, following whose defeat he was imprisoned; on his release, passed into the service of Ṭashtamur ad-Dawādār. After al-Malik al-Ashraf Shaʿbān's death made Amir of Ten in Aleppo, thence transferred to Damascus as Commander of a Thousand; succeeded Arghūn al-Isʿardī as Governor of Hama, in Rajab 780 (began 24th October 1378) appointed Viceroy of Syria, arrested in 782 (began 7th April 1380), some time later released and the same year appointed Governor of Safad, after six months transferred to Tripoli,[2] then to Damascus as Commander (*atābak*), twenty days later arrested, imprisoned for four months and finally exiled to Baalbek. Spent about a year in Safad as Governor, transferred to Tripoli for a second time, and remained there for about four and a half years; recalled to Damascus and confined to prison for ten months and ten days. In 791 (1389) appointed Governor of Aleppo, fought Minṭāsh, on his return to Aleppo fortified it, later appointed Commander-in-Chief in Cairo, on the 29th Muḥarram 800 (22nd October 1397) arrested and imprisoned in Alexandria, where he died the 28th[3] Ramaḍān 801 (3rd June 1399).

BLAZON: *Upper field blank, on both the middle and lower field a cup.*

CITY GATE, Aleppo, called Bāb Anṭākiya.

Above the entrance gate, underneath the arch.

Inscription flanked by two shields. The essential portion runs as follows:

[1] Maqrīzī, *Muqaffā*, s.v. (MS. Leyden, cod. 1366 a, fo. 18^r and ^{v}); *Nujūm* (MS. Paris, Ar. 1786, fo. 222^r, l. 6); *Nujūm*, VI, p. 137, l. 1, 140, l. 18–141, l. 8, 143, l. 20; *Manhal*, s.v. (MS. Paris, Ar. 2072, fo. 46^v–48^r); *Ḍau'*, s.v. (MS. Leyden, 369 a, Warn., p. 400); Ibn Iyās, cf. Index, especially I, pp. 276, l. 11, 281, l. 10, 282, l. 16, 287, l. 17, 292, l. 11 b ff., 294, l. 7, 295, l. 5, 308, l. 4; Weil, IV. 564 f., V. 4, 8; Ṭabbākh, *Aʿlām* II. 466–71.

[2] He was Governor of Tripoli in 783; *CIA. Égypte*, I. 225.

[3] *Nujūm*, VI, p. 140, l. 20: on the 20th Ramaḍān.

(3) . . . جدّد هذا الباب المبارك فى أيّام مولانا السلطان (4) الملك الظاهر

أبى سعيد برقوق خلّد الله ملكه بنظر مولانا المقرّ الأشرف السيفى كمشبغا الظاهرى

كافل المملكة (5) الحلبيّة المحروسة وتولّى عمارته أقلّ عباد الله تعالى [2–3 words]

قاضى المسلمين ?بحلب (6) بإشارة الجناب العالى الشهابى أحمد بن سلار وذلك فى

شهر رمضان المعظّم سنة ?اثنين وتسعين وسبعمائه

. . . *This blessed gate was renewed in the days of our Lord the Sultan al-Malik aẓ-Ẓāhir Abū Sa'īd Barqūq, may God make his reign eternal, under the supervision of our Lord, His Most Noble Excellency, Kumushbughā aẓ-Ẓāhirī, Viceroy of the protected province of Aleppo. The work was carried out by the poorest of God's servants . . . qāḍī of the Muslims at Aleppo, under the supervision of His High Excellency* (janāb), *Shihāb ad-dīn Aḥmad b. Salār. This (was done) in the month Ramaḍān, the August, of the year* 792 (began 13th August 1390).

BIBLIOGRAPHY: Van Berchem, *Inschriften Oppenheim*, p. 41 f., and figs. 4, 5.

KUNJAK AL-KHʷĀRIZMĪ

BLAZON: *Sword on undivided shield.*

LINTEL STONE, cemetery on the Ṣafḥ, Damascus. Pl. XLIX. 2.

Right-hand portion of the inscription broken off, shield to the left.

. . . بعمارته المقر المرحوم الا . . ى !كنجك !الخوارزمى . . فى أيّام . . . الله تعالى

أحمد بن علىّ . . . شهور سنة خمس وستّين وسبعمائة [Van Berchem]

[*Ordered?*] *to build it His late Excellency, Saif ad-dīn* (?) *Kunjak al-Khʷārizmī . . . in the days of . . .* [*the servant yearning for?*] *God the Exalted, Aḥmad b. 'Alī . . .* [*during*] *the months of the year* 765 (1363/4).

BIBLIOGRAPHY: Unpublished.

LĀJĪN[1]

Ḥusām ad-dīn Lājīn b. ʿAbdallāh al-Manṣūrī, called *aṣ-ṣaghīr* (i.e. the small one), originally a mamluk of al-Malik al-Manṣūr ʿAlī b. Aybak, then mamluk of Qalāūn, held a number of small offices such as page, *ūshāqī*, and armour-bearer, *silaḥdār*. After Qalāūn's accession he was dubbed amir and appointed Governor of the Fortress of Damascus, and the 11th Rabīʿ I 679 (11th July 1280) Viceroy of Syria. After a term of eleven years he was imprisoned by Khalīl b. Qalāūn in 690 (1291). On 10th Muḥarram 694 (30th November 1294) appointed Viceroy by Kitbughā, a position he held till he ascended the throne as 'al-Malik al-Manṣūr' on the 28th Muḥarram 696 (26th November 1296). Died Thursday, 10th Rabīʿ II 698 (15th January 1299).

BLAZON: *Three-fielded round shield.*

1. COPPER COIN (*fils*), Palestine Archaeological Museum, Jerusalem.

Obv. Within dotted circle,

[ال]سلطا

[ن ا]لملك

[المنـ]صور

Rev. In centre, blazon.

Around, within dotted circle

حسام [الدنيا والدين [2] لاجين

1·6 gr. Clipped. Maximum width 17·5 mm.

BIBLIOGRAPHY: Unpublished.

Mentioned: Mayer, *Guide to the Exhibition of Moslem Heraldry in Palestine*, p. 5.

[1] Abu-l-Fidā', ed. Reiske, V. 52, 100, 120, 130–2, 150–4; ed. Constantinople, IV, pp. 14, ll. 8, 11, 27, ll. 7–9, 33, l. 4, 35–42, l. 3; Zetterstéen, *Beiträge*, pp. 1, l. 10, 2, l. penult., 21, l. 10, 33, l. 11, 41–50, 53, l. 13, 223, l. 18; Ibn al-Wardī, II, pp. 227, ll. 7 b ff., 239, l. 3 b, 241–5; Ibn Ḥabīb, pp. 266, 288, 292, 296; Ṣāliḥ b. Yaḥyā, pp. 108, l. 8, 109, l. 6, 174, ll. 5 ff.; *Khiṭaṭ*, II, p. 239, ll. 20 ff. (2nd ed., III, 389 t); *SM.*, II a, pp. 11, 21, n. 20, 23 m, 37, 110 m, 116, 129, 134, 145, 153; II b, pp. 23, 40–114; *Manhal*, s.v. (MS. Paris, Ar. 2072, fo. 52ᵛ–55ᵛ); Jalāl ad-dīn as-Suyūṭī, *Ḥusn al-muḥāḍara* (Cairo, 1327 A.H.), II. 74–5; Mujīr ad-dīn, *al-Uns al-jalīl*, p. 437, ll. 7–15; Ibn Iyās, I, pp. 115, l. 1, 124, l. 18 ff., 136–9; Weil, IV, cf. Index, Cheikho in Ṣāliḥ b. Yaḥyā, p. 47, n. 2.

[2] On a much obliterated specimen of the same coin recently found at ʿAjlūn, now in the Government Museum, Amman, the words [ا]لدين لاجـ[ـين] are quite legible.

2. COPPER COIN (*fils*), Palestine Archaeological Museum, Jerusalem.

Obv. Within double circle, plain and dotted,

السلطا

ن الملك

المنصور

Rev. In centre, blazon.

Around, within dotted circle

ضرب بدمشق لاجين

Dots, annulets, small ornaments, differentiating marks. 1·57 gr. Clipped, maximum width 18 mm.

BIBLIOGRAPHY: As above.

MAḤMŪD AL-ʿAINĪ[1]

B. Maḥmūd b. Aḥmad b. Mūsā b. Aḥmad, born at ʿAintāb, the 17th Ramaḍān 762 (21st July 1361), son of a qāḍī, received a good ecclesiastical education, lived for a time as a wandering scholar; appointed Chief of Police (*muḥtasib*) in Cairo the 1st Dhu-l-Ḥijja 801 (4th August 1399); repeatedly dismissed from office but reappointed, in 803 (1400/1) became Inspector of Pious Foundations (*nāẓir al-aḥbās*), under Shaikh reinstated as Chief of Police; the 27th Rabīʿ II 829 (8th March 1426), became Qāḍī of the Hanafites; deposed, appointed for a second time, in 836 (1433) accompanied Barsbāy to Amid, in 842 (1438/9) dismissed from his office of qāḍī, in 846 (1442/3) was again holder of three different offices, namely: Chief of Police, Inspector of Pious

[1] Aḥmad b. ʿAbd as-Salām, *al-Badr aṭ-ṭāliʿ*, s.v. (MS. Leyden, Cod. 518 Warn.); *Khiṭaṭ*, II, p. 330, l. 15 (2nd ed. IV. 139 m); *SM.* I b, 219 ff.; *Nujūm*, especially VI, pp. 594, l. 5, 595, l. 12, 598, l. 7, 651, ll. 5, 11, 673, l. 2, 692, l. 13, 722, l. 21, 774, l. 23; VII, pp. 2, l. 1, 127, l. 14, 363, l. ult.–366, l. 10; *Manhal*, s.v. (MS. Cairo, III, fo. 337r–339v); Ibn Iyās, especially II, p. 33, l. 6 b; Weil, V. 185, 212 f.; Wüstenfeld, *Die Geschichtschreiber der Araber*, p. 218 f.; Brockelmann, *Geschichte der arabischen Litteratur*, II. 52 f.; Marçais in *The Encyclopaedia of Islām*, s.v. (Engl. ed. I. 213 f.).

It should be pointed out that up to the beginning of the ninth (fifteenth) century, the office of a Chief of Police was exclusively reserved for ecclesiastical officials. Beginning with the reign of Sultan Shaikh, this post was open to military men as well, Minklībughā having been the first amir to be invested with it (Qalqashandī, *Ṣubḥ*, XI. 210). Al-ʿAinī's blazon being accompanied by an inscription in which he is given the title of *al-maqarr*, it does not seem unreasonable to conclude that notwithstanding his ecclesiastical past, he was then considered a military man.

Foundations, and Chief Judge; in 853 (1449/50) lost these posts. Died the 4th Dhu-l-Ḥijja 855 (28th December 1451).

BLAZON: *Two fielded round shield. On red upper field a white pen-box, on dark-brown lower field a yellow vase placed between two white six-petalled rosettes.*

MADRASA and MAUSOLEUM, Cairo. Pl. LXI. 3.

Heraldic shields on the ceiling of the vestibule, the inscription on the frieze immediately below. The essential portion of the inscription runs as follows:

أمر بتجديد هذا السقف بانى هذه المدرسة السعيد الفقير الى الله تعالى

ابو محمّد محمود ابن أحمد العينى الحنفى . . . وذلك بتأريخ الثالث والعشرين

من شهر ربيع الآخر سنة خمسة وثلاثين وثمان مائة من الهجرة النبويّة . . .

Ordered the renovation of this ceiling the founder of this madrasa . . . Abū Muḥammad Maḥmūd b. Aḥmad al-ʿAinī, the Hanafite. . . . The date of this was the 23rd of the month Rabīʿ II of the year 853 *of the Hijra* (15th June 1449).

BIBLIOGRAPHY: Creswell, *Brief Chronology*, p. 120 (inscription without blazon).

Blazon reproduced and described: Wé, *Das Wappen des Sultans Mu'ayyed*, p. 139 (as the title indicates with a wrong attribution); Artin, *Contribution*, No. 100, p. 123.

Blazon reproduced: Franz, *Die Baukunst des Islam*, p. 93 and pl.; Karabacek, *Abendländische Künstler*, p. 88 (where it is attributed to Sultan Shaikh).

Mentioned: Devonshire, *Sultan Salâh ed Dîn's Writing-Box*, p. 245.

MAḤMŪD B. SHIRWĪN[1]

Najm ad-dīn Maḥmūd b. ʿAlī b. Shirwīn, one of the few amirs who, even though of foreign origin, did not start their career as slaves, came to Cairo in 738 (1337/8) after having served for some time as vizier in Baghdad, appointed Amir of a Hundred and Commander of a Thousand[2] following upon his presentation to Muḥammad b. Qalāūn, became Vizier under al-Malik al-Manṣūr Abū Bakr, dismissed by al-Malik al-Kāmil Shaʿbān, reinstated in

[1] Ṣafadī, *Aʿyān*, s.v. (MS. Berlin, fo. 161^{r}); *Khiṭaṭ*, II, p. 425, l. 28 f.; *Durar*, s.v. (MS. Br. Mus., Or. 3044, fo. 142^{v}); *Manhal*, s.v. (MS. Cairo, III, fo. $343^{r, v}$); Weil, IV. 473.

[2] *Durar*, l.c.: Amir of Forty.

office by Ḥājjī, towards the end of Jumādā II or early in Rajab[1] 748 (first half of October 1347) sent to Syria, killed by Manjak al-Yūsufī on arrival at Gaza.

BLAZON: *Upper field self-coloured, on united white middle and lower fields a red fleur-de-lis.*

1. GLASS LAMP, Royal Scottish Museum, Edinburgh, formerly collection Myers. Pl. XVIII.

Six shields.

Inscription on neck:

ممّا عمل برسم المقرّ الأشرف العالى العالمى العا|دلى المهدّى المشيرى

Inscription on body:

المدبّرى الوزيرى النجمى | محمود بن علىّ بن شروين ا | لملكى المظفّرى مدبّر

الممالك [ا]لشريفة الإسلاميّة أعزّ الله تعالى أنصاره

This is one of the objects made for His Most Noble and High Excellency, the Learned, the Just, the Administrator, the Councillor, the Regent, the Vizier, Najm ad-dīn Maḥmūd b. ʿAlī b. Shirwīn, (officer) of al-Malik al-Muẓaffar, Regent of the Noble Islamic Provinces, may God the Exalted make his victories glorious.

DATE: Between Ḥājjī's accession to the throne and Rajab 748.

BIBLIOGRAPHY: Unpublished.

Blazon reproduced: Schmoranz, p. 18, fig. 13; Artin, *Contribution*, p. 58, fig. 8.

Mentioned: Lavoix, *Galerie orientale du Trocadéro*, p. 780; van Berchem, *Notes*, III. 79, n.; Prinet, *De l'origine*, p. 3; Migeon, *Manuel* (2nd ed.), II. 134; Wiet, *Lampes*, p. 164.

2. GLASS LAMP, once in the collection Posno, then Gustave de Rothschild; present owner unknown.

Same inscription and shields.

BIBLIOGRAPHY: Unpublished.

Reproduced: Migeon, *L'Exposition des Arts Musulmans au Musée des Arts Décoratifs*, p. 25.

Mentioned: ll.cc. supra; Lamm, p. 448.

[1] *Manhal*, l.c.: Jumādā I.

MAḤMŪD B. ZANKĪ (NURADIN)

On two buildings closely connected with Nūr ad-dīn the fleur-de-lis appears in an heraldic form. I mention these arms with a great deal of hesitation, since none of them are accompanied by an historical inscription.

1. MĀRISTĀN, Damascus. Pl. XIX. 1.

(*a*) Since the Great War, two shields were discovered by M. de Lorey each underneath the plaster of a small room.

(*b*) A shield on the door seen before 1880 seems to have disappeared since.

DATE: The Māristān was erected by Nūr ad-dīn in 1154.

BIBLIOGRAPHY: (*a*) Unpublished.

Mentioned: Creswell, *Works of Bibars*, p. 153, n. 4.

(*b*) Mentioned and reproduced: Rogers, p. 106, fig. 7.

2. MAIN MOSQUE, Hims.[1] Pl. XIX. 3.

On a capital of a column at the door of the pulpit fleur-de-lis alternating with rosettes; the capitals are set upside down.

BIBLIOGRAPHY: Unpublished.

MALAKTAMUR

BLAZON: *On the middle field of a three-fielded shield a sword. On both the upper and lower fields, traces of red paint.*

COMB, National Museum of Arab Art, Cairo, No. 4926.

One shield.

Inscription on the side of the comb.

سيف الدين ملكتمر السلاحدار

Saif ad-dīn Malaktamur, the armour-bearer.

BIBLIOGRAPHY: Unpublished.

[1] Herzfeld in Sobernheim, 'Die Inschriften der Moschee von Ḥimṣ' (in *Janus*, I), p. 234.

MĀMĀY[1]

S. Māmāy b. Khudād, originally a mamluk of Qāytbāy and his page (*khāṣṣakī*), in Rajab 897 (May 1492) appointed Second Dawādār, repeatedly sent on diplomatic missions to Constantinople, in Ṣafar 901 (began 21st October 1495) promoted to the rank of a Commander of a Thousand. Following a revolt, after a lost battle at Khān Yūnus beheaded in 902 (first days of March 1497).

BLAZON: *On the upper field a napkin, on the middle field a cup charged with a pen-box and placed between a 'pair of trousers', on the lower field a cup.*

PALACE of Māmāy, Cairo, nowadays used as a law-court.
Several shields on the façade.[2]
Inscription in the bay of the portal, of which the visible portion runs as follows:

. . . ك المقرّ الكريم العالى السيفى ماماى عين مقدّمين [1] الألوف بالديار المصريّة

الملكى الأشرفى عزّ نصره بتأريخ شهر [ذى القعدة ?] الحرام سنة إحده (!) وتسعمائة

[*Ordered the construction of this bless*]*ed* [*palace*] *His Honourable and High Excellency, Saif ad-dīn Māmāy, Commander designate of a Thousand in Egypt of al-Malik al-Ashraf, may his victory be glorious. On the date of the month Dhu-l-Qa'da* (?) *of the year* 901 (July–August 1496).

BIBLIOGRAPHY: Kay, l.c., p. 146 f.; *CIA. Égypte*, I, No. 362, p. 541, figs. *a* and *b*.
Reproduced: P[ier], *Saracenic Heraldry*, fig. 18, p. 10.
Mentioned: *CR.*, l.c., p. 150 and n. 1.

MANJAK AL-YŪSUFĪ[3]

S. Manjak al-Yūsufī, a freed mamluk of Muḥammad b. Qalāūn, served as armour-bearer (*silaḥdār*), employed on special missions, made Amir of a

[1] *Ḍau'*, s.v. (MS. Leyden, Cod. 369 a, Warn. p. 406); Ibn Iyās, cf. Index, s.vv., M. al-khāṣṣakī and M. ad-dawādār, especially II, pp. 274, l. 16, 281, l. 18 ff., 292, l. 10 b, 315, l. 4, 316, l. penult.–317, l. 2; Weil, V. 351; Kay, 'Arabic Inscriptions in Egypt' (in *JRAS.* 1896), p. 148; *CIA. Égypte*, I. 542, 545 f.; *CR.* Exerc. 1902, fasc. 19, p. 151.

[2] These shields are badly preserved; some charges have become obliterated on this, others on another shield, a fact which misled van Berchem into assuming, l.c., p. 541, that there were two different shields to be distinguished on this monument.

[3] *Khiṭaṭ*, II, pp. 317, l. 10, 320–4 (2nd ed. IV. 118–19, 124–30); *Durar*, s.v. (MS. Br. Mus., Or. 3044,

Hundred and Great Chamberlain (*ḥājib al-ḥujjāb*) in Damascus, which he entered on 28th Rajab 748 (3rd November 1347). Appointed Vizier and Major-domo in Shawwāl 748 (January 1348), an office that with one interruption (forty days from the 3rd Rabīʿ I 749 (1st June 1348) onward) he held until Saturday, 24th Shawwāl 751 (25th December 1350). Subsequently his possessions were confiscated and he himself put into prison, where he remained until he was freed by Ṭāz under al-Malik aṣ-Ṣāliḥ Ṣāliḥ, and made Commander of a Thousand. Governor of Tripoli 755–9 (1354–8). For a short time during 759 Governor of Aleppo; Viceroy of Syria from 771 (1369/70)[1] to 775 (1373/4), then Viceroy of Egypt and Commander-in-Chief down to his death, Thursday, 29th Dhu-l-Ḥijja 776 (31st May 1375). Buried in his mausoleum near his mosque and khānqāh opposite the Citadel, near the Bāb al-Wazīr.

BLAZON: *On the middle field of a three-fielded shield a scimitar.*

1. PALACE in the Sūq as-Silāḥ, Cairo.

Inscription above the pendentives, intersected by shields, the essential portion of which runs as follows:

. . . أمر بإنشاء هذا المكان المبارك المقرّ الأشرف العالى المولوى الأميرى

الكبيرى . . . السيفى سيف الدين منجك السلاح دار الملكى المظفّرى . . .

Ordered to build this blessed place His Most Noble and High Excellency, our Lord, the Great Amir . . . Saif ad-dīn Manjak, the armour-bearer, (officer) of al-Malik al-Muẓaffar. . . .

DATE: During the reign of al-Malik al-Muẓaffar Ḥājjī 747–8.

BIBLIOGRAPHY: *CR.* fasc. IX, p. 45, pls. I, II; *CIA. Égypte*, I, No. 532, p. 737 f.
Blazon reproduced: Artin, *Contribution*, fig. 131, p. 130 (without attribution).

2. BATH, Bosra; slab of stone now serving as a lintel in the house of the shaikh of the village.

fo. 147ᵛ–148ʳ); *Nujūm*, obituaries, s.a. 776 (MS. Paris, Ar. 1786, fo. 189ʳ,ᵛ); *Manhal*, s.v. (MS. Cairo, III, fo. 364ʳ–366ᵛ); Ibn Iyās, cf. Index, especially I, pp. 190, l. 13, penult., 193, l. 4b, 195, ll. 7, 9, 205–6, 207, l. 16, 208, l. 15, 225, l. 6 b, 228, l. penult., 230, l. 10 ff.; Weil, IV. 477–9, 485, 492, 502, n. 1, 522; *CIA. Égypte*, I. 208 f., 226, 738.

[1] According to *Khiṭaṭ*, II, p. 323, l. 32, from Jumādā I 769 onward, *Manhal*, l.c., from 769 onward.

Shield between two halves of the inscription.

(١) أنشأ هذا الحمّام المباركة المقرّ الأشرف السيفى (2) منجك الأشرفى كافل المالك الشريفة با[لشأم [three words missing] (3) [a few words missing متولّى بصرى وأعمالها الخاصّ [1] والعام يرجو ان يرحمه الله تعالى فى شهور [a few words missing] (Van Berchem)

Constructed this blessed bath His Most Noble Excellency Saif ad-dīn Manjak al-Ashrafī, Viceroy of the Noble provinces of S[yria . . . under the supervision of . . .] the District Officer of Boṣra and its districts, for high and low, praying that God the Exalted have mercy upon him. In the months . . .

DATE: The extreme limits for the date of this building are 769–75.

BIBLIOGRAPHY: Unpublished.

3. MADRASA, Damascus, Rue Midan.
In 1927, M. E. de Lorey told me that prior to the disturbances in 1925, there was in this madrasa an heraldic shield cut in stone. The blazon, *a scimitar on the middle field of a three-fielded shield*, being identical with Manjak's arms and the mosque built by him, there is little doubt as to its identity. The stone has disappeared since.

MANKUWĪRISH

Perhaps identical with R. Mankuwīrish al-Fāruqānī[2] who died in 688 (1289).

BLAZON: *Napkin on undivided field.*

SLAB OF LIMESTONE used as lid of a cistern near the Mosque in the medieval town of Qalʿat ar-Rabaḍ on the right-hand side of the road leading to the Castle of ʿAjlūn. Pl. XXIX.

(١) بسمله . . . إِنَّمَا يَعْمُرُ مَسَاجِدَ ٱللَّهِ مَنْ آمَنَ بِٱللَّهِ وَٱلْيَوْمِ ٱلْآخِرِ وَلَمْ يَخْشَ إِلَّا ٱللَّهَ

[1] Probably a mistake for للخاص.
[2] Ṣafadī, *Wāfī*, s.v. (MS. Br. Mus., 23359, fo. 25r); *SM.* II a, 45, 103.

(2) ① جدد عمارة هذا المسجد المبارك العبد الفقير إلى ② الله تعالى الأمير

الأجلّ ركن الدين منكويرش ③

(3) الجمدار المنصورى النائب بعجلون فى أيّام مولانا السلطان الملك المنصور

خلّد الله ملكه فى جمادى الأوّل سنة ستّ وثمانين وستّمائة

In the name of the most merciful God. He only shall visit the Mosques of God who believeth in God and the last day and feareth God alone (Qur'ān, IX. 18, omitting four words). *Renewed the building of this blessed mosque the servant yearning for God the Exalted, the most magnificent Amir Rukn ad-dīn Mankuwīrish, the jamdār of* (*al-Malik*) *al-Manṣūr, Governor of 'Ajlūn. In the days of our Lord, the Sultan al-Malik al-Manṣūr, may God make his reign eternal, in Jumādā I of the year* 686 (began 14th June 1287).

BIBLIOGRAPHY: Van Berchem, *Arabische Inschriften aus Syrien*, II, pp. 58 ff., fig. 44.

On Schumacher's squeeze, published by van Berchem, l.c., the three heraldic shields look all different, the first like a crescent, the second like a horseshoe, the third like a table. Three different blazons in a text mentioning only two names excluded the possibility of one being the blazon of the amir and the other of his master and the problem seemed to be the more difficult as none of the three emblems was the symbol of office of a jamdār. As Schumacher's squeeze had to be retouched before it was fit for publication, and a misinterpretation of the original was not impossible, I asked Major Horsfield, the Director of Antiquities in Transjordan, for a photograph of this blazon. Major Horsfield most obligingly supplied me with a new squeeze of the whole inscription, which proves (*a*) that the first emblem visible on fig. 44 in van Berchem's article is only one of the dots filling intervening spaces between letters, (*b*) that the second line begins with a shield, which has been cut off Schumacher's squeeze, and (*c*) that all three emblems are absolutely identical, and all of them show a napkin on a round shield. Therefore it is the ordinary blazon of a jamdār and forms no exception to the rule.

MUBĀRAK

BLAZON: *Upper and lower fields self-coloured, on yellow middle field red cup.*

GLASS LAMP, Royal Scottish Museum, Edinburgh, formerly collection Myers. Pl. XXVIII. 1.

Six shields.

Inscription on neck: Qur'ān, II. 256 up to

وما فى الأرض

Inscription on body:

العبد الفقير الى | الله تعالى الجناب العالى | الأميرى الكبيرى ا | لغازى

المالكى | المخدومى الزينى مبارك | الملكى الصالحى |

The servant yearning for God the Exalted, His High Excellency (janāb), *the Great Amir, the Vanquisher, the Royal, the Well-Served, Zain ad-dīn Mubārak,* (*officer*) *of al-Malik aṣ-Ṣāliḥ.*

BIBLIOGRAPHY: Artin, *Contribution*, No. 77, p. 116 (without name and surname).
Mentioned: *CIA. Égypte*, I. 661, n. 6; Wiet, *Lampes*, p. 164, No. 50; Lamm, p. 442 f.

MUBĀRAK B. ṢĀLIḤ

BLAZON: *Cup placed between two daggers on the middle field of a three-fielded shield.*

SHRINE at Jinsāfūt, District of Nablus, locally known as az-Zāwiya. Pl. XXIV. 3.
Inscription over the entrance-door; two lines, intersected by one shield.

(1) لا اله الّا الله ○ محمّد رسول الله

(2) عمّر هذا المكان مبارك ابن صالح ○ الوسى بتأريخ سنة أحد وتسعين وسبع مائة عمل داوود

There is no God but Allah, Muḥammad is His Apostle. This place has been built by Mubārak b. Ṣāliḥ Alūsī (?) *in the year* 791 (1389). *Work of Dāwūd.*

BIBLIOGRAPHY: Unpublished.

SĪDĪ MUḤAMMAD

BLAZON: *Pen-box* (*without the third element*) *on the middle field of a three-fielded shield.*

METAL BOX, Fitzwilliam Museum, Cambridge. Pl. XXXVI. 2.

Two shields on the sides of the box facing each other.

The historical inscription runs as follows:

ممّا عمل برسم العبد الفقير الى الله تعالى سيّدى محمّد الناصرى

This is one of the objects made for the servant yearning for God the Exalted Sīdī Muḥammad an-Nāṣirī.

BIBLIOGRAPHY: Unpublished.

MUḤAMMAD B. AḤMAD

BLAZON: *Emblem No. 8 on undivided shield.*

WINDOW of the Mausoleum of Baraka Khān, known as the Khāldiyya Library, Jerusalem. Pl. XL. 2.

Two shields flanking the inscription:

(١) أنشأ هذا الشبّاك والقبّة بتربة المرحوم الشهيد الملك حسام الدين بركة خان

والقنطرة وعلوّها والبوّابة المباركة والمسقاة (2) والحوانيت وعلوّهم وخمس بيوت بدار

الوقف الفقير الى الله تعالى محمّد بن أحمد بن تمر العلائى لطف الله به فى

مستهلّ القعدة الحرام سنة اثنين وتسعين وسبعمائة

This window and the dome in the mausoleum of the late martyr Prince Ḥusām ad-dīn Baraka Khān and the arch and the [rooms] above it and the blessed portal and the trough and the shops and the [rooms] above them and five houses[1] *in the Waqf-house have been constructed by the one yearning for God the Exalted, Muḥammad son of Aḥmad, son of Timur*[2] *al-ʿAlāʾī, may God show kindness unto him, on the 1st of the sacred Dhu-l-Qaʿda of the year* 792 (11th October 1390).

BIBLIOGRAPHY: *CIA. Jérusalem, Ville*, No. 63, pp. 192 ff., fig. 30, pl. XLVIII.

Blazon reproduced: Rogers, fig. 54.

[1] The word بيوت here probably means 'rooms' as in the present vulgar Arabic of Palestine.

[2] In reading this name, van Berchem hesitated between نمر and يمن, then decided to adopt the latter. I am inclined to consider either تمر or نمر as the more satisfactory from the point of view of palaeography, and تمر, being a Turkish name, as the more probable.

MUḤAMMAD AL-ʿALAWĪ

BLAZON: *On undivided shield emblem No. 33.*

CANDLESTICK, Metropolitan Museum of Art, New York. Pl. XLVIII.

Inscription on body of the candlestick intersected by two shields, two other shields on the top part of the neck:

ممّا عمل برسم الجناب العالى العاملى الشريفى ○ الناصرى السيّد ! ناصر

الدين محمّد العلوى دامت سعادته ○

This is one of the objects made for His High Excellency (janāb), *the Learned, the Governing, the Noble, the Master, Nāṣir ad-dīn Muḥammad al-ʿAlawī, may his happiness last for ever.*

BIBLIOGRAPHY: Unpublished.

MUḤAMMAD AL-KHAZINDĀR

BLAZON: *Cup on undivided shield, later replaced by a three-fielded shield with a napkin on the middle field.*

BRONZE EWER, Metropolitan Museum of Art, New York, formerly in the Edward C. Moore Collection. Pl. XXIII.

Three shields on the body of the ewer underneath the inscription.

Inscription on neck:

ممّا عمل برسم (الجناب) العالى المولوى السيفى (ناصر) الدين محمّد الخزندار

This is one of the objects made for His High Excellency (janāb), *our Lord, as-Saifī Nāṣir ad-dīn Muḥammad, the Treasurer.*

The two words in round brackets are not visible on the photograph, but can be reconstructed from the second inscription.

Inscription on body:

ممّا عمل برسم الجناب العالى المولوى المالكى المخدومى المجاهدى المرابطى السيفى

الناصرى ناصر الدين محمّد الخزندار

This is one of the objects made for His High Excellency (janāb), *our Lord, the Royal, the Well-Served, the Defender of the Faith, the Warrior at the Frontiers, as-Saifī Nāṣir ad-dīn Muḥammad, the Treasurer.*

BIBLIOGRAPHY: Unpublished.

Mentioned and reproduced: A.M.S., 'Saracenic Metalwork' (in *BMMNY*. 1907, p. 152); Dimand, *BMMNY*. 1926, p. 198, fig. 3; id. *Handbook*, p. 115, fig. 54.

MUḤAMMAD B. KITBUGHĀ

BLAZON: *On lower field of a two-fielded shield a red cup.*

1. BRASS DISH, collection R. A. Harari, Esq., London. Pl. XXII. 3.
Nine pointed shields changed, with a visible effort, by a rather unskilled later hand into *round shields, upper and lower fields white* (silver inlay), *on the middle field a cup.* Three inscriptions in concentric circles.

The outer inscription:

ممّا عمل برسم الجناب الكريم العالى ○ المولوى الناصرى امير محمّد بن

المقرّ ○ الشريف المرحوم الزينى كتبغا عزّ نصره ○

This is one of the objects made for His Honourable and High Excellency (janāb), our Lord, Nāṣir ad-dīn Amīr Muḥammad, son of His Noble Excellency, the late Zain ad-dīn Kitbughā, may his victory be glorious.

The middle one:

ممّا عمل برسم الجناب الكريم العالى المولوى الأميرى الكبيرى الغازى

المجاهدى المر|ابطى المثاغرى المالكى العالمى العاملى العادلى الكفيلى الظهيرى

ا|لكافلى النظامى القوامى المخدومى الناصرى أمير محمّد بن المقرّ المرحوم الزينى |

This is one of the objects made for His Honourable and High Excellency (janāb), *our Lord, the Great Amir, the Vanquisher, the Defender of the Faith, the Warrior at the Frontiers, the Warden of the Marches, the Royal, the Learned, the Governor, the Just, the Viceroyal,*[1] *the Protector, the Regent, the Well-Served, Nāṣir ad-dīn Amir Muḥammad, son of His late Excellency Zain ad-dīn.*

[1] For *al-kāfilī* and *al-kafīlī*.

The central inscription contains merely an abridgement of the middle one.

BIBLIOGRAPHY: Unpublished.
Mentioned: Wiet, *Lampes*, p. 71.

2. CANDLESTICK, National Museum of Arab Art, Cairo, No. 2331.
Inscription on body:

ممّا عمل برسم الجناب الكريم العالى الناصرى ○ أمير محمّد بن المقرّ الشريف

المرحوم الزينى كتبغا عزّ نصره ○

This is one of the objects made for His Honourable and High Excellency (janāb), *Nāṣir ad-dīn Amir Muḥammad, son of His Noble Excellency, the late Zain ad-dīn Kitbughā, may his victory be glorious.*

The same inscription repeated on the upper part of the body and on the mouth-piece of the candlestick. On the latter with the addition of the words المولوى ال *our Lord, the* and suppressing the pious wish عزّ نصره at the end.

BIBLIOGRAPHY: Herz, *Catalogue*, p. 172 f.
Mentioned: Wiet, *Lampes*, p. 71.

3. CANDLESTICK, National Museum of Arab Art, Cairo, No. 2332.
Same as above.

BIBLIOGRAPHY: Mentioned: Herz, l.c., p. 172; Wiet, l.c.

MUḤAMMAD AL-MALAṬĪ

BLAZON: *On upper field two napkins, on middle field a cup, on lower field a cup.*

COPPER BASIN, tinned over, Max Freiherr von Oppenheim-Stiftung, Berlin. Pl. LVI. 2, 3.
Inscription:

مما عمل برسم المقرّ العالى الناصرى محمّد الملطى غفر له

This is one of the objects made for His High Excellency, Nāṣir ad-dīn Muḥammad al-Malaṭī, may he be pardoned.

BIBLIOGRAPHY: Unpublished.

MUḤAMMAD B. MUBĀRAKSHĀH AL-'ALĀ'Ī

BLAZON: *Pen-box on middle field of a three-fielded shield.*

PUBLIC FOUNTAIN, Tripoli, locally known as 'Ain at-tīna.
Four shields in the corners of the inscription embedded in the rear wall of the niche of the fountain.

(1) بسمله . . . (2) أنشأ هذا السبيل الفقير الى الله تعالى (3) محمّد بن المرحوم زين الد[ين] مباركشاه العلائى (4) فى مستهلّ [one word] سنة ستّ عشرة وثم[نم]ئه

. . . *Constructed this public fountain, the servant yearning for God the Exalted, Muḥammad, son of the late Zain ad-dīn Mubārakshāh al-'Alā'ī, the 1st . . . of the year* 816 (began 3rd April 1413).

BIBLIOGRAPHY: *CIA. Syrie du Nord*, No. 53, p. 123 f., fig. 12, pl. XIII (left).

MUḤAMMAD B. AN-NASHĀSHĪBĪ[1]

Na. Muḥammad b. an-Nashāshībī, treasurer (*khāzindār*) of Qāytbāy, in Muḥarram 875 (July 1470) appointed Superintendent of the two Harams in Jerusalem and in Hebron. Died after 893 (1488).

BLAZON: *On upper field a napkin, on middle field a cup charged with a pen-box (of which the third element is missing) and placed between a 'pair of trousers', on the lower field a cup.*

MADRASA ASHRAFIYYA, Jerusalem.
Above the northern windows overlooking the small entrance-place to the Haram in front of the Bāb as-Silsila, one shield to the right of the inscription:

A أمر بإنشاء هذه المدرسة الشريفة مولانا السلطان الملك الأشرف أبو النصر قايتباى عزّ نصره

[1] Mujīr ad-dīn, pp. 621 f., 672; *CIA. Jérusalem, Ville*, pp. 342, 364.

To the left of this text in a circle:

B (1) بتأريخ مستهلّ شهر ربيع الأوّل (2) سنة خمس وسبعين وثمانى مائة

وذلك فى (3) أيّام مولانا المقرّ الأشرف الناصرى سيّدى محمّد (4) الخازندار ناظر

الحرمين الشريفين (5) عظّم الله شأنه

A. *Ordered to construct this Noble Madrasa, our Lord, the Sultan al-Malik al-Ashraf Abu-n-Naṣr Qāytbāy, may his victory be glorious,*

B. *on the date of the 1st Rabīʿ I of the year* 875 (28th August 1470), *and this (was done) in the days of our Lord, His Most Noble Excellency, Nāṣir ad-dīn Sīdī Muḥammad, the treasurer, Superintendent of the two Noble Harams, may God increase his dignity.*

BIBLIOGRAPHY: *CIA. Jérusalem, Ville*, No. 105, figs. 65, 66, p. 358.

MUḤAMMAD B. QALĀŪN

Al-Malik an-Nāṣir Muḥammad b. Qalāūn, held the throne three times, during the years 693–4 (1293–4), 698–708 (1299–1309), and 709–41 (1310–41).

There is a number of objects with inscriptions with the formula *ʿizz li-maulānā . . . al-Malik an-Nāṣir Muḥammad* or even *Muḥammad b. Qalāūn*, and showing blazons of amirs whose names are not mentioned in the accompanying texts, such as the glass lamp in the Musée Jacquemart-André. These objects need not be discussed, as there is no proof whatever that their coats of arms are those of Muḥammad b. Qalāūn,[1] but we have to consider another group of blazons none of which could be attributed to Muḥammad with full certainty, but which, considered as a whole, seem to indicate that it is not only possible, but perhaps even probable, that they are his arms.

BLAZON: *Brown rosette on undivided pink shield.*

1. Fragment of GLASS LAMP, National Museum of Arab Art, Cairo, No. 4070.
Inscription on neck intersected by three shields: Qur'ān, XXIV. 35.
Inscription on body:

[1] The same applies to the theory that his arms were fishes, cf. p. 26.

. . . السلطانيّة الملكيّة الناص[ر]يّة . . .

. . . *of the Sultan al-Malik an-Nāṣ[ir]* . . .

DATE: Wiet attributes this lamp to the first reign of Muḥammad b. Qalāūn.

BIBLIOGRAPHY: Wiet, *Lampes*, p. 137 f., pl. XII.

Mentioned: *CR*. Exerc. 1914, fasc. 31, pp. 70–1; Lamm, p. 435, No. 28.

2. COPPER COIN (*fils*), British Museum, London, Palestine Archaeological Museum, Jerusalem.

Obv. Six-petalled rosette.

Rev.

السلط[ا]

ن الملك

الناص[ر]

BIBLIOGRAPHY: Lane-Poole, *Catalogue of Oriental Coins in the British Museum*, IV, No. 528 a, p. 159.

3. COPPER COIN (*fils*), British Museum, London.

Obv. In centre, six-petalled rosette.

Around

ضرب . . . سبعمائة

Rev.

السلطان

الملك الناصر

عزّ نصره

BIBLIOGRAPHY: Lane-Poole, l.c., IX, No. 528 b, p. 349.

MUḤAMMAD B. UZBAK[1, 2]

Na. Muḥammad, son of Uzbak min Ṭuṭukh, through his mother grandson of al-Malik aẓ-Ẓāhir Jaqmaq, in 887 (1482) dubbed Amir of Ten, in 898 (1493) headed the pilgrims' caravan to Mecca (*amīr rakb al-awwal*). Died after 904.

BLAZON: *On upper field a napkin, on middle field a cup placed between a 'pair of trousers', on lower field a cup.*[3] *Napkin, cup on middle field and the lower field covered with ornaments.*

BASIN, Victoria and Albert Museum, London, No. 206—1892.
Inscription on the rim intersected by four shields, repeated on body.

ممّا عمل برسم المقرّ ا لأشرف الكريم

العالى الناصرى سيّدى محمّد نجل المقرّ

الأشرف الكريم العالى المولوى

الأتابكى السيفى أزبك الملكى الأشرفى

This is one of the objects made for His Most Noble and Honourable and High Excellency, Nāṣir ad-dīn Sīdī Muḥammad, son (najl) *of His Most Noble and Honourable and High Excellency, our Lord, the Commander-in-Chief Saif ad-dīn Uzbak,* (*officer*) *of al-Malik al-Ashraf.*

DATE: Some time after 887 and prior to 904 (date of death of Uzbak).

BIBLIOGRAPHY: Unpublished.

Blazon reproduced: Artin, *Contribution*, fig. 84, p. 118 (without identification).

MUḤIBB AD-DĪN

BLAZON: *On each of the ornamented upper and lower fields a napkin, on middle field a pen-box.*

1. COPPER DISH tinned over, Victoria and Albert Museum, London, No. 856—1901.
Inscription round heraldic shield in the centre of the dish.

[1] *Ḍau'*, s.v. (MS. Leyden, Cod. 369a, Warn., p. 610); Ibn Iyās, II, pp. 214, l. 6 b, 278, l. 19, 279, l. 9 b, 355, l. 18.

[2] Cf. the biography of his father, p. 244.

[3] Cf. the blazon of his father, p. 244.

مماّ عمل برسم المقرّ الأشرف محبّ الدين مستوفى الخاصّ الشريفة عظم شأنه

This is one of the objects made for His Most Noble Excellency, Muḥibb ad-dīn, Keeper of the Noble Privy Purse, may his dignity increase.

BIBLIOGRAPHY: Unpublished.

2. COPPER BASIN tinned over, collection H. E. Bowman, Esq., Jerusalem. Four shields and inscription on the outer side of the basin.

○ مماّ عمل برسم الجناب العالى المجبى محبّ الدين كاتب ا ○ ○ الخزانة

الشريفة بالشأم المحروس عظّم المولا شأنه ○

This is one of the objects made for His High Excellency (janāb), *Muḥibb ad-dīn,*[1] *Scribe in the Noble Treasury in Damascus, the protected. May the Lord increase his dignity.*

BIBLIOGRAPHY: Unpublished.

MUḤSIN[2]

Z. Muḥsin al-Fatḥī al-Manūfī, an Abyssinian eunuch, under Qāytbāy succeeded Sunbul as Archivist (*khāzin*),[3] in 904 (1498/9) appointed Chief of the Corps of Cup-bearers (*ra's naubat as-suqāt*), repeatedly subjected to heavy fines and confiscation of property.

BLAZON: *On upper field a napkin, on middle field a cup charged with a pen-box placed between a 'pair of trousers', on lower field a cup.*

COPPER LUNCH-BOX (*maṭbaqiyya*) tinned over, in possession of R. A. Harari, Esq., London.

Identical inscriptions on receptacle and lid.

[1] Most probably not identical with Muḥibb ad-dīn al-Aslamī, in 885 *kātib al-khizāna* in Damascus; Ibn Ṭūlūn, p. 82 (r), l. 18.

[2] *Ḍau'*, s.v.(MS. Leyden, Warn. 369 a, p. 410); Ibn Iyās, II, pp. 352, l. 15, 360, l. 11, 373, ll. 2, 9.

[3] So styled in the inscription and by Sakhāwī; Ibn Iyās calls him *khāzindār*, which, seeing that the khazindārs were usually eunuchs, is self-explanatory.

ممّا عمل برسم الجناب الزينى محسن الخازن الأشرفى عزّ نصره

This is one of the objects made for His Excellency (janāb), *Zain ad-dīn Muḥsin, khāzin of* (*al-Malik*) *al-Ashraf, may his victory be glorious.*

BIBLIOGRAPHY: Unpublished.

MUḤYĪ AD-DĪN AL-QĀDIRĪ

BLAZON: *On upper field a napkin, on middle field a pen-box, on lower field a napkin.*

LUNCH-BOX, copper tinned over. Collection Prof. Riẓā Bey Taufīq, Amman. Main inscription [1] intersected by four shields.

ممّا عمل برسم العبد الفقير [ا]لراجى عفو ربّه ○ ○ ربّه القدير محيى الدين

القادرى ○ ○

This is one of the objects made for the poor servant, hoping for forgiveness from his Omnipotent Lord, Muḥyī ad-din al-Qādirī.

BIBLIOGRAPHY: Unpublished.

MUQBIL AR-RŪMĪ[2]

Z.[3] Muqbil al-Ḥusāmī, of Anatolian origin, an amir at Damascus, originally a mamluk of Ḥusām ad-dīn Lājīn, served under Shaikh, who, on ascending the throne, made him a page, *khāṣṣakī*, and Chief of the Masters of the Robes (*ra's naubat al-jamdāriyya*). Advanced in his career till he was appointed Second Dawādār and following the appointment of Jaqmaq al-Arghūnshāwī as Governor of Damascus, he became Grand Dawādār, the 3rd Shawwāl 822

[1] From a rubbing kindly supplied by Saʿīd Eff. Riẓā.

[2] *Manhal*, s.v. (MS. Cairo, III, fo. 360v–361r); *Nujūm*, VI, cf. Index, especially pp. 394, l. 9, 406, l. 12 f., 480, ll. 19 ff., 481, ll. 7 ff., 483, l. 1, 560, l. 15 f., 572, l. 20 f., 713, l. 17, 828, ll. 18 ff.; *Ḍau'* s.v.; Weil, V. 169, 192; Ibn Iyās, II, p. 163, ll. 2–3, mentioned the death of another Muqbil ad-Dawādār under the events of Ramaḍān 880 (began 29th December 1475). This Muqbil was originally a mamluk of Taghrībirdī al-Mu'ayyadī.

[3] In *Nujūm*, VI, p. 828, l. 18, called Saif ad-dīn.

(23rd October 1419). Remained in office until the death of al-Malik al-Mu'ayyad Shaikh. Under al-Malik al-Muẓaffar Aḥmad fled to Damascus and became a partisan of Jaqmaq. On the latter's capture, Muqbil was imprisoned for a time, then freed and appointed Grand Chamberlain, *ḥājib al-ḥujjāb*, of Damascus. In Jumādā II 825 (began 23rd May 1422), under Barsbāy, appointed Governor of Safad, confirmed Monday, 2nd Muḥarram 827 (6th December 1423), remained there up to the time of his death, Friday, the 29th Rabīʿ I 837 (13th November 1433).

BLAZON: (a) *on golden upper field a self-coloured pen-box, on golden middle field self-coloured cup, on self-coloured lower field golden cup charged with a napkin.*

BLAZON: (b) *golden shield, on upper field a napkin, on middle field a cup, on bottom field possibly also a cup.*

CHAMFRON, Musée de la Ville, Lyon. Pl. LX.

Inscription:

المقرّ الأشرف الزينى مقبل الدوادار الملكى المؤيّد[ى] عزّ نصره للغرّة المباركة

His Most Noble Excellency, Zain ad-dīn Muqbil, the Dawādār of al-Malik al-Mu'ayyad, may his victory be glorious. For the blessed blaze.

The ى of المؤيّدى may have been merged into the arabesque between the د of المؤيّدى and the صر of نصره.

Blazon (a) is placed below the inscription, blazon (b) on both sides of it, but the latter appears on the ear pieces of the chamfron which were made of separate sheets of metal. Date: Between 822 (his appointment as Grand Dawādār) and 824 (Shaikh's death).

BIBLIOGRAPHY: Unpublished.

MŪSĀ[1]

Sh. Mūsā an-Nāṣirī, Chamberlain of Aleppo, some time after 751 appointed Governor of Bīreh, died there in 756 (1355) as a septuagenarian.[2]

[1] Ṣafadī, *Aʿyān*, s.v. Āqūsh (MS. Berlin, fo. 29ʳ) and s.v. Arghūn al-Kāmilī (ib., fo. 24ʳ, l. 11); Ibn Ḥabīb, pp. 381, 402; *Durar*, s.v. (MS. Br. Mus., Or. 3044, fo. 150ᵛ); Rāghib Ṭabbākh, *Aʿlām an-nubalāʾ*, V. 23.

[2] Ibn Ḥajar, l.c. (fo. 152ʳ) gives the biography of a certain Mūsā, *ḥājib* of Aleppo, who became Governor of Bīreh and died there in Rabīʿ II 750 (began 19th June 1349). This is probably only another version of the biography of our Mūsā.

BLAZON: *Horse with ceremonial saddle on undivided shield.*

CARAVANSERAI in ruins, known as Khān al-ʿAsal, south-west of Aleppo, on the way to at-Tarib.

Inscription over the arch, flanked by two shields.

(1) جدد هذا الخان المبارك بتدبير المقرّ الأشرف العالى الشرفى موسى أمير

(2) حاجب بالمملكة الحلبيّة عزّ نصره وكان الفراغ منه فى شهر جمادى الآخر

سنة اربعة واربعين وسبعمائة

This blessed caravanserai was renewed owing to the care of His Most Noble and High Excellency, Sharaf ad-dīn Mūsā, Amīr Chamberlain in the province of Aleppo, may his victory be glorious. Completed in the month of Jumādā II 744 (began 21st October 1343).

BIBLIOGRAPHY: Unpublished.

MŪSĀ B. ʿALĪ B. QALĀŪN[1]

Muẓaffar ad-dīn Mūsā b. al-Malik aṣ-Ṣāliḥ ʿAlī b. Qalāūn born in 687 (1288) at the latest, in 698 (February 1299) on Muḥammad b. Qalāūn's second accession to the throne dubbed amir, in 704 (1304/5) married Salār's daughter, in 710 (1310/11) put in prison, later sent to Qūṣ. Died in 718[2] (began 5th March 1318). Built a house in the Gharabliyyīn Quarter, Cairo.

BLAZON: *Crested eagle looking to the right.*

TITLE-PAGE of *ar-Rauḍ az-zāhir min sīrat . . . al-Malik an-Nāṣir*, a history of Muḥammad b. Qalāūn's expedition against Quṭlūshāh, Asiatic Museum, Leningrad. Pl. XIV. The coat of arms in the centre of the page, the inscription on the lower margin.

برسم الخزانة العالية المولويّة السيّديّة المخدوميّة المظفريّة موسى بن السلطان الشهيد

الملك الصالح قدّس الله روحه

[1] Zetterstéen, *Beiträge*, pp. 145, l. 9, 154, l. 13; Ibn Ḥabīb, p. 315; *SM.* II b, 127, 246; *Durar*, s.v. (MS. Br. Mus., Or. 3044, fo. 150^v–151^r); Ibn Iyās, I, p. 118, l. 11; Weil, IV. 306 f.

[2] Zetterstéen and Ibn Ḥabīb, ll.cc., mention his death under the events of the year 710.

For the library of (His) High (Excellency), our Lord, the Master, the Well-Served, Muẓaffar ad-dīn Mūsā, son of the late Sultan al-Malik aṣ-Ṣāliḥ, may God sanctify his soul.

BIBLIOGRAPHY: Rosen, *Notices sommaires des manuscrits arabes du Musée Asiatique*, No. 164, pp. 102 ff.

MŪSĀ B. ARUQṬĀY[1]

Muẓaffar ad-dīn Mūsā b. Ḥājj Aruqṭāy (q.v.), Commander of a Thousand under Ḥasan b. Muḥammad b. Qalāūn, died as Governor of Safad in 774 (1372).

BLAZON: *Napkin on undivided shield.*

CENOTAPH, Zāwiyat Banāt Ḥāmid, Safad.

Blazon on each of the two pillars flanking the inscription.[2]

(١) بسمله . . . (2) كُلُّ مَنْ عَلَيْهَا فَانٍ وَيَبْقَى وَجْهُ رَبِّكَ ذُو ا(3)لْجَلَالِ وَالْإِكْرَامِ

توفّى العبد الفقير الى الله (4) تعالى موسى بن أرقطاى فى سادس ربيع الآخر

سنة أربعة وسبعين وسبعمائة

In the name of the most merciful God. Every creature which liveth on the earth is subject to decay: but the glorious and honourable countenance of thy Lord shall remain for ever (Qur'ān, IV. 26, 27) *The servant yearning for God the Exalted, Mūsā, son of Aruqṭāy, passed away on the 6th Rabīʿ II* 774 (5th September 1372).

BIBLIOGRAPHY: Unpublished.

This blazon is of particular interest for the study of the problem of heredity. Consisting as it does of an emblem on an undivided shield, it is more suggestive of the days of the first reign of Muḥammad b. Qalāūn, when Ḥājj Aruqṭāy was dubbed amir, than of those of 1347 (Ḥasan's first accession to the throne) or 1354. The device, too, the sign of office of a *jamdār*, is indicative of his father's early career, so that the conclusion that we are

[1] *Durar*, s.v. (MS. Br. Mus., Or. 3044, fo. 150ᵛ); *Nujūm*, s.a. 774 (MS. Paris, Ar. 1786, fo. 183ʳ and ᵛ); Ibn Iyās, I, p. 210, l. 9. Incidentally, this passage enables us to understand the expression *awlād an-nās*, meaning 'sons of military dignitaries'. Cf. similar passages: I. Iyās, I, pp. 235, ll. 4, 9; II, 118, l. 9; III, 52, l. 12 b.

[2] A similar arrangement on the tomb of Quṭlū Khātūn (q.v.).

here dealing with the blazon of Ḥājj Aruqṭāy, inherited by his son, can hardly be considered far-fetched. As for the blazon of Aruqṭāy himself,[1] I can only repeat that as neither the emblem nor the division of the shield seems to agree with the data known about him, it would seem advisable to refrain from expressing an opinion until the vase published by Rogers, and at present completely lost sight of, be found, when we shall be able to ascertain whether the blazon and the inscription mentioning Aruqṭāy's name are in any way connected.

MŪSĀ B. YAGHMŪR[2]

J. Mūsā b. Yaghmūr b. Jaldak (?) al-Yārūqī, born in the province of Ṣa'īd in 599 (1202/3), Governor of Cairo under al-Malik aṣ-Ṣāliḥ, subsequently Governor of Damascus, under al-Malik al-Mu'aẓẓam Tūrānshāh in 648. Appointed major-domo in Cairo under Baybars. Died 663 (1264/5) at Quṣair in Egypt.

BLAZON: *White eight-petalled rosette without shield.*

COPPER VASE, collection R. A. Harari, Esq., London. Pl. XXXIV. 2.
Six shields, silver inlaid, three intersecting the inscription, three on the lower half of the vase.
Inscription:

برسم ○ الأمير الكبير ○ جمال الدين موسى ○ ابن يغمور

For the Great Amir Jamāl ad-dīn Mūsā b. Yaghmūr.

BIBLIOGRAPHY: Unpublished.

NĀNIQ AL-ASHRAFĪ

Perhaps identical with Nāniq aẓ-Ẓāhirī[3] in the service of al-Malik al-Ashraf Aynāl, killed before the 9th Sha'bān 863 (11th June 1459), or, what is less probable, with Nāniq al-Muḥammadī aẓ-Ẓāhirī,[4] the 7th Dhu-l-Ḥijja 867

[1] Cf. p. 78.
[2] Mufaḍḍal, ed. Blochet, p. 143; Ṣafadī, *Wāfī*, s.v. (MS. Br. Mus., Add. 23359, fo. 58ʳ–59ʳ); Ibn Ḥabīb, p. 251; *SM.* I b, 23; *Manhal*, s.v. (MS. Cairo, III, fo. 378ʳ–379ʳ).
[3] *Nujūm*, VII, p. 519, l. 1; Weil, V. 267.
[4] *Nujūm*, VII, pp. 717, l. 18, 743, ll. 2, 5, 12, 744, l. 5, 747, l. 12, 749, l. 7; Ibn Iyās, II, pp. 92, l. 7 b, 103, l. 10; Weil, V. 329 f.

(23rd August 1463) appointed Junior Marshal (*amīr akhūr thānī*), served in Ṣafar 871 (September–October 1466) as Superintendent of the Cellar (*shādd ash-sharābkhānā*), shortly afterwards appointed Chief of the Corps of the Mamluks, in 872 (1468) fell in the expedition against Siwār.[1]

BLAZON: *On upper field a pen-box, on middle field two cups, on lower field a napkin.*

COPPER DISH tinned over, in the collection of Sir Ronald Storrs, Governor of Cyprus. Four shields, the fifth, in the centre, is now entirely obliterated. Of the three inscriptions the middle one is of historical interest. Pl. LVIII. 5, 7.

ممّا عمل برسم المقرّ العالى ○ المولوى السيّدى المالكى ○ المخدومى الأميرى

نانق ○ الملكى الأشر(ف)ى عزّ انصاره ○

This is one of the objects made for His High Excellency, our Lord, the Master, the Royal, the Well-Served, Amir Nāniq, (officer) of al-Malik al-Ashraf, may his victories be glorious.

BIBLIOGRAPHY: Unpublished.

Mentioned: Mayer, *Guide to the Exhibition of Moslem Heraldry*, p. 5, No. 6.

NAURŪZ AL-ḤĀFIẒĪ[2]

S. Naurūz al-Ḥāfiẓī, originally a mamluk of Barqūq, served as one of his pages, became Amir of a Hundred and Commander of a Thousand, in 797 succeeded Taghrībirdī, the father of the historian, as Chief of the Corps of the Mamluks (*ra's naubat an-nuwwāb*), in Rabīʿ II 800 (began 22nd December 1397) appointed Grand Marshal, the 13th Ṣafar 801 (25th October 1398) arrested and imprisoned in Alexandria, because he took part in a rebellion against Barqūq, in 802 released, became again Chief of the Corps of the

[1] A third amir of this name, Nāniq al-Yashbakī (Bertrandon de la Broquière, ed. Schefer, p. xxxix, *Nujūm*, VI, p. 606, l. 11), who fell in 829 in the campaign against Cyprus, need not be considered.

[2] *Ḍau'*, s.v.; *Nujūm*, cf. Index, especially VI, pp. 23, l. 13, 25, l. 7, 27, l. 10, 70, l. 3, 98, l. ult., 126, l. 11, 129, l. 5, 168, l. 7, 173, l. 19, 178, l. 16, 183, l. 16, 187, l. 8, 204, l. 12, 230, l. 19, 318, l. 4, 334, l. 1, 339, l. 14, 442–3; *Manhal*, s.v. (MS. Cairo, III, fo. 388r–390v); Ibn Iyās, I, pp. 308, ll. 7, 12, 312, ll. 22, 26, 320, l. ult., 321, l. 4 f., 328, l. 19, 336, ll. 5 b, 337, l. 18, penult., 341, l. 5, 344, ll. 10, 21, 346, ll. 8 f., 13 f., 351, l. penult., 352, l. 15, 353, ll. 3, 5, 354, ll. 2, 5, 3 b, 355, ll. 16, 20, 25, ult., 356, l. 3, 357, l. ult., 358, ll. 7 ff.; II. 3 b–5, l. 2. Weil, especially V. 13, 75, 104, 106, 109, 111, 113–20, 123, 127, 130, 131, 133; Sobernheim, *Die Inschriften der Zitadelle von Damaskus*, p. 20 f.

Mamluks (*ra's naubat al-umarā'*) and one of the most powerful amirs, in the course of the following years several times appointed Viceroy of Syria; together with Shaikh al-Maḥmūdī stirred up a rebellion against Sultan Faraj and murdered him in Ṣafar 815 (May 1412), under al-Musta'īn billāh confirmed as Viceroy of Syria, opposed Shaikh after the latter's accession, was defeated and executed the 21st[1] Rabī' II 817 (10th July 1414). Built a dome over the fountain in the Khānqāh Shaikhūniyya, Cairo.

1. MAIN MOSQUE, Damascus. Pl. LIV. 3.

Inscription on the bronze revetment of the North Gate.

Upper half:

eastern wing

بسم الله الرحمن ○ الرحيم أُدْخُلُوهَا

western wing

بِسَلَامٍ آمِنِينَ جدّد هاذا الباب ○ المبارك فى شهر الله المحرّم سنة تسع وثمان مائة

In the name of the most merciful God. Enter ye therein in peace and security (Qur'ān, XV. 46). *This blessed door was renewed in the month of God Muḥarram of the year* 809 (began 18th June 1406).

Lower half:

eastern wing

عمّر هذا الباب المبارك ○ في أيّام مولانا السلطان

western wing

الملك الناصر فرج ابن برقوق ○ باشره مولانا ملك الأمرآء نوروز

This blessed door was built in the days of our Lord, the Sultan al-Malik an-Nāṣir Faraj, son of Barqūq. Our Lord the Governor-General, Naurūz, carried it out.[2]

BIBLIOGRAPHY: Wulzinger und Watzinger, *Damascus, eine islamische Stadt*, pp. 11, fig. 1B, 155 f., with portions of the text published by Littmann, pl. 3 d (eastern wing).

[1] *Nujūm*, VI, p. 442, l. 17: 28th Rabī' II.

[2] The consonants admit of only one reading, viz. بَاشَرَهُ, instead of the usual باشارة which would read better.

2. CITADEL, Damascus.

Inscription over the entrance gate to the middle tower of the North wall. The historical portion of it runs as follows:

. . . عمّر هذه القلعة المنصورة مولانا ○ ملك الأمرآء نوروز الحافظى أعزّ الله
تعالى أنصاره فى شهور سنة تسع وثمان مائة

. . . *Built this victorious fortress our Lord, the Governor-General, Naurūẓ al-Ḥāfiẓī, may God the Exalted make his victories glorious, during the months of the year* 809 (1406/7).

BIBLIOGRAPHY: Sobernheim, l.c., No. 17, p. 20 f.

Mentioned: Wulzinger und Watzinger, *Damaskus, die islamische Stadt*, p. 181.

3. CITADEL, Damascus.

Another shield is visible on the same wall, to the west of the above-mentioned tower. The badly damaged inscription contains traces of Naurūz' name and his appellative *al-Ḥāfiẓī*.

BIBLIOGRAPHY: Unpublished.

QAJMĀS[1] AL-ISḤAQĪ[2]

S. Qajmās al-Isḥāqī, originally a mamluk of Jaqmaq, became Aghā of Qāytbāy, in Jumādā II 875 (began 25th November 1470) appointed Junior Treasurer (*khāzindār*), in Rajab of the same year Governor of Alexandria, in Jumādā I 880 (September 1475) appointed Grand Marshal, in 885 appointed Viceroy of Syria for a second time. Died in Damascus the 2nd Shawwāl 892 (21st September 1487).

BLAZON: *On upper field a napkin, on middle field a cup charged with a pen-box placed between a 'pair of trousers', on lower field a cup.*

1. MOSQUE, Darb al-Aḥmar, Cairo.

Blazon engraved on knots of grating.

DATE: Between 885 and Muḥarram 886.

[1] Spelt قجماس, قچماس and قچماز.

[2] *Ḍau'*, s.v. (MS. Leyden, Cod. Warn. 369 a, p. 384); Ibn Iyās, II, pp. 124, l. 18, 125, l. 4, 159, l. 3 b. 173, ll. 1, 4 b, 180, ll. 18 ff., 182, l. 18, 185, l. 21, 201, l. 15, 203, l. 19, 245, l. ult.–246, l. 2; Ibn Ṭūlūn, pp. 82 [٣], ll. 24, 26, 80 [٥], ll. 17, 22, 24, 79 [٦], l. 27 ff.; Weil, V, 343; *CR*. Exerc. 1892, fasc. 9 (2nd ed.), p. 86 (quoting 'Alī Pāshā Mubārak's *al-Khiṭaṭ at-Taufīqiyya*); *CIA*. *Égypte*, I. 513.

BIBLIOGRAPHY: Unpublished.

Mentioned: Herz, *Catalogue* (Engl. ed.), p. 194.

2. LANTERN, National Museum of Arab Art, Cairo, No. 242. Pl. LXIII.

Six shields; the essential portion of the inscription runs as follows:

ممّا عمل برسم المقرّ الأشرف العالى . . . السيفى قجماس أمير آخور كبير الملكى الأشرفى

This is one of the objects made for His Most Noble and High Excellency, Saif ad-dīn Qajmās, Grand Marshal of al-Malik al-Ashraf.

BIBLIOGRAPHY: *CIA. Égypte*, I, No. 493, p. 674; Herz, *Catalogue*, p. 193 f., where the beginning and the end of the inscription are given.

QĀNĪBĀY

BLAZON: ***On upper field a napkin, on middle field a cup charged with a pen-box and placed between a 'pair of trousers', on lower field a cup.***

COPPER DISH tinned over, in the collection of M. Ant. E. Benachi, Athens.

One shield in the centre of the dish, the main inscription round it.

ممّا عمل برسم المقرّ الأشرف العالى المولوى المخدومى السيفى قانيباى مولانا ملك الأمراء عزّ نصره

This is one of the objects made for His Most Noble and High Excellency, our Lord, the Well-Served, Saif ad-dīn Qānībāy, our Lord the Governor-General, may his victory be glorious.

On the back an inscription giving the name of one of the later possessors of the dish:

برسم المقرّ الأشرف السيفى آقباى ملك الأمرآء بالشرقيّة

For His Most Noble Excellency Saif ad-dīn Āqbāy, Governor-General of the Sharqiyya (-district in Egypt).

DATE: The *terminus ad quem* of the dish is 888 A.H., Āqbāy having been transferred in Dhu-l-Qaʿda of that year (December 1483) from Sharqiyya to Gaza.[1]

BIBLIOGRAPHY: Unpublished.

QĀNIBĀY (?) AL-BAWWĀB

BLAZON: *On upper field a napkin, on middle field a cup charged with a pen-box and placed between a 'pair of trousers', on lower field a cup.*

FLAT DISH, National Museum of Arab Art, Cairo, formerly in the possession of Artin Pasha.

In the centre of the dish a shield with a much obliterated inscription round it.

On the back inscription intersected by three shields.

ممّا عمل برسم الجناب العالى المولوى ○ الأميرى الكبيرى المخدومى السيفى ○

قانباى ؟ البوّاب من طبقة رفرف عزّ أنصاره ○

This is one of the objects made for His High Excellency (janāb), *our Lord, the Great Amir, the Well-Served, Saif ad-dīn Qānibāy* (?), *the Doorkeeper, of the Rafraf-Barracks, may his victories be glorious.*

BIBLIOGRAPHY: Unpublished.

QĀNĪBĀY AL-JARKASĪ[2]

S. Qānībāy, originally a mamluk of Yashbak ash-Shaʿbānī, who presented him to Jarkas al-Qāsimī al-Muṣāriʿ, some time after the death of his master became a sultanian mamluk and a page (*khāṣṣakī*) either under al-Malik al-Mu'ayyad Shaikh or under his son Aḥmad, the 27th Dhu-l-Ḥijja 841 (21st June 1438) dubbed Amir of Ten, later became Chief of a Corps of Mamluks (*ra's nauba*), in 842 (1438), after Jaqmaq's accession to the throne, appointed Superintendent of the Cellar (*shādd ash-sharābkhānā*), on the 10th Rajab 844 (5th December

[1] Ibn Iyās, II, p. 220, l. 12 b.

[2] *Nujūm*, cf. Index, especially VII, pp. 8, l. 9, 38, l. 7, 115, l. 18, 126, l. 17, 144, l. 2, 167, l. 18, 249, l. 18, 250, l. 7, 417, l. 4, 424, l. 20, 568, l. 15, 657, l. 14, 687, l. 9, 770 f.; *Manhal*, s.v. (MS. Paris, Ar. 2072, fo. 6v–7r); Sakhāwī, *Tibr*, pp. 122, l. 10, 256, l. 7 b; *Ḍau'*, s.v. (MS. Leyden, Cod. 369 a, Warn. p. 368 f.); Ibn Iyās, cf. Index, especially II, pp. 29, l. 7 b, 35, l. 7 b, 40, ll. 9, 6 b; Weil, V. 253, 260; *CIA. Égypte*, I. 382; Wiet, *Lampes*, p. 99.

1440) made Amir of Forty and on the 13th Jumādā II 846 (19th October 1442) Amir of a Hundred, the 3rd Sha'bān 849 (4th November 1445) appointed Grand Dawādār, the 23rd Ṣafar 853 (17th April 1449) Grand Marshal. On al-Malik al-Ashraf Aynāl's accession to the throne imprisoned in Alexandria, released by al-Malik aẓ-Ẓāhir Khushqadam, died in Damietta the 14th Rabī' II 866 (16th January 1462) as an octogenarian. Built a monastery (*zāwiya*), a mosque, and a mausoleum in Cairo.

BLAZON: *On red upper field a blue scimitar, on golden middle field a white pen-box, on green lower field a red cup placed between a white 'pair of trousers' with golden openings.*

1. MOSQUE, Cairo.

A fragment of a badly damaged inscription painted on the cornices of the ceiling, intersected by shields, now in the National Museum of Arab Art, Cairo, No. 3387.

Name, title, and date as seen by van Berchem before the restoration of the Mosque.

. . . السيفى قانباى الجركسى أمير آخور الملكى الظاهرى . . . وذلك بتاريخ

سنة خمس وأربعين وثمانمائة

. . . *Saif ad-dīn Qānibāy al-Jarkasī, Marshal of al-Malik az-Ẓāhir . . . and this on the date of the year* 845 (1441/2).

BIBLIOGRAPHY: *CIA. Égypte*, I. 381–3, fig.

Mentioned: Herz, *Catalogue* (Engl. ed.), p. 309, n. 1.; *Deux lampes*, p. 184; *CR*. Exerc. 1909, fasc. 26, p. 62, Exerc. 1911, fasc. 28, p. 51 f.; Creswell, *Brief Chronology*, p. 129 f.

2. GLASS LAMP, National Museum of Arab Art, Cairo, No. 332.

Three shields intersecting the qur'ānic inscription on the neck (xxiv. 35) and three others on the lower part of the body.

Inscription on the upper part of the body:

مّما عمل برسم المقرّ الأشرف العالى السيفى قانى باى الجركسى نضام! الملك

This is one of the objects made for His Most Noble and High Excellency, Saif ad-dīn Qānībāy al-Jarkasī, Regent of the Kingdom.

BIBLIOGRAPHY: Artin, *Trois différentes armoiries*, pp. 70 ff., fig. 2; *CIA. Égypte*, I, No. 488, p. 670 f.; Herz, *Catalogue* (Engl. ed.), p. 308 f.; Wiet, *Lampes*, pp. 97 ff., pl. LXXXIX.

Reproduced: Lane-Poole, *History of Egypt*, p. 348, fig. 91; P[ier], *Saracenic Heraldry*, p. 10, fig. 15; Devonshire, *Sultan Salâh ed-Dîn's Writing-Box*, p. 243, fig. D.

Mentioned: Artin, *Six lampes*, p. 130; van Berchem, *Notes*, III. 57, 76, n. 1; Herz, *Deux lampes*, p. 184; Schmoranz, p. 71; Lamm, p. 482, No. 227.

QĀNṢŪH

BLAZON: *On upper field a napkin, on middle field a cup charged with a pen-box placed between a 'pair of trousers', on lower field a cup.*

COPPER DISH, tinned over. Collection M. François Marcopoli, Consul of Portugal, Aleppo.

Blazon in the centre, a much obliterated inscription round it.

ممّا عمل برسم المقرّ الأشرف العالى قانصوه بهرامى (?) أمير آخور عزّ أنصاره

This is one of the objects made for His Most Noble and High Excellency, Qānṣūh Bahrāmī (?), *the Marshal, may his victories be glorious.*

BIBLIOGRAPHY: Unpublished.

QĀNṢŪH AL-GHAURĪ[1]

Al-Malik al-Ashraf S. Qānṣūh min Baybirdī al-Ghaurī served as page (*khāṣṣakī*), then as *jamdār*; in Dhu-l-Qa'da 886 (began 22nd December 1481) appointed Governor of the Southern District of Egypt (*kāshif al-wajh al-qiblī*); in Rabī' II 889 (May 1484) dubbed Amir of Ten; in 894 (1489) appointed Grand Chamberlain of Aleppo; in 903 (1497) promoted to the rank of a Commander of a Thousand; in Sha'bān 905 (March 1500) appointed Chief of the Corps of the Mamluks (*ra's naubat an-nuwwāb*); in 906 (1500), under Jānbalāṭ, became Grand Dawādār, Majordomo, Vizier, and *kāshif al-kushshāf*; shortly afterwards dismissed from office, but reinstated by Ṭūmānbāy. On the 1st Shawwāl 906 (20th April 1501) proclaimed sultan, acceded to the throne

[1] Ibn Iyās, especially II, pp. 211, l. 11 b, 222, l. 10, 259, l. 9 b, 366, l. 3, 379, l. 5 b, 380, l. 18, 390, l. 19, III, p. 58; Ibn Ṭūlūn, p. 62 (٣٣), ll. 24 ff.; Weil, V. 382, 383, 385 f., 414; Muir, *The Mameluke Slave Dynasty*, pp. 187, 199; Lane-Poole, *History of Egypt*, pp. 349, 354; Sobernheim, *The Encyclopaedia of Islām*, s.v. Ḳānṣūh (Engl. ed. II, p. 720 f.), with full literature; Rāghib Ṭabbākh, *A'lām an-nubalā'*, III. 99, 106, V. 390–5.

as al-Malik al-Ashraf. Met his death on the battle-field of Marj Dābiq, the 25th Rajab 922 (24th August 1516).

BLAZON: *On upper field a napkin, on middle field a cup charged with a pen-box and placed between a 'pair of trousers', on lower field a cup.*

COPPER BOWL on foot, tinned over, in possession of the present writer.
Inscription intersected by two shields:

ممّا عمل برسم المقرّ الأشرف الكريم العالى المولوى المخدومى السيفى قانصوه

الغورى أميرة ! حاجب الحجّاب بحلب المحروسة عزّ انصاره

This is one of the objects made for His Most Noble and Honourable and High Excellency, our Lord, the Well-Served, Saif ad-dīn Qānṣūh al-Ghaurī, Amir Grand Chamberlain in Aleppo, the protected, may his victories be glorious.

DATE: 894–903 (1489–97).
BIBLIOGRAPHY: Unpublished.

QĀNṢŪH AL-MUḤAMMADĪ[1]

Probably identical with S. Qānṣūh al-Muḥammadī, a page (*khāṣṣakī*) of al-Malik al-Ashraf Barsbāy; dubbed amir by al-Malik al-Manṣūr; under Khushqadam sent to Damascus. Died during an expedition against Siwār in Ṣafar 872 (September 1467).

BLAZON: *On upper field a napkin, on both the middle and lower fields a cup.*

COPPER VESSEL,[2] present owner unknown.
Inscription:

عمل برسم الجناب العالى المولوى الأشرفى [3] المخدومى السيفى قانصوه المحمّدى

عزّ نصره

[1] *Ḍau'*, s.v. (MS. Leyden, Cod. 369 a. Warn., p. 371).

[2] Rogers described it as a 'coffret en cuivre', by which he probably meant a lunch-box (*maṭbaqiyya*) made of copper tinned over.

[3] This word being either misread or inserted by Rogers out of its proper place, it was put between asterisks in the translation.

[*This is one of the objects*] *made for His High Excellency* (janāb), *our Lord,** (*officer*) *of* (*al-Malik*) *al-Ashraf,* the Well-Served, Saif ad-dīn Qānṣūh al-Muḥammadī, may his victory be glorious.*

BIBLIOGRAPHY: Rogers, No. 8, p. 116, fig. 28.

Reproduced: P[ier], *Saracenic Heraldry*, p. 10, fig. 10.

Mentioned: *CIA. Égypte*, I, p. 475, n.

QĀNṢŪH AL-YAḤYĀWĪ[1]

S. Qānṣūh al-Yaḥyāwī, originally a mamluk of Jaqmaq; appointed in turn Governor of Alexandria, Safad, Tripoli in 873 (1468), and Aleppo in Rabī' II 874 (began 8th October 1469); in 884 (1479) Viceroy of Syria; in 885 (1480) taken prisoner by Ya'qūb Beg b. Ḥasan; on his return in Rajab 886 (began 26th August 1481) exiled to Jerusalem, where in 888 (1483) he renewed the water-supply from 'Ain al-'Arrūb; in 892 (1487) for a second time appointed Viceroy of Syria; died in Damascus as Viceroy in 902 (1497).

BLAZON: *On the upper field a napkin, on the middle field a cup between a pen-box placed vertically and a horn* (?), *on the lower field a cup.*

1. PUBLIC FOUNTAIN, Aleppo, Sāḥat Bizzeh.

Three shields.

Inscription[2] at the rear wall of the fountain.

(١) بسمله . . . وَهُوَ ٱلَّذِى يُنَزِّلُ ٱلْغَيْثَ مِنْ بَعْدِ مَا قَنَطُوا وَيَنْشُرُ رَحْمَتَهُ وَهُوَ

ٱلْوَلِىُّ ٱلْحَمِيدُ

[1] *Nujūm*, VII, pp. 703, l. 15, 841, l. 1, 849, l. 19, 850, l. 2; *Ḍau'* s.v. (MS. Leyden. Cod. 369 a. Warn., p. 371); Ibn Iyās, cf. Index, especially II, p. 322, l. 14 b; Mujīr ad-dīn, *al-Uns al-jalīl*, pp. 413, 661/2 (Sauvaire, pp. 197, 293); Ibn Ṭūlūn, p. 83 (٢), l. 26, 82 (٣), l. 16, 81 (٤), ll. 9, 11 b, 79 (١), l. 12 b, 72 (١٣), ll. 15, 19; Weil, V. 342, 343, 367; Sobernheim, *Baalbek in islamischer Zeit*, p. 38.

[2] The inscription was hitherto illegible, several words having been mutilated and the whole slab covered over with at least three coatings of whitewash and oil-paint, on top of which somebody had painted what he believed to be the original text, an effort that rendered decipherment practically impossible. Thanks to the good offices of the French Commandant of Police at Aleppo, I was afforded an opportunity of at least partially clearing the inscription, as the result of which I submit the above reading.

(2) أمر بإنشاء [هذا السبيل] المبارك المقرّ العالى المولوى الأميرى الكبيرى

العضدى الذخرى [1 word] السيفى قانصوه اليحياوى

(3) [3–4 words] كافل المملكة الحلبيّة المحروسة أعزّ الله أنصاره وذلك فى

عاشر محرّم سنة ثلاث وثمانين وثمانمائة

In the name of the most merciful God. It is He who sendeth down the rain after men have despaired thereof, and spendeth abroad His mercy, and He is the patron firstly to be praised (Qur'ān, XLII. 27). *Ordered to build this blessed fountain His High Excellency, our Lord, the Great Amir, the Supporter, the Treasure,* [1 word] *Saif ad-dīn Qānṣūh al-Yaḥyāwī* [3–4 words] *the Viceroy of the protected province of Aleppo, may God make his victories glorious. This was done the* 10*th Muḥarram* 883 (13th April 1478).

BIBLIOGRAPHY: Unpublished.

Blazon mentioned and reproduced: Creswell, *Two Khâns at Khân Ṭûmân*, p. 137, pl. XXVII A.

2. PUBLIC FOUNTAIN, Damascus, 26 Rue Camahin.

Inscription at the back wall of the fountain:

(1) فى خامس عشرين ربيع الآخر سنة أربعة (!) وO تسعمائة أحسن الله على

[2 words not clear]

(2) آمين يا ربّ العالمين صلّى الله على O سيّدنا محمّد وآله وصحبه وسلّم

(3) العالى المولوى الأميرى السيفى أزدمر نقيب القلعة المنصورة بالشأم المحروس

اعزّ الله أنصاره وتقبّل منه بتربة المرحوم أستاذه المقرّ الأشرف السيفى قانصوه

اليحياوى الكاف[لى]

On the 25*th Rabī' II* 904 (10th December 1498), *may God bestow his gifts upon ... Amen. O Lord of the Worlds! May God bless our Lord Muḥammad and his family and his companions and give them peace.*

... [*His*] *High* [*Excellency*], *our Lord, the Amir, Saif ad-dīn Uzdamur,*[1] *Commandant of the victorious fortress in the protected Damascus. May God make his victories glorious and accept this offering in the mausoleum of his late master, His Most Noble Excellency, Saif ad-dīn Qānṣūh al-Yaḥyāwī, the Viceroy.* ...

I presume that behind the back wall of the fountain there was the mausoleum of Qānṣūh which I could not examine at the time of my last visit to Damascus. The fragmentary text of lines 1 and 2 containing Qānṣūh's blazon and a date—two years after his death—but no name, obviously belongs to line 3 (the beginning and end of which are both covered by the comparatively modern side-walls of the fountain) although the relation between the two is not clear. It is quite possible that the upper one is not in situ.

S. Uzdamur is probably identical with Uzdamur *al-mushidd*, Commandant of the fortress of Damascus in 902 (1496/7), who may have remained in office till 906.[2] What he did in or for the mausoleum of Qānṣūh is not clear, except that he did not establish any endowment in its favour, as in that case the Arabic text would have had على تربة instead of the present بتربة.

BIBLIOGRAPHY: Unpublished.

Blazon reproduced with inaccurate description in Artin, *Contribution*, No. 99 *bis*, p. 123.

3. COPPER BOWL, tinned over, in possession of Professor C. H. Becker, Berlin, late Minister of Education of the State of Prussia.

Two shields, two texts without historical interest, viz.:

(1) الصبر عبادة ا (2) الخير عبادة لم

BIBLIOGRAPHY: Unpublished.

4. FAÇADE of a ruined house, Aleppo, Rue Djoub Esadallah, opposite the Dār Shībānī. Pl. LXVI. 4.

BIBLIOGRAPHY: Unpublished.

Although blazons 3 and 4 are anonymous, I venture to class them here because of the peculiar combination of emblems unknown from other blazons.

A plate, with blazon and inscription, of which M. J. Sauvaget has kindly sent me a sketch and a copy, is deserving of special mention.

BLAZON: *A pen-box on the middle field of a three-fielded shield.*

[1] In vocalizing the name ازدمر I am guided by Ibn Taghrībirdī, *Manhal*, s.v. (MS. Paris, Ar. 2068, fo. 167ᵛ). Cf. L. A. Mayer, *Arabic Inscriptions of Gaza III*, p. 223 f.

[2] Ibn Ṭūlūn, p. 26(٥٩).

The inscription reads as follows:

مما عمل برسم المقر الكبير ا ۞ العالي المولوي الكبيري ۞ السيفي كؤور؟؟؟ ما ا الحجياي ۞

كافل المملكة الحلبية عز أنصاره ۞

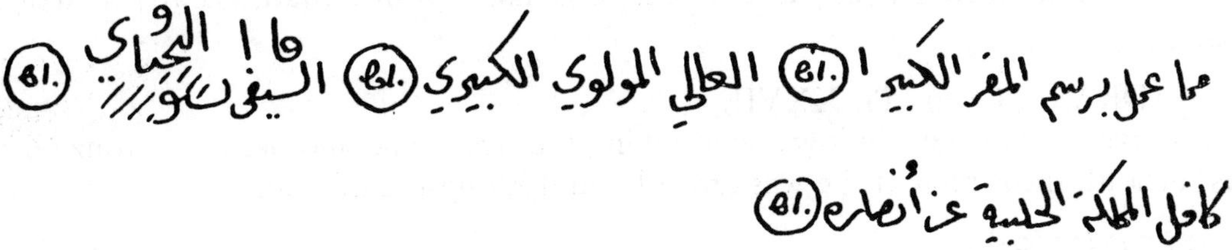

This is one of the objects made for His Great[1] and High Excellency, our Lord, the Great (Amir),[2]
Saif ad-dīn Qānṣūh al-Yaḥyāwī, Viceroy of the province of Aleppo, may his victories be glorious.

A glance at the facsimile shows that there are corrections just in the portions containing
the name, suggestive of this object having been made for a governor of Aleppo, probably a century before Qānṣūh was dubbed amir. When it passed into the latter's
possession, the name of the original owner was obliterated and Qānṣūh's engraved in
its place.

QARĀSUNQUR[3]

Sh. Qarāsunqur al-Jarkasī al-Manṣūrī, bought by Qalāūn, before the latter
became Sultan; first made a page and polo-master, then Governor of Hama;
in 681[4] appointed Governor of Aleppo; remained in office till al-Malik al-
Ashraf's accession to the throne; recalled to Egypt as *amīr jandār*; under Lājīn,
Viceroy of Egypt till replaced by Mankūtamur in Dhu-l-Qaʿda 696 (began
21st August 1297); Governor of Ṣubaiba under Muḥammad b. Qalāūn; in
698 appointed Governor of Hama; in 699 transferred to Aleppo as Governor;
on Muḥammad b. Qalāūn's third accession to the throne, appointed Viceroy
of Syria; entered Damascus in Dhu-l-Qaʿda 709 (April 1310); remained in

---

[1] الكبير was perhaps intended for الكريم 'Honourable'.

[2] الأميري being omitted, due, perhaps, to carelessness on the part of the engraver.

[3] Zetterstéen, *Beiträge* esp. pp. 43, l. 12, 80, l. 15, 82, l. 1, 96, l. 17, 108, l. 11, 129, l. 1, 130, l. 15,
131, l. 19, 133, l. 21, 134, l. 17, 145, l. 21, 151, ll. 4, 14, 154, l. 10, 155, l. 1, 157, ll. 4, 9, 180, l. 1.
Ibn Baṭṭūṭa, I. 167–72; Ibn Ḥabīb, pp. 269, 293, 296, 298, 313, 317; *SM.* II a, pp. 53, 62, 110,
139, 141, 143, II b, pp. 42, 50 f., 127, 133, 139 n. 10, 169, 281; *Khiṭaṭ*, II. 388–90 (2nd ed., IV.
232–5); *Durar*, s.v. (MS. Br. Mus. Or. 3044, fo. 38ʳ and ᵛ); *Manhal*, s.v. (MS. Paris. Ar. 2072, fo. 15ʳ
and ᵛ); Ibn Iyās, I, pp. 126, l. 5 b, 136, l. 15, 137, l. 3, 152, l. 6, 157, l. 8 b.; Weil, cf. Index, where
several details concerning this Qarāsunqur are mentioned under Q. al-Muʿizzī; *CR.* Exerc. 1891, fasc. 7,
p. 44; Rāghib Ṭabbākh, *Aʿlām*, II. 335–8, 347, 350, 352, 359, 361–7.

[4] *Khiṭaṭ*, II, p. 388, l. 28: in Shaʿbān, 682.

office till 711,[1] when he fled to the Tartars. Died in Marāgha 27th Shawwāl 728 (14th September 1328) as a septuagenarian. Built a madrasa and a ribāṭ in Cairo.

1. MADRASA, Cairo. Pl. XXVII. 1, 2.
Shield over one of the windows overlooking the street, and another on a bronze band just beneath the capital of the western column flanking the mihrab.

DATE: 700 (1300–1).

BIBLIOGRAPHY: Unpublished.

2. PUBLIC FOUNTAIN, locally known as Qasṭal Maqāmāt, in a lane leading to the Jāmiʿ al-Maqām, Aleppo-Firdaus. Pl. XXVII. 3, 4.

Inscription flanked by two shields.

(1) بسمله . . . أمر بإنشآء هذا السبيل المبارك المولى الأمير الكبير المجاهد المرابط الخاضع لربّه المنان المفتقر الى

(2) عفو الله والرضوان شمس الدنيا والدين قراسنقر الجوكندار المنصورى الناصرى نائب السلطنة الشريفة بحلب المحروسة اثابه

(3) الله تعالى وضاعف له الحسنات وجعل ذخره الباقيات الصالحات كُتب فى المحرّم سنة ثلاث وسبع مائة من الهجرة النبويّة

In the name of the most merciful God. Ordered to construct this blessed public fountain the Lord, the Great Amir, the Defender of the Faith, the Warrior at the Frontiers . . . Shams ad-dunyā wa-d-dīn Qarāsunqur, the polo-master, (officer) of (al-Malik) al-Manṣūr and (al-Malik) an-Nāṣir, Governor of the Noble Sultanate in Aleppo, the protected, may God the Exalted give him reward and multiply the good deeds for him and make his treasure the pious deeds that last. Written in Muḥarram of the year 703 (began 15th August 1303) *of the Hijra of the Prophet.*

BIBLIOGRAPHY: Unpublished.

[1] According to Zetterstéen, l.c., and Ibn Taghrībirdī, l.c., he was appointed Governor of Aleppo for a third time, remained in office a short time (فاستمّر بها أيّاما) and then fled.

QAṢRAUH[1]

S. Qaṣrauh b. ʿAbdallāh,[2] originally a mamluk of Timrāz aẓ-Ẓāhirī, passed into the service of Sultan Barqūq; under al-Malik al-Mu'ayyad Shaikh became Amir of Ten; the 1st Rabīʿ II 816 (1st July 1413) arrested and imprisoned in Alexandria; released the 7th Ramaḍān 821 (8th October 1418); the 3rd Ramaḍān 824 (1st September 1421) became Chief of the Corps of Mamluks and Amir of a Hundred; the 13th Dhu-l-Ḥijja 824 (9th December 1421); appointed Grand Marshal; on the 26th[3] Ṣafar 826 (8th February 1423) appointed Governor of Tripoli; in 830 (1426/7) transferred to Aleppo as Governor; the 29th Rajab 837 (12th March 1434) appointed Viceroy of Syria, a post he held till his death, 3rd Rabīʿ II 839 (26th October 1435). Built a dome over the shrine of ʿAbdallāh al-Anṣārī, near Aleppo.

BLAZON: *A napkin on top, a pen-box in the middle, a cup at the bottom displayed on a napkin without dividing lines. Round shield.*

PUBLIC FOUNTAIN, Aleppo, known as Qasṭal Bāb al-Maqām.
Inscription in the niche. On the façade to the left of the onlooker a shield; on the other side of the façade there was probably originally another shield, hidden to-day by a mean shop.

(1) أنشأ هذا السبيل المبارك فى ايّام مولانا السلطان الملك الأشرف برسباى خلد الله ملكه وأدام اقتداره

(2) فى كفالة المقرّ الأشرف قصروه كافل المملكة الحلبيّة المحروسة اعز الله أنصاره المقرّ السيفى بالك الأشرفى نائب القلعة

[1] *Nujūm*, VI, especially pp. 327, l. 5, 388, l. 1, 493, l. 18, 504, l. 6, 512, l. 1, 521, l. 21, 532, l. 5, 563, l. 16, 596, l. 16, 597, l. 20, 620, l. 12, 714, l. 22, 735, l. 19, 738, l. 17, 796, l. 21, 809, l. 1, 839, l. 16, 840, l. 10; *Manhal*, s.v. (MS. Paris, Ar. 2072, fo. 23r–24r); *Ḍau'*, s.v. (MS. Leyden, Cod. 369 a. Warn. p. 393); Ibn Iyās, II, p. 16, l. 20, p. 18, l. 6 b; Sobernheim, *CIA. Syrie du Nord*, pp. 63 ff.; Weil, V. 165 f., 187, 192, 203; Rāghib Ṭabbākh, *Aʿlām*, III. 23 f.

[2] Ibn Iyās calls him Q. b. ʿUthmān.

[3] *Nujūm*, VI, p. 563, l. 20: on the 12th Ṣafar.

(3) المنصورة بحلب المحروسة أعزّ الله أنصاره فى العشر الأوّل من شهر ذو القعدة سنة أحد وثلاثين وثمان مائة

Constructed this blessed public fountain in the days of our Lord, the Sultan al-Malik al-Ashraf Barsbāy, may God make his reign eternal and make his power last, under the viceroyalty of His Most Noble Excellency, Qaṣrauh, Viceroy of the protected province of Aleppo, may God make his victories glorious, His Excellency Saif ad-dīn Bāk al-Ashrafī,[1] *Governor of the victorious fortress of Aleppo, the protected, may God make his victories glorious; in the first ten days of the month Dhu-l-Qa'da of the year* 831 (12th–21st August 1428).

BIBLIOGRAPHY: Unpublished.

QAUṢŪN[2 3]

S. Qauṣūn came to Egypt as a merchant in 720 (began 12th February 1320), became cupbearer of Muḥammad b. Qalāūn, attained within a short time to the grade of Amir of a Hundred and Commander of a Thousand. Married in 727 the Sultan's daughter. After Muḥammad's death became Commander-in-Chief (*atābak*) during the short reign of al-Malik al-Manṣūr Abū Bakr and *atābak* and Viceroy of his successor al-Malik al-Ashraf Kujuk. Arrested in 742 (1341/2); remained in prison until strangled by Aḥmad b. Muḥammad b. Qalāūn in Shawwāl (or in Dhu-l-Qa'da) 742 (March–April 1342).

BLAZON: ***Upper field self-coloured, on united golden middle and lower fields a red cup.***

1. GLASS LAMP. Metropolitan Museum of Art, New York. Originally collection Mannheim, then J. Pierpont Morgan.

Inscription on neck, intersected by two shields: First words of Qur'ān, XXX. 35.

Inscription on body:

[1] S. Bāk, a mamluk of amir Ṭaṭar, became Chief of a Corps of Mamluks, the 11th Sha'bān 824 (11th August 1421); appointed Governor of the fortress of Aleppo; died there after the year 833. *Nujūm*, VI, p. 503, l. 12; *Manhal*, s.v. (MS. Paris, Ar. 2069, fo. 50^{r}).

[2] Zetterstéen, *Beiträge*, pp. 191, l. 1, 201, l. 2, 203, l. 2 ff., 217, l. 12, 226, ll. 10, 16, 227, l. 20. Ṣafadī, *A'yān*, s.v. (MS. Berlin, fo. 114^{v}–115^{v}); Ibn Ḥabīb, p. 375 f.; *Khiṭaṭ*, II. 72–3, 307 (2nd ed., III. 116–18, IV. 104 f.); *Durar*, s.v. (MS. Br. Mus. Or. 3044, fo. 40^{r} and ^{v}); *Manhal*, s.v. (MS. Paris, Ar. 2072, fo. 36^{v}–37^{v}); Ibn Iyās, I. 167 f., 176–9; Weil, IV. 369–70, 415–17, 420, 422–4, 428, 431, 432, 434, 441.

[3] Spelling indicated by vowel-signs in *A'yān*, s.v. (l.c., fos. 26^{r}, l. 10 b, 22^{v}, l. 6 b, 114^{v}).

مما عمل برسم المقرّ ا | العالى المولوى المالكى | المخدومى السيفى | قوصون

الساقى | الملكى الناصرى

This is one of the objects made for His High Excellency, our Lord, the Royal, the Well-Served, Saif ad-dīn Qauṣūn, the cup-bearer of al-Malik an-Nāṣir.

DATE: Having been made for Qauṣūn's mosque in Cairo, this lamp should be dated 730 (1329).

BIBLIOGRAPHY: Schmoranz, pp. 66–7, 69, figs. 66–8, pl. XXXIV; Artin, *Quatre lampes*, pp. 81 ff., pl. IV, where قوصون is spelt with a *sīn* and الملكى with an additional *alif*.

Mentioned and reproduced: Molinier, *Collection Mannheim*, p. 39 and fig.; Dimand, *Handbook*, p. 196, fig. 120.

Mentioned: *CIA. Jérusalem, Ville*, p. 289, n. 4; Wiet, *Lampes*, p. 159, No. 26.

2. GLASS LAMP. Originally collection Gérôme, present owner unknown.

BIBLIOGRAPHY: *CIA. Égypte*, I. 179, n. 2.

Mentioned: Schmoranz, p. 69; Wiet, *Lampes*, p. 159, No. 27; Lamm, p. 438, No. 41.

3. CARAVANSERAI (*wakālah*), Cairo.

Two shields in the upper angles of the frame in which the doorway is set.

Inscription to the right and left of the entrance:

. . . انشأ هذا الخان المبارك المقرّ الأشرف العالى . . . قوصون الساقى الملكى

الناصرى . . .

. . . *Constructed this blessed caravanserai His Most Noble and High Excellency . . . Qauṣūn the cup-bearer, (officer) of al-Malik an-Nāṣir . . .*

BIBLIOGRAPHY: *CIA. Égypte*, I. 180 f. without mentioning the blazon.

Mentioned: *CR.* Exerc. 1901, fasc. 18, p. 88; Creswell, *Brief Chronology*, p. 97.

4. FOUNDATION TEXT of a cistern used as tombstone at Qalansuweh (Map of the Palestine Exploration Fund, Sheet XI, J.n.). Pl. XXXV. 3.

Three shields in the fourth line of the inscription.

Inscription not in situ.

(1) بسمله . . . وَلَنَجْزِيَنَّهُمْ أَجْرَهُمْ بِأَحْسَنِ مَا كَانُوا يَعْمَلُونَ

(2) امر بإنشاء هذا الحوض المبارك السعيد فى أيّام مولانا السلطان ا

(3) الملك الناصر العبد الفقير الى الله تعالى المقرّ الأشرف السيفى عون

(4) ○ الأمّة كهف الملّة ضوء ○ الدولة قوصون الناصرى ○

(5) الساقى أعزّ الله تعالى أنصاره وختم بالصالحات أعماله ابتغاء لوجه الله تعالى

(6) للسبيل لسائر خلق الله والوقف عليه القطعة الأرض غربى الحوض

(7) (1 word) فى العشر الآخر من ربيع الأوّل سنة تسع وثلاثين وسبعمائة

والله (1 word)

In the name of the most merciful God. And we will give them their reward, according to the utmost merit of their actions (Qur'ān, XVI. 99). *Ordered the construction of this blessed and gladdening cistern in the days of our Lord, the Sultan, al-Malik an-Nāṣir, the servant yearning for God the Exalted, His Most Noble Excellency Saif ad-dīn, the Support of the Nation, the Refuge of the Religion, the Light of the Government, Qauṣūn an-Nāṣirī, the cup-bearer, may God, the Exalted, make his victories glorious, and his last works pious ones, in his desire to please God, the Exalted, as a pious foundation for all creatures of God. Its waqf consists of a plot of land to the west of the cistern.... In the last ten days of Rabī' I of the year* 737 (28th October–6th November 1336), *and God . . .*

BIBLIOGRAPHY: Unpublished.
Mentioned: *CIA. Jérusalem, Ville*, p. 289, n.

QĀYTBĀY[1]

BLAZON: *On upper field a napkin, on both middle and lower fields a cup.*

COPPER BASIN, in 1888 in the collection Garnier de Heldévire, Cairo, present owner unknown.

[1] Identified by Artin, l.c., with Sultan Qāytbāy. Van Berchem has pointed out, l.c., that this identification is void of foundation.

Inscription:

ممّا عمل برسم الجناب العالى | المو[و]ى الأميرى | illegible | السيفى قايتباى
عزّ أنصاره

This is one of the objects made for His High Excellency (janāb), *our Lord, the Amir . . . Saif ad-din Qāytbāy, may his victories be glorious.*

BIBLIOGRAPHY: Artin, *Trois différentes armoiries de Kaït Bay*, p. 72 f.

Mentioned: van Berchem, *Notes*, III. 76, n. 1.

QĀZĀN

BLAZON: *Upper field blank, on united middle and lower fields a pair of polo-sticks*.

COPPER DISH tinned over. Collection R. A. Harari Esq., London. Pl. XXVI. 3. Inscription intersected by four shields.

ممّا عمل برسم الجناب ○ العالى المولوى الأ○ميرى السيفى قازان ○ الجمدار
العلائى ○

This is one of the objects made for His High Excellency (janāb), *our Lord, the Amir, Saif ad-dīn Qāzān, the jamdār of 'Alā' ad-dīn.*

BIBLIOGRAPHY: Unpublished.

QIJLĪS[1 2]

S. Qijlīs an-Nāṣirī, originally a mamluk of Muḥammad b. Qalāūn and his armour-bearer, charged with various missions such as the transmitting of news, of insignia of appointments, of Sultanian orders, the accompanying of

[1] Abu-l-Fidā', s.a. 710, ed. Reiske, V, p. 232, l. 6, 238, ll. 7, 12; Zetterstéen, *Beiträge*, pp. 159, l. 4 b, 162, l. 5 b, 163, ll. 1, 7, 9, 167, l. 1, 171 ult., 176, l. 3 b, 182, l. 21; *Durar*, s.v. (MS. Br. Mus. Or. 3044, fo. 37v–38r); Ibn Ḥabīb, p. 342; *Manhal*, s.v. (MS. Paris, Ar. 2072, fo. 12r); Ibn Iyās, I, pp. 159, l. 7, 161, l. 20.

[2] Spelt by European scholars *Caglis* (Reiske), *Kaḥlīs* (Lane-Poole, van Berchem), *Kahtis* (Artin), *Kadjlich* (Migeon). In the printed text of Ibn Iyās قجليش. The proper spelling was first established by Wiet, *Lampes*, p. 159.

princes and princesses, the escorting of prisoners; in Shawwāl 717 (began 7th December 1317) leader of the pilgrimage; appointed *Amīr silāḥ* with the rank of an Amir of Forty not later than 721 (1321). Died the 15th Ṣafar 731 (28th November 1330).

BLAZON: *Upper and lower fields red, on self-coloured middle field black scimitar with white bands.*

GLASS LAMP, Victoria and Albert Museum, London, No. 580—'75.
Inscription on the neck intersected by three shields: Qur'ān, IX. 18, till الصلاة (... 'and is constant in prayer').
Inscription on the body:

هذا ما أوقفه || العبد الفقير الى | الله تعالى الرا || جى عفو ربّه الكر || يم قجليس

الملكى | الناصرى

This is what was made a waqf by the servant yearning for God, the Exalted, hoping for the pardon of his generous Lord, Qijlīs, (officer) of al-Malik an-Nāṣir.

On the lower part of the body three more shields.

DATE: This lamp has been dated 700 (1300) by Artin Pasha, ll. cc. *infra*; until some reason is given for such a date, it seems very improbable, because Qijlīs appears for the first time in history in 710 in a very inferior position as *silaḥdār*, who brought the letter-patent to Abu-l-Fidā'. The lamp being suggestive of considerable wealth on the part of its owner, we should prefer to assume that it was made at least 15–20 years later.

BIBLIOGRAPHY: Nesbitt, *Catalogue of the Glass Vessels in the South Kensington Museum*, p. 38 f.; Lane-Poole, *The Art of the Saracens*, pp. 258, 272.
Blazon described and reproduced: Schmoranz, pp. 12 f., 20, fig. 9; Artin, *Contribution*, No. 133, pp. 130, 237; Rogers, p. 124, No. 21, fig. 41.
Mentioned: Artin, *Quatre lampes*, p. 85, n. 1; Migeon, *Manuel* (2nd ed.), II. 135; Wiet, *Lampes*, p. 159 f., No. 28; Lamm, p. 439, No. 42.

QULUNJAQ[1]

S. Qulunjaq, appointed Amir of a Thousand on Qalāūn's accession to the throne.

[1] *SM.* I b, p. 171; Ibn Iyās, I, p. 115, l. 3 قلجق, Sobernheim, *Arabische Gefässinschriften von der Ausstellung islamischer Kunst in Paris*, p. 178.

BLAZON: *White pointed shield.*

BRONZE PLATE, Musée Jacquemart-André, Paris.

Twenty-four shields, three of which intersect the shorter of the two inscriptions here reproduced:

مماّ عمل برسم الامير الاجلّ الكبير المجاهد المرابط المثاغر المجتبى المرتضى

المخدوم عضد الملوك واختيار السلاطين سيف الدين قلنجق الظاهر[ى] السعيدى

دام عزّه

This is one of the objects made for the Most Magnificent and Great Amir, the Defender of the Faith, the Warrior at the Frontiers, the Warden of the Marches, the Elect, the Chosen, the Well-Served, the Supporter of the Kings and the Chosen of the Sultans, Saif ad-dīn Qulunjaq, (officer) of (al-Malik) aẓ-Ẓāhir and (al-Malik) as-Sa'īd, may his glory last for ever.

DATE: Between 663, the year in which Baraka Khān assumed the title al-Malik as-Sa'īd, and Dhu-l-Qa'da 678 (March 1280), the date of his death.

BIBLIOGRAPHY: Sobernheim, l.c. *infra*, No. 1, pp. 177–9, pl. VI a, inscription without blazon.

Mentioned: Van Berchem, *Notes*, III. 36 and n.; Bertaux, *Musée Jacquemart-André*, No. 978 (6th ed.), p. 136; Migeon, *Manuel* (2nd ed.) II, p. 69.

QUMĀRĪ[1 2]

Probably identical with S. Qumārī, a junior amir during the lifetime of his brother Baktamur as-Sāqī; in 733 (1332) promoted to the rank of an Amir of a Hundred; in 742 (1341/2) appointed Grand Marshal, later Major-domo of al-Malik aṣ-Ṣāliḥ Isma'īl; on the 11th Rabī' II 746 (11th August 1345) appointed Governor of Tripoli. Arrested towards the end of Dhu-l-Ḥijja 746 (April 1346); imprisoned in Alexandria; executed early in 747 (1346).

BLAZON: *A pair of polo-sticks on the united middle and lower field of a two-fielded shield.*

[1] *A'yān*, s.v. (MS. Berlin, fo. 114^{v}); *Manhal*, s.v. (MS. Paris, Ar. 2072, fo. 35^{r}); Ibn Iyās, I, p. 184, l. 5; Weil, especially IV. 441, 453, 463, 466, n. 1; Sobernheim, *CIA. Syrie du Nord*, p. 101 ff.

[2] Spelling indicated in words in *Manhal*, s.v. Mūsā b. Qumārī (MS. Cairo, III, fo. 377^{r}).

Two WOODEN PANELS, National Museum of Arab Art, Cairo, No. 3405; in 1880 in the collection de St. Maurice. Pl. XXVI. 2.
Inscription intersected by one shield:

الجناب العا○لى السيفى قمارى

His High Excellency (janāb), *Saif ad-dīn Qumārī.*

BIBLIOGRAPHY: Rogers, No. 23, p. 125, fig. 43 (who read the name as Kumây). Mentioned: *CIA. Jérusalem, Ville*, p. 269, n. 4.

QUSHTUMUR

BLAZON: *Round shield with five bars.*

BRASS DISH, in the collection of R. A. Harari, Esq., London. Pl. XLII. 6.

One shield in the centre. Inscription intersected by two heraldic shields and two six-petalled whirling rosettes, marked r.

○ الجناب العالى المولوى الأميرى الكبيرى ⊙ العالمى العاملى العادلى الغازى ○

المجاهد المرابطى المثاغرى السيفى سيف الدين ⊙ قشتمر شادّ الدواوين بالديار

المصريّة عزّ أنصاره ○

His High Excellency (janāb), *our Lord, the Great Amir, the Learned, the Governing, the Just, the Vanquisher, the Defender of the Faith, the Warrior at the Frontiers, the Warden of the Marches, Saif ad-dīn Qushtumur, Superintendent of Chanceries in the Kingdom of Egypt, may his victories be glorious.*

BIBLIOGRAPHY: Unpublished.

QUṬB AD-DAMURDĀSHĪ

BLAZON: *On upper field a napkin, on middle field two cups, on lower field a pen-box.*[1]

COPPER VASE, once in the possession of Mason Bey, present owner unknown.

[1] Possibly the blazon should be described as showing *on upper field a pen-box, on middle field two cups, on lower field a napkin.* Artin Pasha did not recognize the two cups ('un ornement que je ne puis déterminer'), moreover, he may have held the vase upside down when describing the shield, as he had done in other cases, cf. e.g. No. 105, a shield showing *on upper field a napkin, on middle field a pen-box, on lower field a cup*, having turned the dish upside down, he failed to recognize the cup.

Inscription:

عمل الجناب العالى المولوى المحمدى الأمير الكبير القطب الدمرداشى دام عزّه [1]

. . . *His High Excellency, our Lord . . . the Great Amir Quṭb* (*ad-dīn*) *ad-Damurdāshī, may his glory last for ever.*

BIBLIOGRAPHY: Artin, *Contribution*, No. 107, p. 125.

QUṬLŪ KHĀTŪN

BLAZON: *Polo-sticks on the combined middle and lower fields of a two-fielded shield.*

CENOTAPH in the courtyard of the Zāwiyat as-Sayyid Aḥmad al-Badawī, Gaza.

A shield on each of the two pillars flanking the inscription, the essential portion of which runs as follows:

. . . هذا ضريح الستّ . . . الشهيدة قطلو خاتون ابنة المقرّ المرحوم بهادر
الجوكندار . . . وكان وفاتها يوم الاثنين الثانى من شهر ربيع الآخر سنة ثلاث
وثلاثين وسبعمائة

. . . *This is the tomb of the Lady . . . the late Quṭlū Khātūn, daughter of His Excellency, the late Bahādur, the Polo-master*[2] . . . *She passed away Monday, the 2nd Rabīʿ II of the year* 733 (21st December 1332).

BIBLIOGRAPHY: Mayer, *Arabic Inscriptions of Gaza*, I, pp. 76 ff., pl. 3.

QUṬLŪBUGHĀ

BLAZON: *Upper field probably self-coloured, on middle field pen-box consisting of ink-pot, three small pots, and three reed-holders, on lower field criss-cross pattern.*

BASIN, collection R. A. Harari, Esq., London. Pl. XXXIV. 1.

Inscription intersected by three shields on the inside of the rim.

[1] The text is obviously corrupt, the words ممّا . . . برسم being missing at the beginning; المحمدى is probably misread for المحترمى.

[2] Bahādur the Polo-master, an Amir of Forty in Damascus, died in Ṣafar 723, *Aʿyān*, s.v. (MS. Aya Sophia, No. 2970); *Durar*, s.v.

مـمّا عمل برسم الجناب العالى المولوى الأميرى الكبيرى ○ السيّدى المالكى

المخدومى السيفى سيف الدين قطلوبغا ○ الدوادر المقرّ الأشرف السيفى ارغون

الإسعردى عزّ نصره ○

This is one of the objects made for His High Excellency (janāb), *our Lord, the Great Amir, the Master, the Royal, the Well-Served, Saif ad-dīn Quṭlūbughā, the dawādār of His Most Noble Excellency, Saif ad-dīn Arghūn al-Is'ardī, may his victory be glorious.*

DATE: The *terminus ad quem* for this object is Arghūn's death, some time after 778.

BIBLIOGRAPHY: Unpublished.

RAZMAK[1]

BLAZON: *Two scimitars placed diagonally on the middle field of a three-fielded shield.*

FOUNDER'S TEXT embedded in the façade of the Mosque, locally known as Jāmi' Ibn 'Uthmān, Gaza. The inscription is probably not *in situ*.

In each of the four corners a shield.
Inscription:

(١) بسمله . . . أنشأ هذه المدرسة المباركة العبد الفقير الى (2) الله تعالى

المقرّ السيفى رزمك الملكى الظاهرى عزّ نصره بتأريخ شهر شعبان سنة سبع

وتسعين وسبعمائة

In the name of the most merciful God. Constructed this blessed school the servant yearning for God the Exalted, His Excellency Saif ad-dīn Razmak, (officer) of al-Malik aẓ-Ẓāhir, [*may God make*] *his victory* [*glorious*], *during the month of Sha'bān of the year* 797 (began 22 May 1395).

BIBLIOGRAPHY: Unpublished.

Mentioned: Mayer, *Arabic Inscriptions of Gaza*, III. 222.

[1] With regard to the spelling of this name, cf. Mayer, l.c., n. 2. In the present case I have chosen the variant Razmak, the *alif* being missing in the above text.

SALADIN

In his *Saladin and the Fall of the Kingdom of Jerusalem*, p. 286, Stanley Lane-Poole quotes a passage from the *Itinerary of King Richard I* (Book III, chap. 1) reading as follows: 'Our men could also see Saladin's own pair of lions and those of his brother Saphadin and Takadin the champion of heathendom.'[1] This would mean that the lion was a family emblem as far back as the early Ayyubids. But there is nothing in the Latin text to justify such an assumption. Stubbs's edition, p. 210 f., says: 'Vident quoque *papiliones*[2] ipsius Salahadini, et *tentoria*[2] fratris ipsius Saphahadini et procuratoris Paganismi Techehedini,' i.e. pavilions and tents, not lions. It should be pointed out that the lion on one of Saladin's copper-coins[3] may be of an astrological character but is doubtless not heraldic, and that the eagle in the Citadel of Cairo[4] is of very uncertain date, probably considerably later than the period of Saladin and Qarāqūsh.

ṢALĀḤ AD-DĪN B. SAMRĪ

BLAZON: *Emblem No. 43 on undivided shield.*

CANDLESTICK, Musée du Louvre, Paris, formerly in the collection Delort de Gléon. Pl. LII. 1.

Inscription flanked by two shields on the socket of the candlestick.

○ مما عمل برسم الأمير صلاح الدين ابن سمرى ○

This is one of the objects made for the Amir Ṣalāḥ ad-dīn, son of Samrī.

BIBLIOGRAPHY: Unpublished.

Mentioned: Migeon, *L'Orient Musulman*, vol. *Sculpture*, &c., No. 108, p. 26.

1 l.c., p. 282 n. + explaining it as 'quoted from T. A. Archer's admirable *Crusade of Richard I*'.
2 Italicized by the present writer.
3 Lavoix, *Catalogue des Monnaies Musulmanes*, vol. *Égypte et Syrie*, No. 491 f., p. 188 f., pl. v.
4 Nützel, *Embleme*, p. 14; Lane-Poole, *History of Egypt*, p. 228, fig. 52.

SALĀR[1]

S. Salār, son of a Master of the Hunt at the Saljūq court, known as the dispatch-rider (*barīdī*), captured by Baybars, bought by Qalāūn, became one of the most important mamluks of the latter, passed first into the service of Khalīl b. Qalāūn, then into that of Muḥammad b. Qalāūn, on Lājīn's accession to the throne took the oath from the Egyptian amirs, the 4th Jumādā I 698 (7th February 1299), appointed Viceroy of Egypt, remained in office as such under Baybars al-Jāshnigīr. On Muḥammad's third accession to the throne at his own request appointed Governor of Kerak. Died in prison either in Rabīʿ II or in Jumādā I 710 (September or October 1310).

BLAZON: *Dark middle field on white three-fielded shield.*

BIBLIOGRAPHY: The colour of this blazon is indicated in *Nujūm*, s.a. 711. وكان رنك سلار أبيض وأسود (MS. Paris, Ar. 1783, fo. 77^v) quoted by *SM.* II a, p. 15, no. 12; Rogers, p. 98; Casanova, 'L'historien Ibn 'Abd aḍh-Ḍhâhir' (in *MMAF.* VI, p. 499); Artin, *Contribution*, p. 135 f.; Lane-Poole, *Art of the Saracens*, p. 270; Prinet, *De l'origine orientale des armoiries européennes*, p. 54; *CIA. Jérusalem, Ville*, p. 235.

SHRINE of Shaikh 'Alī Bakkā', Hebron.

Inscription over the entrance door intersected by two shields.[2]

Repeated on the courtyard side of the gate.

The essential portion of the inscription runs as follows:

. . . امر بانشاء هذه المأذنة المباركة المقرّ العالى السيفى سيف الدين سلار

ابن عبد الله الناصرى نائب السلطنة المعظّمة وكفيل الممالك الشريفة بالديار المصريّة

والشاميّة . . . ○ . . . كتب بتأريخ مستهلّ رمضان ○ المعظّم سنة اثنى وسبعمائة

هجريّة . . .

[1] Zetterstéen, *Beiträge*, cf. Index, especially pp. 54, l. 5, 81, l. 18, 96, l. 14, 108, l. 3, 130, l. 9, 131, l. 12, 133, l. 14, 134, l. 11, 135, l. 17, 137, l. ult., 146, l. 14, 151, l. 1 f., 153, ll. 11, 16; Ṣāliḥ b. Yaḥyā, p. 174 f.; *SM.* II b, pp. 41, 126; *Khiṭaṭ*, II. 417 (2nd ed., IV. 277); *Manhal*, s.v. (MS. Paris, Ar. 2070, fo. 92^r–94^r); Ibn Iyās, I. 155; Weil, IV. 207, 221, 223, 281, 302 f.; *CIA. Égypte*, I. 158–60, 226, 653; Jaussen, 'Inscription Arabe du Khân al-Aḥmar à Beïsân (Palestine)' (in *BIFAO.* t. XXII, 1922, pp. 101–3).

[2] The colour of the fesse is the colour of the stone of which the building was made, viz. dirty dark red.

... *Ordered to construct this blessed minaret His High Excellency, Saif ad-dīn Salār b. 'Abdallāh an-Nāṣirī, Viceroy and Governor-General of the noble provinces of Egypt and Syria ... Written the 1st Ramaḍān* 702 (19th April 1302).

BIBLIOGRAPHY: Mayer, *Le Blason de l'Amîr Salâr*, pp. 58 ff., and pl.

Inscription without blazon: Sauvaire in Duc de Luynes, *Voyage d'exploration à la Mer Morte*, II. 192 ff.; Jaussen, 'Inscriptions arabes de la ville d'Hébron (in *BIFAO*. t. XXV, 1925, pp. 29 ff., pl. VI).

Reproduced: Artin, *Contribution*, No. 237, with wrong description on p. 138.

SALMĀ, WIFE OF 'ALĪ

A. 'Alī is perhaps the brother of B. Muḥammad, son of the Amir Fakhr ad-dīn 'Isā, the Turcoman, dubbed Amir of Ten by Muḥammad b. Qalāūn.[1]

BLAZON: *Emblem No. 27 on the middle field of a three-fielded shield.*

FOUNDATION TEXT of a public fountain, now embedded in the wall of the mausoleum of the Turkumānī-Mosque, Cairo, pl. XL. 4.

The essential portion of the inscription runs as follows:

. . . هذا السبيل المبارك . . . الحاجّة سلما زوجة الجناب المرحوم [ال]علائى أمير علىّ بن التركمانى ○ وذلك فى شهر ربيع الأوّل سنة . . . أربعين وسبعمائة من الهجرة . . .

[*Ordered the construction?*] *of this blessed public fountain ... the pilgrim Salmā, wife of His Excellency* (janāb), *the late 'Alā' Amir ad-dīn 'Alī b. at-Turkumānī. This was done in the month Rabī' I of the year* 740 *of the Hijra* (began 6th September 1339) ...

BIBLIOGRAPHY: *CR.* Exerc. 1909, fasc. 26, pp. 62 f.

Blazon reproduced: Rogers, No. 30, fig. 50, p. 131; P[ier], *Saracenic Heraldry*, p. 10, fig. 11.

SANJAR AL-JĀWLĪ[2]

Al. Sanjar al-Jāwlī, born in 653 (began 10th February 1255) in Āmid as son of an Inspector of Works (*mushidd*), originally a mamluk of amir Jāwul, first

[1] *Khiṭaṭ*, II, p. 313, l. 25 (2nd ed., IV, p. 113, l. 13).

[2] Zetterstéen, *Beiträge*, pp. 140, l. 6, 155, l. 20, 170, l. 3 b, 180, l. 6, 222, l. penult.; *A'yān*, s.v. (MS.

Governor of Shaubak, dubbed amir under Baybars II, in 698 (1299) appointed Major-domo, remained in office till 706, became Superintendent of Chanceries, the 6th Jumādā I 711 (began 20th September 1311) appointed Governor of Gaza, in Dhu-l-Ḥijja 712 (April 1313) commissioned to make the cadaster in Syria; arrested the 28th Sha'bān 720 (3rd October 1320), released the 9th Dhu-l-Ḥijja 728 (15th October 1328), lived as amir in Cairo till al-Malik aṣ-Ṣāliḥ Isma'īl appointed him Governor of Hama, about three months after that appointment transferred to Gaza as Governor for a second time. Died in Cairo the 9th Ramaḍān 745 (14th January 1345). Constructed many buildings in Gaza, of which he made a town (*maddana Ghazza wa-maṣṣarahā*), erected the Main Mosque at Hebron (over the tombs of the Patriarchs), built a caravanserai at Qāqūn, another in the village of Ludd, a bridge (*qanāṭir*) in the 'forest' of Arsūf, an aqueduct running from Hebron to Jerusalem, built Salār's caravanserai at Baisan, and a mausoleum for himself in Cairo.

BLAZON: *Identical with the blazon of Salār.*

وكان الجاولى ينتمى الى سلار ويحمل رنكه[1]

BIBLIOGRAPHY: *A'yān*, s.v. (MS. c., fo. 50^r, l. 8).

Two blazons, both on buildings erected by Sanjar, but neither of them accompanied by an historical inscription, should be attributed therefore to amirs who repaired the building in course of time.

(1) The Mamluk GOVERNMENT HOUSE, Jerusalem, known to-day as the *Rauḍat al-Ma'ārif-School.*

BLAZON: *A table (khānjā) on the middle field of a three-fielded shield.*

Two shields over the arch of the main hall. Most probably the *khānjā* originally consisted of a piece of coloured stone or paste.

(2) GOVERNMENT HOUSE (*qaṣr an-niyāba*), Gaza, now used as Police-barracks. Pl. XXXV. 2.

Berlin, fo. 49^v f.); Ibn Ḥabīb, pp. 320, 382; *SM.* II b, pp. 127, 133, 203, 262, 266, 284; *Khiṭaṭ*, II, 398, ll. 9 ff. (2nd ed., IV. 247 f.); *Durar*, s.v. (MS. Br. Mus. Or. 3043, fo. $134^{r, v}$); *Manhal*, s.v. (MS. Paris, Ar. 2070, fo. $107^{r, v}$); Ibn Iyās, I, pp. 155, ll. 10 ff., 166, l. 17; Weil, IV. 303; *CIA.É.* I. pp. 159, 160, 732 f.; de Luynes, *Voyage d'exploration*, II, pp. 190 ff.

[1] It is possible that in the passage, *Khiṭaṭ*, II, p. 398, l. 3 b (2nd ed., IV, p. 248, l. 13), وكان ينتمى الى الأمير سلار ويبجّل ذكره, the last two words stand for ويحمل رنكه, the whole chapter, containing a list of buildings erected or renewed by Sanjar, having been copied by Maqrīzī, almost verbatim, from Ṣafadī.

BLAZON: *Crescent on the middle field of a three-fielded shield.*

Two shields flanking an ornamented slab over a window above a side-entrance door, blocked, according to local information, for more than fifty years.

SHA'BĀN[1]

Al-Malik al-Ashraf Abu-l-Mafākhir Sha'bān b. Ḥusain b. Muḥammad b. Qalāūn, born 754, acceded to the throne Tuesday, the 15th Sha'bān 764 (30th May 1363), died the 5th Dhu-l-Qa'da 778 (16th March 1377).

BLAZON: *Fleur-de-lis on undivided shield.*

COPPER COIN (*fils*), British Museum, London; Bibliothèque Nationale, Paris; Palestine Archaeological Museum, Jerusalem.

Obv.

اربعة بحماة
سنة

ضرب

ستّين

Rev. Fleur-de-lis between annulets.[2]

BIBLIOGRAPHY: Lane-Poole, *Catalogue of Oriental Coins*, IX, No. 606 q, p. 362, pl. XIX; Lavoix, *Catalogue des Monnaies Musulmanes*, vol. *Égypte et Syrie*, No. 908, p. 375 f.[3]

SHĀDBAK

Probably identical with S. Shādbak,[4] [5] originally a mamluk of Jakam min 'Iwaḍ, passed into the service of Ṭaṭar, on whose accession to the throne he

[1] *Durar*, s.v. (MS. Br. Mus. Or. 3043, fo. 138r, dates missing, space provided for them being left blank); *Manhal*, s.v. (MS. Paris, Ar. 2070, fo. 147r–151v); Ibn Iyās, I, pp. 212, ll. 6 b ff., 234, l. 9; Weil, IV. 510 f., 530; Sobernheim in *Encyclopaedia of Islām*, s.v. (Engl. ed., Fasc. D, p. 239 f.).

[2] The sequence of words varies in each of the three specimens. The text reproduced above is the one visible on the coin in the Palestine Archaeological Museum.

[3] There is no proof whatsoever that two other copper coins struck at Tripoli for a certain al-Malik al-Ashraf, were made for Sha'bān. Cf. Lane-Poole, l.c., IV, Nos. 604–6, p. 185, and Lavoix, l.c., Nos. 912–13, pp. 377 f.

[4] *Manhal*, s.v. (MS. Paris, Ar. 2070, fo. 138r, v).

[5] Name explained by Taghrībirdī, l.c., last words, as Joy-Prince (امير فرح).

was made a page (*khāṣṣakī*); dubbed amir by Barsbāy in the early days of the latter's reign, became Chief of a Corps of Mamluks, was promoted to the rank of an Amir of Forty; succeeded Aynāl al-'Alā'ī as Governor of Edessa, was recalled some years later to Cairo, where he lived as Amir of Forty, made Amir of a Hundred by Jaqmaq, in 848 or 849 appointed Governor of Hama, dismissed from office, in 850 (began 29th March 1446) lived in Jerusalem without office, in 852 (1448) arrested and confined to the prison of Marqab, released the following year, returned to Jerusalem, where he died the 2nd Rabī' I 854 (15th April 1450).

BLAZON: *On upper field a pen-box, on middle field a cup charged with a napkin, on lower field a fleur-de-lis.*

COPPER DISH, in the collection of J. Home, Esq., Cairo.

Three very much obliterated shields. Inscription on rim:

ممّا عمل برسم المقرّ الأشرف العالى المولوى الأميرى الكبيرى المخدومى

المجاهدى السيفى شاد بك الملكى الأشرفى عزّ نصره

This is one of the objects made for His Most Noble and High Excellency, our Lord, the Great Amir, the Well-Served, the Defender of the Faith, Saif ad-dīn Shādbak, (officer) of al-Malik al-Ashraf, may His victory be glorious.

BIBLIOGRAPHY: Unpublished.

SHAIKH[1]

S. Shaikh al-Maḥmūdī, in 782 (began 7th April 1380) sold to Barqūq by the slave-merchant Maḥmūdshāh al-Yazdī, became Master of the Robes (*jamdār*), subsequently page (*khāṣṣakī*), finally cup-bearer, after the battle of Shaqḥab made Amir of Ten, then Amir of Forty, under Faraj Amir of a Hundred, in 802 (1399/1400) appointed Governor of Tripoli, remained in office till Dhu-l-Ḥijja 804 (July 1402) with the exception of some months spent in Mongol captivity; Viceroy of Syria till the end of 807 (June 1405), following upon the Syrian riots in 808 appointed at his own request Governor

[1] Ṣāliḥ b. Yaḥyā, p. 57; *Manhal*, s.v. (MS. Paris, Ar. 2070, fo. 154^{v}–168^{v}); *Nujūm*, VI, cf. Index; Ibn Iyās, especially I, pp. 322, l. 4, 324, l. 10, 334, l. 12, 336, l. penult., 337, l. 1, 342, l. 11, 352, l. 15, 355, l. ult., 358, ll. 9, 7 b; II, pp. 2, 3, ll. 1 ff., 8, l. 16; Weil, V. 78, 102 f., 106, 109, 113–30, 150; *CIA. Égypte*, I. p. 341, 345.

of Safad, in 813 (1410/11) after the revolt of Syrian amirs appointed Governor of Aleppo, in 815 (1412) appointed Commander-in-Chief of the Khalif and Sultan al-Musta'īn billāh, acceded to the throne Monday, the 1st Sha'bān 815 (6th November 1412), assuming the title al-Malik al-Mu'ayyad. Died Monday, the 9th Muḥarram 824 (14th January 1421).

BLAZON: *Upper field blank, on middle field a cup charged with two small cups, on lower field a cup.*

EAST DOOR[1] of the Main Mosque, Damascus, Pl. LIV. 1, 2. Each half[2] consists of four panels, the uppermost showing an inscribed shield giving the name of al-Malik al-Manṣūr,[3] the second one an historical inscription, the third one the blazon described above, the fourth one rosettes and two other blazons showing *a cup on the middle field of a three-fielded shield.*[4] Inscription on the left half.

عمل هذا الباب المبارك فى أيّام مولانا السلطان الملك المنصور عبد العزيز

Continued on the right half:

بإشارة المقرّ الأشرف العالى المولوى شيخ الخاصّكى عزّ نصره

This blessed door was made in the days of our Lord, the Sultan al-Malik al-Manṣūr 'Abd al-'Azīz, under the direction of His Most Noble and High Excellency, Shaikh al-Khāṣṣakī, may his victory be glorious.

DATE: 'Abd al-'Azīz occupied the throne between the 26th Rabī' I and 4th Jumādā II 808 (21st September–20th November 1405), the door was made, therefore, in the course of these two months.

[1] The door was destroyed during or shortly after the Great War. Portions of the bronze revetment are now kept in the National Museum, Damascus.

[2] The revetment as seen on the photograph Bonfils, No. 785, has been disfigured by many patches and additions, among the latter being an inscription dated 1222 A.H.

[3] (b) *izz li-maulānā as-sulṭān al-malik*; (a) *al-manṣūr*; (c) *'azza naṣruhu.*

[4] As neither of the heraldic shields intersects the inscription, it is not beyond the bounds of possibility that the lower one is Shaikh's. On the other hand, the size and position of the shields in such an inconspicuous place as the fourth panel makes it improbable that it represents the blazon of the Viceroy of Syria, under whose supervision the revetment was made. The shields in the fourth panel will, therefore, have to be considered as those of an official in charge of the work, conceivably of the *shādd al-'amā'ir*, who at some time was an Amir of Ten; cf. L. A. Mayer, 'The Inspector of Monuments under the Mamluks', in *Bulletin of the Institute of Jewish Studies of the Hebrew University*, II. 87 ff. (in Hebrew).

BIBLIOGRAPHY: Artin, *Contribution*, Nos. 80 and 81, p. 117 f. (with several mistakes such as العالم for العالى, هذه for هذا, ايبك for عبد العزيز).

Mentioned: Wulzinger and Watzinger, *Damaskus, die islamische Stadt*, p. 156.

Reproduced: Saladin-Migeon, *Manuel*, I, fig. 40, p. 75; II, fig. 194, p. 235.

SHAIKHŪ[1]

S. Shaikhū al-ʿUmarī, originally a mamluk of Muḥammad b. Qalāūn, became under al-Malik al-Muẓaffar Ḥājjī one of the prominent amirs and under al-Malik an-Nāṣir Ḥasan Chief of a Corps of Mamluks, in 751 (1350) appointed Governor of Tripoli, but prior to assuming the post imprisoned first in Damascus and later in Alexandria, in Rajab 752 (began 24th August 1351) on Ṣāliḥ's accession to the throne released and restored to his former office, subsequently promoted to the rank of *ra's naubat an-nuwwāb*; on Ḥasan's second accession in 755 (1354), appointed Commander-in-Chief and Great Amir (the first atābak to be so called), died the 26th Dhu-l-Qaʿda (or Dhu-l-Ḥijja) 758 (end of 1357), over 50 years old. Built a monastery (*khānqāh*) and a Mosque at aṣ-Ṣalība.

BLAZON: *Upper field red, on a self-coloured or golden middle field a red cup, lower field black.*[2]

1. GLASS LAMP, National Museum of Arab Art, Cairo, No. 328, formerly in the collection Linant de Bellefonds, then Rostowitz Bey.

Three shields[3] on neck and three on the lower part of the body.

Inscription on neck: Qur'ān, XXIV. 35.

Inscription on body:

برسم المقرّ الأ | شرف العالى | المولوى | المخدومى | السيفى | شيخو الناصرى

For His Most Noble and High Excellency, our Lord, the Well-Served, Saif ad-dīn Shaikhū, (officer) of (al-Malik) an-Nāṣir.

[1] *Aʿyān*, s.v. (MS. Berlin, fos. 51^{v}–52^{v}); Ibn Ḥabīb, p. 404; *Durar*, s.v. (MS. Br. Mus. Or. 3043, fo. 139^{r}); *Manhal*, s.v. (MS. Paris, Ar. 2070, fos. 153^{r}–154^{v}); *Khiṭaṭ*, II. 313 f. (2nd ed., IV. 113–15); Ibn Iyās, especially I, pp. 195, l. 7, 202, l. 20, 203, l. 11, 204, l. 25, 205, l. 9; Weil, IV. 477, 486, 491 f., 498, 500–2; Nesbitt, *Catalogue Collection Slade*, p. 62; *CIA. Égypte*, I. 234, 236, 239, 244, 275, 290.

[2] Cf. the descriptions following. Most likely the lower field was originally a very dark blue which turned black. Some authors describe it as being dark green.

[3] Middle field golden.

DATE: Either 750 (1349/50) or 756 (1355), these being the respective dates of the erection of his mosque and khānqāh.

BIBLIOGRAPHY: Rogers, *Blason*, p. 112, No. 2, fig. 22; Artin, *Six lampes*, pp. 143–5, pl. II; *CIA. Égypte*, I, No. 475, p. 662 f.; Herz, *Catalogue* (Engl. ed.), pp. 294 f.; Wiet, *Lampes*, pp. 92 f., pl. XXI.

Blazon mentioned and reproduced: Ströhl, *Heraldischer Atlas*, p. 3, fig. 12; Prinet, *De l'origine orientale*, p. 54; Fox-Davies, *Guide*, p. 13, fig. 10.

Mentioned: Lane-Poole, *Art*, pp. 250, 272; Schmoranz, p. 70; van Berchem, *Notes*, III. 79 f. n.; Artin, *Une lampe armoiriée*, pp. 7, 9; *Contribution*, p. 237; Lamm, *Gläser*, p. 450, No. 89.

2. GLASS LAMP, National Museum of Arab Art, Cairo, No. 4257, formerly in the possession of H.H. Prince Yusuf Kamal.

Blazons (except for the middle field which is self-coloured) and text of inscriptions as in No. 1.

BIBLIOGRAPHY: Wiet, *Lampes*, p. 138 f., pl. XX.

Main inscription published (with omissions) in *CR.* Exerc. 1913, p. 133.

Reproduced: Wiet, 'Le Musée Arabe' (in *L'Art Vivant*, 1929, p. 52).

Mentioned and reproduced: Wiet, *Album*, No. 95.

Mentioned: Lamm, *Gläser*, p. 450, No. 84.

3. GLASS LAMP, fragment of neck. National Museum of Arab Art, Cairo, No. 4465.

DATE: The provenance of this fragment being well established, namely from Shaikhū's mosque, and the blazon being identical with other blazons of this amir,[1] it should be dated 750 (1349/50).

Blazon as in No. 2.

BIBLIOGRAPHY: Wiet, *Lampes*, p. 146; Lamm, *Gläser*, p. 450, No. 83 a.

4. GLASS LAMP, Stieglitz Museum, Leningrad.

Inscription on neck, intersected by shields: Qur'ān, XXIV. 35.

Inscription on body (so far as visible on photograph):

... | المخدومى | السيفى شيخو | ...

... *the Well-Served, Saif ad-dīn Shaikhū* ...

[1] In view of the facts stated above, no serious doubt as to the attribution of this fragment can be entertained.

BIBLIOGRAPHY: Unpublished.

Reproduced: Migeon, *Arts Musulmans*, pl. LIII.

Mentioned: Wiet, *Lampes*, p. 165, No. 59; Lamm, *Gläser*, p. 451, No. 94.

5. GLASS LAMP, British Museum, London, formerly Slade Collection.

Blazons and inscriptions as in No. 1. The inscription on the body contains an additional eulogy أعزّ الله نصره *May God make his victory glorious.*

BIBLIOGRAPHY: Lane-Poole, *Art*, pp. 258 f., 272; Nesbitt, *Catalogue Collection Slade*, p. 61, No. 333, pl. VIII.

Mentioned: Nesbitt, *Catalogue of Glass Vessels*, p. lxv; Garnier, *Collection Spitzer*, p. 295; Schmoranz, p. 70; Migeon, *Manuel*, 2nd ed., II. 135; Wiet, *Lampes*, p. 165, No. 60. Lamm, *Gläser*, p. 451, No. 92.

6. GLASS LAMP, Metropolitan Museum, New York, formerly collection Moore.

Inscription on the neck: Qur'ān, XXIV. 35, intersected by three shields (two of which are visible on the photograph).

Inscription on body (so far as visible on photograph):

. . . [الا]شرف العالى | المولوى | المخ[د]و[م]ى | . . .

BIBLIOGRAPHY: Unpublished.

Reproduced: *Bulletin of the Metropolitan Museum*, II. 105; Pier, *Saracenic Glass*, p. 189, pl. XXXVII, fig. 2.

Mentioned and reproduced: Lamm, *Gläser*, p. 450, No. 88, pl. 202, No. 4.

Mentioned: Wiet, *Lampes*, p. 165, No. 61; Dimand, *Handbook*, p. 196.

7. GLASS LAMP, Musée du Petit Palais, Paris, formerly collection Dutuit.

Three shields on neck.

Inscription on body:

ممّا عمل برسم المقرّ الأشرف العالى | المولوى الأميرى الكبيرى المحترمى
المخدومى | السيّدى السيفى شيخو الناصرى عزّ نصره

This is one of the objects made for His Most Noble and High Excellency, our Lord, the Great

Amir, the Honoured, the Well-Served, the Master Saif ad-dīn Shaikhū, (officer) of (al-Malik) an-Nāṣir, may his victory be glorious.

BIBLIOGRAPHY: Artin, *Une lampe armoiriée de l'Émir Scheikhou*, pp. 7 ff., fig. 1.

Reproduced: Migeon, *Les Objets d'Art de la Collection Dutuit*, p. 23.

Mentioned: Wiet, *Lampes*, p. 166, No. 62; Lamm, *Gläser*, p. 449, No. 82 (with full lit.), pl. 192, fig. 7 (sketch).

8. GLASS LAMP, once in the collection Bourgeois, Cologne.

Inscription on neck: Qur'ān, XXIV. 35.

Inscription on body (so far as visible on photograph):

... | المولوى | المخدومى | ...

BIBLIOGRAPHY: Unpublished.

Reproduced: Hirth, *Formenschatz*, 1905, No. 3; Glück and Diez, pp. 428 (fig.), 574; Cohn-Wiener, *Kunstgewerbe des Ostens*, p. 133, fig. 102.

Mentioned: Wiet, *Lampes*, p. 166, No. 63; Lamm, *Gläser*, p. 449 f., No. 83 (with sketch).

9. GLASS LAMP, collection Cook, formerly collection Linant de Bellefonds, then Rostowitz Bey.

BIBLIOGRAPHY: Artin, *Six lampes*, p. 146, pl. II.

Mentioned: Wiet, *Lampes*, p. 166, No. 64; Lamm, *Gläser*, p. 450 f., No. 90.

10. GLASS LAMP, collection Demotte.

Blazons and inscriptions as in No. 2.

Mentioned: Wiet, *Lampes*, p. 166, No. 65;[1] Lamm, *Gläser*, p. 450, No. 86.

11. GLASS LAMP, Musée du Louvre, Paris, formerly in the collection S. de Rothschild.

Blazon and inscriptions as in No. 1, except that the middle fields of shields on the neck are golden, and those of the shields on the lower part of the body are self-coloured.

BIBLIOGRAPHY: Unpublished.

Mentioned and reproduced: Lamm, *Gläser*, p. 450, No. 87, pl. 202, No. 2.

[1] There is another lamp of Shaikhū, once in the collection Spitzer, which is most probably identical with one of those preceding, as suggested by Wiet, l.c., p. 166, No. 65 bis.

12. PUBLIC FOUNTAIN (*sabīl*), near the Citadel, Cairo, pl. XXIV. 2.

Above the inscription blazons alternating with cartouches each set in a niche. The historical portion of the inscription runs as follows:

. . . أمر بانشاء هذا السبيل المبارك المبرور العبد الفقير الى الله تعالى شيخوا

الملكى الناصرى وكان الفراغ فى شهر ذ(ى) القعدة سنة خمس وخمسين وسبعمائة

. . . Ordered the construction of this blessed public fountain, a pious work, the servant yearning for God, the Exalted, Shaikhū, (officer) of al-Malik an-Nāṣir. (The work) was finished in the month of Dhu-l-Qa'da of the year 755 (began 17th November 1354).

BIBLIOGRAPHY: *CR*. Exerc. 1894, p. 115 (without mentioning the blazon); *CIA*. *Égypte*, I. 229 f., and fig.[1]

Reproduced: *CR*. Exerc. 1895, fasc. 12, pl. XIV.

Mentioned: Artin, *Une lampe armoiriée*, pp. 10–12.

13. KHĀNQĀH, Ṣalība-Quarter, Cairo.

Shields engraved on the grille of one of the windows.

DATE: 756 (1355).

BIBLIOGRAPHY: Artin, *Contribution*, p. 115, No. 60, p. 198, No. 310; *Une lampe armoiriée*, p. 11, figs. 2–6.

Artin considered one of these blazons to be a *tamgha*. Needless to say that all these blazons (with the exception of fig. 4) consisting as they do of a cup on an *undivided* field are absolutely identical; fig. 4 shows the usual blazon of Shaikhū, viz. *a cup on the middle field of a three-fielded shield.*

SHIHĀB AD-DĪN B. FARAJĪ

BLAZON: *Upper field creamy, on united creamy middle and lower fields a reddish brown emblem No. 26.*

EARTHENWARE BASIN, National Museum of Arab Art, Cairo, No. 3945.
Inscription outside the bowl intersected by three shields:

[1] The little loop or handle on the cup is due to a mistake of van Berchem's draughtsman. It does not exist on the original.

ممّا عمل برسم الأمير الأجلّ المخدوم الأعزّ ○ الأخصّ شهاب الدين ابن

الجناب العالى المولوى ○ الأميرى الكبيرى السيفى فرجى ادام عزّه ○

This is one of the objects made for the Most Magnificent Amir, the Well-Served, the Most Glorious, the Favourite, Shihāb ad-dīn, son of His High Excellency (janāb), *our Lord, the Great Amir, Saif ad-dīn Farajī, may (God make) his glory last for ever.*

The same inscription is repeated on the inside of the basin with the exception of the words الأميرى الكبيرى and أدام عزّه omitted and the words المحترمى *the honoured* and الملكى الناصرى (*officer*) *of al-Malik an-Nāṣir* added after الأجلّ *the Most Magnificent* and *Farajī* respectively.

The name of Shihāb ad-dīn probably was Aḥmad, but being unable to identify him, I prefer to list him under his honorific surname.

BIBLIOGRAPHY: Unpublished.

Mentioned and reproduced: Wiet, *Album du Musée Arabe du Caire*, No. 68.

SĪBĀY B. BUKHT JUKHĀ[1]

S. Sībāy b. Bukht Jukhā, originally a mamluk freed by Qāytbāy, in 892 (1486) appointed Governor of Sis, in 894 (1488) made Amir of Ten, in 906 (1500) appointed Governor of Hama,[2] in the same year transferred as Governor to Aleppo; in 906 appointed Grand Marshal. In 910 (1504) refused the post of an Amīr Majlis in Cairo. Subsequently deposed, he rebelled against the sultan, but surrendered in 911 (1505) and became Amīr Silāḥ. In 911 appointed Viceroy of Syria, he kept this post till he was killed in the battle of Marj Dābiq, the 25th Rajab 922 (24th August 1516).

BLAZON: *On upper field napkin, on middle field cup charged with a pen-box and placed between a 'pair of trousers', on lower field cup.*

[1] Ibn Iyās, II, pp. 247, l. 9 f., 261, l. 11 b, 391, l. 9; III, pp. 18, l. 1, 40, l. 10, 43, l. 10, 46, ll. 11, 10b, 47, l. 3 b, penult., 51, l. 6 b, 62, l. 4; Ibn Ṭūlūn, pp. 60 [٢٥], ll. 8 b ff., 58 [٢٧], ll. 2, 8, 16, 57 [٢٨], ll. 16, 19, 8 b, penult., 56 [٢٩], ll. 13, penult.; Weil, V. 373, 374, 379, 391, 412–14; Massignon, *Six plats de bronze de style mamelouk*, No. 2, p. 83 [7].

[2] Sībāy, the Governor of Hama, is perhaps for two reasons not identical with our Sībāy: (1) in an inscription at Hama (Max van Berchem, *Inschriften Oppenheim*, p. 30) dating from the beginning of the tenth century of the Hijra, the Governor is called Sībāy son of *ʿAbdallāh*; (2) Ibn Iyās, II, p. 391, l. 9, spells his name سنباى instead of سيباى, although on the other hand he says in the same sentence that Sībāy was at the time of his promotion Governor of Sis. There was another Sībāy, Governor of Hama, who died in 893; cf. *Ḍau'*, s.v. Aynāl al-ḥaṣīf; Ibn Ṭūlūn, p. 78 [٧], l. 7 b.

COPPER PLATE, tinned over, Palestine Archaeological Museum, Jerusalem. Pl. LXII. 3.

One shield in the centre of the plate, inscription around it:

مِمّا عمل برسم المقرّ العالى السيفى سيباى مولانا ملك الأمرآء بالشأم عزّ أنصاره

This is one of the objects made for His High Excellency, Saif ad-dīn Sībāy, our Lord, the Governor-General in Syria, may his victories be glorious.

BIBLIOGRAPHY: Unpublished.

SĪBĀY MIN JĀNIBĀY

BLAZON: *On upper field a napkin, on middle field a cup charged with a pen-box placed between a 'pair of trousers', on lower field a cup.*

COPPER BOWL, tinned over, once in the possession of A. Gamsaragan Bey, Ramleh-Alexandria.

Inscription:[1]

مِمّا عمل برسم الجناب العالى ○ المولوى الاميرى الكبيرى ○ المخدومى السيفى سيباى ○ من جانباى الملكى! عزّ أنصاره ○

This is one of the objects made for His High Excellency (janāb), *our Lord, the Great Amir, the Well-Served, Saif ad-dīn Sībāy min Jānibāy,* (*officer*) *of al-Malik* (*al-Ashraf?*), *may his victories be glorious.*

BIBLIOGRAPHY: Unpublished.

ṢIRGHITMISH[2]

S. Ṣirghitmish, brought to Cairo by Khawājā Ibn aṣ-Ṣawwāf in 737 or 738, sold to Muḥammad b. Qalāūn, at the time of whose death he was in the

[1] From a rubbing obligingly put at my disposal by the owner, and a photograph kindly lent me by Husain Eff. Rashid of the National Museum of Arab Art, Cairo.

[2] *Aʿyān*, s.v. (MS. Berlin, fo. 53^{r}–54^{r}); *Durar*, s.v. (MS. Br. Mus. Or. 3043, fo. 140^{v} f.); *Khiṭaṭ*, II, p. 404, ll. 8 b ff. (2nd ed., IV. 257 f.); *Manhal*, s.v. (MS. Paris, Ar. 2070, fo. 174^{v}–175^{r}); Ibn Iyās, I, pp. 196, l. 13, 200, l. 16, 202, l. 4 b, 205–6, 207–8; Weil, IV, especially 502 f.; *CIA. Égypte*, I. 241 f., 768; Artin, *Lampe en verre émaillé portant armoirie*, pp. 162 ff.

corps of *jamdārs*, rose by degrees till in 749 (1348/9) he became Amir of a Hundred and Commander of a Thousand, in 751 Inspector of Roads and Bridges, in Muḥarram 752 (March 1351) appointed Chief of the Corps of Mamluks; arrested the 20th Ramaḍān 759 (26th August 1358), died in Alexandria in Dhu-l-Ḥijja of the same year.[1]
Built a khanqah and a madrasa in Cairo, a madrasa at Amman, carried out work both at a place for ablutions in Mecca and at the Haram there.

BLAZON: *Upper field self-coloured, on white middle field a red napkin, lower field red.*

1. GLASS LAMP, collection Arakel Pasha Nubar, formerly in the collection Schefer, then in that of Messrs. Stora, Paris, subsequently in that of Boghos Pasha Nubar.

Six shields, three on the neck, and three on the lower part of the body.

Inscription on neck: Qur'ān, XXIV. 35.

Inscription on body:

المقرّ الكريم | العالى المولوى المالكى | المخدومى السيفى صرغتمش رأس

نوبة ||لملكى الناصرى

His Honourable and High Excellency our Lord, the Royal, the Well-Served, Saif ad-dīn Ṣirghitmish, Chief of a Corps of Mamluks of al-Malik an-Nāṣir.

BIBLIOGRAPHY: *CIA. Égypte*, I. 241, n.; Artin, l.c., pp. 159 ff., pl. 1.

Mentioned: Lavoix, *Galerie Orientale du Trocadéro*, p. 780; Migeon, *L'Exposition des Arts Musulmans*, p. 22; *Catalogue de l'Exposition de 1903*, No. 652; *Catalogue de la Collection Schefer*, p. 24, No. 167; Wiet, *Lampes*, p. 167, No. 69; Cordier, *La Collection Schefer*, p. 254; Lamm, *Gläser*, p. 453, No. 102.

2. LAMP 'EGG', Coptic Museum, Cairo.

Inscription intersected by two shields:

المقر الكريم العالى المولوى ○ المالكى المخدومى السيفى صرغتمش ○

His Honourable and High Excellency, the Royal, the Well-Served, Saif ad-dīn Ṣirghitmish.

BIBLIOGRAPHY: Wiet, *Lampes*, p. 167, No. 68.

[1] Ibn Iyās, I. 208 l. 11, mentions his death among the events of the year 761.

3. LAMP 'EGG', National Museum of Arab Art, Cairo, No. 3748. Pl. XXXI. 2.

Inscription intersected by two shields:

المقرّ الكريم العالى المولوى ○ المالكى المخدومى السيفى صرغتمش ○

His Honourable and High Excellency, our Lord, the Royal, the Well-Served, Saif ad-dīn Ṣirghitmish.

DATE: Ṣirghitmish's madrasa, in which this ovoid has been found was built in 757 (1356).

BIBLIOGRAPHY: Wiet, *Lampes*, p. 128, pl. XCII (second row, to the left).

Mentioned: *CR*. Exerc. 1911, fasc. 28, p. 13, Lamm, *Gläser*, p. 453, No. 104.

4. Another 'EGG' in the same Museum, No. 3749, evidently forming a pair with the preceding one, shows the same blazon, but only a qur'ānic inscription (IX. 18 till الصلوة).

BIBLIOGRAPHY: Wiet, *Lampes*, p. 129, pl. XCII (second row, to the right).

On the strength of an identical blazon and—in the case of No. 5—a similar decoration I should like to mention here two other objects in the same Museum without any historical inscription.

5. GLASS LAMP, National Museum of Arab Art, Cairo, No. 4054.

BIBLIOGRAPHY: Wiet, *Lampes*, p. 129, pl. XVI.

6. BRASS LANTERN, National Museum of Arab Art, Cairo, found in the mosque of Ṣirghitmish.

Shields on each of its seven sides.

BIBLIOGRAPHY: Herz, *Catalogue* (Engl. ed.), p. 101; *Le Musée National*, p. 58 f. and fig.

SŪDŪN B. JĀNĪBAK[1]

S. Sūdūn b. Jānībak, called al-ʿAjamī (= the Persian), originally a mamluk of Qāytbāy, in 906 appointed Chief of the Corps of Mamluks, in Rabīʿ I 908 (began 4th September 1502), appointed Amīr Majlis, in Rabīʿ II 910 (began

[1] Ibn Iyās, II, p. 380, l. 17; III, pp. 2, l. ult., 25, l. 9 b, 7 b, 52, ll. 6 b ff.; IV (ed. Kahle), pp. 40, l. 19, 213, l. 20, 220, l. 8 (these three passages kindly communicated by the editor); Ibn Ṭūlūn, pp. 60 [٦٠], l. 5 b, 59 [٥٩], l. 4, 58 [٥٨], l. 10, 57 [٥٧], l. 5, 55 [٥٥], l. 6 b, 54 [٥٤], ll. 12 b ff.; Weil, V. 365, 379, 411, 414; *CIA. Égypte*, I. 585 f.; Massignon, *Six plats*, p. 80 [4].

11th September 1504), appointed Viceroy of Syria, returned two months later to Cairo serving again as Amīr Majlis, in Ṣafar 917 (May 1511) appointed Amīr Silāḥ, in Rabīʿ I 917, Commander-in-Chief, a post he occupied till he met his death on the battlefield of Marj Dābiq, the 24th Rajab 922 (24th August 1516).[1]

BLAZON: *On upper field a napkin, on middle field a cup placed between a 'pair of trousers', on lower field a cup.*

1. BRONZE DISH, collection Consul Ledoulx, Constantinople.

Inscription round the shield in the centre of the dish:

ممّا عمل برسم الجناب العالى المولوى الأميرى سودون العجمى عين مقدمى

الأولوف ! بالديار المصريّة

This is one of the objects made for His High Excellency (janāb), *our Lord, the Amir Sūdūn al-ʿAjamī, Commander designate of a Thousand in the province of Egypt.*

BIBLIOGRAPHY: Massignon, *Six plats*, No. 1, pp. 79 f. [3 f.].

2. MAUSOLEUM, Cairo.

Heraldic shields intersecting a qur'ānic inscription.

The essential portion of the historical inscription:

امر بإنشاء هذا المكان المبارك . . . المقرّ الأشرف الكريم العالى المولوى الأميرى

الكبيرى . . . السيفى سودون أمير مجلس بالديار المصريّة الملكى الأشرفى

Ordered the construction of this blessed place . . . His Most Noble and Honourable High Excellency, our Lord, the Great Amir . . . Saif ad-dīn Sūdūn, Amīr Majlis in the province of Egypt, (officer) of al-Malik al-Ashraf.

DATE: Between 908 (S.'s appointment as *amīr majlis*) and 917 (his promotion to the rank of an *amīr silāḥ*).

BIBLIOGRAPHY: *CIA. Égypte*, I, No. 397, pp. 584 ff., fig.

Blazon reproduced: P[ier], *Saracenic Heraldry*, fig. 20, p. 10.

[1] According to Ibn Ṭūlūn, p. 54 [٣١], l. 12 b, Sūdūn died in Rabīʿ II 921 (began 15th May 1515).

SŪDŪN AL-QAṢRAWĪ[1]

S. Sūdūn, originally a mamluk of Qaṣrauh min Timrāz, Viceroy of Syria, passed into the service of the Sultan, became a page, under Aynāl a Junior Dawādār, under Khushqadam dubbed Amir of Ten, in 865 (1461) appointed Governor of the Citadel of Cairo in lieu of Khāirbak al-Qaṣrawī, the 11th Rabī' II 872 (9th November 1467) received the fief of a Commander of a Thousand, in 873 became Chief of the Corps of Mamluks. Died in Aleppo in 873 (1469).

BLAZON: *A composite blazon containing among other emblems a pen-box.*

MOSQUE, Cairo.

Shields on the ceiling of the Mosque.

Inscription on the western entrance door, the essential portion of which runs as follows:

. . . أنشأ هذا الجامع المبارك . . . عبد الله محمّد سودون القصروه ! نائب القلعة

الشريفة الملكى الظاهرى . . .

. . . *Constructed this blessed Mosque . . . 'Abdallāh Muḥammad Sūdūn al-Qaṣrauh, Governor of the Noble Citadel, (officer) of al-Malik aẓ-Ẓāhir . . .*

BIBLIOGRAPHY: *CIA. Égypte*, I, No. 288, p. 424, without mentioning the blazon.

Blazon mentioned: Herz, *Deux lampes en verre*, p. 184.

SŪDŪN AL-YASHBAKĪ[2]

S. Sūdūn, originally a mamluk of Yashbak al-Jakamī, Governor of several fortresses in Syria, appointed Governor of the fortress of Safad, then Governor of the fortress of Damascus, subsequently Commander of a Thousand in Damascus, leader of the Syrian pilgrimage in 868 (1464), died leaving Medina on his way back to Syria.

BLAZON: *On upper field a pen-box, on middle field a cup charged with two small cups, on lower field a cup placed between two napkins.*

[1] *Ḍau'*, s.v.; *Nujūm*, VII, p. 831, l. ult.; Ibn Iyās, II, pp. 103, l. 9, 111, l. 6, 115, l. 19; Weil, V. 333 f.; *CR.* Exerc. 1890, fasc. 7, p. 56 f.; *CIA. Égypte*, I. 425; Creswell, *Brief Chronology*, p. 137.

[2] *Ḍau'*, s.v.

COPPER PLATE, tinned over. In the collection of M. Eustache de Lorey, Paris.[1] Pl. LIX. 4. 5.

Inscription intersected by three shields:

مما عمل برسم المقرّ العالى المولوى الأمير ○ الأميرى الكبيرى السيفى سودون

اليشبكى الأشرفى ○ نائب القلعة المنصورة بالشام المحروس عزّ أنصاره ○

This is one of the objects made for His High Excellency, our Lord, the Great Amir, Saif ad-dīn Sūdūn al-Yashbakī, (officer) of (al-Malik) al-Ashraf, Governor of the victorious fortress of Damascus, the protected, may his victories be glorious.

BIBLIOGRAPHY: Unpublished.

SUNQUR AS-SAʿDĪ[2]

Sh. Sunqur as-Saʿdī in 708 (1309) Inspector of the Army (*naqīb al-jaish*), in 715 Chief of the Sultanian Mamluks, in 723 (1323) sent to Tripoli. Died there in 728.[3] Built the Madrasa Saʿdiyya and a convent (*ribāṭ*) for women in Cairo, a mosque, a mill, and a caravanserai in the village of Naḥrīriyya, Gharbiyya province.

BLAZON: *Emblem No. 41 on undivided shield.*

GLASS LAMP, in the possession of M. Ispenian, Cairo, formerly in the collection Brocard, then Demotte.

Six shields, three on the neck, and three on the lower part of the body.

Inscription on neck: Qur'ān, XXIV. 35.

Inscription on body:

مما عمل برسم المدرسة المباركة والقبّة الشريفة الذى أنشأها المقرّ العالى الشمسى

شمس الدين سنقر السعدى الملكى الناصرى عزّ نصره

This is one of the objects made for the blessed school and the noble dome founded by His High

[1] This plate, together with other objects in the collection of M. de Lorey, will be fully published by Prof. G. Wiet.

[2] Zetterstéen, *Beiträge*, p. 136, l. 12; *Durar*, s.v. (MS. Br. Mus. Or. 3043, fo. 135v); *Khiṭaṭ*, I, pp. 226, ll. 24 ff., 250, ll. 5 ff.; II, p. 397, l. 14 (2nd ed., I, pp. 365, ll. 17 ff., 403 m.; IV, p. 245 f.; ed. Wiet, IV. 82 f., 174 f.); *SM.* II b, p. 284; Ibn Iyās, I. 164 b; *CIA. Égypte*, I. 733–5.

[3] According to Ibn Iyās, l.c., I. 3 b, he died in 727.

Excellency, Shams ad-dīn Sunqur as-Saʿdī, (officer) of al-Malik an-Nāṣir, may his victory be glorious.

BIBLIOGRAPHY: Wiet, *Lampes*, p. 156, No. 15.

Blazon reproduced: Artin, *Contribution*, p. 198, No. 311.

TAGHRĪBIRMISH

BLAZON: *Upper field blank, on both the middle and the lower field a cup.*

MOSQUE and MAUSOLEUM, Tripoli, locally known as al-Madrasa aẓ-Ẓāhiriyya. One shield at the beginning of the fifth line of the inscription on the lintel of the entrance door. The essential portion runs as follows:

. . . عمّر هذا المكان المبارك المقرّ السيفى تغرى برمش الظاهر[ى] . . . مسجدًا لله تعالى وتربةً لدفن ولديه . . . وذلك فى ثالث شهر الله المحرّم سنة تسع وتسعين وسبعمائة

. . . His Excellency Saif ad-dīn Taghrībirmish aẓ-Ẓāhirī built this blessed place, as a mosque for God the Exalted and a mausoleum for his two sons . . . this (was done) on the 3rd Muḥarram of the year 799 (7th October 1396).

BIBLIOGRAPHY: *CIA. Syrie du Nord*, No. 52, pp. 122 f., fig. 11.

TAGHRĪWIRMISH

BLAZON: *On upper field a napkin, on middle field a cup charged with a pen-box and placed between a 'pair of trousers', on lower field a cup.*

COPPER DISH, tinned over, with lid, Museum für Völkerkunde, Munich, No. 26 N. 41 a, formerly in the National Museum, Munich. Pl. LXII. 13.

Inscriptions on lid and body of the dish. The fullest historical inscription is on the lid.

ممّا عمل برسم المقرّ الأشرف الكريم العالى المولوى الأميرى | الكبيرى السيّدى

المالكى المخدومى العضدى الذخرى | السيفى تغرى ورمش أمير دوادار الدوادار |

كبير المقام الشريف عزّ أنصاره وأدام لك السعادة والسلامة

This is one of the objects for His Most Noble and Honourable and High Excellency, our Lord, the Great Amir, the Master, the Royal, the Well-Served, the Supporter, the Treasure, Saif ad-dīn Taghrīwirmish, Amīr Dawādār, Grand Dawādār of His Noble Majesty, may his victories be glorious, and may [God] make thy happiness and well-being last for ever.[1]

BIBLIOGRAPHY: Unpublished.

TANAM AL-ASHRAFĪ

BLAZON: *On upper field a napkin, on middle field a cup charged with a pen-box placed between a 'pair of trousers', on lower field a cup.*

MOSQUE, Damascus, locally known as the Jāmi' aṣ-Ṣuwafā.[2]

Inscription in one line over the windows, flanked on each side by a shield.

بسمله . . . أنشأ هذا المكان المبارك المقرّ الكريم العالى المولوى السيفى تنم

الأشرفى عين مقدمى الألوف وحاجب ثانى بالشأم المحروسة عزّ نصره بتأريخ سنة

سبعة وتسعين وثمانمائة

In the name of the most merciful God. Constructed this blessed place His Honourable and High Excellency, our Lord, Saif ad-dīn Tanam al-Ashrafī, Commander designate of a Thousand and Second Chamberlain in the protected Damascus, may his victory be glorious. On the date of the year 897 (began 4th November 1491).

BIBLIOGRAPHY: Unpublished.

Blazon reproduced and mentioned: Artin, *Contribution*, No. 88, p. 119.

[1] The last words are addressed to the owner of the dish. Such texts, usually beginning with the words يا ايّها المولى, are by no means rare in Mamluk epigraphy and form a special group among the inscriptions containing pious wishes for the welfare of owners of objects of this kind.

[2] The inscription has been recently transferred to the National Museum, Damascus.

TANBAK[1]

S. Tanbak al-Ḥasanī, called Tanam, a freed mamluk of Barqūq, made a page early in the latter's first sultanate, dubbed amir in 791 (1389), sent to Damascus as an Amir of a Hundred, some time later appointed Commander (*atābak*) at Damascus, in Muḥarram 795 (began 17th November 1392), Viceroy of Syria. Stirred up an unsuccessful revolt, arrested and executed the 4th Ramaḍān 802 (29th April 1400). Built a caravanserai near al-Qaṭīfa and a mausoleum in Damascus.

BLAZON: *Upper field blank, on middle field a blue cup, on grey lower field a reddish cup between two reddish napkins.*

MAUSOLEUM, Sūq al-Mīdān, between Nos. 369 and 381, Damascus.

One shield in an ornamented panel above the main door.

Inscription in one line stretching across the whole façade, a portion hidden by a modern building, in 1926 used as a store-room; the inscription ends in this store-room.

بسمله . . . ذَلِكَ فَضْلُ ٱللّهِ يُؤْتِيهِ مَنْ يَشَآءُ وَٱللّهُ وَاسِعٌ عَلِيمٌ أمر بإنشاء هذه
التربة المؤسّسة على التقوى المعدلة الممهّد قدرها بفعل الخير المستصحب فى الدنيا
والآخرة سيّدنا ومولانا المقرّ الأشرف العالى المولوى الأميرى الكبيرى العالمى العادلى
العونى الغياثى الممهّدى المشيدى المحسنى المتصدّقى الكافلى المخدومى السيفى معزّ
الإسلام والمسلمين سيّد ملوك الأمرآء فى العالمين ركن الغزاة والمجاهدين عون الأمّة
غياث الملّة ناشر العدل ناصر الحقّ عضد الملوك والسلاطين تنبك الحسنى الظاهرى
كافل السلطنة الشريفة بالشام المحروس أعزّ الله تعالى أنصاره . . . وكان الفراغ من
هذه التربة المباركة فى شهور سنة سبع وتسعين وسبعمائة [Sobernheim]

[1] *Nujūm*, especially VI, pp. 3, l. 11, 7, l. ult., 8, l. 1, 35, l. 15, 36, ll. 4, 12, 38, l. 16, 41, l. 3 ff., 143, l. 4, 146, l. 20–147, l. 15; *Manhal*, s.v. (MS. Paris, Ar. 2069, fo. 161v–163v); Ibn Iyās, especially I, pp. 298, l. 9, 318, l. 18, 319, l. 16, 322, ll. 7 ff., 323, ll. 6, 15, 324, l. 23; Weil, V, pp. 9, n. 2, 73–8.

. . . Qur'ān, V, end of v. 59 . . . *Ordered the construction of this mausoleum . . . His Most Noble and High Excellency, our Lord, the Great Amir . . . Saif ad-dīn . . . Tanbak al-Ḥasanī, (officer) of (al-Malik) aẓ-Ẓāhir, Viceroy of Syria, the protected . . . this blessed mausoleum was completed during the months of the year* 797 (began 27th October 1394).

BIBLIOGRAPHY: Unpublished.

Blazon reproduced: Bourgoin, *Précis de l'art arabe* II, p. 11, pl. 29, Rogers, fig. 58.

ṬANBUGHĀ[1]

BLAZON: *Cup on undivided shield.*

DISH, once in the possession of Messrs. Stora, Paris, present owner unknown.

برسم المقرّ العالى المولوى المخدومى العلائى طنبغا حاجّى الساقى [Van Berchem]

For His High Excellency, our Lord, the Well-Served, 'Alā' ad-dīn Ṭanbughā Ḥājjī, the cup-bearer.

BIBLIOGRAPHY: Unpublished.

TĀNĪBAK[2]

BLAZON: *On upper field a napkin, on middle field a cup placed between a 'pair of trousers', on lower field a fleur-de-lis.*

COPPER BOWL on foot, in 1910 in the collection of M. H. Marcopoli, Aleppo.

Inscription:

(1) ممّا عمل برسم المقرّ الأشرف العالى المولوى الأميرى (2) الكبيرى المخدومى السيفى تانى‌بك أمير دوادار المقام الشريف أعز أنصاره [Herzfeld]

This is one of the objects made for His Most Noble and High Excellency, our Lord, the Great Amir, the Well-served, Saif ad-dīn Tānībak, Amīr Dawādār of His Majesty, may (*God make*) *his victories glorious.*

BIBLIOGRAPHY: Unpublished.

[1] Not having seen the original, I follow the transcription of van Berchem. The name Ṭaybughā is more common; a certain Ṭaybughā Ḥājjī was appointed Governor of Gaza in Dhu-l-Ḥijja 736, dismissed from office before the 13th Jumādā I 739 (Zetterstéen, *Beiträge*, pp. 192, l. 17, 200, l. 5).

[2] The position of this name in biographical dictionaries, such as *al-Manhal aṣ-ṣāfī* and *ad-Durar al-kāmina*, proves that the first consonant is *t* and not *th*.

TĀNĪBAK AL-KHĀZINDĀR

Either identical with Tānībak *al-khāzindār*,[1] who died in Shawwāl 899 (began 5th July 1494) or with his namesake, also a *khāzindār*,[2] son-in-law of Khāirbak min Aynāl (q.v.), District Officer (*kāshif*) of the Gharbiyya-province, arrested in 905 (1499/1500), in 922 (began 5th February 1516) Commander of a Thousand without office, took part in the expedition against the Ottoman Sultan Selim, executed by the latter together with many other amirs, on Saturday, 5th Rabīʿ I 923 (28th March 1517).

BLAZON: *On upper field a napkin, on middle field a cup charged with a pen-box placed between a 'pair of trousers', on lower field a cup.*

1. COPPER DISH, tinned over. Collection F. T. Dallin, Esq., Chieveley, Newbury, Berks. Pl. LXII. 10.

One shield in the centre of the plate. Inscription on the outside:

برسم المقرّ الأشرف السيفى تانى بك أمير خازندار كبير الملكى الأشرفى

For His Most Noble Excellency, Saif ad-dīn Tānībak, Grand Amīr Treasurer of al-Malik al-Ashraf.

BIBLIOGRAPHY: Unpublished.

2. COPPER DISH, tinned over. Collection W. A. Stewart, Esq., Jerusalem.

In the centre a shield with inscription round it:

ممّا عمل برسم الجناب العالى المولوى تانى بك الخازندار عزّ أنصاره

This is one of the objects made for His High Excellency (janāb), *our Lord, Tānībak, the Treasurer, may his victories be glorious.*

BIBLIOGRAPHY: Unpublished.

TANKIZ [3]

S. Tankiz al-Ḥusāmī an-Nāṣirī, originally a mamluk of Sultan Lājīn, passed after the latter's death into the service of Muḥammad b. Qalāūn, became

[1] Ibn Iyās, II, p. 284, ll. 14 b f.

[2] Ibn Iyās, II, p. 371, l. 5 b; III, pp. 3, l. 10, 21, l. 9 b, 25, l. 3 b, 26, l. 16, 29, l. 10 b, 56, l. ult., 106, l. 12, 111, l. 6.

[3] Abu-l-Fidā', ed. Reiske, V, p. 264, l. 9–11, ed. Constantinople, IV, p. 71, ll. 16 f.; Nuwairī, s.a. 708

Amir of Ten before Muḥammad left for Kerak (24th Ramaḍān 708 = 7th March 1309), remained in his service at Kerak, appointed Governor of Damascus in Rabīʿ II 712 (which began on 6th August 1312), arrested in the last days of 740 (June 1340), died in the prison of Alexandria on Tuesday, 14th[1] Muḥarram 741 (10th July 1340) in his sixties.

BLAZON: *Golden cup on undivided red field.*

1. SHRINE OF NABĪ YAMĪN, Qalqīlieh.

One cup intersecting lines 2 and 3.

Inscription in the annex:

(1) بسمله . . . أمر بتجديد هذا الحـ[وض؟ الخان؟]

(2) المبارك المقرّ الأشرف O العالى المولوى الأميرى الكبير

(3) ى السيّدى العالمى العا ! O دلى المثاغرى المرابطى الكا

(4) فلى السيفى تنكز نائب السلطنة الشريفة بالشأم المحروس عزّ نصره

In the name of the most merciful God. Ordered to renew this blessed tank (or *caravanserai*) *His Most Noble and High Excellency, our Lord, the Great Amir, the Master, the Learned, the Just, the Warden of the Marches, the Warrior at the Frontiers, the Viceroy Saif ad-dīn Tankiz, Governor of the Noble Sultanate in Damascus, the protected, may his victory be glorious.*

The inscription continues on the cup itself, but only the first word *bi-ta'rīkh* 'on the date of' is legible. The cup is displayed in the centre of the inscription without a shield. This monument does not appear in the list of buildings copied by Ṣafadī[2] from the official inventory of the property of Tankiz made after his imprisonment, perhaps because the repairs were of no consequence and the whole building of little value. In

(MS. Leyden, Cod. 20, fo. 48ᵛ, l. 7); Zettersteen, *Beiträge*, especially pp. 158, l. 7, 211, l. 4 ff., 212, l. 20; Ibn al-Wardī, II, p. 261, l. 10 b, 329 m.; Ibn Baṭṭūṭa, I. 121; Kutubī, *Fawāt*, I. 91–5; Ṣafadī, *Tuḥfa*, s.v., *al-Wāfī*, s.v., *Aʿyān*, s.v. (MS. Istanbul, AS. 2970); Ibn Ḥabīb, II, especially pp. 319, 373; Qalqashandī, *Ṣubḥ*, XII. 16–19 (Letter of Appointment); Ṣāliḥ b. Yaḥyā, p. 175; *Khiṭaṭ*, II, p. 54, ll. 20 ff. (2nd ed., III. 87 f.); *Durar*, s.v. (MS. Br. Mus. Or. 3043, fo. 98ᵛ–100ʳ); *Manhal*, s.v. (MS. Paris, Ar. 2069, fo. 158ᵛ–161ᵛ); Mujīr ad-dīn, *al-Uns al-jalīl*, p. 387 (Sauvaire 142–3); Ibn Iyās, I, pp. 171, l. 10–173, l. 5 (biography); Weil, IV, cf. Index; *CIA. Égypte*, I. 213 n.; Cheikho in Ṣāliḥ, p. 61, n. 1 (biography with incorrect details); Lammens, *La Syrie*, II. 5 f.; Zambaur, *Manuel de Généalogie et de Chronologie*, p. 31, n. 2.

[1] According to Maqrīzī, l.c., l. penult., and Mujīr ad-dīn he died on the 21st Muḥarram, according to Ibn Taghrībirdī in the middle of the month.

[2] Quoted by al-Kutubī, *Fawāt*, I. 94 f., where p. 95, l. 8 b طحولية should be corrected into جلجولية; *Manhal*, s.v. Tankiz (MS. Paris, Ar. 2069, fo. 160ʳ–161ᵛ).

any case, it should not be identified with the 'very fine khan at Jiljūlieh'[1] referred to in the same list, the ruins of the latter being still visible in Jiljūlieh, a village near Qalqīlieh, unless it is assumed—in itself quite likely—that the inscription was brought thither from the khan at Jiljūlieh. This theory is borne out by the last word of the first line of the Arabic text of the inscription which can be read either الخان or الحوض the first being more acceptable on palaeographical grounds, the second on archaeological evidence

BIBLIOGRAPHY: Unpublished.

2. CARAVANSERAI at Shaqḥab (Marj aṣ-Ṣuffar). Cup without shield, 22 cm. high, engraved on the lintel of the doorway, accompanied by a fragment of an inscription mentioning the name of Tankiz and dated 716 (began 26th March 1316).[2]

BIBLIOGRAPHY: Unpublished.

3. MADRASA, locally known as al-Maḥkama ash-Shar'iyya (Muslim Religious Law Court), Jerusalem.

Three shields intersecting an inscription of the length of the façade:

بسمله . . . أنشأ هذا المكان المبارك ○ راجياً ثواب الله وعفوه المقرّ الكريم ○

السيفى تنكز الملكى الناصرى عفا الله ○ عنه وأثابه [وذلك فى شهور]? سنة تسع

وعشرين وسبعمائة

. . . *Founded this blessed building in the hope of God's reward and forgiveness, His Honourable Excellency Saif ad-dīn Tankiz, (officer) of al-Malik an-Nāṣir, may God forgive him and give him a reward.* [*This was made during*] *the year* 729 (1328–9).

BIBLIOGRAPHY: *CIA. Jérusalem, Ville*, No. 80, pp. 256 ff.

Blazon mentioned and depicted: Artin, *Contribution*, No. 48, p. 114.[3]

4. MAUSOLEUM, locally known as the 'Turbat ash-Shaikh an-Naḥlāwī', Rue el-Nihlaoui, Damascus.

The heraldic shields intersect an unhistorical inscription in stucco in the vestibule leading to the domed chambers. The chalice is taller than on the other blazons of

[1] *Manhal*, l.c., fo. 161^{r}, l. 10.

[2] Information kindly supplied by M. J. Sauvaget, Institut Français d'Archéologie et d'Art Musulmans, Damas.

[3] 'Une coupe sculptée sur la porte du Mehkeme à Jérusalem *sans inscription*' (italicized by the present writer).

Tankiz, but it shows the same characteristic ring between the foot and the bowl of the chalice.

Inscription on the lintel of the entrance gate:

(1) بسمله . . . أمر بإنشاء هذه التربة المباركة المقرّ الشريف العالى المولوى

الأميرى الكبيرى الغازى المجاهدى (2) المالكى المخدومى السيفى سيف الدنيا

والدين تنكز نائب السلطنة المعظّمة بالشأم المحروس عزّ نصره وكان الفراغ في شهر

ذى الحجّة سنة ثلثين وسبعمائة

In the name of the most merciful God. Ordered to construct this blessed mausoleum His Noble and High Excellency, our Lord, the Great Amir, the Vanquisher, the Defender of the Faith, the Royal, the Well-Served, Saif ad-dunyā wa-d-dīn Tankiz, Governor of the August Sultanate in the protected Syria, may his victory be glorious. It was finished in the month of Dhu-l-Ḥijja of the year 730 (September 1330).

BIBLIOGRAPHY: Littmann in Wulzinger und Watzinger, *Damaskus, die islamische Stadt*, pp. 71 f.

5. GLASS LAMP, Main Mosque, Hebron, at present exhibited in the Muslim Museum, Jerusalem. Pl. XLI. 4.

Inscription on neck, intersected by three shields:

إِنَّمَا يَعْمُرُ مَسَاجِدَ ٱللَّهِ ○ مَنْ آمَنَ بِٱللَّهِ وَٱلْيَوْمِ ○ ٱلْآخِرِ وَأَقَامَ ○

He only shall visit the temples of God, who believeth in God and the last day, and is constant (at prayer) (Qur'ān, IX. 18).

Inscription on body:

برسم مدرسة المقرّ العالى المولوى الأميرى السيفى تنكز كافل الممالك الشريفة

بالشأم المحروس

For the school of His High Excellency, our Lord, the Amir Saif ad-dīn Tankiz, Viceroy of the noble provinces of the protected Damascus.

DATE: Tankiz carried out some works in the Haram at Hebron during the year 732 (1331/2), such as lining it with slabs of marble,[1] on which occasion he probably donated the lamp.

BIBLIOGRAPHY: Mentioned and reproduced: Lamm, *Gläser*, p. 439, pl. 196.

6. CARAVANSERAI or BATH, locally known as aṭ-Ṭaḥūna[2] (= the Mill), Jerusalem, Sūq al-Qaṭṭānīn.

Three heraldic shields, one in the centre of the lintel, two on the corbels flanking the inscription.

بسمله . . . المبارك والسوق [3] والربوع على ظهورهم المقرّ ○ الأشرف السيفى تنكز

الناصرى كافل ا[لممالك] الشريفة الشاميّة أعزّ الله أنصاره ○ في شهور سنة ○ . . .

In the name of the most merciful God. [About four words obliterated. Probably: *Ordered to build this*] *blessed* [*khan* or *bath*] *and the market-street and the private houses above them, His Most Noble Excellency Saif ad-dīn Tankiz an-Nāṣirī, Viceroy of the noble* [*provinces*] *of Syria, may God make his victories glorious. In the months of the year . . .*

DATE: According to van Berchem's very plausible suggestion, this building was erected about the same time as the entrance gate to the Sūq al-Qaṭṭānīn dated 737 (1336/7).

BIBLIOGRAPHY: *CIA. Jérusalem, Ville*, No. 81, pp. 262 ff.

Reproduced: *Jerusalem*, ed. Ashbee, I, fig. 57.

Mentioned: Clermont-Ganneau, *Archaeological Researches in Palestine*, I. 127.

7. COPPER BASIN, National Museum of Arab Art, Cairo, No. 7852.

Sixteen shields, eight inside, eight outside.

Inscription inside the basin:

○ ممّا عمل برسم المقرّ الأشرف العالى ا ○ ○ المولوى المالكى العالمى ا ○ ○

العادلى السيفى تنكز كافل ا ○ ○ الممالك الشريفة بالشأم المحروس ○

This is one of the objects made for His Most Noble and High Excellency, our Lord, the

[1] *SM.* I b, p. 246; Mujīr ad-dīn, *al-Uns al-jalīl*, pp. 57, l. 5 f., 438, l. 13; van Berchem, 'Arabische Inschriften aus Syrien' (in *Zeitschrift des Deutschen Palästina-Vereins*, XIX, 1896, No. II, p. 111 f.); Vincent et Mackay, *Hébron, Le Ḥaram el-Khalîl*, p. 212 f.; Jaussen, 'Inscriptions Arabes de la Ville d'Hébron' (in *Bulletin de l'Institut Français d'Archéologie Orientale*, t. XXV, No. 7, pp. 10 ff.)

[2] The Turkish name Khān Otuzbir (cf. *CIA. Jérusalem*, l.c.) is no more in use.

[3] In the list of buildings mentioned above (p. 219, n. 2) this market-street is described as قيسارية مليحة الى الغاية, *Fawāt*, I, p. 92, l. 10 b.

Royal, the Learned, the Just, Saif ad-dīn Tankiz, Viceroy of the noble provinces of Syria, the protected.

The inscription outside the basin is obliterated.

BIBLIOGRAPHY: Unpublished.

8. MOSQUE, Damascus, since the Great War used as barracks.

'Porte sud de la Mosquée. Peinte sur la voûte (diam. o m., 25 env.) [9⅚″]. Coupe réservée en blanc sur fond rouge' [Sauvaget].

BIBLIOGRAPHY: Unpublished.

TANKIZBUGHĀ[1]

S. Tankizbughā al-Māridīnī, Superintendent of the cellar (*sharabkhāna*) under al-Malik an-Nāṣir Ḥasan, became Amir of a Hundred, refused the Viceroyalty of Syria, died as Amir Majlis in Ramaḍān 759[2] (began 7th August 1358).

BLAZON: *Upper and lower fields white, on blue middle field a white cup.*

GLASS LAMP, Louvre, Paris. Formerly collection of Count Lair.

Inscription on neck, intersected by three shields:

ممّا عمل برسم ○ تربة المرحوم ○ المقرّ الأشرف ○

continued on body:

العالى | المولوى ا | لمالكى | المخدومى ا | لسيفى تنكزبغا أمير | مجلس الملكى الناصرى

This is one of the objects made for the mausoleum of His Most Noble and High Excellency, our Lord, the Royal, the Well-Served, the late Saif ad-dīn Tankizbughā, amīr majlis of al-Malik an-Nāṣir.

On the lower part of the body three more shields.

BIBLIOGRAPHY: Migeon, *L'Orient Musulman*, vol. *Cristaux*, p. 12, pl. 8, fig. 19.

Mentioned: Migeon, *Manuel* (2nd ed.) II, 136; Wiet, *Lampes*, p. 173, No. 119; Lamm, *Gläser*, pp. 466 f. (and sketch).

[1] *Durar*, s.v. (MS. Br. Mus. Or. 3042, fo. 100ʳ); Ibn Iyās, I, p. 207, l. 13; Weil, IV. 489; *CIA. Égypte*, I, p. 274, nn. 1, 3.

[2] Ibn Iyās, l.c., mentions his death among the events of the year 760.

ṬĀNYARAQ[1]

S. Ṭānyaraq al-Yūsufī, originally a mamluk of Yūsuf b. al-Malik an-Nāṣir, in Shawwāl 747 (began 15th January 1347) made Amir of a Hundred by al-Malik al-Muẓaffar Ḥājjī (without passing through any of the intermediate grades), Governor of Hama from Monday, 16th Dhu-l-Ḥijja 751 (14th February 1351) until Sha'bān 752 (began 23rd September 1351), then sent to Damascus without any office, for the second time appointed Governor of Hama, entered it towards the end of Ramaḍān 753 (early in November 1352), in 755 dismissed and sent to Damascus, took part in the pilgrimage in the year 756 (1355), imprisoned in 759 (1357/8) in the fortress of Damascus, spent some time without office first in Damascus, then at Safad. By the end of 759 or early in 760 (end of 1358) arrested and put in prison at Alexandria. On al-Malik an-Nāṣir Ḥasan's deposition, Ṭānyaraq was freed, loaded with presents and made Amir of a Hundred and Commander of a Thousand in Damascus, where he arrived on Friday, the 6th Sha'bān 762 (11th June 1361). Early in Shawwāl 762 (August 1361) appointed Governor of Hama for the third time, remained there until the end of 763 (1361/2), when he was dismissed from office and transferred as Amir to Tripoli. Died there in 764 (1362/3).

BLAZON: *Cup on the lower field of a two-fielded shield.*

AQUEDUCT, Hama, at the crossing of the Zuqāq al-'Āṣī and the Zuqāq ad-Dabbāgha, near an-Nā'ūra al-Muḥammadiyya. Coming from town, on the left side of the left arch of the Aqueduct.
Inscription in two lines on the right hand side of the blazon:

(١) أنشئت هذه الناعورة الكبيرة والمباركة [a few words] (2) فى أيّام مولانا المقرّ الأشرف السيفى طان يرق كافل المملكة الحمويّة فى سلخ سنة ثلاث وستّين وسبعمائة

This big and blessed water-wheel was constructed . . . in the days of our Lord, His Most Noble Excellency Saif ad-dīn Ṭānyaraq, Viceroy of the province of Hama, during the last days of the year 763 (October 1362).

BIBLIOGRAPHY: Unpublished.

[1] *A'yān*, s.v. (MS. Berlin, fo. 55ᵛ–56ʳ), s.v. Asandamur (l.c., fo. 27ʳ, l. 21), and s.v. Arghūn al-Kāmilī (l.c., fo. 24ʳ, l. 13); *Durar*, s.v. (MS. Br. Mus. Or. 3043, fo. 142ᵛ); Weil, IV. 474, 478, 486.

ṬASHTAMUR AL-'ALĀ'Ī[1]

S. Ṭashtamur al-'Alā'ī, the dawādār, served for a long time as Grand Dawādār in Egypt, being the first Grand Dawādār with the rank of an Amir of a Hundred and Commander of a Thousand, succeeded 'Alī al-Māridīnī as Viceroy of Egypt in 772 (1370), on 7th Dhu-l-Qa'da 778 (18th March 1377) transferred to Damascus as Viceroy of Syria, became in 779 Commander-in-Chief. In the course of the same year, on the assumption of power by Z. Baraka and S. Barqūq, was arrested by them and sent first to Damietta[2] and then to Jerusalem, where he died in Sha'bān 786 (18th September–16th October 1384), more than fifty years of age.

BLAZON: *Upper and lower fields dark red, on a yellow middle field a black pen-box.*

1. BOWL of bell brass, Victoria and Albert Museum, London, No. 857–1901

Inscription:

المقرّ الكريم العالى ○ المولوى الأميرى الكبيرى ○ السيفى طشتمر أمير دوادار ○ الملكى الأشرفى عزّ نصره ○

His Noble and High Excellency, our Lord, the Great Amir, Saif ad-dīn Ṭashtamur, Grand Dawādār of al-Malik al-Ashraf, may his victory be glorious.

BIBLIOGRAPHY: Unpublished.

Mentioned: van Berchem, *Notes*, III. 77 n.

2. MOSQUE of Khushqadam, Cairo. Pl. LXI. 2.

Heraldic shields on the ceilings of the vestibule and corridor.

The essential portion of the inscription of the frieze in the corridor runs as follows:

. . . أمر بانشاء هذا المكان المبارك . . . المقرّ العالى . . . الأمير سيف الدين طشتمر الدوادار الملكى الأشرفى . . .

. . . Ordered the construction of this blessed place . . . His High Excellency . . . the Amir Saif ad-dīn Ṭashtamur, the dawādār of al-Malik al-Ashraf . . .

[1] Ibn Ḥabīb, 441, 453, 459; *Manhal*, s.v. (MS. Paris, Ar. 2070, fo. 185v); Mujīr ad-dīn, *al-Uns al-jalīl*, I, p. 396, l. 3 b; Ibn Iyās, I, pp. 227, l. 3, 231, l. 15, 233, l. 5, 235, l. ult., 239, ll. 11 f., 242, ll. 16 ff., 243, ll. 2 ff.; Weil, IV. 528, 532, 534 f.; Creswell, *Chronology*, p. 111; *CIA. Jérusalem, Ville*, pp. 295 f.

[2] Ibn Iyās, I, p. 243, l. 5: to Alexandria.

The pen-box has been painted over a white napkin, probably the shield of the first builder of Ṭashtamur's house, which, as is well-known, has been completely restored by Khushqadam al-Aḥmadī.

BIBLIOGRAPHY: Herz, *Mosquée Khochkadam el-Ahmadi, à Darb el-Hosr, au Caire* (*CR.* Exerc. 1909, App. au 26 fasc., p. 161 f.).

Blazon reproduced: Artin, *Contribution*, No. 106, p. 125, with a wrong date and without attribution to Ṭashtamur.

Mentioned: Creswell, *Brief Chronology*, p. 111 f.

Both inscriptions, and consequently the blazons accompanying them, must have been composed under al-Malik al-Ashraf Shaʿbān, i.e. between 764 and 778 (1363–76). The first can be even more closely dated, namely 764–72, as Ṭashtamur, having been appointed in the latter year Viceroy of Egypt,[1] had ceased to be Grand Dawādār (*amīr dawādār*) since 772. Whether the second text also is to be so dated, or whether it can be attributed to any other year of Shaʿbān's reign, depends on whether *dawādār* in that inscription means Grand Dawādār or whether it refers to the insignificant court-office, probably held by Ṭashtamur at the time of his having been dubbed amir and so often found in texts of amirs in the highest positions. The latter interpretation seems to be the more probable of the two.

ṬASHTAMUR AL-BADRĪ[2]

S. Ṭashtamur al-Badrī, nicknamed Green-Pea (*ḥimmiṣ akhḍar*) because of his predilection for this vegetable when in the Training School, served originally under Arghūn ad-Dawādār, became cup-bearer of Muḥammad b. Qalāūn. On the 9th Muḥarram 737 (18th August 1336) appointed Governor of Safad, a post he held until in Muḥarram 741,[3] having successfully carried out the arrest of Tankiz, he was transferred to Aleppo as Governor. Under al-Malik an-Nāṣir Aḥmad appointed Viceroy of Egypt, thirty-five days later arrested, imprisoned at Kerak, executed in Muḥarram 743 (began 6th June 1342). Besides his house in Cairo which was erected under the supervision of the

[1] Ibn Iyās, I. p. 227, l. 3.

[2] Zetterstéen, *Beiträge*, p. 178, ll. 3 f., 192, l. 3 b, 211, l. 2, 212, l. 12, 213, l. 17; Ibn Ḥabīb, pp. 374, 376, 378; *Aʿyān*, s.v. (MS. Berlin, fo. 57^{r}–58^{v}); Ṣāliḥ b. Yaḥyā, p. 175; *Durar*, s.v. (MS. Br. Mus. Or. 3043, fo. $143^{r,v}$); *Manhal*, s.v. (MS. Paris, Ar. 2070, fo. 184^{v}–185^{r}); Ibn Iyās, I, pp. 164, ll. 16 f., 176, l. 9 b, 178, ll. 7 ff., 179, l. 5 b, l. ult., 180, ll. 8, 10, 17; II, p. 390, ll. 11 ff.; Weil, IV. 388 f., 424, 440, 442, 449, n. 1; van Berchem, *Notes III*, p. 77 n.; *CIA. Égypte*, I. 737.

[3] According to Ibn Iyās, I, p. 176, l. 9 b, he was confirmed in his office as Grand Dawādār by al-Malik al-Manṣūr Abū Bakr استقرّ به دواداراً كبيرًا على عادته, but on p. 178, l. 7, he is called 'Governor of Aleppo'.

Qāḍī Karīm ad-dīn, he built a stable with a magnificent portal, a Mosque and a mausoleum in the 'Desert', and his residence close to it, two bath-houses, a qaisāriyya, a mausoleum (Maghārat Yaʿqūb), and a bath at Safad.

BLAZON: *Cup on the middle field of a three-fielded shield.*

MAUSOLEUM, Cairo.

Inscription flanked by two shields.

○ برسم المقرّ العالى الأميرى السيفى طشتمر الساقى | الناصرى ختم الله له بخير

فى ربيع الأوّل سنة خمس وثلثين وسبعمائة ○

For His High Excellency, the Amir Saif ad-dīn Ṭashtamur, the cup-bearer of (al-Malik) an-Nāṣir . . . in the month of Rabīʿ I of the year 735 (November 1334).

BIBLIOGRAPHY: *CIA. Égypte*, I. 736 f. (after Mehren, *Câhirah og Kerâfat*, I. 71) without mentioning the blazon.

Reproduced: Devonshire, *L'Égypte Musulmane*, pl. XXV.

Mentioned: Creswell, *Brief Chronology*, p. 96 f.; *CIA. Jérusalem, Ville*, p. 288, n. 4.

ṬAYBARS AL-ʿALĀʾĪ

BLAZON: *Napkin on middle field of three-fielded shield.*

TOP OF LANTERN (?). Present owner unknown.

Inscription intersected by three shields:[1]

الجناب العالى ○ السيفى طيبرس العلا○ئى راس نوبة الجمدارية ○

His High Excellency (janāb), *Saif ad-dīn Ṭaybars al-ʿAlāʾī, Chief of the Corps of Jamdārs.*

BIBLIOGRAPHY: Unpublished.

[1] Above the napkin a sword, passing through middle and lower fields, engraved by a later hand.

ṬĀZ AN-NĀṢIRĪ[1]

S. Ṭāz b. Quṭghāj,[2] mamluk of Muḥammad b. Qalāūn, a page (*khāṣṣakī*), then amir majlīs, one of the regents under al-Malik al-Muẓaffar Ḥājjī, helped Ṣalāḥ ad-dīn Ṣāliḥ b. Muḥammad b. Qalāūn to the throne in 752 (1351), was Grand Dawādār when imprisoned in 755 (1354), released shortly afterwards and appointed Governor of Aleppo in the same year, imprisoned again early in 759 (1357/8), released through the good offices of Yalbughā al-Khāṣṣakī in 762 (1361). Lived later on in Jerusalem and Damascus without holding further office. Died towards the end of 763 (October 1362).

BLAZON: *Cup on the middle field of a three-fielded shield.*

MADRASA and MAUSOLEUM, Jerusalem, Ṭarīq Bāb as-Silsila (David Street), locally known as Dār Hidāya.

Two shields, flanking an inscription carved on the lintel of the window of the mausoleum.

بسمله . . . هذه تربة العبد الفقير الى الله تعالى المقرّ الأشرف السيفى طاز

توفّى رحمه الله سنة ثلث وستّين وسبعمئة

. . . *This is the mausoleum of the servant yearning for God the Exalted, His Most Noble Excellency, Saif ad-dīn Ṭāz. Passed away—may God have mercy on him—in the year* 763 (1361/2).

BIBLIOGRAPHY: *CIA. Jérusalem, Ville*, No. 86, pp. 286–91, pl. LXX.

Reproduced: Artin, *Contribution*, No. 74, p. 116 (without identification and with the wrong description: Coupe sculptée sur le sebil d'une maison appelée Beit-el-Danaf, dans le Haret-el-Selsileh, à Jérusalem), *Jérusalem* ed. Ashbee, II, figs. 32, 33.
Artin Pasha[3] regarded a composite blazon on a portal in Siufiyya (pl. LXIX. 1) as the blazon of Ṭāz. The attribution is both unfounded and wrong; unfounded, because (*a*) the accompanying inscription contains only the beginning of a series of titles and no name, (*b*) the attribution was made on the basis of an identification of the building

[1] *Aʿyān*, s.v. (MS. Berlin, fo. 54ᵛ–55ᵛ); Ibn Ḥabīb, pp. 399, 411; *Khiṭaṭ*, II. 734 (2nd ed., III. 119 m); *Durar*, s.v. (MS. Br. Mus. Or. 3043, fo. 142ʳ, ᵛ); *Manhal*, s.v. (MS. Paris, Ar. 2070, fo. 178ʳ f.); Mujīr ad-dīn, *al-Uns al-jalīl*, p. 396, l. 10 (Sauvaire, p. 161); Ibn Iyās, cf. Index, especially I, pp. 194, ll. 9 b ff., 202–3, 205, ll. 4 b ff., 211, l. 8; Weil, IV. 475–507; Creswell, *Brief Chronology*, pp. 105 f.; *CIA. Jérusalem, Ville*, p. 287 (lit.); Ṭabbākh, *Aʿlām*, II, 436, 439.

[2] Spelling indicated in *Aʿyān*, and *Durar*, ll. cc.

[3] *Contribution*, No. 97, p. 122.

with the palace of Ṭāz, for which no proof was furnished by Artin;[1] wrong, because the blazon in Siufiyya is about a century later than Ṭāz.

TIMRĀZ[2]

In 918 (1512/13) Governor of the Fortress of Aleppo.

BLAZON: *On upper field a napkin, on middle field a cup charged with a pen-box and placed between a 'pair of trousers', on lower field a cup.*

BASIN, in the possession of Messrs. J. Sassoon, London, formerly in the collection of the Countess of Craven. Pl. LXII. 5, 9.

Inscription on lip, repeated on body.

المقر الاشرف الكريم العالى ○ المولوى الأميرى الكبيرى ○ السيفى تمراز

نائب قلعة حلب ○ المنصورة عزّ المولا أنصاره ○

His Most Noble and Honourable and High Excellency, our Lord, the Great Amir, Saif ad-dīn Timrāz, Governor of the victorious fortress of Aleppo, may the Lord make his victories glorious.

BIBLIOGRAPHY: Unpublished.

TIMRĀZ AL-AḤMADĪ[3]

BLAZON: *On upper field a napkin, on both the middle and the lower field a cup.*

MOSQUE, Cairo.

Beneath the ceiling of the public fountain an inscription intersected by two shields.

أمر بانشاء هذا السبيل المبارك السعيد من فضل الله تعالى ○ وجزيل عطائه

الجناب الكريم العالى المولوى الأميرى السيفى تمراز الظاهرى أمير آخور الملكى

[1] Although the palace must have been situated in the vicinity, cf. Maqrīzī, *Khiṭaṭ*, II, p. 73, l. 10 b (2nd ed., III, p. 119, l. 4).

[2] *CIA. Égypte*, I, p. 222 and n. 2.

[3] I. Iyās II, 134, l. 7, *CIA. Égypte*, I, p. 429.

الظاهرى ○ وكان الفراغ من ذلك فى شهر صفر الخير سنة ستّ وسبعين

وثمان مائة

Ordered to build this blessed fountain . . . His Honourable and High Excellency (janāb), *our Lord, the Amir Saif ad-dīn Timrāz az-Ẓāhirī, Marshal of al-Malik az-Ẓāhir. Finished in Ṣafar* 876 (began 20th July 1471).

BIBLIOGRAPHY: Herz, 'Mosquée Timrâz el-Ahmadi connue aussi sous le nom de Mosquée el-Bahloul' (in *CR*. Exerc. 1911, fasc. 28, pp. 120 f.).

TIMRĀZ AL-MU'AYYADĪ[1]

S. Timrāz al-Mu'ayyadī, originally a mamluk of al-Malik al-Mu'ayyad Shaikh and one of his Junior Treasurers, exiled to Syria, some time after 826 made amir at Damascus by Barsbāy, accompanied the Sultan to Amid in 836 (1433), the 19th Jumādā II 838 (20th January 1435) made Amir of a Hundred and Commander of a Thousand in Damascus, on the 27th Shawwāl 839 (14th May 1436) appointed Governor of Safad, on the 1st Rabī' I 840 (13th September 1436) dismissed from office and later appointed Governor of Gaza.[2] In Jumādā I 841 arrested in Cairo, imprisoned in Alexandria and executed there on the 23rd Jumādā II of the same year (22nd December 1437).

BLAZON: *On upper field a napkin, on middle field a cup charged with two small cups, on lower field two napkins.*

MAQĀM, Nabī Rūbīn, near Jaffa, pl. LIX. 1.

Inscription on slab of marble embedded over the entrance door. Marble in state of decomposition especially noticeable at the ends of the first and third lines.

(1) بسمله . . . أمر بإنشاء هذا القبر المبارك المقرّ العالى السيفى [سيف الدين]?

(2) تمراز المؤيّدى الأشرفى نائب السلطنة ○ بغزّة على نبىّ الله روب[ين] عل[يه

السلام]

[1] *Nujūm*, VI, pp. 574, l. 1, 728, ll. 11, 747, l. 8, 750, ll. 1 ff., 754, ll. 4 ff., 849, l. 7, 853, l. 4; *Manhal*, s.v. (MS. Paris, Ar. 2069, fo. 156v).

[2] This is according to the narrative in *Nujūm*, ll. cc. In his *Manhal* Ibn Taghrībirdī reverses the order stating that Timrāz was first Governor of Gaza and afterwards Governor of Safad.

(3) [. . .] الناصرى فملعون بن ملعون من [. . .] الى سكّانها [. . .]

In the name of the most merciful God. His High Excellency Saif ad-dīn [2 words] *Timrāz al-Mu'ayyadī al-Ashrafī, Governor of Gaza, ordered to construct this blessed tomb for the prophet of God Reu[ben, peace upon h]im* [approx. 3 words] *of an-Nāṣir. And cursed, and son of a cursed one be he who* [1 word] *to its inhabitants* [. . .].

BIBLIOGRAPHY: Unpublished.

TIMUR MIN[1] MAḤMŪDSHĀH[2]

S. Timur min Maḥmūdshāh, a mamluk of Khushqadam, on the latter's accession dubbed amir, in 866 (1462) succeeded Aynāl al-Ashqar as Governor (*wālī*) of Cairo, the 12th Jumādā I 872 (9th December 1467) appointed Grand Chamberlain, died in Ṣafar 880 (began 6th June 1475).

BLAZON: *On upper field a napkin, on middle field a scimitar crossed by a cup, on lower field a cup.*

COPPER BOWL on foot, tinned over, in the collection of Mme Maspero, Paris. Pl. LXVIII. 2, 3.

Inscription intersected by two shields.

ممّا عمل برسم المقرّ الأشرف العالى المولوى الأميرى ○ الكبيرى تمر أمير حاجب

الحجّاب بالقاهرة المحروسة عزّ أنصاره ○

This is one of the objects made for His Most Noble and High Excellency, our Lord, the Great Amir, Timur, Grand Chamberlain in Cairo, the protected, may his victory be glorious.

BIBLIOGRAPHY: Artin, *Un bol compotier en cuivre blasonné du XVe siècle*, pp. 90 ff., figs. 1–3.

TIMURBĀY AL-YAḤYĀWĪ

BLAZON: *On upper field a napkin, on middle field a cup charged with a pen-box placed between 'a pair of trousers', on lower field a cup.*

[1] Ibn Iyās calls him T. *b.* Maḥmūdshāh, in the index Timur appears under three headings: T. b. M., T. ḥājib al-ḥujjāb, and T. aẓ-Ẓāhirī. The fact that he is called also T. al-Maḥmūdī (*Nujūm*, VII, p. 826, l. 6) proves that *min* Maḥmūdshāh is the correct form.

[2] *Nujūm.* VII, p. 851, l. 14f.; Ibn Iyās, II, pp. 74, l. 5, 88, l. 4, 158, l. 10; Artin, *Bol compotier*, p. 92 ff.

COPPER BOWL, once in the collection Siouffi.

ممّا عمل برسم المقرّ العالى المولوى الأميرى الكبيرى السيفى تمرباى اليحياوى

عزّ أنصاره [Van Berchem]

This is one of the objects made for His High Excellency, our Lord, the Great Amir, Saif ad-dīn Timurbāy al-Yaḥyāwī, may his victories be glorious.

BIBLIOGRAPHY: Unpublished.

ṬUGHAYDAMUR

BLAZON: *Upper field blank, on the united middle and lower field two scimitars slanting diagonally towards the bottom of the lower field.*

BASE OF CANDLESTICK, collection R. A. Harari, Esq., London. Pl. XXXVI. 4.

Inscription intersected by three shields:

ممّا عمل برسم الجناب العالى ○ المولوى الأميرى السيفى طغيدمر ○ السلحدار

الملكى الناصرى ○ [Harari]

This is one of the objects made for His High Excellency (janāb), *our Lord, the Amir Saif ad-dīn Ṭughaydamur, the armour-bearer, (officer) of al-Malik an-Nāṣir.*

BIBLIOGRAPHY: Unpublished.

ṬUGHAYTAMUR AN-NAJMĪ[1]

S. Ṭughaytamur an-Najmī, originally a mamluk of Muḥammad b. Qalāūn, dubbed amir by the latter,[2] served as Grand Dawādār under al-Malik aṣ-Ṣāliḥ Isma'īl, al-Malik al-Kāmil Sha'bān and al-Malik al-Muẓaffar Ḥājjī. He was the first dawādār with the rank of an Amir of a Hundred and Commander of a Thousand (to which he was promoted at the beginning of

[1] *A'yān*, s.v. (MS. Berlin, fo. 59[r, v]); *Khiṭaṭ*, II, p. 425, ll. 21 ff. (2nd ed., IV, 290, ll. 2 ff.); *Durar*, s.v. MS. Br. Mus. Or. 3043, fo. 144[r]); *Manhal*, s.v. (MS. Paris, Ar. 2070, fo. 189[v]); Weil, IV. 473; *CIA. Égypte*, I. 661.

[2] According to *Durar*, l.c., dubbed amir during the reign of al-Malik aṣ-Ṣāliḥ Isma'īl.

Ḥājjī's reign). Exiled to Syria, killed in Gaza by Manjak during Jumādā II 748 (began 8th September 1347). Built a *khānqāh*, known as the Najmiyya, in Cairo, a bath-house near it, a drinking trough, and a big house.

BLAZON: *On greenish-brown upper field a golden pen-box, on golden middle field a red cup, lower field greenish-brown.*

1. GLASS LAMP, R. Museo Nazionale, Firenze, originally collection Carrand.

Inscription on neck, three times interrupted by heraldic shields: Qur'ān, II. 256, to نوم. Further three shields on the lower part of the body.

Inscription on body:

ممّا عمل برسم المقرّ العا|لى المولوى الأ|ميرى الكبيرى السيفى طغيتمر ا|النجمى

الدواد|ار الملكى ا|الصالحى عزّ نصره |

This is one of the objects made for His High Excellency, our Lord, the Great Amir, Saif ad-dīn Ṭughaytamur an-Najmī, the dawādār of al-Malik aṣ-Ṣāliḥ, may God make his victory glorious.

BIBLIOGRAPHY: Herz, *Deux lampes*, p. 186, pl. II.

Mentioned: Jacquemart, 'Exposition de l'Union Centrale' (in *GBA*. 1869, II), p. 340; Herz, *Catalogue*, p. 293; Migeon, *Orient Musulman, Cristaux*, p. 12, No. 17 (where it is stated that the blazon is identical with that of Ṭuquztamur); Wiet, *Lampes*, p. 163, No. 46; Lamm, *Gläser*, p. 446, No. 71.

2. GLASS LAMP, National Museum of Arab Art, Cairo, No. 314.

Inscription on neck, three times interrupted by heraldic shields, identical with the inscription on body, except for the last two words which are missing on the neck. Three more shields on the lower part of the body.

Inscription on neck:

برسم المقرّ الشريف العالى المولوى المالكى المخدومى السيفى طغيتمر الدوادار

Repeated on body with the addition of الملكى الصالحى *of al-Malik aṣ-Ṣāliḥ.*

For His Noble and High Excellency, our Lord, the Royal, the Well-Served, Saif ad-dīn Ṭughaytamur, the dawādār.

BIBLIOGRAPHY: *CIA. Égypte*, I, No. 472, pp. 660 f.; Herz, *Deux lampes*, p. 181, pl. I; Herz, *Catalogue*, Engl. ed., p. 293; Wiet, *Lampes*, pp. 70 f., pl. XIII.

Reproduced: Le Bon, *Civilisation*, pl. facing p. 600; Briggs, *Muhammadan Architecture in Egypt and Palestine*, fig. 239

Mentioned and reproduced: Wiet, *Album*, No. 94; Lamm, *Gläser*, p. 446, pl. 192, 1.

Blazon reproduced and described: Artin, *Contribution*, No. 93, p. 121 ('sur une lampe en verre émaillé sans inscription, au Musée Arabe du Caire'!).

ṬUGHĀYTAMUR

BLAZON: *Both the upper and lower field red, on self-coloured middle field a cup.*

CYLINDRICAL BOX, bronze, National Museum of Arab Art, Cairo, No. 3985.

Inscription on lid:

المقرّ العالى المولو○ى الأميرى الكبيرى الغا○زى المجاهدى المرابطى المثا○غرى

المؤيّدى الذخرى العونى ○ الغياثى السيفى طغاى‌تمر ○ الساقى الملكى الناصرى ○

His High Excellency, our Lord, the Great Amir, the Vanquisher, the Defender of the Faith, the Warrior at the Frontiers, the Warden of the Marches, the Helped (by God), the Treasure, the Helper, the Rescuer, Saif ad-dīn Ṭughāytamur, the cupbearer, (officer) of al-Malik an-Nāṣir.

The same inscription but with fewer titles appears on the body of the box, where the name Ṭughāytamur is spelt 'Ṭughātamur' without a 'y'.

BIBLIOGRAPHY: Mentioned and reproduced: Wiet, *Album*, No. 52.

ṬUQṬAMISH

BLAZON: *On upper field a napkin, on middle field a cup charged with a pen-box, placed between a pair of 'trousers', on lower field a cup.*

COPPER BOWL, tinned over, in the possession of Messrs. Ohan & Son, Jerusalem.

Inscription intersected by two shields, the lower portion of both text and shields being damaged.

ممّا عمل برسم الجناب العالى السيفى طقطمش الدوادار المقرّ الأشرف السيفى

جان بلاط

This is one of the objects made for His High Excellency (janāb), *Saif ad-dīn Ṭuqṭamish, dawādā of His Most Noble Excellency Saif ad-dīn Jānbalāṭ.*

BIBLIOGRAPHY: Unpublished.

ṬUQUZTAMUR[1 2]

S. Ṭuquztamur al-Ḥamawī, the cup-bearer, originally a mamluk of Abu-l-Fidā', presented to Muḥammad b. Qalāūn, dubbed amir by the latter, appointed *amīr majlis* in 731 (1330/1), made a pilgrimage in 732, Viceroy of Egypt in 741 (1340/1), Governor of Hama in Rabī' II 742 (September–October 1341), Governor of Aleppo 743 (1342), Viceroy of Syria from middle of Rajab 743 till Rabī' I 746 (middle December 1342–July 1345). Died in Cairo in Jumādā I, 746[3] (September 1345). Built a bridge over the Great Canal of Cairo (*al-khalīj al-kabīr*).

BLAZON: *Two-fielded pointed shield. Upper field self-coloured, on red lower field a white eagle above a white cup.*

1. BRONZE EWER, in the collection R. A. Harari, Esq., London, pl. XVI.

Inscription on neck:

مما عمل برسم المقرّ الأشرف | العالى السيفى طقزتمر | الساقى الملكى
الناصرى

This is one of the objects made for His Most Noble and High Excellency, Saif ad-dīn Ṭuquztamur, the cupbearer, (officer) of al-Malik an-Nāṣir.

Inscription on body:

مما عمل برسم المقرّ الأشرف العالى ◊ المولوى الأميرى الكبيرى السيفى
طقز ◊ تمر الساقى الملكى الناصرى ◊

This is one of the objects made for His Most Noble and High Excellency, our Lord, the Great Amir, Saif ad-dīn Ṭuquztamur, the cupbearer, (officer) of al-Malik an-Nāṣir.

BIBLIOGRAPHY: Unpublished.

[1] Zetterstéen, *Beiträge*, especially pp. 179, l. penult., 218, l. 23; Ibn Ḥabīb, pp. 374, 375, 378, 384; *A'yān*, s.v. (MS. Berlin, fo. 60r, v); *Wāfī*, s.v.; Ṣāliḥ b. Yaḥyā, pp. 141, l. 1, 146–7, 176, l. 8; *Khiṭaṭ*, II. 116 b, 147 (2nd ed., III, pp. 189, l. 7 b, 239, ll. 7 f.); *Durar*, s.v. (MS. Br. Mus. Or. 3043, fo. 144v); *Manhal*, s.v. (MS. Paris, Ar. 2070, fo. 191v–192r), and s.v. Ṭurjī (l.c., fo. 182r, l. 5); Ibn Iyās, especially I, pp. 176, l. 12 b, 177, l. 3 b, 184, l. 6; Cheikho in Ṣāliḥ, p. 141, n. 1.

[2] This is Ṣafadī's spelling, cf. *A'yān*, s.v.; Ibn Baṭṭūṭa, I. 86, spells this name Ṭuquz*du*mur, in *Manhal*, s.v., it is vocalized Ṭuquz*d*amur, in Ibn Ḥabīb, l.c., Ṭ*a*quz*d*amur.

[3] According to *Khiṭaṭ*, II, p. 116, l. ult., Ṭuquztamur died on the 1st Jumādā II.

2, 3. Two GLASS LAMPS, British Museum, London.

Inscription on neck: Qur'ān, XXIV. 35.

Inscription on body:

ممّا عمل برسم المقرّ العالى المولوى الأميرى السيفى طقزدمر أمير مجلس الملكى الناصرى

This is one of the objects made for His High Excellency, our Lord, the Amir Saif ad-dīn Ṭuquzdamur, amīr majlis of al-Malik an-Nāṣir.

The inscriptions are identical on both lamps, save for the words *His High Excellency*, omitted on one of them.

BIBLIOGRAPHY: Lane-Poole, *Art of the Saracens*, p. 259 f., 272; Sobernheim, *Arabische Gefässinschriften*, p. 190, pl. VIII b.

Mentioned and reproduced: Migeon, *Manuel* (2nd ed.) II, p. 135 f., fig. 295; P[ier], *Saracenic Heraldry*, fig. 25, p. 10.

Blazon reproduced and described: Rogers, No. 25, p. 126, fig. 45; Artin, *Contribution*, No. 42, p. 95; Prinet, *De l'origine orientale*, p. 53, fig. 18; reproduced only: Lane Poole, *History of Egypt*, p. 316, fig. 72; Ströhl, *Heraldischer Atlas*, p. 3, fig. 9.

Mentioned: Garnier, *Collections de M. Spitzer*, p. 296; van Berchem, *Notes III*, p. 80 n.; *CR*. fasc. 32, p. 136, n. 2; Wiet, *Lampes*, p. 162 f., Nos. 43, 44; Lamm, *Gläser*, p. 445.

The following objects with the blazon described above should be attributed to Ṭuquztamur, although they were issued by his major-domo. It is worth noting that the customary opening phrase ممّا عمل برسم 'this is one of the objects made for' does not occur in any of the three inscriptions in which Qushtumur is mentioned.

4. CANDLESTICK, in 1876 in the collection of Count Hoyos, Vienna, present owner unknown.

Inscription:

الجناب العالى المولوى الأميرى الكبيرى 0 السيفى قشتمر أستاذ الدار [1] الكريمة طقزتمر أمير مجلس عزّ نصره 0

His High Excellency (janāb), *our Lord, the Great Amir, Saif ad-dīn Qushtumur, major-domo of the noble house of Ṭuquztamur, amīr majlis, may his victory be glorious.*

[1] In the facsimile published by Karabacek there is only one *alif* visible in this word. Either involutio or a mistake on the part of the draughtsman.

BIBLIOGRAPHY: J. Karabacek, *Ein damascenischer Leuchter des XIV. Jahrhunderts*, pp. 265–82 and figs.; Sobernheim, *Arabische Gefässinschriften von der Ausstellung islamischer Kunst in Paris*, pp. 186 f., pl. VIII c, d, e, who corrected several mistakes made by Karabacek such as *qasīm* for *Qushtumur*, *al-karīmī* for *al-karīma*, *Toka* for *Ṭuquz*.

Described and reproduced: *Katalog der Kunstsammlung Graf Rudolf Hoyos*, No. 283.

Blazon reproduced: Fox-Davies, *Guide*, p. 13, fig. 7.

Mentioned: *CIA. Égypte*, I. 387, n. 4; Migeon, *Manuel* (2nd ed.), II, p. 136.

5. COPPER BOWL, Kunstgewerbe-Museum, Hamburg, No. 1906, 577. Formerly in the possession of Husain Eff. Siouffi, Damascus, then in that of Messrs. Tabbagh, Paris.

Three shields alternating with three non-heraldic cartouches.

Inscription:

الجناب العالى المولوى الأميرى الكبيرى ا0 لمالكى العالمى الغازى السيفى قشتمر 0

أستاذ الدار الكريمة طقزتمر أمير مجلس عزّ نصره 0

His High Excellency (janāb), *our Lord, the Great Amir, the Royal, the Learned, the Vanquisher, Saif ad-dīn Qushtumur, major-domo of the noble house of Ṭuquztamur, amīr majlis, may his victory be glorious.*

BIBLIOGRAPHY: Unpublished.

Reproduced: Ahlenstiel-Engel, *Arabische Kunst*, fig. 9.

6. COPPER BOWL, collection R. A. Harari, Esq., London.

Three heraldic shields.

Inscription on outside of bowl.

الجناب العالى المولوى الأميرى الكبيرى المالكى ا0لعالمى العاملى العادلى الغازى

المجاهدى المرا0بطى المخدومى السيفى قشتمر أستاذ الدار الكريمة طقزتمر أمير

مجلس عزّ نصره 0

His High Excellency (janāb), *our Lord, the Great Amir, the Royal, the Learned, the Just, the Vanquisher, the Defender of the Faith, the Warrior at the Frontiers, the Well-Served, Saif ad-dīn Qushtumur, major-domo of the noble house of Ṭuquztamur, amīr majlis, may his victory be glorious.*

BIBLIOGRAPHY: Unpublished.

Five more objects showing a blazon in every detail of design and colour identical with authentic examples of the blazon of Ṭuquztamur may be tentatively attributed to him.

7. GLASS BOTTLE, Musée du Louvre, Paris, formerly in the collection Spitzer, then in that of Goupil.

Three shields.

Inscription:

ممّا عمل برسم الشرب‌خانا السعيدة المخدوميّة الناصر [1 word] عزّ الله أنصاره

الملكى الكاملى

This is one of the objects made for the gladdening cellar of the Well-Served, Nāṣir ad-dīn (?) . . . may God make his victories glorious, (officer) of al-Malik al-Kāmil.

The text is not sufficiently clearly worded to allow of a good translation, and it is not evident whether the object was made for Ṭuquztamur's own cellar or for somebody else's cellar to whom the bottle was offered by Ṭuquztamur, the last-mentioned alternative being by far the most probable. As to the designation 'officer of al-Malik al-Kāmil', it will be remembered that Ṭuquztamur was in the service of al-Malik al-Kāmil Sha'bān, as Viceroy of Syria, from the latter's accession to the throne in Rabī' II 746, until Ṭuquztamur's death a few weeks later.

BIBLIOGRAPHY: Unpublished.

Reproduced and described: Migeon, *L'Orient Musulman*, vol. *Cristaux*, p. 11, pl. 6, where the reference to Herz and the statement that there are two similar bottles, one in Florence and another in Cairo, should be deleted. In his notes Migeon mixed up this bottle with the lamp of Ṭughāytamur an-Najmī.

Mentioned: Schmoranz, p. 3; Lavoix, *Galerie orientale du Trocadéro*, p. 780; Lavoix, *La Collection Albert Goupil*, p. 303; Migeon, *Manuel* (2nd ed.), II. 135 f.; Wiet, *Lampes*, p. 164, No. 54; Lamm, p. 410 f., where additional literature can be found.

8. GLASS LAMP, Kunst und Altertumssammlungen, Veste Coburg, in 1855 acquired in Cairo.

Three shields, the inscription rubbed off.

BIBLIOGRAPHY: Reproduced: Kämmerer 'Schöne Gläser aus der Sammlung der Veste Coburg', in *Illustrierte Zeitung*, Leipzig, No. 4442, 1st May 1930, p. 600.

9, 10. TWO SLABS OF WHITE MARBLE, National Museum of Arab Art, Cairo, found in a bath at Darb al-Gamamiz, Cairo.

Without inscription.

BIBLIOGRAPHY: Herz, *Catalogue*, p. 45, fig. 10; Artin, *Contribution*, Nos. 39 and 40, p. 95.

Reproduced: Migeon, *Le Caire, le Nil et Memphis*, p. 72; Rogers, fig. 49 (Germ. ed.).

Mentioned: Herz, *Le Musée National*, p. 51.

11. POTSHERD, once in the collection Fouquet, present owner unknown.

BIBLIOGRAPHY: Artin, *Contribution*, No. 41, p. 95.

ṬURGHĀY[1] [2]

S. Ṭurghāy, originally a mamluk of aṭ-Ṭabbākhī, passed into the service of Muḥammad b. Qalāūn, became his taster (*jāshnigīr*), the 3rd Rabīʿ II 739 (19th October 1338) appointed Governor of Aleppo, after the arrest of Tankiz dismissed from office together with other governors of Syria, returned to Cairo, where he lived in retirement till in Rajab 743 (December 1342) he was sent to Tripoli as Governor. Remained there till his death, 6th Ramaḍān 744 (22nd January 1344).[3]

BLAZON: *Table (khānjā) probably on the middle field of a three-fielded shield.*

ورنك المتّصل خونجا

. . . *and the blazon of the arriving* [i.e. Ṭurghāy] *was a table* . . .

BIBLIOGRAPHY: Abu-l-Fidā', ed. Constantinople, IV, p. 132, l. 18; Ibn al-Wardī, II, p. 324, l. 7 b.

[1] Zetterstéen, *Beiträge*, pp. 162, l. 16, 163, l. 11, 173, l. 1, 183, l. 16, 199, l. 11, 212, l. 14, 214, l. 21, 218, l. 15, 222, l. 9; Abu-l-Fidā', ed. Constantinople, IV, p. 132, l. 15; Ibn al-Wardī, II, p. 324, l. 10 b; Ibn Ḥabīb, pp. 370, 379 (with vowel-signs); *Aʿyān*, s.v. (MS. Berlin, fo. 56r); *Khiṭaṭ*, II, p. 51, ll. 9 f. (2nd ed., III, p. 81, l. penult.); *Durar*, s.v. (Mus. Br. Mus., Or. 3043, fo. 143r); *Manhal*, s.v. (MS. Paris, Ar. 2070, fo. 182r); Tabbākh, *Aʿlam*, II, 399–401.

[2] Spelling in words in *Manhal*, l.c., where the name is explained as meaning a bird in Turkish.

[3] *Manhal*, l.c.: Shaʿbān 743.

ṬURJĪ[1 2]

S. Ṭurjī, one of the mamluks of Muḥammad b. Qalāūn, originally his cupbearer, later silaḥdār, elevated by him to the rank of an amīr majlis. In 719 (1319) and 725 (1325) leader of the pilgrimage. Died on the 5th Rabī' II 731 (16th January 1331).

BLAZON: *Cup on the red middle field of a three-fielded shield.*[3]

1. CANDLESTICK, in the collection of Mr. Theron Damon, Robert College, Constantinople. Pl. XXII. 1, 2.

Inscription on neck: Essential portion illegible on the photograph.

Inscription on body:

مما عمل برسم المقرّ العالى ○ السيفى طرجى الساقى الناصرى ○

This is one of the objects made for His High Excellency Saif ad-dīn Ṭurjī, the cupbearer of (al-Malik) an-Nāṣir.

BIBLIOGRAPHY: Unpublished.

2. COPPER BASIN, tinned over, collection R. A. Harari, Esq., London.

Inscription intersected by four shields:

○ المقرّ الأشرف العالى المولوا ○ ○ السيفى طرجى أمير مجلس [ا]لملكى [ا]لنا ○

His Most Noble and High Excellency, our Lord, Saif ad-dīn Ṭurjī, amīr majlis of al-Malik an-Nā[ṣir].

BIBLIOGRAPHY: Unpublished.

ṬURUNṬĀY AṬ-ṬABBĀKHĪ

BLAZON: *Barry of five pieces.*

EWER, Museo Civico, Bologna, No. 'Università 5'.

[1] Zetterstéen, *Beiträge*, pp. 169, l. 10, 172, l. 6, 176, l. 7, 183, l. 3; *Durar*, s.v. (MS. Br. Mus., Or. 3043, fo. 142ᵛ); *Manhal*, s.v. (MS. Paris, Ar. 2070, fo. 181ᵛ, 182ʳ); Ibn Iyās, I, p. 161, l. 3 b.

[2] I am spelling the name according to the *A'yān*, s.v. (MS. Berlin, fo. 56ʳ, l. 11), although the amir dealt with there is not identical with our Ṭurjī. Zetterstéen spells it Ṭurjī and Uṭarjī (اطرجى).

[3] Traces of incrustation are visible on the photographs of the candlestick, which I owe to the good offices of the owner and of Prof. R. M. Riefstahl.

One shield immediately below the spout.

Inscription round the spout:

برسم الجناب العالى طرنطاى الطبّاخى

For His High Excellency (janāb), *Ṭuruntāy aṭ-Ṭabbākhī.*

BIBLIOGRAPHY: Unpublished.

ULMĀS[1]

S. Ulmās, originally a mamluk of Muḥammad b. Qalāūn, became taster (*jāshnigīr*), the 21st Rajab 717 appointed Grand Chamberlain, on Arghūn's transfer to Aleppo acted as Viceroy of Egypt (although without the title of such), arrested the 20th Dhu-l-Ḥijja 733. Executed the 12th Ṣafar 734[2] (22nd October 1333).

BLAZON: *Yellow emblem No. 26 with whitish crescent, on whitish undivided field.*

GLASS LAMP, National Museum of Arab Art, Cairo, No. 3154, originally in the collection Linant de Bellefonds, subsequently in that of Rostovitz Bey.

Six shields, three intersecting the inscription on the neck (Qur'ān, IX. 18, to الآخر), and three on the lower part of the body.

Inscription on body:

ممّا عمل برسم الجامع المعمو بذكر | الله تعالى وقف المقرّ العالى | السيفى الماس

أمير حاجب الملكى الناصرى

This is one of the objects made for the Mosque that prospers by the worship of God the Exalted, a pious foundation of His High Excellency, Saif ad-dīn Ulmās, Amir-Chamberlain of al-Malik an-Nāṣir.

BIBLIOGRAPHY: Rogers, No. 26, pp. 127 ff., fig. 46; Artin, *Six lampes*, No. 6, pp. 148 ff., pl. II; Herz, *Catalogue*, Engl. ed., pp. 290 ff., fig. 56; Wiet, *Lampes*, pp. 122 ff., pl. VIII.

Mentioned: Lane-Poole, *Art of the Saracens*, pp. 250, 272; *CR*. Exerc. 1903, fasc. 20, p. 58; Lamm, *Gläser*, p. 437 f., No. 38 (with sketch).

Blazon reproduced: P[ier], *Saracenic Heraldry*, p. 10, fig. 17.

[1] Zettersteén, *Beiträge*, pp. 147, l. 9, 166, l. 19, 187, ll. 8, 15, 226, l. 10; *Durar*, s.v. (MS. Or. 3043, fo. 77ʳ); *Khiṭaṭ*, II, pp. 74, l. 12, 307, ll. 9 ff.; *Manhal*, s.v. (MS. Paris, Ar. 2069, fo. 19ᵛ–20ʳ); Rogers, l.c.; Artin, l.c.

[2] *Durar*, l.c.: the last days of Dhu-l-Ḥijja 732; *Manhal*, l.c.: the 2nd Ṣafar.

ULMĀS

BLAZON: *On upper field a napkin, on middle field a cup charged with a pen-box placed between a 'pair of trousers', on lower field a cup.*

COPPER BOWL, tinned over, in the possession of the present writer.

Four shields.

Inscription:

مما عمل برسم المقرّ الأشرف الكريم ا ○ العالى المولوى الأميرى الكبير[ى] ○

السيفى ألماس [2-3 words] [1] السعيد أعزّ ○ الله تعالى أنصاره وادام عزّ[ه] ○

This is one of the objects made for His Most Noble and Honourable and High Excellency, our Lord, the Great Amir, Saif ad-dīn Ulmās . . . may God the Exalted make his victories glorious and his strength eternal.

BIBLIOGRAPHY: Unpublished.

ULMĀS AL-ASHRAFĪ [2]

Probably identical with Ulmās, originally in the service of al-Malik al-Ashraf Barsbāy, made amir in Aleppo, occupied various posts there, became *atābak* of Aleppo, was killed in battle against Siwār, on the 5th Rabīʿ I 872 (4th October 1467), over 50 years old.

BLAZON: *On upper field a pen-box, on middle field two cups, on lower field a napkin.*

COPPER BASIN tinned over. Collection R.A. Harari, Esq., London, once in the possession of Husain Eff. Siouffi, Damascus. Pl. LVIII. 3, 4.

Inscription:

المقرّ الكر [patch] ○ السيّدى المالكى المخدومى | السيفى ألماس الملكى ا○الأشرفى

أمير [patch] | المقام الشريف بحلب المحروس ○ أعزّ أنصاره لصاحبه لسعادة

His Hono[urable] Excellency, the Master, the Royal, the Well-Served, Saif ad-dīn Ulmās,

[1] These words are entirely obliterated except for three letters ب ا ب (or و).

[2] *Ḍau'*, s.v. (MS. Leyden, Cod. 369 b Warn., p. 732).

(officer) of al-Malik al-Ashraf, amir . . . of His Majesty in Aleppo, the protected. May (God) make his victories glorious. Happiness to its proprietor.

BIBLIOGRAPHY: Unpublished.

'UMAR AL-'ĀQIL

BLAZON: *On the middle field of a three-fielded shield a pen-box without the middle part.*

PERFUME SPRINKLER, in 1880 in possession of A. Baudry, present owner unknown. Inscription:

مماّ عمل برسم العبد الفقير الحاجّ عمر العاقل

This is one of the objects made for the servant yearning for God, the Mecca-pilgrim 'Umar al-'Āqil (=the wise).

BIBLIOGRAPHY: Rogers, No. 16, p. 122, fig. 36.

'UMAR B. SHĀHĀNSHĀH

The blazon of al-Malik al-Muẓaffar Taqī ad-dīn 'Umar, the Ayyubid, was described by St. Ambroise, *L'Estoire de la Guerre Sainte,* ed. Gaston Paris, v. 6563 ff., p. 175: *La iert l'amiralz Dequedin, un des parenz Salahadin, qui ot portrait en sa baniere enseignes d'estrange maniere: ço estoit une baniere as braies, c'erent ses enseignes veraies,* and by the author of the *Itinerarium Regis Ricardi,* ed. Stubbs, p. 272, as *habens baneriam insignitam miro genere distinctionis, scilicet incisarum schemate braccarum.*[1] In the absence of a concrete example of his arms we can only register this statement, although it would seem much more probable that the emblem seen by the Frankish knight was a shield divided by bends like the arms of other Ayyubids of Hama, e.g. Abu-l-Fidā' or Nūr ad-dīn b. 'Imād ad-dīn. Assuming the badge to be somewhat disfigured, either because the banner had a hole or the embroidery had been unpicked or—should the emblem have been sewn on—a piece of cloth had been torn off, the remaining portion could have easily justified such a statement.

In the past 'Umar's emblem has been considered to be either a pen-box[2] or a pair of polo-sticks.[3]

[1] Often quoted, among others, by Wilken, *Geschichte der Kreuzzüge,* IV, p. 416, n. 85; Lane-Poole, *Saladin,* p. 320; Artin, *Contribution,* p. 131.

[2] Lane-Poole, l.c., note *: 'a well-known *renk* . . . copied from an ancient Egyptian hieroglyphic cartouche.'

[3] Artin, *Contribution,* p. 132; Mayer, *Arabic Inscriptions of Gaza,* I. 74.

UZBAK[1]

S. Uzbak min Ṭuṭukh bought by al-Ashraf Barsbāy in 841, passed into the service of aẓ-Ẓāhir Jaqmaq, became a cup-bearer, in 852 (began 7th March 1448) dubbed Amir of Ten, then appointed Chief of a Corps of Mamluks (*ra's nauba*), under al-Malik al-Manṣūr succeeded Qarājā as Amir of Forty and Second Treasurer (*khāzindār*), arrested by al-Malik al-Ashraf Aynāl, imprisoned in Alexandria and Safad, released early in 858 (1454), lived in Jerusalem without office, in 861 (began 29th November 1456) recalled to Cairo, made Amir of Ten, 9th Jumādā I 868 (19th January 1464) appointed Grand Chamberlain (*ḥājib al-ḥujjāb*), then Chief of the Corps of Mamluks (*ra's naubat an-nuwwāb*), towards the end of Rabīʿ I 872 (began 30th September 1467) appointed Viceroy of Syria. In Muḥarram 873 (began 22nd July 1468) appointed Commander-in-Chief, remained in office until 900. In 902 appointed Commander-in-Chief for a second time, died the 24th Ramaḍān 904 (5th May 1499). Built a mosque, a bath, and a caravanserai (*wakālah*) in Cairo.

BLAZON: *On upper field a napkin, on middle field a cup placed between 'a pair of trousers', on lower field a cup.*

COPPER DISH, tinned over, in the collection of R. A. Harari, Esq., London.

On the back of the dish two inscriptions and two shields.

Inscription (A):

المقرّ الأشرف الكريم العالى المولوى الأميرى الكبيرى | السيفى ازبك أتابك

العساكر المنصورة بالممالك الاسلاميّة عظم شأنه

His Most Noble and Honourable and High Excellency, our Lord, the Great Amir, Saif ad-dīn Uzbak, Commander-in-Chief of the victorious armies in the Islamic provinces, may his dignity increase.

Inscription (B):

[1] *Manhal*, s.v. (MS. Paris, Ar. 2068, fo. 167v); *Ḍau'*, s.v. (MS. Leyden, Cod. 369 b Warn., pp. 677–9); Ibn Iyās, especially II, pp. 100, l. 4, 282, ll. 3 b ff., 291, l. 12, 355, l. 4 ff.; Weil, V. 256, 300, 329 f., 333, 366, 373 f.; *CIA. Égypte*, I. 459 f., 471, 530, n. 3.

ممّا عمل برسم الزينى سرور من اقبردى غفر له | فى خدمة امير دواد[ا]ر
كبير طومان باى عزّ نصره

This is one of the objects made for Zain ad-dīn Surūr min Āqbirdī, may he be pardoned, in the service of the Grand Dawādār Ṭūmānbāy, may his victory be glorious.

To judge from their position the shields belong to the first inscription, although the second one is so worded as if the dish had been made originally for Surūr and not for Uzbak.

DATE: The second text mentions a Grand Dawādār Ṭūmānbāy, during whose term of office the dish was made. Now there are two Ṭūmānbāys to be considered: one appointed Grand Dawādār the 17th Rabīʿ I 904, on al-Malik aẓ-Ẓāhir Qānṣūh's accession to the throne, remained in office till he was elected Sultan in 906; the other Ṭūmānbāy b. Qānṣūh, nephew of Sultan Qānṣūh al-Ghaurī, in 913 appointed Grand Dawādār, remained in office till he, too, was elected Sultan in 922. Theoretically there is the possibility of both inscriptions having been engraved within six months between Rabīʿ I and Ramaḍān 904, during which period Uzbak was still Commander-in-Chief and Ṭūmānbāy already Grand Dawādār. As the data do not suffice to identify this Surūr with any of his several namesakes mentioned by Ibn Iyās, it might be assumed for the sake of argument that Surūr had this dish made to order after the 17th Rabīʿ I 904, that he died, or that his property was confiscated or otherwise disposed of later, but still in time for Uzbak to acquire this dish and add his inscription prior to his own death in Ramaḍān of the same year. But this hypothesis seems far-fetched and improbable. It is far more likely that the initial phrase 'this is one of the objects made for' is not to be taken literally, and that it is, in this as in a few other instances, merely a later addition, so that we may not unreasonably consider this object as having been made for Uzbak and acquired by Surūr after Uzbak's death.
BIBLIOGRAPHY: Unpublished.

2. BRONZE DISH, in possession of Mme Maspero, Paris.

One shield in the centre, four on the border.

Inscription:

ممّا عمل برسم المقرّ الأشرف الكريم العالى ○ المولوى الأميرى الكبيرى
السيّدى ○ المالكى المخدومى السيفى أزبك ○ أتابك العساكر المنصورة بالديار ○
المصريّة الملكى الأشرفى عزّ نصره ○

This is one of the objects made for His Most Noble and Honourable and High Excellency, our

Lord, the Great Amir, the Master, the Royal, the Well-Served, Saif ad-dīn Uzbak, Commander-in-Chief of the victorious army in Egypt, (officer) of al-Malik al-Ashraf, may his victory be glorious.

BIBLIOGRAPHY: Jean Maspero, *Deux vases de bronze arabes du XVe siècle*, pp. 173 f.

UZBAK AL-YŪSUFĪ[1]

S. Uzbak al-Yūsufī, originally a mamluk of Jaqmaq, became known as Treasurer and Keeper of the Privy Purse, in Ṣafar 876 (began 20th July 1471) appointed Governor of ʿAintāb in sign of disgrace, but pardoned and allowed to remain in Cairo, until in Rabīʿ I 880 (began 5th July 1475), dismissed from office of Grand Treasurer, became Commander of a Thousand, in 886 Leader of the pilgrimage, in 894 (1489) appointed Chief of the Corps of Mamluks, in Ṣafar 901 (began 21st October 1495) appointed Amīr Silāḥ, towards the end of the same year appointed Amīr Majlis, in Jumādā II 902 (began 4th February 1497), replaced by Tānībak Qarā, in Muḥarram 903 (September 1497) appointed Councillor to the Government (*mushīr al-mamlaka*), died the 24th Ramaḍān 904 (5th May 1499).

BLAZON: *On upper field a napkin between a 'pair of trousers' pointing outwards, on middle field a cup between another 'pair of trousers'* (?), *on lower field a cup between two napkins.*

1. MOSQUE, Cairo, pl. LXIX. 2.

Two shields flanking the windows above the main entrance gate. The upper and lower fields and the charges of the middle field are sunk *en creux*, whereas the remaining charges and the middle field are raised, i.e. are level with the surface of the stone.

Inscription to the right of the shields:

أمر بانشاء هذا المسجد الجامع المقرّ الأشرف الكريم العالى السيفى أزبك اليوسفى
امير رأس نوبة النوّاب الملكى الأشرفى بتأريخ شهر شعبان المكرّم سنة تسعمائة
من الهجرة

Ordered to build this Mosque His Most Noble and Honourable and High Excellency Saif ad-dīn

[1] *Ḍau'*, s.v. (MS. Leyden, Cod. 369 b. Warn. p. 679 f.); Ibn Iyās, especially II, pp. 129, l. penult., 158, l. 23, 213, l. 5, 232, l. 22, 259, l. 6, 292, l. 16, 304, l. 8 b, 312, l. penult., 332, l. 23, 353, l. 15, 356, ll. 13 ff.; Weil, V. 348, n. 2, 366, 374 n.; Herz., *La Mosquée d' Ezbek el-Yussufy*, pp. 16 f.; Artin, *Un sabre de l'Émir Ezbek el Yussufi el Zahery*, pp. 253 ff.; *CIA. Égypte*, I. 536–8.

Uzbak al-Yūsufī, Amir Chief of the Mamluks of al-Malik al-Ashraf. On the date of the honoured Sha'bān of the year 900 of the Hijra (May 1495).

BIBLIOGRAPHY: Herz, *La Mosquée de Ezbek el-Yussufy*, pp. 16 ff., fig. 6; Artin, *Un sabre de l'Émir Ezbek*, p. 252, fig. 3; *CIA. Égypte*, I, No. 350, p. 528, fig. on p. 530, and pl. XL, 1.

Reproduced and described: Rogers, No. 10, p. 116, fig. 30.

Reproduced: Lane-Poole, *History of Egypt*, p. 349, fig. 92; P[ier], *Saracenic Heraldry*, fig. 19, p. 10; fig. 16 shows in the upper field a cup instead of a napkin.

2. SWORD, National Museum of Arab Art, Cairo, formerly in the collection Artin Pasha. Pl. LXVIII. 1.

On the blade inscription in one line accompanied by a shield.

A comparison of this shield with any one of those on the Mosque reveals two changes in the shape of the emblems on the upper field. The napkin is misformed, which made Artin Pasha describe it as a 'vase fermé', and the 'pair of trousers' is turned with its points towards the napkin and not away from it. The first point of difference is certainly due to the carelessness of the engraver, whose lack of skill is illustrated by the clumsy character of the script.

The essential portion of the text runs as follows:

وقف المقرّ الأشرف السيفى أزبك أمير ر[أ]س نوبة النوب الملكى الأشرفى . . .

Waqf of His Most Noble Excellency Saif ad-dīn Uzbak, Amir Chief of the Corps of the Mamluks of al-Malik al-Ashraf . . .

BIBLIOGRAPHY: Artin, *Un sabre*, pp. 249 ff., figs. 1 and 2.

UZDAMUR[1] [2]

Perhaps identical with S. Uzdamur, originally a mamluk of Barqūq, promoted after the death of the latter, under Shaikh became Amir of a Hundred, arrested by Ṭaṭar, died in 824 (1421).

BLAZON: *On upper field a pen-box, on middle field two cups, on lower field a napkin.*

[1] *Manhal*, s.v. (MS. Paris, Ar. 2068, fo. 168v–169r). The main reason for suggesting this identification is the surname Saif ad-dīn, most other Uzdamurs having borne the surname *'Izz* ad-dīn.

[2] With regard to the pronunciation of this name, cf. Mayer, *Arabic Inscriptions of Gaza*, III. 223 f.

COPPER BASIN, tinned over, Max Freiherr v. Oppenheim-Stiftung, Berlin. Pl. LVIII. 1, 2.

Two shields.

Inscription:

ممّا عمل برسم الجناب العالى | المالكى المخدومى | السيفى أزدمر امير عشروات

This is one of the objects made for His High Excellency (janāb), *the Royal, the Well-Served, Saif ad-dīn Uzdamur, Amir of Ten.*

BIBLIOGRAPHY: Unpublished.

YALBUGHĀ AN-NĀṢIRĪ[1]

S. Yalbughā, originally a mamluk of al-Malik an-Nāṣir Ḥasan, held many offices, in 775 appointed Grand Chamberlain (*ḥājib al-ḥujjāb*). Died in 776 (1374/5).

BLAZON: *Upper field red, on self-coloured middle field a blue sword with white sword-knot and white bands, lower field black.*

GLASS LAMP, in the possession of M. Ispenian, Cairo, formerly in the collection J. Dixon.

Three shields on neck, three on the lower part of the body.

Inscription on neck:

المقرّ الكريم العالى المولوى الأميرى الكبيرى المالكى المخدومى

continued on body:

السيفى يلبغا الناصرى الأشرفى امير حاجب بالأبواب الشريفة اعلاه الله تعالى

His Honourable and High Excellency, our Lord, the Great Amir, the Royal, the Well-Served, Saif ad-dīn Yalbughā an-Nāṣirī, (*officer*) *of al-Malik al-Ashraf, Amir Chamberlain at the Noble Gates, may God, the Exalted, elevate him.*

DATE: Between 775 (date of his appointment as Amir Chamberlain) and 776 (his death).

BIBLIOGRAPHY: Lane-Poole, *Art of the Saracens*, p. 261; Wiet, *Lampes*, p. 174, No. 127.

[1] *Nujūm*, obituaries, s.a. 776 (MS. Paris, Ar. 1786, fo. 189v); *Manhal*, s.v. (MS. Cairo, III, fo. 440v) *CIA. Égypte*, I. 679, n. 2.

Mentioned and reproduced: *Illustrated Catalogue of Specimens of Persian and Arab Art*, Burlington Fine Arts Club, 1885, No. 256, p. 32, pl. 18; Schmoranz, p. 21.

Mentioned: *CIA. Égypte*, I. 679, n. 2; Migeon, *Manuel* (2nd ed.), II. 134; Lamm, *Gläser*, p. 470, No. 180.

YALBUGHĀ AL-ʿUMARĪ[1]

S. Yalbughā al-ʿUmarī, known as 'the page' (*khāṣṣakī*), a freed mamluk of al-Malik an-Nāṣir Ḥasan, dubbed Amir of Ten by his master, later promoted to the rank of an Amir of Forty, became Major-domo, in 760 appointed Amīr Majlis, in 762 murdered Ḥasan, on the accession of al-Malik al-Manṣūr Muḥammad b. Ḥājjī became Commander-in-Chief, remained in office till he met his death during a revolt the 10th[2] Rabīʿ II 768 (14th December 1366).

BLAZON: *On the middle field of a three-fielded shield a cup.*

MADRASA, Ramleh.

Inscription, now disappeared:

. . . هذه المدرسة المباركة المقرّ العالى المولوى السيفى يلبغا الخاصّكى أعزّ الله أنصاره

فى جمادى الأوّل سنة ستّين وسبعمائة [van Berchem]

[*Ordered to build*] *this blessed school His High Excellency, our Lord, Saif ad-dīn Yalbughā al-khāṣṣakī, may God make his victories glorious, in Jumādā I* 760 (April 1359).

BIBLIOGRAPHY: Unpublished.

YALBUGHĀ AL-YAḤYĀWĪ[3]

S. Yalbughā b. S. Ṭābṭā al-Yaḥyāwī, a favourite mamluk of Muḥammad b. Qalāūn and his cup-bearer. In 743 (1342/3) Governor of Hama. After the

[1] Ibn Ḥabīb, p. 419; *Ṣubḥ*, VII. 60; Ṣāliḥ b. Yaḥyā, p. 51, l. ult., 52, l. ult., 213, l. 5, 279, l. 12; *Khiṭaṭ*, II, p. 399, l. 20 (2nd ed., IV. 249, l. 8); *Durar*, s.v.; *Manhal*, s.v. (MS. Cairo, III, fo. 432v–434v); Ibn Iyās, especially I, pp. 207, l. 15, 209, ll. 5, 17 ff., 211, l. 5, 212, l. 6, 213, l. 13–218, l. 4 b, 219, ll. 7 ff.; Weil, especially IV, 503 f., 508, 511–18; *CIA. Égypte, I.* 274, n. 3; Cheikho in Ṣāliḥ, p. 51, n. 5.

[2] Ibn Iyās, I, p. 218, l. 4 b: the 9th; *Khiṭaṭ*, l.c.: in Shawwāl.

[3] *Aʿyān*, s.v. (MS. Berlin, fo. 170r–171v), and s.v. Ṭābṭā (l.c., fo. 54r); Ibn Ḥabīb, pp. 379, 383, 387, Ṣāliḥ b. Yaḥyā, pp. 146, l. ult., 176, l. 11, 177, ll. 2 ff.; *Durar*, s.v. (MS. Br. Mus., Or. 3044, fo. 162r) *Manhal*, s.v. (MS. Cairo, III, fo. 430r–432v); Ibn Iyās, I, pp. 184, l. 6, 187–8; Weil, IV. 453, 460, 463, 472, 473; Cheikho in Ṣāliḥ, p. 146, n. 2 (where the date of his death is wrongly stated to be 747).

death of Alṭunbughā appointed Governor of Aleppo in 744 (1343/4); under al-Malik al-Kāmil Sha'bān appointed Viceroy of Syria, which he entered on Saturday, the 12th Jumādā I 746 (10th September 1345). Made prisoner, executed, and buried at Qāqūn, Jumādā I 748 (9th August–7th September 1347). Built the stable in the Sūq al-Khail, which was later turned into the Madrasa of Sultan Ḥasan, Cairo. Repaired the Qubbat an-Nāṣir at the Masjid al-Qadam, qaisariyyas outside Bāb al-Faraj, two baths outside the Bāb al-Jābiyah (Damascus), and started working on a mosque in the Sūq al-Khail in Damascus in 748 (1347).

BLAZON: *Cup on middle field of a three-fielded shield.*

PUBLIC FOUNTAIN, Maḥall Muḥammad Bey, Bāb an-Nairab-quarter, Aleppo. Locally known as 'Qasṭal Shabāraq'.

Four heraldic shields had to be placed in the four corners of the slab of stone, but only the bottom ones have been fully carved out, of the upper shields only the two horizontal lines dividing the fields being marked.

(1) أمر بإنشاء هذا السبيل المبارك المقرّ الأشرف العالى المولوى المالكى المخدومى

(2) الكافلى السيفى يلبغا الساقى الصالحى كافل الممالك الحلبيّة المحروسة أعزّ الله أنصاره من ماله

(3) ابتغاء لوجه الله تعالى يسقيه العطش الأكبر يَوْمَ لَا يَنْفَعُ مَالٌ وَلَا بَنُونَ الّا مَنْ أَتَا ٱللَّهَ بِقَلْبٍ سَلِيمٍ (Qur'an XXVI. 88 f.)

(4) وذلك فى شهر ربيع الأوّل سنة ستّة واربعين وسبعمئة بنظر الفقير الى الله تعالى إبرهيم بن محمّد الحرّانى عفا الله عنه

His Most Noble and High Excellency, our Lord, the Royal, the Well-Served, the Viceroy, Saif ad-dīn Yalbughā, the Cup-bearer of (al-Malik) aṣ-Ṣāliḥ, Viceroy of the protected provinces of Aleppo, may God make his victories glorious, ordered to construct this blessed public fountain out of his own fortune, in his desire to please God the Exalted, may He quench his greatest thirst the day in which neither riches nor children shall avail, unless unto him who shall approach God with a pure heart. This was done in Rabīʿ I 746 (July 1345) *under the supervision of the servant yearning for God the Exalted Ibrahīm b. Muḥammad al-Ḥarrānī, may God forgive him.*

BIBLIOGRAPHY: Bishoff, *Tuḥaf al-anbā'*, pp. 157f. (several mistakes, blazon not mentioned).

YASHBAK AL-ḤAMZĀWĪ[1]

S. Yashbak al-Ḥamzāwī, mamluk of Sūdūn al-Ḥamzāwī aẓ-Ẓāhirī, appointed by Jaqmaq Dawādār of the Sultan at Aleppo, in 851 (1447) appointed Governor of Gaza, in the same year Governor of Safad, died there the 27th Ramaḍān 855 (23rd October 1451).

BLAZON: *On upper field a pen-box, on middle field a cup charged with two small cups and placed between two emblems No. 46, on lower field a cup.*

BODY OF CANDLESTICK, made of copper, inside tinned over, Düsseldorf, Kunstgewerbe-Museum, No. 16151. Pl. LXV. 3.

Inscription intersected by three shields:

ممّا عمل برسم المقرّ الأشرف العالى المولوى ○ السيّدى السيفى يشبك الحمزاوى

نقيب ○ القلعة المنصورة بدمشق المحروسة عزّ أنصاره ○

This is one of the objects made for His Most Noble and High Excellency, our Lord, the Master, Saif ad-dīn Yashbak al-Ḥamzāwī, Commandant of the victorious fortress in the protected Damascus, may his victories be glorious.

None of the passages mentioned in the note records the fact that Yashbak ever was commandant (*naqīb*) of the fortress of Damascus, but the high title given him in the text of the inscription makes it plausible that he occupied this post between 851 and 854. The date of this candlestick must therefore lie within these four years.

BIBLIOGRAPHY: Unpublished.

YASHBAK MIN MAHDĪ[2]

S. Yashbak min Mahdī, originally a mamluk of Jaqmaq, in 859 still in the ranks, became Junior Dawādār, in 871 (1466/7) dubbed Amir of Ten and

[1] *Manhal*, s.v. (MS. Cairo, III, fo. 426ᵛ, 427ʳ); *Ḥawādith*, s.aa. 851, 854; *Nujūm*, VII, cf. Index; Sakhāwī, *at-Tibr al-masbūk*, p. 381, ll. 11 ff.; *Ḍau'*, s.v.

[2] *Ḍau'*, s.v.; *Nujūm*, VII, pp. 753, l. 5, 866, l. 5, 868, l. 2; Ibn Iyās, especially II, pp. 51, l. 4, 90,

appointed District Officer of the Southern District of Egypt, on Qāytbāy's accession in 872 (1468) appointed Grand Dawādār, in addition to which he was given, in 873, the posts of Vizier and Major-domo, and shortly afterwards those of a First General (*bāsh al-ʿaskar*), Amir Silāḥ, Inspector-General (*kāshif al-kushshāf*) and Regent (*muddabir al-mamlaka*), in Shawwāl 878 (began 19th February 1474) resigned from the posts of Vizier and Major-domo, in Rajab 883 (October 1478) appointed Major-domo for a second time. Died during the last ten days of Ramaḍān 885[1] (24th November–3rd December 1480).

BLAZON: (*a*) *On upper field a napkin, on middle field a cup charged with a pen-box and placed between a 'pair of trousers', on lower field a cup.*[2] (*b*) *A lion.*[3]

1. COPPER DISH, in 1880 in the collection A. Baudry, present owner unknown.

Inscription:

ممّا عمل برسم المقرّ الأشرف العالى المولوى الأميرى الكبيرى السيفى يشبك

من مهدى أمير دوادار كبير الملكى الأشرفى

This is one of the objects made for His Most Noble and High Excellency, our Lord, the Great Amir, Saif ad-dīn Yashbak min Mahdī, Grand Amir Dawādār of al-Malik al-Ashraf.

BIBLIOGRAPHY: Rogers, No. 6, pp. 114 f., fig. 26; *CIA. Égypte*, I. 454 and n. 3, where the mistakes in Rogers's text were corrected.

2. PALACE, Cairo, locally known as Ḥosh Bardaq.

Two painted shields, one on each side of the portal. The colours faded and most of the charges undistinguishable.

The essential portion of the inscription on the façade runs as follows:

. . . ممّا أمر بإنشائه برسم المقرّ الأشرف العالى . . . يشبك من مهدى أمير

l. 16, 92, l. 10, 102, l. 20, 107, l. 4, 124, l. 3, 127, ll. 3 ff., 141, l. 5 b, 149, l. 8, 152, l. 4 b, 154, l. 11, 184, l. 1, 199, ll. 9, 7 b ff., 202, l. 8; Weil, V. 328, 335, 342; *CIA. Égypte*, I. 440, 451, 455, 457, n. 2, 515, 721–3, 749 f.

[1] With regard to this date, cf. *CIA. Égypte*, I. 455, n. 5, 457, n. 2, 515, n. 1.

[2] Although there are no 'trousers' on Rogers' drawing, l.c. fig. 26, he assures us that the blazons are in both cases identical.

[3] Known only from a passage in Ibn Iyās وصنع فى رنكه صفة سبع (II, p. 127, l. 9), mentioned by Weil, V. 335, and quoted by Artin, *Bol compotier*, p. 94, n. 1.

دوادار كبير وباش العساكر المنصورة ومدبّر الممالك الاسلاميّة . . . [وذلك فى شهر رمضان المعظّم سنة ثمانين وثمانمائة]

. . . *This is one (of the buildings) the construction of which was ordered for His Most Noble and High Excellency . . . Yashbak min Mahdī, Grand Amīr Dawādār and Head of the Victorious Army and Regent of the Islamic provinces . . . during the month of Ramaḍān of the year* 880 (began 29th December 1475).

BIBLIOGRAPHY: *CIA. Égypte*, I. 440, 454, n. 3, 459 and n. 2.

Mentioned: Rogers, l.c., p. 115; Herz, *Deux lampes*, p. 182, n. 3.

Reproduced: *CR.* Exerc. 1894, fasc. 11, pl. V; Lane-Poole, *History of Egypt*, p. 319, fig. 75 (only the pen-box visible); Migeon, *Le Caire, le Nil et Memphis*, p. 19; Creswell, *Brief Chronology*, pl. XVI. A ; Tarchi, *L'Architettura e l'Arte Mussulmana*, pl. LXXXI.

YASHBAK ASH-SHAʿBĀNĪ [1]

S. Yashbak ash-Shaʿbānī aẓ-Ẓāhirī, originally a mamluk of Barqūq, made by him Amir of a Hundred and Commander of a Thousand in 800 (1397), Treasurer (*khāzindār*) in 801 (1399), guardian (*lālā*) of Faraj, later Grand Dawādār. Following upon the execution of Tanam and Aytmish in 802, became the real regent of the country. In 803 captured by Jakam al-ʿIwaḍī and on the 16th Shawwāl (30th May 1401) put into prison, but on the 24th Dhu-l-Qaʿda 804 (25th June 1402) reinstalled in office. On the 7th Jumādā II 808 (30th November 1405), appointed Commander-in-Chief. Some time later fled to Syria, revolted, beat the Sultan at Bilbais, but, abandoned by the Syrian Amirs, was compelled to hide himself in Cairo till Faraj pardoned him. Arrested on the 25th Ṣafar 810 (1st August 1407) fled, revolted again, finally slain in the battle of Baalbek, 13th Rabīʿ II 810 (16th September 1407).

BLAZON: *On each of the middle and lower fields of a three-fielded shield a cup.*

MAUSOLEUM, Baalbek, locally known as the 'Dome of the Monkeys'.

Inscription over the lintel of the entrance door, four shields in the corners:

[1] *Manhal*, s.v. (MS. Cairo, III, fo. 417^v–419^v) and s.v. Yūsuf al-Bajāsī, l.c. 445^v, l. 8; *Nujūm*, VI, cf. Index; Ibn Iyās, I, pp. 308, l. 14, 314, l. 13, 320, l. 3, 337–9, 346, l. 4 b, 347 t, 348, l. 4, 349, ll. 5 b f., 350, l. 5; Weil, V. 99, 100, 101, 107, 108; Sobernheim, *Baalbek in islamischer Zeit*, p. 28 (of the offprint).

(1) بسمله . . . انشأ هذه التربة المباركة المقرّ الأشرف شيخ كافل المملكة الشاميّة

(2) أعزّ الله تعالى انصاره وجعلها وقفًا محبّسًا على المقرّ الأشرف المرحوم يشبك

(3) تغمّده الله برحمته ومن جاوره المقرّ المرحوم جركس وكان الفراغ فى سنة اثنى عشرة وثمانمئة

(4) وكان المشيد شيخ القوم جلال

In the name of the most merciful God. Constructed this blessed mausoleum His Most Noble Excellency, Shaikh, Viceroy of Syria, may God the Exalted make his victories glorious, and made it a waqf for His Most Noble Excellency, the late Yashbak, may God cover him with His mercy, and his neighbour, His Excellency, the late Jarkas. Completed in the year 812 (1409/10). *The head-mason Jalāl was in charge of the work.*

BIBLIOGRAPHY: Sobernheim, *Baalbek in islamischer Zeit*, No. 24 (pp. 27 ff. of the offprint).

YŪNUS AD-DAWĀDĀR[1]

Sh.[2] Yūnus an-Naurūzī, or an-Nayrūzī, originally a mamluk of Jurjī an-Naurūzī, first served under Yalbughā al-ʿUmarī, then under the Atābak Asandamur, and finally as Dawādār under Barqūq, who, on ascending the throne, appointed him Grand Dawādār in 784 (towards the end of 1382). Took part in the expeditions against Timur in 789 (1387), and against Yalbughā and Minṭāsh in 791. Killed at little over 60 years of age, in flight, near Khurbat al-Luṣūṣ, on the 23rd[3] Rabīʿ II 791 (21st April 1389).

BLAZON: *On upper field a pen-box, and on each of the middle and lower fields a cup.*[4]

[1] Ibn Ḥabīb, II. 470; *Khiṭaṭ*, II, p. 426, l. 11 (2nd ed., IV, p. 291, l. 8); *Durar*, s.v. (MS. Br. Mus., Or. 3044, fo. 172^{r}, where 791 should be read for 771); *Manhal*, s.v. (MS. Cairo, III, fo. 472^{v}); Ibn Iyās, I, pp. 260, l. 8, 267, l. 10 b, 271, ll. 8, 16, 18; Weil, IV. 543, 550, 551.

[2] Ibn Taghrībirdī and Ibn Iyās call him wrongly Saif ad-dīn.

[3] According to Ibn Iyās, I, p. 271, l. 18: on the 21st Rabīʿ II; *Khiṭaṭ*, l.c.: Tuesday, the 22nd.

[4] Cf. Introduction, chap. Colours, p. 28.

1. MAUSOLEUM, Cairo. Pl. LV. 1.

Inscription round the base of the dome on the outside.

امر بانشاء هذه التربة المباركة من فضل الله تعالى وجزيل عطائه المقرّ العالى

الأميرى الكبيرى الأجلّى المحترمى المخدومى الشرفى يونس النيروزى الدوادار الملكى

الظاهرى

The foundation of this blessed tomb was ordered, through the grace of God and the abundance of his gifts, by His High Excellency, the Great Amir, the Magnificent, the Honoured, the Well-Served, Sharaf ad-dīn Yūnus an-Nayrūzī, the dawādār of al-Malik aẓ-Ẓāhir.

DATE: On the basis of a statement of Ibn Taghrībirdī that Barqūq's father Anaṣ, who died on the 18th Shawwāl 783 (5th January 1382) was buried in the mausoleum of Yūnus ad-Dawādār, Creswell,[1] concluded that the mausoleum must have been built before that date. This does not agree with the text of the inscription in which Yūnus styled himself as 'dawādār of al-Malik aẓ-Ẓāhir', i.e. of Sultan Barqūq, who acceded to the throne only 11 months later, on Wednesday, the 19th Ramaḍān 784 (26th November 1382). Consequently we shall have to consider the latter date as the *terminus a quo* for the blazon and inscription and to assume that either Anaṣ was buried in the building before the dome was finished, or that he was temporarily buried elsewhere and transferred to the mausoleum of Yūnus after its completion. For both cases there are precedents. In any case the building must have been finished during the year 784, as in another inscription at Damascus (cf. No. 2). Yūnus was given higher titles than those figuring in this inscription.

BIBLIOGRAPHY: Creswell, l.c., for the inscription and greater part of the translation. Blazon mentioned l.c. and *CR.* 1889, p. 146, depicted in Artin, *Contribution*, pp. 122–3, fig. 98 bis, who read (very imperfectly) a few words of the inscription.

2. MOSQUE, called 'aṭ-Ṭāwūsiyya', Damascus, Zuqāq al-Baḥṣa al-barrāniyya (behind the Hotels Victoria and Grand Hôtel d'Orient). Pl. LV. 2.

Inscription in one line on both sides of the main-entrance gate.

(1) بسمله أنشأ هذا المكان المبارك المقرّ الأشرف الكريم العالى المولوى الأميرى

الكبيرى العالمى ○ المجاهدى المرابطى المثاغرى السيّدى السندى الذخرى العونى

الغياثى الهمامى النظامى القومى المالكى الكافلى المؤيّدى الظفرى

[1] *Brief Chronology*, p. 115.

(2) العضدى الذخرى العونى الغياثى الزعيمى الملاذى المخدومى الشرفى يونس

أمير دو[ا]دار بالأبواب الشريفة أعزّ الله أنصاره وضاعف اقتداره بتأريخ شهور

سنة أربع وثمانين وسبعمائة

In the name of the most merciful God. Founded this blessed place His Most Noble and Honourable and High Excellency, our Lord, the Great Amir, the Learned, the Defender of the Faith, the Warrior at the Frontiers, the Warden of the Marches, the Master, the Treasure, the Helper, the Rescuer, the Shelter, the Regent, the Royal, the Viceroy, the Helped by God, the Victorious, the Supporter, the Treasure, the Helper, the Rescuer, the Chieftain,[1] *the Well-Served, Sharaf ad-dīn Yūnus, Amīr Dawādār at the Noble Gates, may God render his victories glorious and multiply his power. During the months of the year* 784 (17th March 1382–5th March 1383).

BIBLIOGRAPHY: Half of the inscription read and translated by Littmann and the blazon described in Wulzinger and Watzinger, *Damaskus, die islamische Stadt*, p. 51.

3. PUBLIC FOUNTAIN, Damascus, Bāb al-Baḥṣa, adjoining the Ṭāwūsiyya-Mosque. Beginning of the inscription obliterated, end missing. One line of text intersected by shields.

[. . . الع]الى المولوى الأميرى الكبيرى ○ العالمى العادلى المالكى المخدومى

الشرفى يونس الدوادار الملكى الظاهرى أعزّ الله أنصاره

. . . our Lord, the Great Amir, the Learned, the Just, the Royal, the Well-Served, Sharaf ad-dīn Yūnus, Dawādār of al-Malik aẓ-Ẓāhir, may God make his victories glorious.

DATE: Probably contemporary with the adjoining mosque, i.e. built in 784 A.H.

BIBLIOGRAPHY: Unpublished.

4. CARAVANSERAI, Khan Yunus, near Gaza, pl. LV. 3, 4.

Inscription on both sides of the main-entrance gate:

(1) بسمله . . . ذَلِكَ فَضْلُ ٱللَّهِ يُؤْتِيهِ مَنْ يَشَآءُ وَٱللَّهُ ذُو [ٱ]لْفَضْلِ ٱلْعَظِيمِ

أنشأ هذه الخان السبيل في أيّام سيّدنا

[1] The text of this inscription is evidently not in order, probably through the fault of the mason. Some titles are repeated, others copied with mistakes, e.g. *al-muẓaffarī* without the *mīm*, *dawādār* with one *alif* only.

(2) ومولانا السلطان الملك الظاهر سيف الدنيا والدين ابى سعيد برقوق خلّد

الله سلطانه وشدّ بالصالحات أركانه

(3) أوقفه المقرّ الشريف العالى المولوى الأميرى الزعيمى السفيرى الشرفى ظهير

الملوك والسلاطين المعروف بحبّ الفقرآء والمساكين

(4) امير (about one word weathered) التقى يونس النوروزى الدوادار مولانا

السلطان الملك الظاهرى أعزّ الله تعالى أنصاره وضاعف جزاه

In the name of the most merciful God. This is the free grace of God, he bestoweth the same on whom he pleaseth: and God is endued with great beneficence (Qur'ān, LXII. 4). *This public caravanserai was founded in the days of our Lord and Master the Sultan al-Malik aẓ-Ẓāhir Saif ad-dunyā wa-d-dīn Abū Sa'īd Barqūq, may God make his sultanate eternal and keep him firmly established in good works, and was made a waqf by His Noble and High Excellency, our Lord, the Amir, the Chieftain, the Envoy Sharaf ad-dīn, Protector of Kings and Sultans, known for his love for the poor and destitute*[1] . . . *the pious Amīr Yūnus an-Naurūẓī, the Dawādār of our Lord the Sultan al-Malik aẓ-Ẓāhir, may God the Exalted make his victories glorious and multiply his reward.*

BIBLIOGRAPHY: Unpublished.

Blazon mentioned and depicted: Artin, *Contribution*, p. 122, fig. 98, where it is described as having been 'relevée sur le minaret de la mosquée du sultan Barkouke, à Khan Zumer'. I have to thank Professor Sayce, who supplied Artin Pasha with a drawing of this blazon, for the information that he copied it at Khan Yunus. For a drawing of the façade of this khan showing the emplacement of the blazon, but not the emblems, cf. Briggs, *Muhammadan Architecture in Egypt and Palestine*, p. 119, fig. 107.

YŪSUF AL-BAJĀSĪ[2]

J. Yūsuf b. Aḥmad b. Muḥammad b. Aḥmad b. Ja'far b. Qāsim al-Bīrī al-Bajāsī, known as Yūsuf the Major-domo, son of a preacher at Bireh, became *ballāṣī*

[1] No titles except 'Sīdī' are allowed to be placed between the surname composed of ad-dīn and the proper name of an amir. The position of the intrusive phrase *ẓahīr . . . at-taqī* is quite exceptional.

[2] *Khiṭaṭ*, II, pp. 402, l. 10, 403, ll. 2 f. (2nd ed., IV, pp. 253, l. 16, 254, ll. 4 b f); *Nujūm*, especially VI, pp. 92, l. 6, 115, l. 21, 167, l. 4 f., 183, l. 3, 217, ll. 5, 18, 220, l. 22–222, l. 4, 291, l. 16–292, l. 5; *Manhal*, s.v. (MS. Cairo, III, fo. 445ʳ–448ᵛ); Weil, V. 116, n. 1; *CIA. Égypte*, I. 314 f., 333, 404.

of Shaikh ʿAlī, District Officer of Damascus (*kāshif barr Dimishq*), in Dhu-l-Ḥijja 803 (July–August 1401) served as Major-domo of the Marshal Sūdūn Ṭāz, afterwards became Major-domo of Bajās, after whose retirement he passed into the service of Taghrībirdī, the father of the historian; on the 4th Rajab 807 (6th January 1405) succeeded Ibrahīm b. Ghurāb as Major-domo, in Shaʿbān 809 (began 11th January 1407) appointed Vizier and Keeper of the Privy Purse and finally District Officer of the Northern District of Egypt (*kāshif al-wajh al-baḥrī*) in addition to his post of Major-domo; arrested early in Jumādā I 812, executed the 11th Jumādā II[1] of the same year (21st October 1409).

BLAZON: *On upper field a pen-box, on middle field a scimitar with sword-knot and bands, on lower field emblem No. 26.*

MADRASA, Cairo.

The blazon of Yusuf the Major-domo was effaced in 812 by Sultan Faraj,[2] but one shield has escaped the notice of his masons.

BIBLIOGRAPHY: Reproduced: Briggs, *Muhammadan Architecture*, fig. 185.

YŪSUF AẒ-ẒĀHIRĪ

BLAZON: *Upper field blank, on middle field a cup crossed by a sword, on lower field a cup.*

SLAB OF MARBLE at a public fountain in the Main Bazaar, Hama. Pl. LIII. 2.

Two shields below the inscription, an inscribed shield above it.[3]

(1) بسمله . . . أنشأ هذا السبيل المبارك المقرّ العالى

(2) المولوى السيّدى الأشرفى المالكى المخدومى يوسف[4] . . .

[1] *Khiṭaṭ*, II, p. 402, l. 10: Jumādā I.

[2] A well-known passage in *Khiṭaṭ*, II, p. 402, l. 6 b, ثمّ . . . محى من هذه المدرسة اسم جمال الدين ورنكه often quoted, among others, by *SM.* II a, p. 15 n.; Rogers, *Blason*, p. 96; *CIA. Égypte*, I. 315, n. 1; *CR.* Exerc., 1915–19, fasc. 32, p. 118.

[3] Cf. p. 33 (2).

[4] The end of the line partly hammered away.

(3) الظاهرى اعزّ الله أنصاره وكان الفراغ [1] منه فى شهر جمد الأوّل سنة
سبعة وتسعين وسبع مائة

In the name of the most merciful God. Ordered the construction of this blessed public fountain His High Excellency, our Lord, the Master, the Most Noble, the Royal, the Well-Served, Yūsuf . . . aẓ-Ẓāhirī, may God make his victories glorious. Completed in the month of Jumādā I of the year 797 [2] (began 22nd February 1395).

BIBLIOGRAPHY: Unpublished.

[1] The text has الفارغ.

[2] Perhaps 799 (February 1397).

ADDITIONS

AḤMAD AD-DAWĀDĀR

BLAZON: *Pen-box on the middle field of a three-fielded shield.*

COPPER BOWL with spout, tinned over, National Museum of Arab Art, Cairo, No. 4442.

Inscription and three shields on the outside of the bowl.

ممّا عمل برسم الجناب العالى ○ المولوى السيفى ○ سيّدى أحمد الدوادار ○

This is one of the objects made for His High Excellency (janāb), *Saif ad-dīn Sīdī Aḥmad, the dawādār.*

BIBLIOGRAPHY: Unpublished.

Mentioned: *CR.* Exerc. 1915–1919, p. 496.

ʿALĪ B. BAKTAMUR

BLAZON: *Upper and lower fields white, on red middle field horse with ceremonial saddle.*

GLASS LAMP, once in the collection of the late Baron Gustave de Rothschild, present owner unknown. A copy, signed by Brocard, kept in the British Museum.
Three shields on the neck.

Inscription on body (identical with inscription on neck)

ممّا عمل برسم تربة الأمير المرحوم علاء الدين علىّ ولد المقرّ المرحوم السيفى
بكتمر الحاجب تغمّده الله برحمته

This is one of the objects made for the mausoleum of the late Amir ʿAlāʾ ad-dīn ʿAlī, son of His Excellency the late Saif ad-dīn Baktamur, the Chamberlain, may God cover him with his mercy.

DATE: After the 20th Rabīʿ II 729 (21st February 1329), the date of Baktamur's death.[1]

[1] Zetterstéen, *Beiträge*, p. 180, l. 17; according to *Khiṭaṭ*, II, p. 64, l. 12 ff. and *Durar*, s.v.: 728.

BIBLIOGRAPHY: Unpublished.

Reproduced: Migeon, *Manuel* (2nd ed.) II, fig. 292.
Mentioned: Jacquemart, *Exposition de l'Union Centrale*, p. 340; Wiet, *Lampes*, p. 182 f.; Lamm, *Gläser*, p. 449 (and sketch pl. 192, fig. 6).

ʿALĪ B. SHĀHĪN[1]

Possibly identical with A. ʿAlī b. Shāhīn al-ʿUthmānī, appointed Governor of the Citadel of Damascus in or before 882 (1477–8). Died in 891 (1486).

BLAZON: *On upper field a napkin, on each of the middle and lower fields a cup.*

LUNCH-BOX (maṭbaqiyya) tinned over, without lid. Collection Prof. E. Nord, German Consul-General, Jerusalem. Pl. LVI. 4.
Inscription:

مّما عمل برسم المقرّ الأشرف الكريم العالى المولوى المخدومى O سيّدى علىّ
ابن شاهين نائب القلعة بدمشق المحروسة عزّ أنصاره

This is one of the objects made for His Most Noble and Honourable and High Excellency, our Lord, the Well-Served, Sīdī ʿAlī, son of Shāhīn, Governor of the Citadel of Damascus, the protected, may his victories be glorious.

BIBLIOGRAPHY: Unpublished.

TO ĀQBIRDĪ B. ʿALĪBĀY

BLAZON: *On upper field a napkin, on middle field a cup charged with a pen-box and placed between a 'pair of trousers', on lower field a cup.*

ĀQŪSH AL-AFRAM[2]

Ja. Āqūsh al-Afram, originally a mamluk of al-Malik al-Manṣūr Qalāūn and his armour-bearer, in Jumādā I 698 (February 1299) appointed Viceroy of

[1] *Al-qaul al-mustaẓraf* transl. Devonshire (in *BIFAO*. XX. 1922, p. 27); *Ibn Iyās II*, p. 238, l. 10.
[2] Abu-l-Fidā', ed. Reiske, V, pp. 154, 166, 198, 214, 216, 220, 232, 252, 254, 268, ed. Constantinople, IV, pp. 42, l. 14, 45, l. 20, 54, l. 9, 58, l. 19 f., 59, l. 1, 60, l. 18, 62, l. penult., 68, l. 13 ff., 69, l. 11, 72,

Syria, on Muḥammad b. Qalāūn's third accession sent to Ṣarkhad,[1] in the middle of Rajab 710 (first half of December 1310) took office as Governor of Tripoli,[2] in Muḥarram 711 (began 20th May, 1311) joined Qarāsunqur in his flight to the Tartars.[3] Died in Hamadhan in 716.[4] Built a mosque in the Ṣāliḥiyya-Quarter, Damascus.

BLAZON: *A red sword placed across the white upper and lower fields and the green middle field.*

كان رنكه دائرة بيضاء يشقها شطب اخضر عليه سيف احمر يمرّ فى البياض

الفوقانى البياض التحتانى على الشطب الاخضر

BIBLIOGRAPHY: Ṣafadī, *Tuḥfa*, s.v. (MS. Paris, Ar. 5827, fo. 192r–193r) quoted in *Manhal*, l.c., fo. 3r, l. 3 ff., and from the *Manhal* in *SM.* II a, p. 15, n. 12; Prisse d'Avennes, *L'Art Arabe*, p. 66; Rogers, p. 98, who, against the evidence of the text, attributed it to Ānūk al-Ashrafī, a relative of Sultan Barsbāy; Lane-Poole, *Art of the Saracens*, p. 270; Gayet, *L'Art Arabe*, p. 281 f.; Karabacek, *Führer*, p. 272; Artin, *Contribution*, p. 237, who, in his turn, attributed it to Āqṭūh, a mistake repeated by P[ier], *Saracenic Heraldry*, p. 10, fig. 7; Prinet, *De l'origine orientale*, p. 4.

TO AYNĀL AL-YŪSUFĪ

2. GLASS LAMP, Hermitage-Museum, Leningrad, once in the collection Basilewski. Shields on neck and on lower part of the body.

l. 15 ff.; Nuwairī s.a. 710 (quoted by Sobernheim, *CIA. Syrie du Nord*, p. 45, n.2); Zetterstéen, *Beiträge*, especially pp. 46, l. 17, 54, l. 10, 57, l. 17, 81, l. 22, 96, l. 16, 108, l. 10, 130, l. 14, 131, l. 18, 133, l. 20, 134, l. 16, 138, l. ult., 143, ll. 2, 21, 144, l. 4, 145, l. 18, 151, ll. 4, 15, 153, l. 7, 157, l. 3 ff.; Dhahabī, *Duwal* II, pp. 156, l. 13, 165, l. 3 b, 166, l. 8, 167, ll. 1, 12, 168, l. 7; Mufaḍḍal, pp. 453, 457, 507; Ibn Ḥabīb, pp. 296, 307, 309, 314, 317; Ṣafadī, *Tuḥfa*, s.v.; Ṣāliḥ b. Yaḥyā pp. 49, l. 4, 116, l. 12, 119, l. 11, 137, l. 10 ff., 175, l. 7 (in the index Cheikho mistook Āqūsh an-Najībī for Ā. al-Afram); *SM.* II b, pp. 114, 123, 126, 128, 169 f.; *Manhal*, s.v. (MS. Paris, Ar. 2069, fo. 2r–3r); Ibn Iyās I. 139, l. 7b, 151, l. 20, 152, l. 4, who confused Ā. al-Afram with Ā., Governor of Kerak, (pp. 157, l. 19, 171, l. 17), whilst further confusion arose in the index over references to Ā. ash-Shamsī; Weil, cf. Index, especially IV. 221, 223, 236, 293 f., 308 f; *Durar*, s.v.

[1] It is doubtful whether as governor or as exile. The first alternative is possibly indicated by Abu-l-Fidā' V. 220 (IV. 60): ثم رسم السلطان للأمير جمال الدين آقوش الافرم بصرخد, and by Zetterstéen, l.c. p. 145, l. 18: وأنعم على آقوش الأفرم بصرخد, the expressions used in the text being rather ambiguous; the second very clearly by *Manhal*, s.v.: قبض عليه وبعثه الى صرخد بطالاً and less clearly by Zetterstéen, l.c. 153, l. 7: وكان مقيماً بصرخت.

[2] According to *Manhal*, l.c., appointed in 711, served a term of six months.

[3] According to Abu-l-Fidā', l.c., p. 252, in 712.

[4] Cheikho in Ṣāliḥ b. Yaḥyā, p. 49, n. 1; according to *Manhal*, l.c., either in 716 or in 720.

Inscription, so far as visible on the reproduction:

. . . المقرّ الأشرف | . . . [اينا]ل اليوسفى . . .

. . . *His Most Noble Excellency* . . .[*Aynā*]*l al-Yūsufī* . . .

BIBLIOGRAPHY: Prisse d'Avennes, p. 211; Lamm, *Gläser*, p. 480 f., pl. 205, fig. 1 (without text or translation of the inscription).

Mentioned: Schmoranz, pp. 21, 71; *CIA. Égypte* I, p. 679; Wiet, *Lampes*, p. 180, No. 169.

Although Prisse d'Avennes was the first to read the name of Aynāl al-Yūsufī correctly, Lamm was the first to re-establish the name of the Amir, who, in the literature very fully quoted by him, for a long time past had been called Aynāl al-Ya'qūbī. On the other hand, it should not be forgotten that in attributing this lamp to A. al-Ya'qūbī, Schmoranz, van Berchem and Wiet only rely on Rogers, p. 114, No. 4, or Jacquemart, *Exposition de l'Union Centrale*, p. 340, according to whom the blazon on the lamp was a *cup*, so that there is a possibility of there having been two different lamps in the Basilewski collection. Whether the one examined by Rogers was rightly attributed to al-Ya'qūbī is another matter which, in the absence of a photograph, it is impossible to decide.

TO BASHTĀK

4. PALACE, Naḥḥasīn-Quarter, Cairo.

Inscriptions and heraldic shields in the sunk panels (*maqālī*) of the wooden ceiling of the western liwan.

Inscription:

ممّا عمل برسم المقرّ الأشرف العالى المولوى الأميرى السيفى بشتاك الملكى الناصرى

This is among what was made for His Most Noble and High Excellency our Lord, the Amir Saif ad-dīn Bashtāk, (officer) of al-Malik an-Nāṣir.

DATE: 738 or 740 (1337 or 1339).[1]

BIBLIOGRAPHY: Herz, *C.R.* Exerc. 1909, p. 174, pl. XX.

Reproduced: Migeon, *Manuel* (2nd. ed.), I, fig. 133.

[1] *CIA. Égypte*, I, p. 182; Creswell, *Brief Chronology*, p. 100.

BIRDIBAK

BLAZON: *On upper field a napkin, on middle field a cup charged with a pen-box placed between a 'pair of trousers', on lower field a cup.*

COPPER DISH, tinned over, M. v. Oppenheim-Stiftung, Berlin.

Shields on the border and one in the centre of the dish.

Inscription round the shield in the centre.

ممّا عمل برسم المقرّ الأشرف العالى المولوى المخدومى السيفى بردبك عزّ أنصاره

This is one of the objects made for His Most Noble and High Excellency, our Lord, the Well-Served, Saif ad-dīn Birdibak, may his victories be glorious.

BIBLIOGRAPHY: Unpublished.

BIRDIBAK AẒ-ẒĀHIRĪ[1]

S. Birdibak al-Fārisī, called *al-Bashmaqdār*, i.e. shoe-bearer, a mamluk of al-Malik aẓ-Ẓāhir Jaqmaq, dubbed Amir of Ten by his master, became Amir of Forty and Second *ra's nauba* under Aynāl, leader of the Mecca caravan, Grand Chamberlain (*ḥājib al-ḥujjāb*), appointed Governor of Aleppo under Khushqadam, arrested and exiled to Jerusalem, returned to Aleppo as Governor, twice Viceroy of Syria. Died in Damascus either in Muḥarram or in Ṣafar 875 (July–August 1470).

BLAZON: *On upper field a napkin, on middle field a cup placed between a 'pair of trousers', on lower field a cup.*

COPPER DISH, in 1880 in the possession of A. Baudry, Cairo, present owner unknown.

Two inscriptions; the longer one runs as follows:

ممّا عمل برسم المقرّ الأشرف الكريم العالى المولوى السيفى بردبك مولانا ملك
الأمراء كافل المملكة بالشأم المحروس الملكى الظاهرى عزّ نصره

This is one of the objects made for His Most Noble and Honourable and High Excellency, our

[1] Ibn Taghrībirdī, *Nujūm*, VII, cf. Index; *Manhal*, s.v. (MS. Paris, Ar. 2069, fo. 53ʳ); Sakhāwī, *aḍ-Ḍau' al-lāmi'*, s.v.; Ibn Iyās, cf. Index, especially II, pp.100, l. penult., 122, l. 5 ff.; Rogers, *Blason*, p. 119 (quoting *aḍ-Ḍau'*); Ṭabbākh, *A'lām* III 59–64.

Lord, Saif ad-dīn Birdibak, our Lord the Governor-General, Viceroy of the protected province of Syria, (officer) of al-Malik aẓ-Ẓāhir, may his victory be glorious.

DATE: Between the 28th Ṣafar 871 and Rabiʿ I 872.

BIBLIOGRAPHY: Rogers, l.c., No. 12, fig. 32, p. 118.

FĀRIS

BLAZON: *On upper field a napkin, on middle field a cup charged with a pen-box and placed between a 'pair of trousers', on lower field a cup.*

FLAT DISH, National Museum of Arab Art, Cairo, formerly in the collection of Artin Pasha.

One shield in the centre, an obliterated inscription round it.

ممّا عمل برسم الجناب العالى السيفى فارس من طبقة العشر . . .[1]

This is one of the objects made for His High Excellency (janāb) *Saif ad-dīn Fāris, of the Ten-Barracks . . .*

BIBLIOGRAPHY: Unpublished.

TO JĀNĪBAK

Since the first item on p. 131 was printed, M. Sauvaget published the candlestick in *Syria*, XI. 239 f. The full inscription contains an additional section كافل الممالك المحروسة عزّ انصاره *Viceroy of the protected provinces (of Syria), may his victories be glorious,* which proves that Jānībak's master was Tanam min ʿAbd ar-Razzāq al-Mu'ayyadī.

TO MAḤMŪD B. SHIRWĪN

3. BASIN, sometime on offer in the Cairo art market. Inscription (A) intersected by circles each containing in the centre a shield with inscription (B) round it.

A. (1) ممّا عمل برسم المقرّ العالى المولوى الأميرى الكبيرى ا

(2) لغازى المجاهدى المرابطى العونى الذخرى الهمامى ا

[1] This is the inscription mentioned on p. 176, s.v. Qānibāy (?) al-Bawwāb.

(3) لعضدى السيّدى المخدومى المشيرى الظهيرى النصيرى المالكى

(4) الذخرى العونى الغيائى النجمى نجم الدين محمود الملكى الناصرى

This is one of the objects made for His High Excellency . . . Najm ad-dīn Maḥmūd, (officer) of al-Malik an-Nāṣir.

B. [Wiet] المقرّ العالى المولوى الأميرى الكبيرى الغازى البدرى لؤلؤ الناصرى

His High Excellency, our Lord, the Great Amir, the Vanquisher, Badr ad-dīn Lu'lu' an-Nāṣirī.

BIBLIOGRAPHY: Unpublished.

MUḤAMMAD B. AL-KHIḌR

BLAZON: *Pen-box on the middle field of a three-fielded shield. The upper and lower fields of the shield show a criss-cross pattern.*

COPPER DISH tinned over, collection W. A. Stewart, Esq., Jerusalem.

In the centre a shield with inscription round it.

ممّا عمل برسم الخواجا شمس الدين محمّد ابن الخضر [يـ]ـر[جـ]ـو المغفرة

This is one of the objects made for the Khawājā Shams ad-dīn Muḥammad b. al-Khiḍr, who hopes for forgiveness.

BIBLIOGRAPHY: Unpublished.

TO NAURŪZ AL-ḤĀFIẒĪ

BLAZON: *On upper field two cups, on both middle and lower fields a cup.*

TO QARĀSUNQUR

BLAZON: *A pair of polo-sticks on undivided shield.*

TIMRĀZ ASH-SHAMSĪ[1]

S. Timrāz ash-Shamsī, a freed mamluk of Barsbāy and his jamdār, under Aynāl became cupbearer, later dubbed Amir of Ten, under Khushqadam exiled to Damietta, recalled to Cairo by Timurbughā, on the accession of his uncle Qāytbāy made Commander of a Thousand, in Jumādā I 875 (began 26th October 1470) took part in an expedition against Siwār, in Ṣafar 878 (June 1473) appointed Ra's Nauba Kabīr, in Shawwāl 886 (began 23rd November 1481) Amīr Silāḥ, in Dhu-l-Ḥijja 900 (began 23rd August 1495) succeeded Uzbak min Ṭuṭukh as Commander-in-Chief, in Dhu-l-Qa'da 901 imprisoned in Alexandria, half a year later released, reinstated in office, on the 27th Dhu-l-Ḥijja 902 (26th August 1497) killed and buried in the mausoleum of Qāytbāy.

BLAZON: *On ornamented upper field pen-box, on dotted middle field ornamented cup charged with plain napkin and placed between a pair of ornamented 'trousers', on ornamented lower field fleur-de-lis.*

BASIN,[2] present owner unknown.

Inscription, so far as visible in the reproduction:

. . . ى الاميرى الكبيرى ○ السيفى تمراز رأس نوبة ا . . .

. . . *The Great Amir, Saif ad-dīn Timrāz, Chief of a Corps . . .*

BIBLIOGRAPHY: Unpublished.

Mentioned and reproduced: Prisse d'Avennes, *L'Art arabe*, pl. CLIX; Artin, *Contribution*, No. 92, pp. 57, 121.

[1] Ibn Iyās cf. Index, s.vv. T., T. amīr silāḥ, T. Altmishī, T. ra's nauba and T. ash-Shamsī, especially II, pp. 38, l. 22, 72, l. 22, 91, l. 8, 104, l. 17, 124, l. 4, 131, l. 7 ff., 135, l. 4 b, 136, l. 1 ff., 147, l. 4,159, l. 11, 172, l. 6 b, 180, l. 22, 194, l. 8, 201, l. 9 ff., 207, l. 10, 210, l. 4 b, 211, l. 17, 216, l. 7, 222, l. 15, 231, l. 4, 232, l. 18, 251, l. 3, 257, l. 24, 282, l. 3 b, 289, l. 17, 292, l. 14, 296–7, 303, ll. 9, 22, 306, l. 14, 311, l. 22, 312, ll. 8 ff., 25, 313, l. 10, 314, l. 13, 315, l. 17, 316, l. 21, 319, l. 8, 321, l. 20, 323, ll. 16, 26, 325, l. 7, 329, ll. 9 ff., 27 ff., 330, l. 1 ff. ; Weil, V. 256, 335 f., 343, 347, 353 f., 358, 361, 363, 365 f.

[2] There is another vessel with the same blazon, but without inscription, Prisse d'Avennes, l.c., pl. CLXV.

COLLECTIONS

THIS list contains all the collections examined for the compilation of the Armorial Roll, in which at least one Muslim object with a coat of arms was found, no matter whether the objects in question were of sufficient historical or other interest to merit inclusion in the present survey or not. Collections marked with a cross are known to the present writer merely from photographs and rubbings. Those marked with an asterisk denote dealers. Most of the above collections having been visited only once, and the majority prior to 1928, it is conceivable that they may now contain additional objects with blazons not known to the present writer.

ALEPPO: M. Eugen Marcopoli,
,, M. François Marcopoli, Consul of Portugal,
,, M. Henri Marcopoli,
,, M. Poché,
ALEXANDRIA: +M. A. Gamsaragan Bey,
,, Mme. Sinadino,
AMMAN: Government Museum,
,, +Prof. Riza Bey Taufiq,
AMSTERDAM: Nederlandsch Rijks-Museum,
ATHENS: M. A. E. Benachi,
BASLE: Ethnographisches Museum,
BERLIN: Kaiser-Friedrich-Museum,
,, Max Freiherr v. Oppenheim-Stiftung,
,, Prof. C. H. Becker,
BEYROUTH: Musée Municipal,
,, M. Claude Prost,
BOLOGNA: Museo Civico,
BONN a/R.: +Prof. P. Kahle,
BOSTON, Mass.: +Museum of Fine Arts,
BROCKENHURST, Hants.:
H. N. Bowden-Smith, Esq.,
CAIRO: National Museum of Arabic Art,
,, Coptic Museum,
,, Library Ahmed Zeki Pasha,
,, Dr. Kamil Bey Ghalib,
,, Major Gayer-Anderson,
,, J. Home, Esq.,
,, Dr. Max Meyerhof,
,, M. Maurice Nahman,*
,, Mr. Ispenian,*
,, M. Tano,*
,, M. Vitali Maggiar,*
,, -Matariya: H. H. Prince Yusuf Kamal,
CAIRO-Zeitun: M. E. Paravicini,
CAMBRIDGE: Fitzwilliam Museum,
CHIEVELEY, Newbury, Berks.:
F. T. Dallin, Esq.,
COBURG, Veste: +Kunst und Altertumssammlung,
CONSTANTINOPLE *see* ISTANBUL,
CYPRUS: *see* NICOSIA,
DAMASCUS: National Syrian Museum,
,, Husain Eff. Siouffi,*
DÜSSELDORF: Kunstgewerbe Museum,
EDINBURGH: Royal Scottish Museum,
FAENZA: Museo delle Ceramiche,
FLORENCE: R. Museo Nazionale,
,, Museo Stibbert,
HAMBURG: Kunstgewerbe Museum,
ISTANBUL: Çinili Köşk,
,, Treasury (Top Kapu Serai),
,, Theron Damon, Esq.,
JERUSALEM: Palestine Archaeological Museum,
,, Muslim Museum, Haram,
,, H. E. Bowman, Esq.,
,, Prof. E. Nord,
,, Messrs N. Ohan & Sons,*
,, W. A. Stewart, Esq.,
LENINGRAD: +Asiatic Museum,
LONDON: British Museum,
,, Victoria and Albert Museum,
,, C. B. Clapcott, Esq.,
,, R. A. Harari, Esq.,
,, Messrs. J. Sassoon,*
,, J. W. A. Young, Esq.,
LYONS: Musée de la Ville,
MILANO: Museo Artistico,

MUNICH:	Museum für Völkerkunde,	PARIS:	M. Eustache de Lorey,
,,	National Museum,	,,	Mme. Maspero,
NEW YORK:	+Metropolitan Museum,	,,	M. G. Pauilhac,
NICOSIA:	Sir Ronald Storrs,	,,	Messrs. M. & R. Stora,*
OXFORD:	Ashmolean Museum,	,,	Messrs. Tabbagh,*
,,	Prof. A. H. Sayce,	ROSLAGS-NÄSBY:	+Dr. C. J. Lamm,
PARIS:	Bibliothèque Nationale,	SÈVRES:	Musée de Sèvres,
,,	Musée Jacquemart-André,	VENICE:	Museo Civico,
,,	Musée du Louvre,	VIENNA:	Naturhistorisches Museum,
,,	Musée du Petit Palais,	,,	Österreichisches Museum,
,,	M. Henri Léman,*	,,	Graf Lanckoronski.

BIBLIOGRAPHY

NOTE the following abbreviations: BIE. = Bulletin de l'Institut Égyptien; BIFAO. = Bulletin de l'Institut Français d'Archéologie Orientale; CR. = Comité de Conservation des Monuments de l'Art Arabe; GBA. = Gazette des Beaux Arts; JA. = Journal Asiatique; JPOS. = Journal of the Palestine Oriental Society; JRAS. = Journal of the Royal Asiatic Society; MIFAO. = Mémoires de l'Institut Français d'Archéologie Orientale; MMAF. = Mémoires de la Mission Archéologique Française; ZDMG. = Zeitschrift der Deutschen Morgenländischen Gesellschaft; ZDPV. = Zeitschrift des Deutschen Palästina-Vereins.

Ahlenstiel-Engel, Elisabeth: Arabische Kunst (in Jedermanns Bücherei, Abteilung: Bildende Kunst), fig. 9. Breslau, 1923.

A. M. S.: Saracenic Metal Work (in Bulletin of the Metropolitan Museum of Art, New York, vol. II, No. 9, Sept. 1907), p. 152.

Artin Pacha, Yacoub: Description de six lampes de mosquée en verre émaillé (in BIE., 2e série, No. 7, 1886, pp. 120–54). Le Caire, 1887.

Artin Pacha, Yacoub: Trois différentes armoiries de Kaït Bay (in BIE., 2e série, No. 9, 1888, pp. 67–77). Le Caire, 1889.

Artin Pacha, Yacoub: Un sabre de l'émir Ezbek el Yussufi el Zahéry (in BIE., 3e série, No. 9, fasc. 2, 1898, pp. 249–59, 3 figs.). Le Caire, 1899.

Artin Pacha, Yacoub: Contribution à l'étude du blason en Orient. London, 1902.

Artin Pacha, Yacoub: Un flacon à eau (Zemzemieh) en terre grise portant des armoiries (in BIE., 4e série, No. 4, fasc. 6, 1903, pp. 459–61, 2 pls.). Le Caire, 1904.

Artin Pacha, Yacoub: Une lampe armoiriée de l'émir Scheikhou (in BIE., 4e série, No. 6, fasc. 1, 1905, pp. 7–13, 6 pls.). Le Caire, 1906.

Artin Pacha, Yacoub: Un brûle-parfum armoirié (in BIE., 4e série, No. 6, fasc. 1, 1905, p. 15, 3 pls.). Le Caire, 1906.

Artin Pacha, Y.: Les Armes de l'Égypte aux XVe et XVIe siècles (in BIE., 4e série, No. 7, 1906, pp. 87–90, 4 pls.). Le Caire, 1907.

Artin Pacha, Y.: Nouvelles preuves concernant la signification du meuble 'cachet' dans les armoiries orientales (in BIE., 4e série, No. 7, 1906, pp. 101–10). Le Caire, 1907.

Artin Pacha, Y.: Description de quatre lampes en verre émaillé et armoiriées (in BIE., 5e série, t. I, 1907, pp. 69–92, 6 pls.). Le Caire, 1908.

Artin Pacha, Yacoub: Lampe en verre émaillé portant armoirie apartenant à S. E. Boghos Pacha Nubar (in BIE., 5e série, t. I, 1907, pp. 159–70, 2 pls.). Le Caire, 1908.

Artin Pacha, Yacoub: Un troisième tableau italien du XVIe siècle blasonné aux armes d'Égypte (in BIE., 5e série, t. II, 1908, pp. 37–40, pls. VI, VII). Alexandrie, 1908.

Artin Pacha, Yacoub: Un bol compotier en cuivre blasonné du XVe siècle (in BIE., 5e série, t. III, fasc. 2, pp. 90–6). Alexandrie, mars 1910.

Artin Pacha, Yacoub: Quatrième et cinquième tableaux italiens blasonnés aux armes de l'Égypte du XVe siècle (in BIE., 5e série, t. III, fasc. 2, pp. 97–100). Alexandrie, mars 1910.

Bahgat, Aly Bey: Histoire de la Houdjra de Médine ou salle funéraire du Prophète à propos d'un chandelier offert par Qayt-Bey (in BIE.). Le Caire, 1914.

Bahgat, Aly Bey: cf. Céramique Égyptienne.

Bahgat, Aly Bey et Gabriel, Albert: Fouilles d'Al-Fousṭâṭ. Paris, 1921, pls. 32.

Beaumont, A. de: Recherches sur l'origine du blason, et en particulier sur la fleur de lis. Paris, Leleux, 1853.

Berchem, Max van: Inscriptions Arabes de Syrie (in Mémoires de l'Institut Égyptien, t. III, pp. 417–520). Le Caire, 1897.

Berchem, Max van: Matériaux pour un Corpus Inscriptionum Arabicarum. Première partie, Égypte (in MMAF., t. XIX, fascs. 1–4). Paris, 1894–1903.

Berchem, Max van: Arabische Inschriften aus Syrien II (in Mitteilungen und Nachrichten des Deutschen Palästina-Vereines, 1903), p. 59, fig. 44.

Berchem, Max van: Notes d'archéologie arabe, III. (in JA., 10e série, III, pp. 5–96). Paris, 1904.

Berchem, Max van: Arabische Inschriften aus Armenien und Diyarbekr (in Lehmann-Haupt, Materialien zur älteren Geschichte Armeniens und Mesopotamiens, Abhandlungen der K. Gesellschaft der Wissenschaften zu Göttingen, Phil. hist. Klasse, Neue Folge, Bd. IX, 3, pp. 8–13, 27 f. of the offprint). Berlin, 1907.

Berchem, Max van: Arabische Inschriften (in Inschriften aus Syrien, Mesopotamien und Kleinasien gesammelt . . . von Max Freiherrn von Oppenheim). Leipzig, 1909, pp. 3 (Abb. 1), 29 (inscribed shield), 42–4, (Abb. 4, 5), 47 (inscribed shield), 47 n., 51 (Abb. 6, 7), 53 (Abb. 8), 54 and n. 4, 105 (inscribed shield).

Berchem, Max van: Matériaux pour un Corpus Inscriptionum Arabicarum. Deuxième partie, Syrie du Sud, Jérusalem (in MIFAO., t. XLIII f.). Le Caire, 1920–7.

Berchem, Max van, et Fatio, Edmond: Voyage en Syrie (in MIFAO., t. XXXVII–VIII). Le Caire, 1914–15.

Berchem, Max van, and Strzygowski, Josef: Amida. Heidelberg, 1910.

(Bertaux, Émile): Musée Jacquemart-André, Catalogue itinéraire, 6th ed., Paris (1929).

Björkman, Walther: Sirwāl (in The Encyclopaedia of Islam, fasc. H, s.v.; Engl. ed., p. 452).

Bourgeois Frères: cf. Collection.

Bourgoin, Jules: Les Arts Arabes . . . et le Trait Général de l'Art Arabe. Paris, 1873, I. 74, 78.

Bourgoin, J[ules]: Précis de l'art arabe et matériaux pour servir à l'histoire, à la théorie et à la technique des arts de l'Orient Musulman (in MMAF. t. VII). Paris, Leroux, 1892.

B(reck), J(oseph): A Masterpiece of Egypto-Syrian Enamelled Glass (in Bulletin of the Metropolitan Museum of Art, vol. XVIII, No. 12, pp. 277 f., 1 fig. December 1923).

Briggs, Martin S.: Muhammadan Architecture in Egypt and Palestine. Oxford, 1924.

The Burlington Fine Arts Club Exhibition of the Fayence of Persia and the Nearer East. London, 1908.

Casanova, P.: L'Art Musulman d'après l'exposition organisée au Palais des Champs-Élysées à Paris, octobre-novembre 1894 (in Revue Encyclopédique, No. 72, 1. 12, 1894). Reprinted in Revue d'Égypte. Figs. on pp. 1, 22. Cairo, 1895.

Catalogue des Objets d'Art de la Renaissance, Tableaux composant la Collection de feu M. Eugène Piot. Paris, mai 1890.

Catalogue des Objets d'Art composant l'importante et précieuse Collection Spitzer... Paris, 1893.

Catalogue des Objets d'Art et de Haute Curiosité... composant la collection de feu M. Leroux. Paris, avril 1896.

Catalogue des Objets d'Art et de Haute Curiosité arabe et européens... composant la Collection Hakky-Bey. Paris, mars 1906.

Catalogue des Objets d'Art et de Haute Curiosité . . . composant la collection Paul Garnier. Paris, décembre 1916.

La Céramique Égyptienne de l'époque musulmane. Musée de l'Art Arabe du Caire. Bâle, 1922, pls. 104, 106, 119, 141, 142.

Clermont-Ganneau, Charles: Notes d'épigraphie et d'histoire arabes (in JA., 8e série, t. X, 1887, pp. 509 ff.; t. XII, 1888, pp. 305 ff. Lydda Bridge and Abu-l-Munajjā Bridge).

Clermont-Ganneau, Charles: Archaeological Researches in Palestine during the years 1873–4. vol. I, p. 127, n. *. London, 1899.

Cohn-Wiener, Ernst: Das Kunstgewerbe des Ostens, fig. 102, p. 133. Berlin, s.a.

Collection Bourgeois Frères. Katalog der Kunstsachen und Antiquitäten des VI. bis XIX. Jhdts. Köln, 1904.

Collection de feu M. Ch. Schefer. Catalogue des objets d'art et de curiosité. Paris, 1898.

Collinot, E., et Beaumont, A. de: Ornements Arabes. Recueil des dessins pour l'art et l'industrie. Paris, Canson, 1883.

C. H.: The Edward C. Moore Collection (in Bulletin of the Metropolitan Museum of Art, New York, vol. II, No. 6, June 1907, p. 105).

CR. Exercice 1889, fasc. 6, p. 146 (Coupole de Monsi). Le Caire, 1890.

Exercice 1891, fasc. 8, p. 86 (inscribed shield of Muḥammad b. Qāytbāy), p. 94 and pl. III (Abū Bakr b. Muzhir). Le Caire, 1891.

Exercice 1892, fasc. 9, p. 45, and pls. I, II (Manjakas-Silaḥdār), p. 69 (Jānībak, governor of Jidda). Le Caire (2e edition), 1903.

Exercice 1893, fasc. 10, p. 37 (identical with Contribution, No. 309, pp. 180 f.), p. 102. Le Caire (2e édition), 1906.

Exercice 1894, fasc. 11, pls. 5, 6 (Palace of Yashbak). Le Caire (2e éd.), 1908.

Exercice 1895, fasc. 12, pl. 14 (Sabīl Shaikhū). Le Caire, 1896.

Exercice 1896, fasc. 13, p. 98. Le Caire, 1897.

Exercice 1897, fasc. 14, p. 58 (Asanbughā), p. 153 (heraldic lions?), Appendix, p. iv, and pl. II (inscribed shield of Qāytbāy), p. vi (Abū Bakr b. Muzhir). Le Caire, 1898.

Exercice 1898, fasc. 15, p. 106. Le Caire, 1900.

Exercice 1900, fasc. 17, pp. 74, 95 (lions from Junainat as-sab' waḍ-ḍab'). Le Caire, 1900.

Exercice 1901, fasc. 18, p. 88 (Qauṣūn). Le Caire, 1901.

Exercice 1902, fasc. 19, p. 149 (inscribed shield of Qāytbāy), p. 150 (Māmāy), pp. 154–5 and pl. VII (Bashtāk). Le Caire, 1902.

Exercice 1903, fasc. 20, p. 58 (Ulmās). Le Caire, 1903.

Exercice 1904, fasc. 21, p. 75 (Āqsunqur). Le Caire, 1904.

Exercice 1905, fasc. 22, pp. 19, 85 (inscribed shield of Qāytbāy), p. 124, n. 1 (Alṭunbughā al-Māridīnī). Le Caire, 1906.

Exercice 1906, fasc. 23, p. 97 (Aḥmad b. Sha'bān), p. 125, and pl. VI (inscribed shield of Qāytbāy). Le Caire, 1907.

Exercice 1907, fasc. 24, p. 135 (inscribed shield of Qānṣūh al-Ghaurī). Le Caire, 1908.

Exercice 1908, fasc. 25, p. 103 (Khudābirdī aẓ-Ẓāhirī), p. 109 (inscribed shield of Qāytbāy). Le Caire, 1909.

Exercice 1909, fasc. 26, p. 62 (Qānībāy al-Jarkasī), pp. 62–3 (Salmā, wife of 'Alī at-Turkumānī), p. 161 (Ṭashtamur ad-Dawādār), pp. 162–3 (Khushqadam al-Aḥmadī, inscribed shield of Sultan Aḥmad b. Aynāl), p. 165 and pl. III (inscribed shield of Qānṣūh al-Ghaurī), p. 174 (Bashtāk). Le Caire, 1910.

Exercice 1910, fasc. 27, p. 156 (Ḥusain b. Abū Bakr b. Isma'īl). Le Caire, 1911.

Exercice 1911, fasc. 28, p. 13 (Ṣirghitmish, Bahādur), pp. 45, 51–2 (Qānībay al-Jarkasī), p. 102 (Yūsuf, naqīb al-jaish), p. 121 (Timrāz), p. 126 (Ibrahīm b. Ghurāb). Le Caire, 1912.

Exercice 1913, fasc. 30, p. 133 (Shaikhū). Le Caire, 1914.

Exercices 1915–19, fasc. 32, p. 118 (Jamāl ad-dīn Yūsuf al-Ustādār), p. 136 (Ṭuquz-damur), p. 155 (Ibn Birdibak ad-Dawādār), pp. 435, 496 (Aḥmad ad-Dawādār), p. 499 (Khudābirdī), p. 746 (Khushkildī al-Khāzindār). Le Caire, 1922.

Cordier, Henri: La Collection Charles Schefer (in GBA., 3e pér., t. 20). Paris, 1898.

Coste, Pascal: Architecture arabe ou Monuments du Caire. Paris, 1839.

Creswell, K. A. C.: Two Khâns at Khân Ṭûmân (in Syria, vol. IV, p. 136). Paris, 1923.

Creswell, K. A. C.: A Brief Chronology of the Muḥammadan Monuments of Egypt to A.D. 1517 (in BIFAO., t. XVI). Le Caire, 1919.

Creswell, K. A. C.: The Works of Sultan Bibars al-Bunduqdârî in Egypt (in BIFAO., t. XXVI, pp. 129–93, 31 pls.). Le Caire, 1926.

Daly, César: Incrustations de Marbre ou Faïence (XV siècle) à Damas (in Revue Générale de l'Architecture et des Travaux Publics, t. XLIII, 4e série, 13e vol., col. 5, pls. 5–6).

Devonshire, Mrs. R. L.: Rambles in Cairo. Cairo, 1917.

Devonshire, Mrs. R. L.: Sultan Sâlah ed-Dîn's Writing Box in the National Museum of Arab Art, Cairo (in The Burlington Magazine, vol. XXXV, pp. 241–5, 1 plate). London, 1919.

Devonshire, Mrs. R. L.: Some Cairo Mosques and their founders. London, 1921.

Devonshire, Mrs. R. L.: Some Mihrab Candlesticks (in The Burlington Magazine, December 1923, pp. 270–6).

Devonshire, Mrs. R. L.: Quatre-vingt mosquées et autres monuments musulmans du Caire. Le Caire, 1925.

Devonshire, Mrs. R. L.: L'Égypte Musulmane et les fondateurs de ses monuments. Paris, 1926.

Devonshire, Mrs. R. L.: Some dated objects in Mr. Ralph Harari's Collection (in Apollo, vol. VI, July-December 1927), pp. 121–6, figs. I–VII.

Devonshire, Mrs. R. L.: Some Moslem Objects in the Benachi Collection (in The Burlington Magazine, October 1928, pp. 189–96, pls. I–III).

Devonshire, Mrs. R. L.: Quelques Influences Islamiques sur les Arts de l'Europe. Le Caire, La Semaine Égyptienne.

Diez, Ernst: Die Kunst der islamischen Völker (in Handbuch der Kunstwissenschaft), fig. 287. Berlin-Neubabelsberg, 1915.

Dimand, M. S.: Near Eastern Metalwork (in Bulletin of the Metropolitan Museum of Art, vol. XXI, 1926), pp. 193–9.

Dimand, M. S.: A Handbook of Mohammedan Decorative Arts. New York, 1930.

Djemal Pascha, Ahmed: Alte Denkmäler aus Syrien, Palästina und Westarabien. Berlin, 1918 (pls. 39, 46).

Eisen, Gustavus A., assisted by Fahim Kouchakji: Glass. Its Origin, History, Chronology, Technic, and Classification to the Sixteenth Century. New York, William Edwin Rudge, 1927.

2e Exposition de peintres orientalistes français. Galeries Durand-Ruel . . . du 26 février au 16 mars 1895. Paris.

Exposition d'Art Musulman (with Preface by Gaston Migeon), Les Amis de l'Art, Alexandrie, mars 1925, pp. 69–71, 73, 75, 75–77.

Ferrari, Giulio: Gli Stili nella forma e nel colore. Rassegna dell'arte antica e moderna di tutti i paesi, vol. II. Torino, C. Crudo Co., s.a.

Fouquet, D.: Contribution à l'étude de la céramique orientale. Pl. XV, fig. 2. Le Caire, 1901.

Fox-Davies, Arthur Charles: A Complete Guide to Heraldry (2nd ed.), p. 13. London, 1925.

Franz Pascha, Julius: Die Baukunst des Islam (in Handbuch der Architektur, II. Teil, Bd. III, zweite Hälfte, p. 93 and pl.). Darmstadt, 1887.

F. V. P.: Oriental Glass (in Museum of Fine Arts Bulletin, Boston, vol. VIII, No. 48, December 1910).

F. V. P.: Gifts from the Western Art Visiting Committee (in Museum of Fine Arts Bulletin, Boston, vol. X, No. 58, August 1912), pp. 28 f.

Garnier, Edouard: Collections de M. Spitzer (in GBA., 2e pér., t. 29). Paris, 1884.

Garnier, Edouard: La Verrerie. La Collection Spitzer. Tome Troisième. Paris, 1891, p. 78 ff.

Garnier, Paul, cf. Catalogue.

Gaudefroy-Demombynes: La Syrie à l'époque des Mamelouks d'après les auteurs arabes (in Bibliothèque Archéologique et Historique III). Paris, 1923, pp. lxi, n. 1, xcii f., p. 171, n. 1.

Gayet, Al.: L'Art Arabe (in Bibliothèque de l'enseignement des Beaux Arts), Paris 1893, pp. 278–84: Les Armoiries.

Gerspach: L'Art de la Verrerie. Paris, A. Quantin, (1885).

Glück und Diez: Die Kunst des Islam, pp. 189, 428, 429, 451, 461. Berlin, 1925.

G., F. D.: The Godman Collection of Oriental and Spanish Pottery and Glass, 1865–1900. London, 1901.

Hakky Bey: Le Miroir de l'Art Musulman. Revue Mensuelle et illustrée consacrée à l'étude de l'art Musulman. No. 1, Paris, 1 mars 1898.

Hakky Bey: cf. Catalogue.

Herz Bey, M.: La Mosquée d' Ezbek el-Yussufy (in Revue Égyptienne, première année, 1er juin 1889, pp. 16 ff.).

Herz Bey, Max: Le Musée National du Caire (in GBA, 3e pér., t. XXVIII. 1902, pp. 45–59, 497–505).

Herz Max: Catalogue Sommaire des Monuments exposés dans le Musée National de l'Art Arabe. Le Caire, 1895. Second edition under the title Catalogue raisonné des monuments exposés dans le Musée National de l'Art Arabe, précédé d'un aperçu de l'histoire de l'architecture et des arts industrials en Égypte. 1906.

Herz Bey, Max: Le bain de l'émir Bechtak (in BIE., 4e série, No. 5, pp. 33–6, 1 pl.; identical with CR. 1902, pp. 154 ff.). Le Caire, 1905.

Herz Bey, Max: A Descriptive Catalogue of the Objects exhibited in the National Museum of Arab Art (translated by G. Foster Smith). Cairo, 1907.

Herz Max: Az Iszlám Müvészete. Budapest, 1907.

Herz Bey, M.: Deux lampes en verre émaillé de l'émir Toghaitimor (in BIE., 5e série, t. I, fasc. 2, 1907, pp. 181–7, 2 pls.). Le Caire, juin 1908.

Herz Bey, Max: Armes et armures arabes (in BIFAO., t. VII, pp. 1–14, pls. I–VIII). Le Caire, 1910.

Huart, Clément: Histoire des Arabes. Paris, 1912 (vol. I), 1913 (vol. II).

Ibn Faḍl Allah al-'Omari: Masālik el Abṣār fi Mamālik el Amṣār. I. L'Afrique, moins l'Égypte. Traduit et annoté avec une introduction et 5 cartes par Gaudefroy-Demombynes (in Bibliothèque des Géographes Arabes publiée sous la direction de Gabriel Ferrand, t. 2). Paris, 1927, pp. xlv, n. 1, 215.

Jacquemart, A.: Exposition de l'Union Centrale des Beaux-Arts appliqués à l'industrie. Musée Oriental (in GBA. 2e pér., t. II. 1869, p. 332 ff.), pp. 340, 342.

Kahle, Paul: Islamische Schattenspielfiguren aus Egypten (in Der Islam, vol. I, figs. 6, 24, 33, pl. 7; vol. II, pp. 144, 145, 152, 160, 177, n. 1, 189 ff., fig. 46).

Kahle, Paul: Der Leuchtturm von Alexandria, ein Schattenspiel aus dem mittelalterlichen Ägypten (in Forschungen und Fortschritte, vol. IV, No. 30, 20th October 1928).

Kahle, Paul: Der Leuchtturm von Alexandria mit Beiträgen von Georg Jacob. Stuttgart, 1930.

Karabacek, J.: Zur orientalischen Münzkunde (in Wiener Numismatische Monatshefte, 1867, No. 10), p. 7 (of the offprint).

Karabacek, Joseph: Die kufischen Münzen des steiermärkisch-ständischen Joanneums in Graz (in Wiener Numismatische Monatshefte, Bd. IV, 1868, p. 62, Nr. XXXVIII a).

Karabacek, Joseph: Beiträge zur Geschichte der Mazjaditen. Leipzig, 1874, p. 5 n.

Karabacek, Joseph: Das angebliche Bilderverbot des Islam. Ein Vortrag gehalten im Bayerischen Gewerbe-Museum in Nürnberg am 7 Februar 1876. Nürnberg, 1876.

Karabacek, Joseph: Ein damascenischer Leuchter des XIV. Jahrhunderts (in Repertorium für Kunstwissenschaft, vol. I, pp. 265–82, 3 fig.).

Karabacek, Joseph v.: Papyrus Erzherzog Rainer. Führer durch die Ausstellung. Wien, 1894, p. 272, No. 1323.

Karabacek, Josef von: Zur Orientalischen Altertumskunde. I. Sarazenische Wappen (Sitzungsberichte der kais. Akademie der Wissenschaften in Wien, Philosophisch-Historische Klasse, Bd. 157). Wien, 1907.

Karabacek, Josef von: Zur Orientalischen Altertumskunde. IV. Muhammedanische Kunststudien (ib. Bd. 172). Wien, 1913, pp. 10–14.

Karabacek, Josef von: Abendländische Künstler zu Konstantinopel im XV. und XVI.

Jahrhundert. I. Italienische Künstler am Hofe Muhammeds II. des Eroberers 1451–81 (in Denkschriften, Phil. hist. Klasse, Kaiserliche Akademie der Wissenschaften in Wien, 62. Band). Wien, 1918, pp. 88 f.

Katalog, Amtlicher, (der) Ausstellung München, 1910.

Katalog der . . . Kunstsammlung Graf Rudolf Hoyos (XCIV. Kunstauktion H. O. Mietke). Wien, 26, iv, 1897.

Kay, H. C.: Al Kāhirah and its Gates (in JRAS. 1882, pp. 229–45).

Kay, Henry C.: Arabic Inscriptions in Egypt, Part II (in JRAS., 1896, pp. 137 f.).

Kendrick A. F.: Catalogue of Muhammadan Textiles of the Mediaeval Period. Victoria and Albert Museum. London, 1924.

Kremer, A. von: Topographie von Damascus (in Denkschriften der phil. hist. Classe d. Akademie d. Wissenschaften, vol. V, p. 34). Wien, 1854.

Kühnel Ernst: Islamische Kleinkunst (in Bibliothek für Kunst- und Antiquitätensammler, Bd. 25). Berlin, 1925, pp. 111 f.

Kühnel, Ernst: Islamische Stoffe aus ägyptischen Gräbern, in der Islamischen Kunstabteilung und in der Stoffsammlung des Schlossmuseums. Berlin, 1927.

Kühnel, Ernst: Die islamische Kunst (in Springer, Anton: Handbuch der Kunstgeschichte, vol. VI). Leipzig, 1929.

Lane-Poole, Stanley: Catalogue of Oriental Coins in the British Museum, vol. IV. The Coinage of Egypt . . . under the Fátimee Khaleefehs, the Ayyoobees and the Memlook Sultans . . . edited by Reginald Stuart Poole. London, 1879.
Vol. IX: Additions to vols. I–IV . . . edited by Reginald Stuart Poole, London 1889.

Lane-Poole, Stanley: The Art of the Saracens in Egypt. London, 1886, chapter IX. 'Heraldry on Glass and Metal', pp. 226–31; ed. 1888 (quoted in this volume) pp. 268–73.

Lane-Poole, St.: A History of Egypt in the Middle Ages. London, 1901, 2nd ed., 1914.

Lane-Poole, Stanley: Saladin and the Fall of the Kingdom of Jerusalem. New York & London, 1908, p. 320, n.

Lammens, H.: Notes épigraphiques et topographiques sur l'Émésène (in Le Musée Belge, vol. VI, 1902, pp. 30–57), pp. 32–3.

Lavoix, Henri: Les Arts Musulmans (in GBA., 2e pér., t. XII). Paris, 1875.

Lavoix, Henri: La Collection Albert Goupil (in GBA., 2e pér, t. XXXII). Paris, 1885.

Lavoix, Henri: Catalogue des Monnaies Musulmanes de la Bibliothèque Nationale, vol. III, Égypte et Syrie. Paris, 1896.

Lavoix, Henri: La Galerie Orientale du Trocadéro (in GBA. 2e pér., t. XVIII). Paris, 1878, pp. 769–91.

Le Bon, Gustave: La Civilisation des Arabes. Paris, 1884.

Leroux: cf. Catalogue.

Lorey, Eustache de: Quelques monuments arabes de Damas (in Actes du Congrès d'Histoire de l'Art, Paris, 26 septembre–5 october 1921. Vol. I. Troisième section. Paris, 1923, pp. 313–17, pl. 16).

Martin, F. R.: Sammlungen aus dem Orient in der Allgemeinen Kunst- und Industrie-Ausstellung zu Stockholm, 1897.

Martin, F. R.: Aeltere Kupferarbeiten aus dem Orient. Stockholm, 1902.

Martinovitch, N.: A Glass Globe of Arghūn (in Eastern Art Annual, vol. II, 1930, p. 245, pl. CXXXVI).

Marye, Georges: L'Exposition d'Art Musulman (in GBA., 3e pér., t. XI). Paris, 1894.

Maspero, Jean: Deux vases en bronze arabes du XVe siècle (in BIFAO., t. 7, pp. 173–5). Le Caire, 1910.

Massignon, Louis: Six plats de bronze de style mamelouk (in BIFAO., t. 10, pp. 79–88, 4 pls.). Le Caire, 1912.

Maundrell, H.: A Journey from Aleppo to Jerusalem at Easter, A.D. 1697. Oxford, 1703, p. 124.

Maunier, René: La fleur de lis dans l'art arabe (in Bulletin de la Societé Nationale des Antiquaires de France, 1925, pp. 215 f.).

Mayer, L. A.: Arabic Inscriptions of Gaza (in JPOS., vol. III, pp. 69–78, 3 pls.). Jerusalem, 1923.

Mayer, L. A.: Arabic Inscriptions of Gaza II (in JPOS., vol. V, pp. 64–8, 1 pl.). Jerusalem, 1925.

Mayer, L. A.: Le Blason de l'Amîr Salâr (in JPOS., vol. V, pp. 58–60, 1 pl.). Jerusalem, 1925.

Mayer, L. A.: Das Schriftwappen der Mamlukensultane (in Jahrbuch der Asiatischen Kunst 1925, Festschrift Sarre), pp. 183–7, 4 Abb.

Mayer, L. A.: Guide to the Exhibition of Moslem Heraldry in Palestine. Jerusalem, 1926 (with a Preface by John Garstang).

Mérionec, A. de: Chagaratt Ouddour (in BIE., 2e série, No. 9, 1888, p. 119). Le Caire, 1889.

Migeon, Gaston: Les Objets d'Art de la Collection Dutuit (in Les Arts, décembre 1902, pp. 22–32), p. 23.

Migeon, Gaston: L'Exposition des Arts Musulmans au Musée des Arts Décoratifs (in Les Arts, avril 1903), pp. 22, 25.

Migeon, Gaston: Manuel d'Art Musulman, 2 vols. Paris, 1927.

Migeon, Gaston: La Collection de M. Octave Homberg (in Les Arts, décembre 1904, pp. 45, 48).

Migeon, Gaston: Le Caire, le Nil et Memphis (in Les Villes d'Art célèbres). Paris, 1906, pp. 14, 19, 72, 138.

Migeon, Gaston: La Collection de M. Piet-Latauderie (in Les Arts, August 1909, p. 24 f.).

Migeon, Gaston: L'Orient Musulman. Paris, 1922.

Migeon, Gaston: Les Arts Musulmans (in Bibliothèque d'histoire de l'art). Paris et Bruxelles, 1926.

Migeon, Van Berchem et Huart: Exposition des Arts Musulmans. Catalogue descriptif. Paris, 1903.

Molinier, Émile: Collection Charles Manheim. Objets d'art. Paris, 1898.

Nesbitt, Alexander: Catalogue of the Collection of Glass formed by Felix Slade with Notes on the History of Glass-making. London, 1871

Nesbitt, Alexander: Glass. London, 1878.

Nesbitt, Alexander: A Descriptive Catalogue of the Glass Vessels in the South Kensington Museum. London, 1878.

Nützel, H.: Embleme und Wappen auf muhammedanischen Münzen (in Festschrift zur Feier des fünfzigjährigen Bestehens der Numismatischen Gesellschaft zu Berlin.). Berlin, 1893.

P(ier), G(arret), C(hatfield): Saracenic Heraldry in Ceramic Decoration (in Bulletin of the Metropolitan Museum of Art, New York, vol. III, 1908, pp. 8–11).

Pier, Garret Chatfield: Pottery of the Near East. G. P. Putnams Sons, New York and London, 1909.

Pier, Garrett Chatfield: Saracenic Glass (in Orientalisches Archiv, Jg. I, pp. 189–90, pls. 37–8). Leipzig, 1911.

Piot: cf. Catalogue.

Prinet, Max: De l'origine orientale des armoiries européennes (in Archives Héraldiques Suisses 1912, fasc. 2, pp. 53–58).

Prisse d'Avennes: L'Art Arabe d'après les monuments du Kaire. Paris, 1877, pp. 63–8, 164, fig. 21.

Quatremère, Étienne: Histoire des Sultans Mamlouks de l'Égypte écrite en arabe par Taki-eddin-Ahmed-Makrizi, traduite en français et accompagnée de notes philologiques, historiques, géographiques. Paris, Oriental Translation Fund, t. I, 1837, p. 2, n. 4; t. II, 1842, pp. 14–15, n. 12.

Reinaud, M.: Observations générales sur les médailles musulmanes à figures (in JA., 2e année, cahier 6, 1823, pp. 352 ff.).

Reinaud, M.: Histoire de guerres des croisades sous le règne de Bibars, Sultan d'Égypte, d'après les auteurs arabes (in JA., 6e année, 1827, p. 74).

Rivière, H.: La Céramique dans l'art musulman. Paris, 1913.

Rödiger, E.: Ueber einen Helm mit arabischen Inschriften (in ZDMG., Bd. XII, 1858, pp. 300–4).

Rogers, Bey, E. T.: Le blason chez les princes musulmans de l'Égypte et de la Syrie (in BIE., 2 série, No. 1, pp. 83–131, 14 pls.). Le Caire, 1882. Revised German translation under the title: Das Wappenwesen der muhamedanischen Fürsten in Egypten und Syrien (in Vierteljahrsschrift für Heraldik, Sphragistik und Genealogie, vol. XI, 1883, pp. 407–30, pls. III–VIII).

S., A. M.: cf. A. M. S.

Saladin, H. et Migeon G.: Manuel d'art musulman. Paris, 1907.

Sarre, Friedrich: Islamische Tongefässe aus Mesopotamien (in Jahrbuch der Kgl. Preussischen Kunstsammlungen, Bd. XXVI, 1905).

Sarre, F.: Vergoldete u. emaillierte syrische Gläser. Leihgaben in der islamischen Kunstabteilung (in Amtliche Berichte aus den kgl. Kunstsammlungen XXXII. Jg. No. 6, 1911, pp. 138–41).

Sarre, Friedrich: Keramik und andere Kleinfunde der islamischen Zeit von Baalbek (in Baalbek, Ergebnisse der Ausgrabungen und Untersuchungen in den Jahren 1898 bis 1905, vol. III). Berlin und Leipzig, 1925.

Sarre, F. und Martin, F. R.: Die Ausstellung von Meisterwerken Muhammedanischer Kunst in München 1910. München, 1912.

Sarre, F. and Mittwoch, E.: Sammlung F. Sarre. Erzeugnisse islamischer Kunst, Teil I., Metall. Berlin, 1906.

Schefer: cf. Collection.

Schmoranz, Gustav: Old Oriental Gilt and Enamelled Glass Vessels. Vienna and London, 1899.

Schumacher, G.: Researches in Southern Palestine (in Quarterly Statements of the Palestine Exploration Fund, 1886, p. 181).

Sobernheim, M.: Arabische Gefässinschriften von der Ausstellung islamischer Kunst in Paris ⟨1903⟩ (in ZDPV. vol. XXVIII, 1905, pp. 176–205, Taf. VI, VIII).

Sobernheim, Moritz: Matériaux pour un Corpus Inscriptionum Arabicarum. Deuxième partie. Syrie du Nord (in MIFAO, t. XXV). Le Caire, 1909.

Sobernheim, M.: Die Inschriften der Zitadelle von Damaskus (in Der Islam, Bd. XII), p. 20.

Sobernheim, Moritz: Baalbek in islamischer Zeit (in Baalbek, Ergebnisse der Ausgrabungen und Untersuchungen in den Jahren 1899 bis 1905, vol. III). Berlin, 1922.

Sobernheim, M.: Die arabischen Inschriften von Aleppo (in Der Islam, Bd. XV., pp. 161–210).

Spitzer: cf. Catalogue.

Ströhl, H. G.: Heraldischer Atlas. Eine Sammlung von heraldischen Musterblättern für Künstler, Gewerbetreibende, sowie für Freunde der Wappenkunde. Stuttgart, 1899, p. 3.

Tizengauzen, W. G.: Materialy dlya bibliografii musulmanskoy archeologii iz bumag Barona W. G. T. izdaly K. A. Inostrancew i Ya. I. Smirnow (in Zapiski Vostočnavo Otdyeleniya Imperatorskavo Russkavo Archeologičeskavo Obščestva, vol. XVI, pp. 79–145, 213–416). St. Petersburg, 1906. Chapter IX: Heraldry sphragistics and metrology, pp. 231–7.

Uspenskiy, Th. N.: Archeologičeskie pamiatniki Siryi (in Izv. Rusk. Arch. Instit. v Konstantinopolye, vol. VII, pp. 1–212), pp. 99, 140, 147, fig. 2, 30, 31, 46.

Vincent, Hugues et Abel, F. M.: Jérusalem, Recherches de topographie, d'archéologie et d'histoire. Tome second, Jérusalem Nouvelle. Paris, 1926, fasc. 4, pp. 977, 981 f., fig. 411.

Wallace-Dunlop, Madeline, A.: Some Oriental Brasswork (in The Magazine of Art, vol. VIII, 1885, pp. 56–60, 109–12).

(Wallis, Henry): Illustrated Catalogue of Specimens of Persian and Arab Art exhibited in 1885. London, 1885.

Wé, P.: Das Wappen des Sultans Mu'ayyed (in Der Deutsche Herold, Bd. XIX, p. 139).

Weissbach, F. H.: Die Denkmäler und Inschriften an der Mündung des Nahr el-Kalb (in Wissenschaftliche Veröffentlichungen des deutsch-türkischen Denkmalschutz-Kommandos, Heft 6). Berlin und Leipzig, 1922, pp. 43–8, pl. XIV.

Wiet, Gaston: Le Musée Arabe (in L'Art Vivant, January 1929, pp. 52 f.).

Wiet, Gaston: Lampes et bouteilles en verre émaillé. Catalogue général du Musée Arabe du Caire. Le Caire, 1929.

Wiet, Gaston: Album du Musée Arabe du Caire. Le Caire, 1930.

Wilken, Friedrich: Geschichte der Kreuzzüge, Vierter Teil, Leipzig, 1826, p. 416, n. 85. (Taqī ad-dīn).

Woodward, John: A Treatise on Heraldry, British and Foreign. Winburgh and London, 1896, pp. 36–9.

Wulzinger, Karl und Watzinger, Carl: Damaskus, die islamische Stadt (in Wissenschaftliche Veröffentlichungen des deutsch-türkischen Denkmalschutz-Kommandos. Heft V). Berlin-Leipzig, 1924.

Zéki Pacha, Ahmed: Les Couleurs Nationales de l'Égypte Musulmane, p. 26. Le Caire, 1921.

INDEX

In this index figures refer to pages, an asterisk (*) denoting the occurrence of the word so marked more than once on that page, e.g. p. 62 f.* meaning that the word appears once on p. 62 and several times on p. 63. The Arabic text of the inscriptions has not been indexed. In arranging the index no notice has been taken of the Arabic article. Words either restored or doubtful and marked accordingly in the text appear in the index usually without any brackets, question-marks, or like signs.

Buildings are indexed under the names of the builders, unless known by a designation in which the name of the founder does not appear; in the latter case the name is indexed under the town in which the building is to be found.

Emblems and heraldic devices are indexed under the English names given them in the Armorial Roll, those unnamed under 'emblems'.

Public collections are indexed under the names of the respective towns, private ones under the names of their owners. All collections examined during the compilation of this book also appear in the list on p. 269 f.

Titles of offices are given in their Arabic form with cross-references from the English translation.

PLATE I

PLATE II

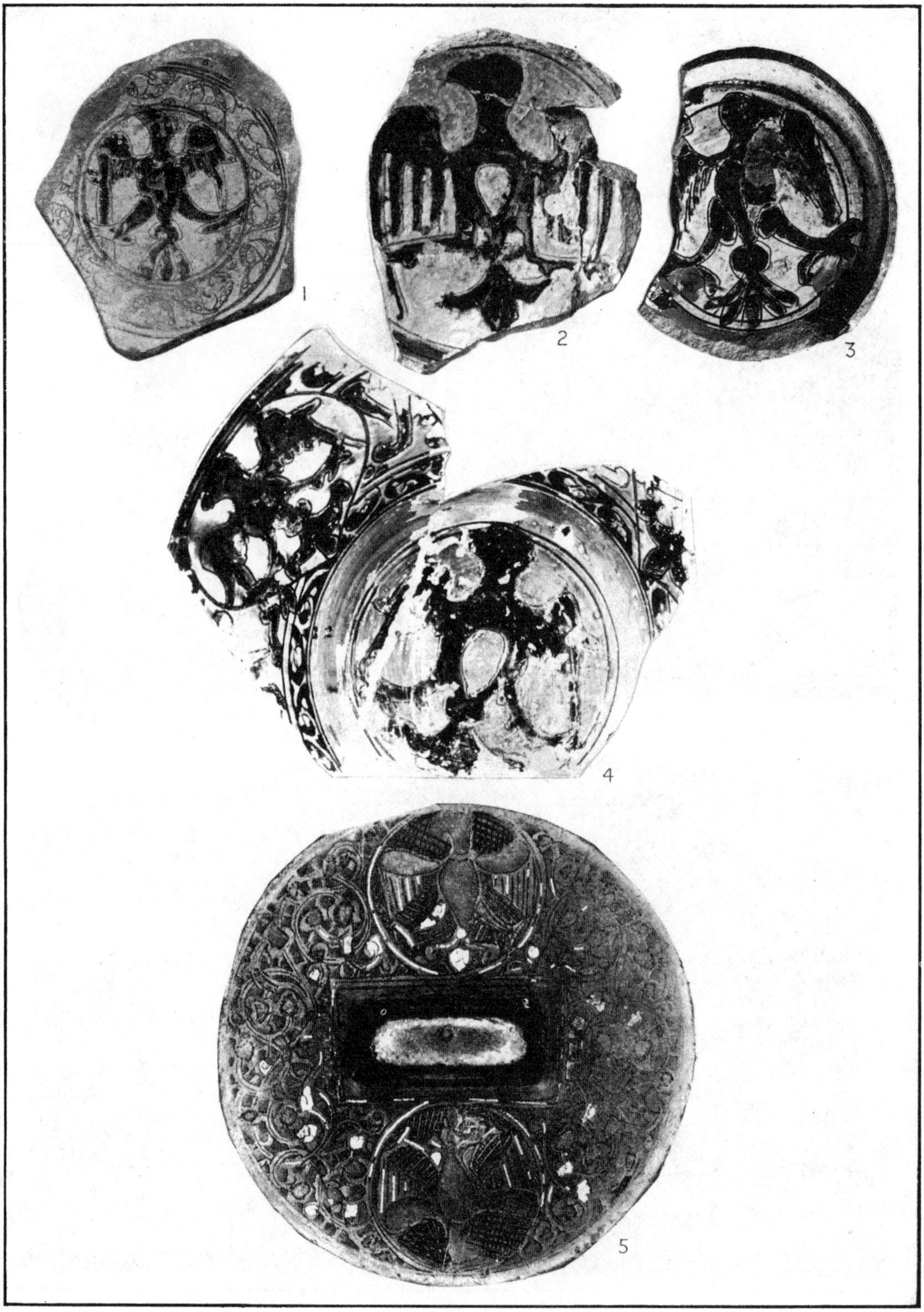

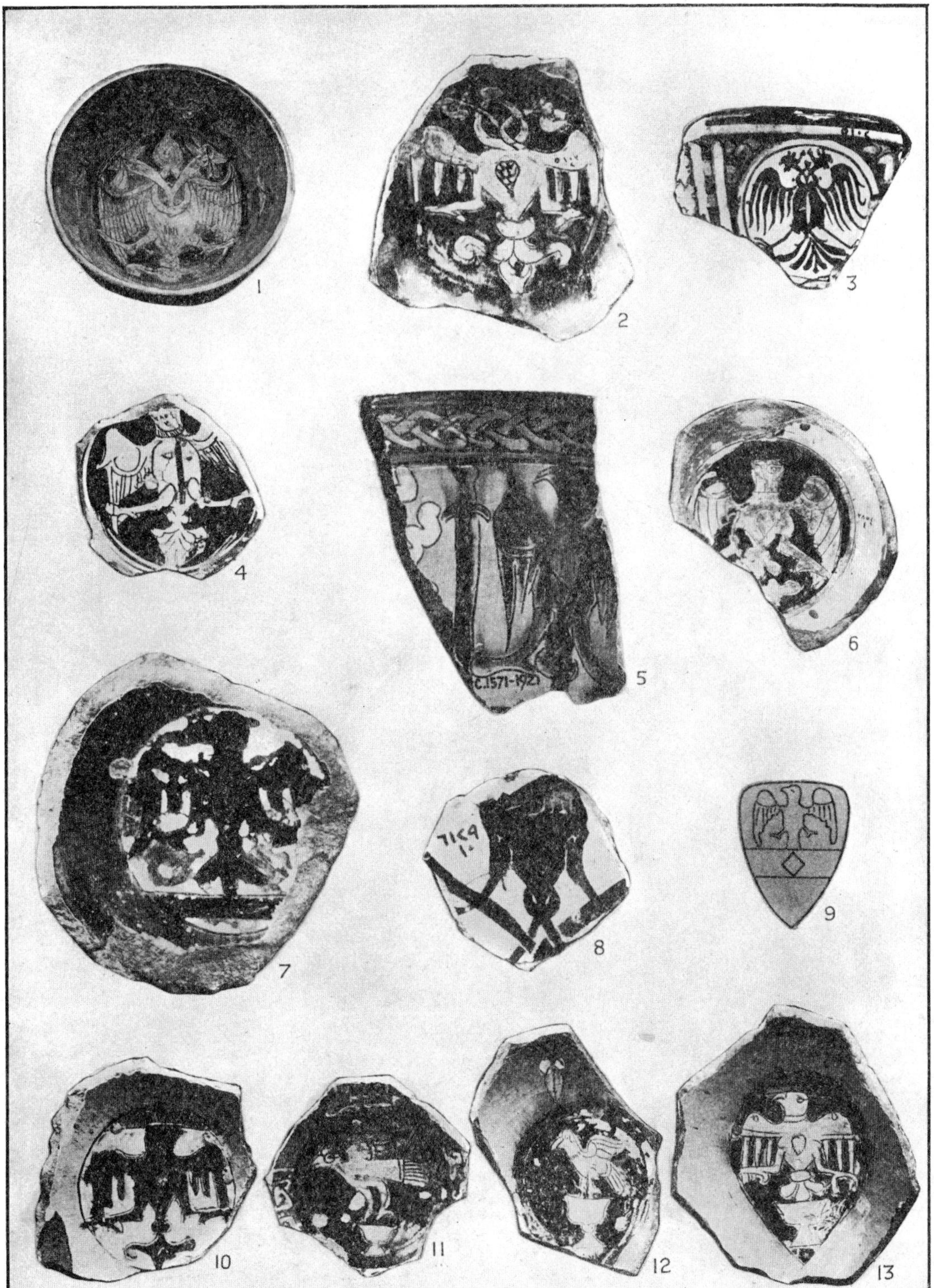
1
2
3
4
C.1571-1921
5
6
7
8
9
10
11
12
13

PLATE IV

1
2
3
4
5
6
7
8
9
10
11
12
13
14
15
16
17

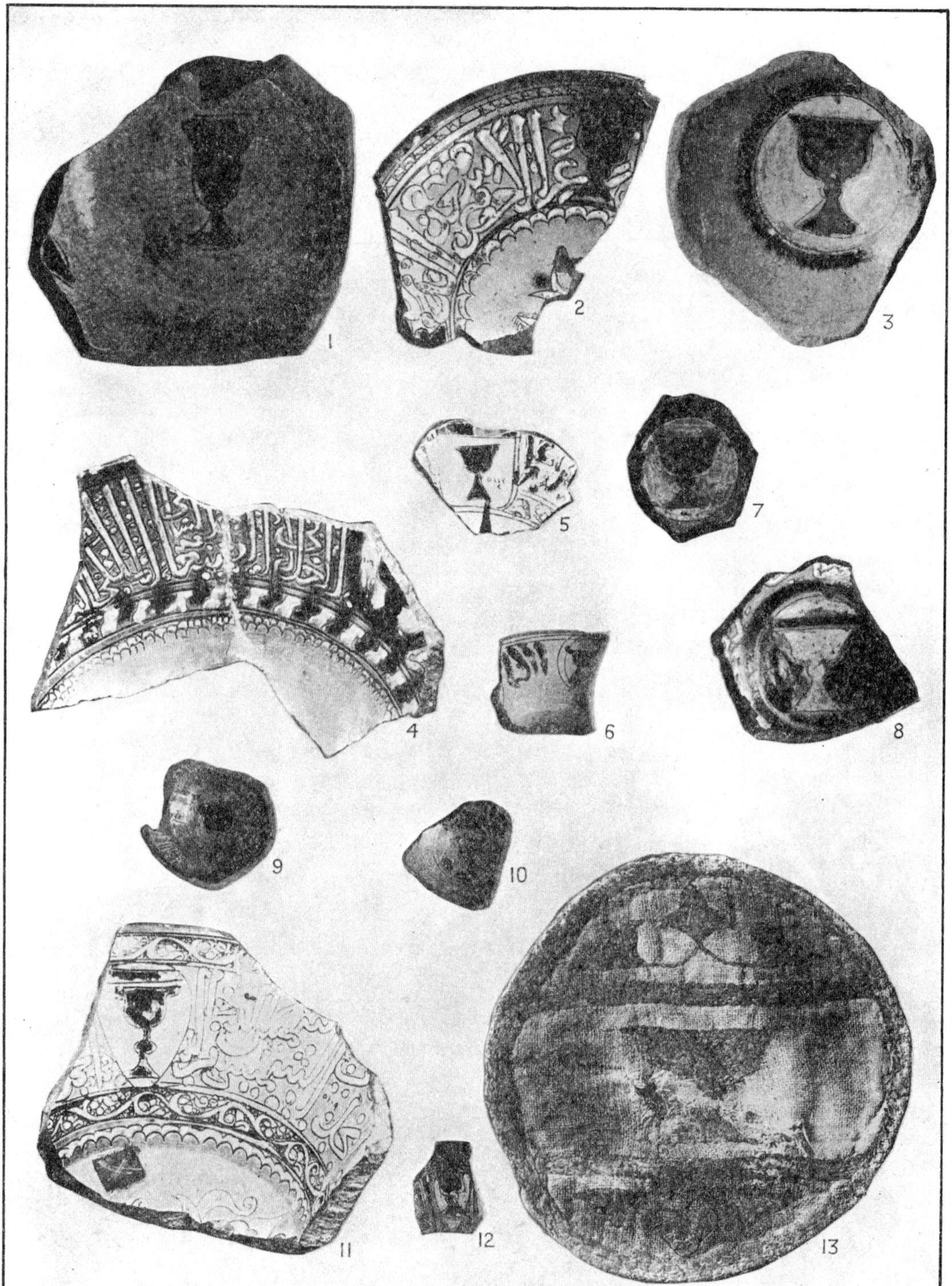
1
2
3
4
5
6
7
8
9
10
11
12
13

1
2
3
4
5
6
7
8
9
10
11
12
13
14
15
16
17

PLATE VIII

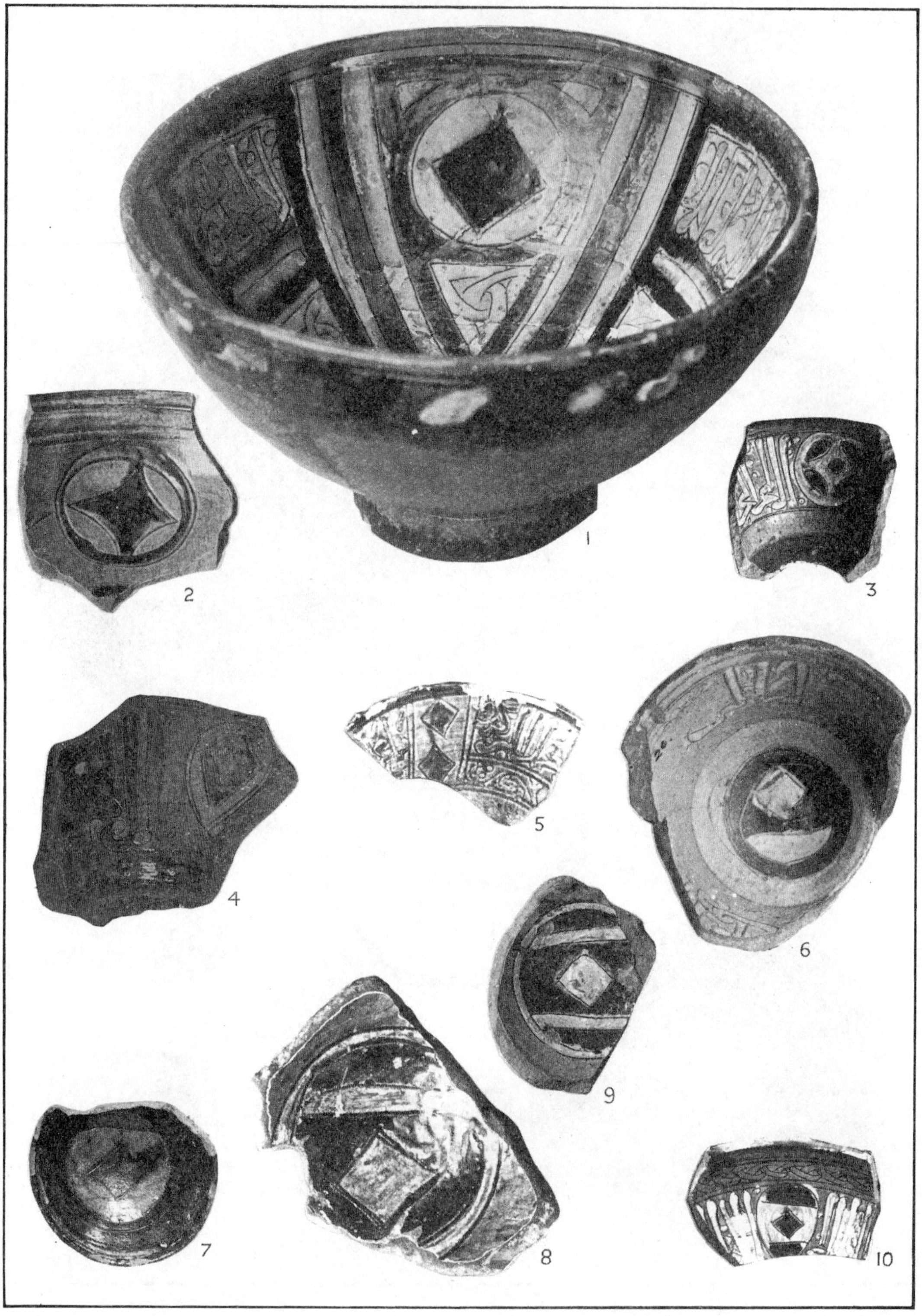

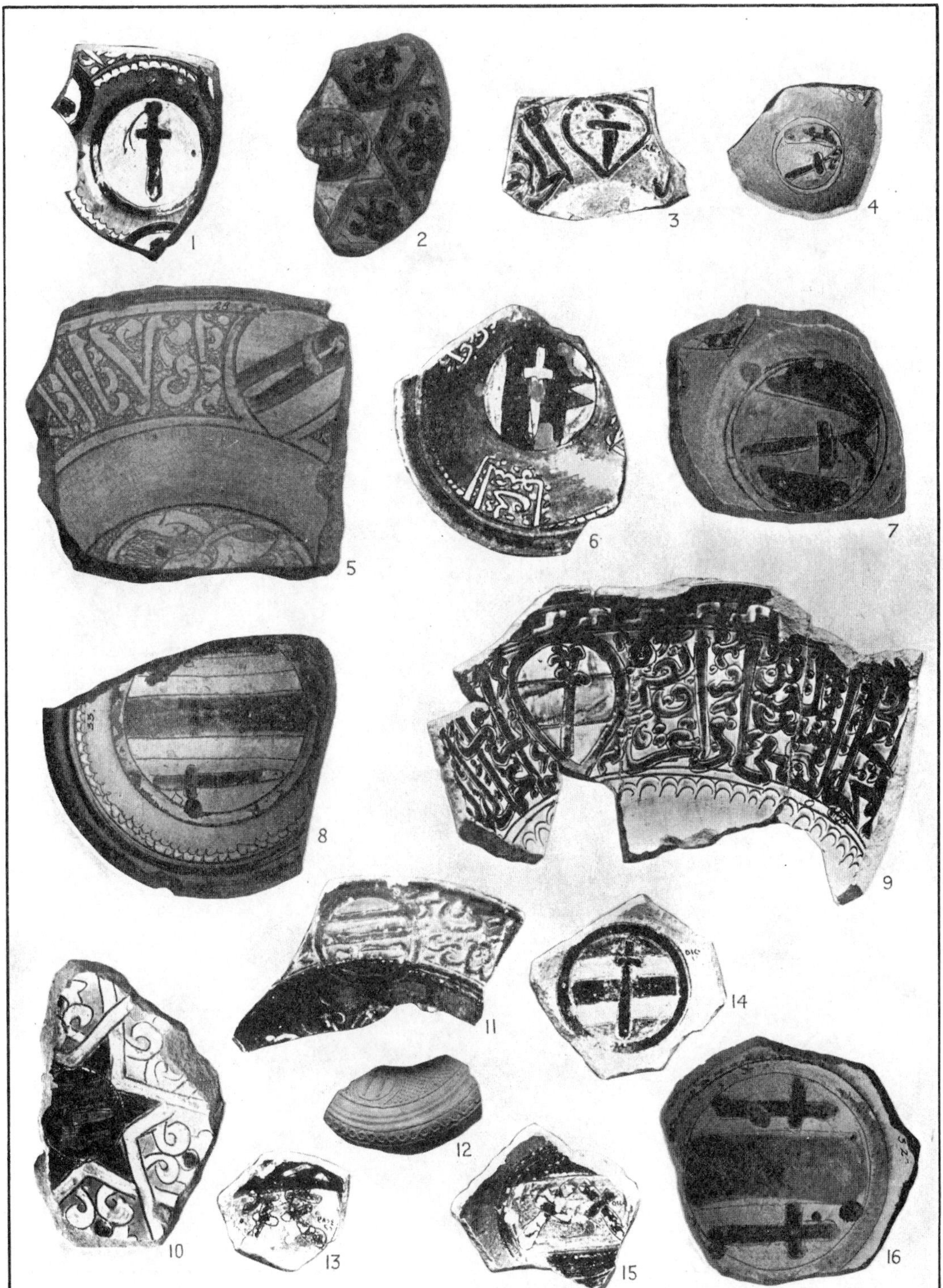
1
2
3
4
5
6
7
8
9
10
11
12
13
14
15
16

PLATE X

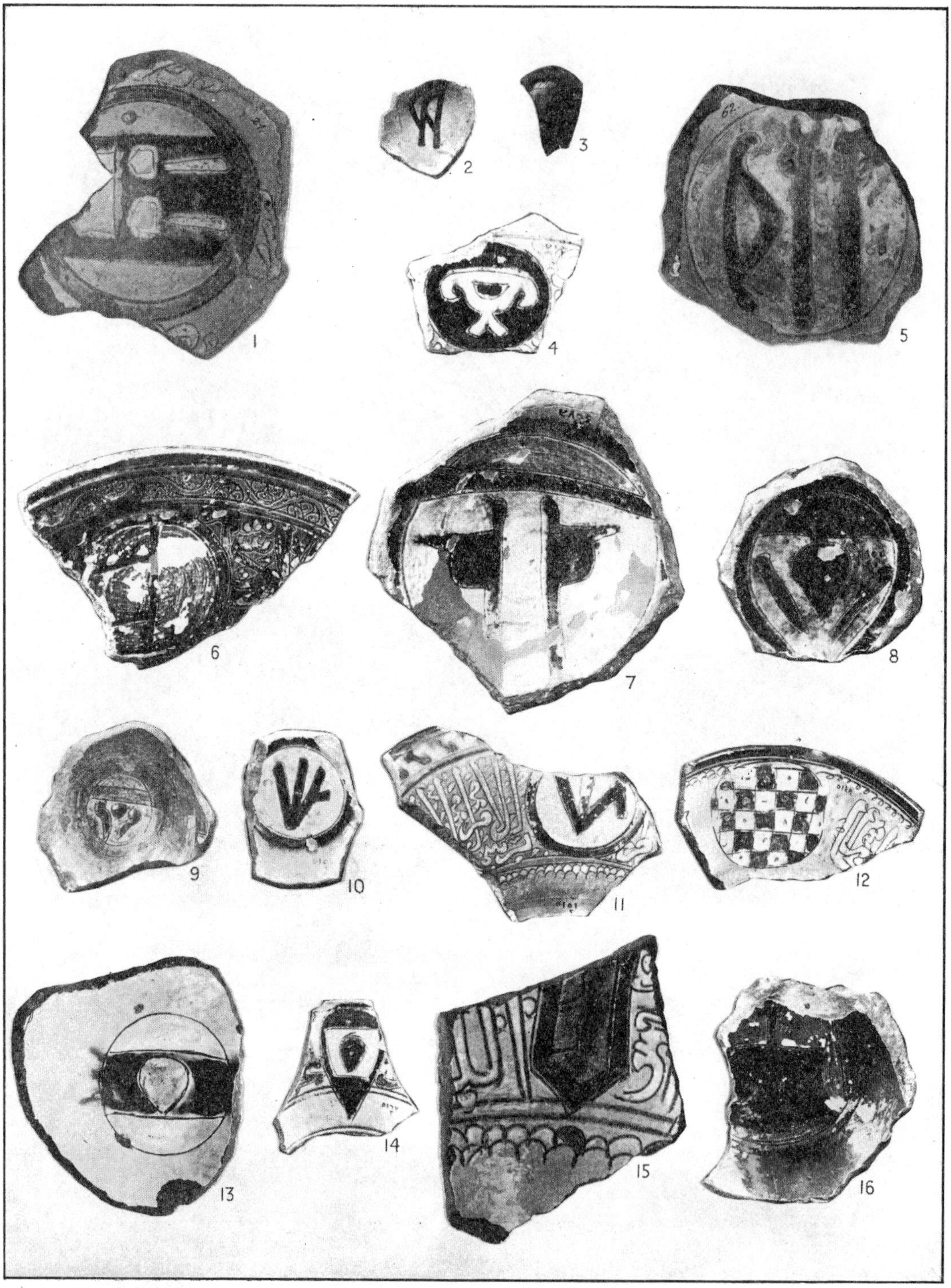

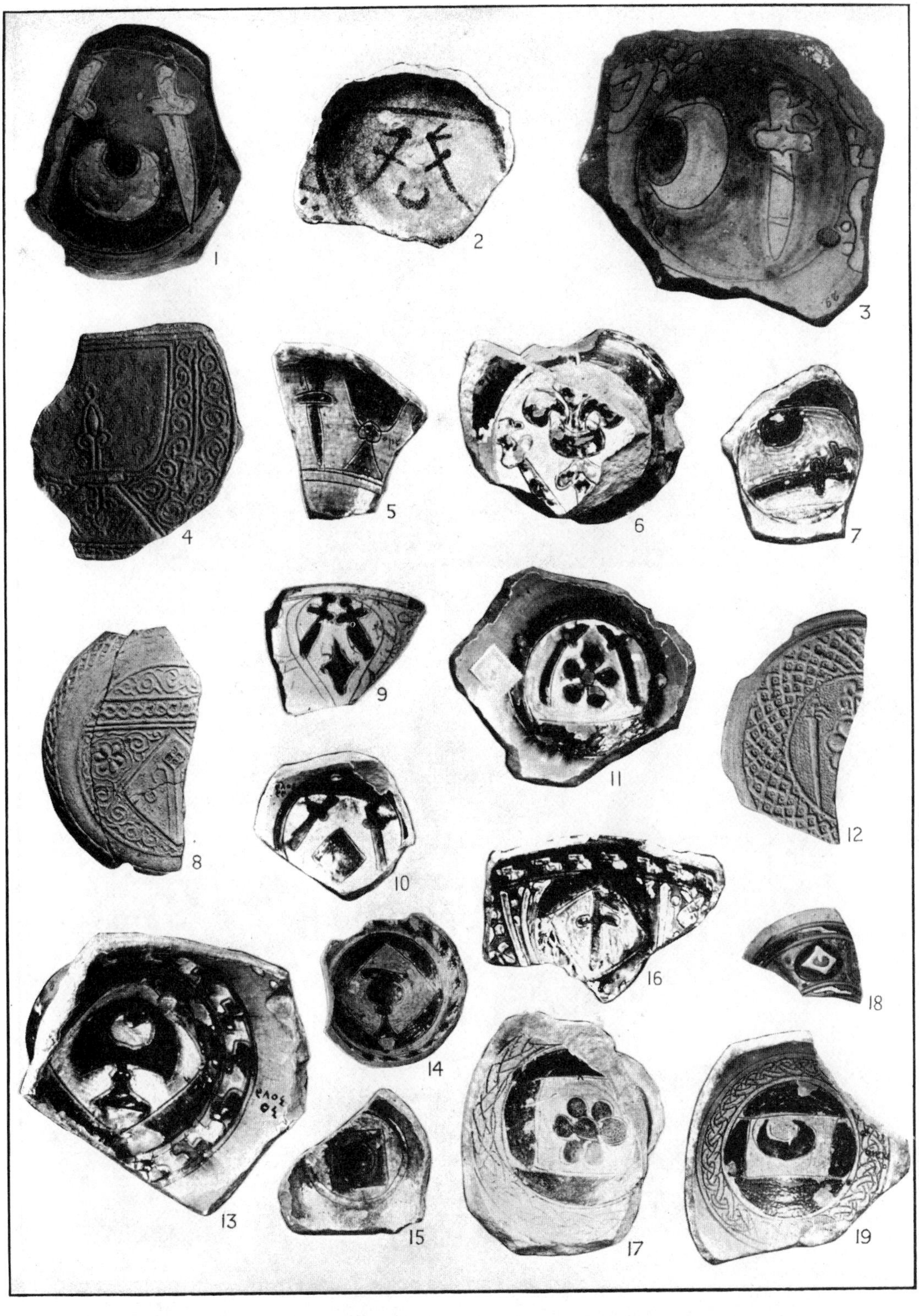

PLATE XII

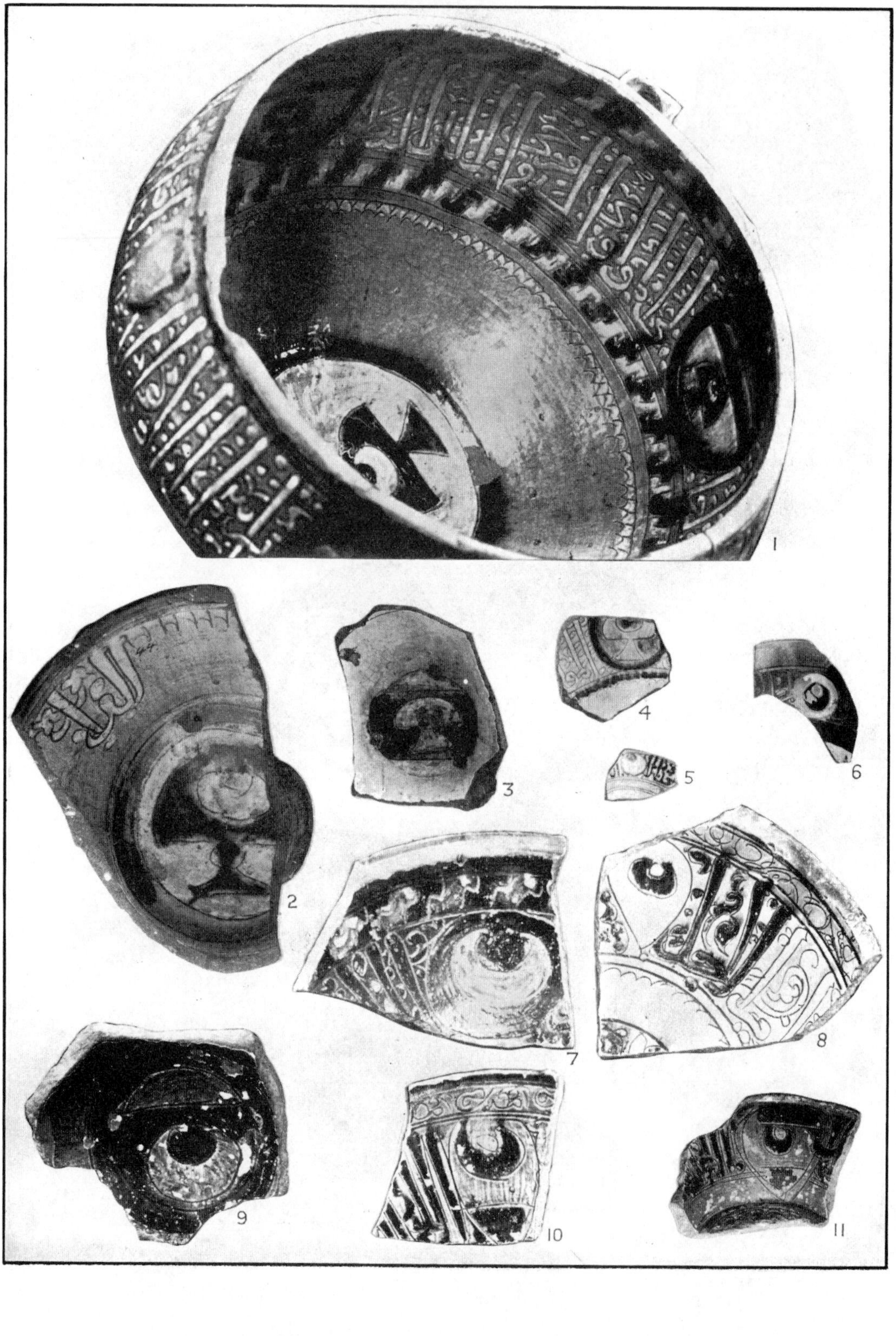

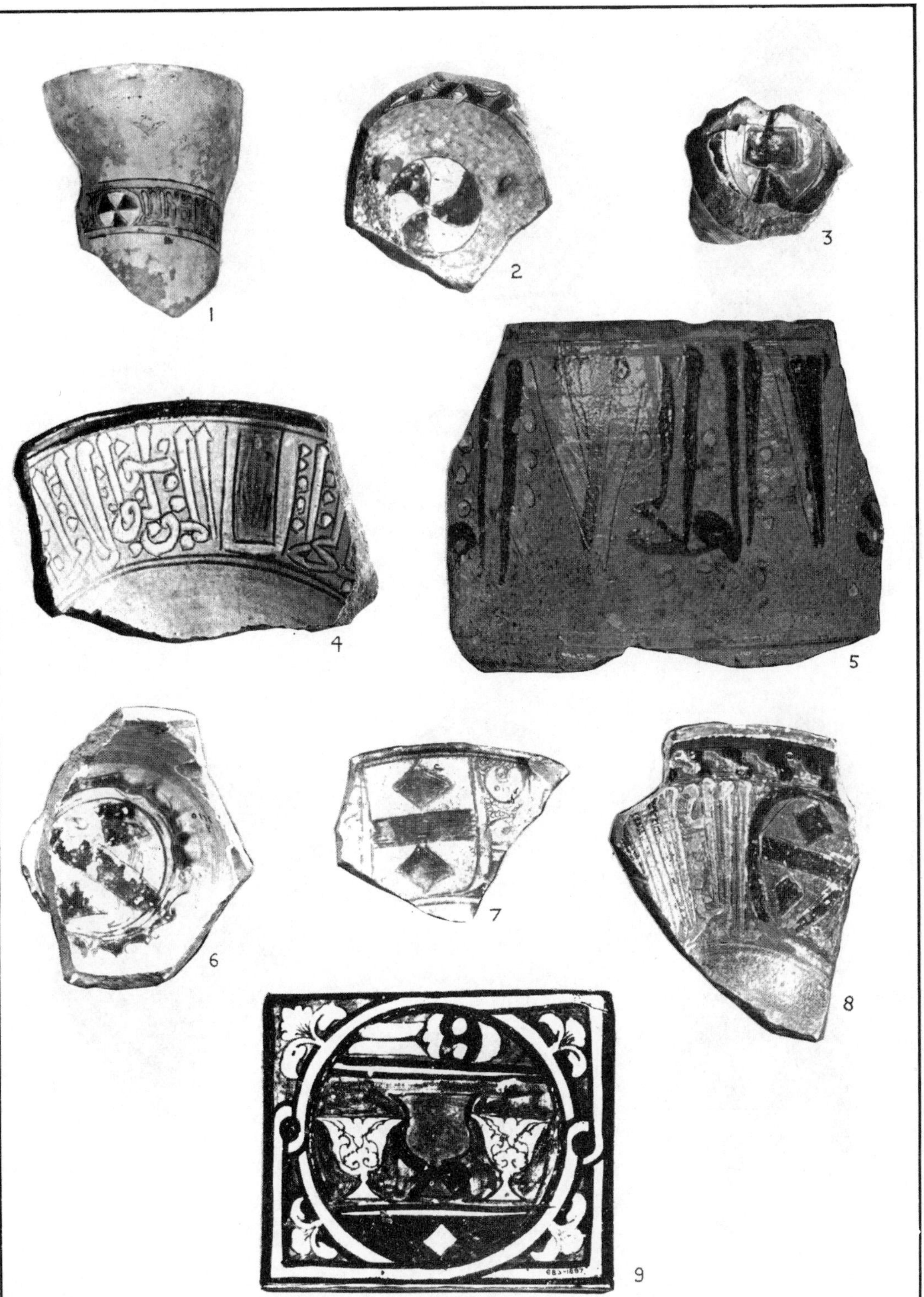
1
2
3
4
5
6
7
8
9

PLATE XII*b*

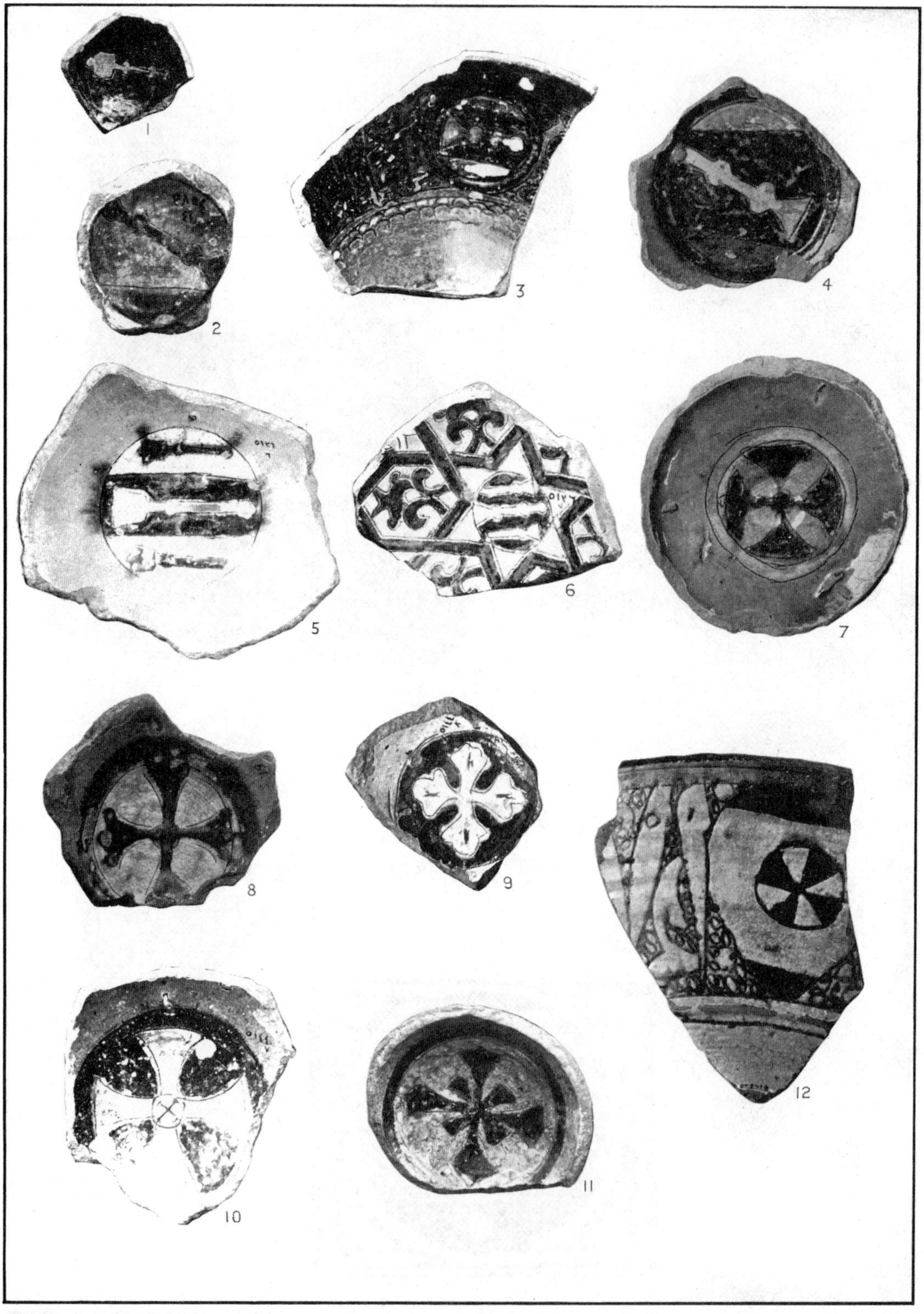

1
2
3
4
5
6
7
8
9
10
11
12
13
14
15
16
17
18
19
20

PLATE XIV

PLATE XVI

PLATE XVIII

1

2

3

4

PLATE XX

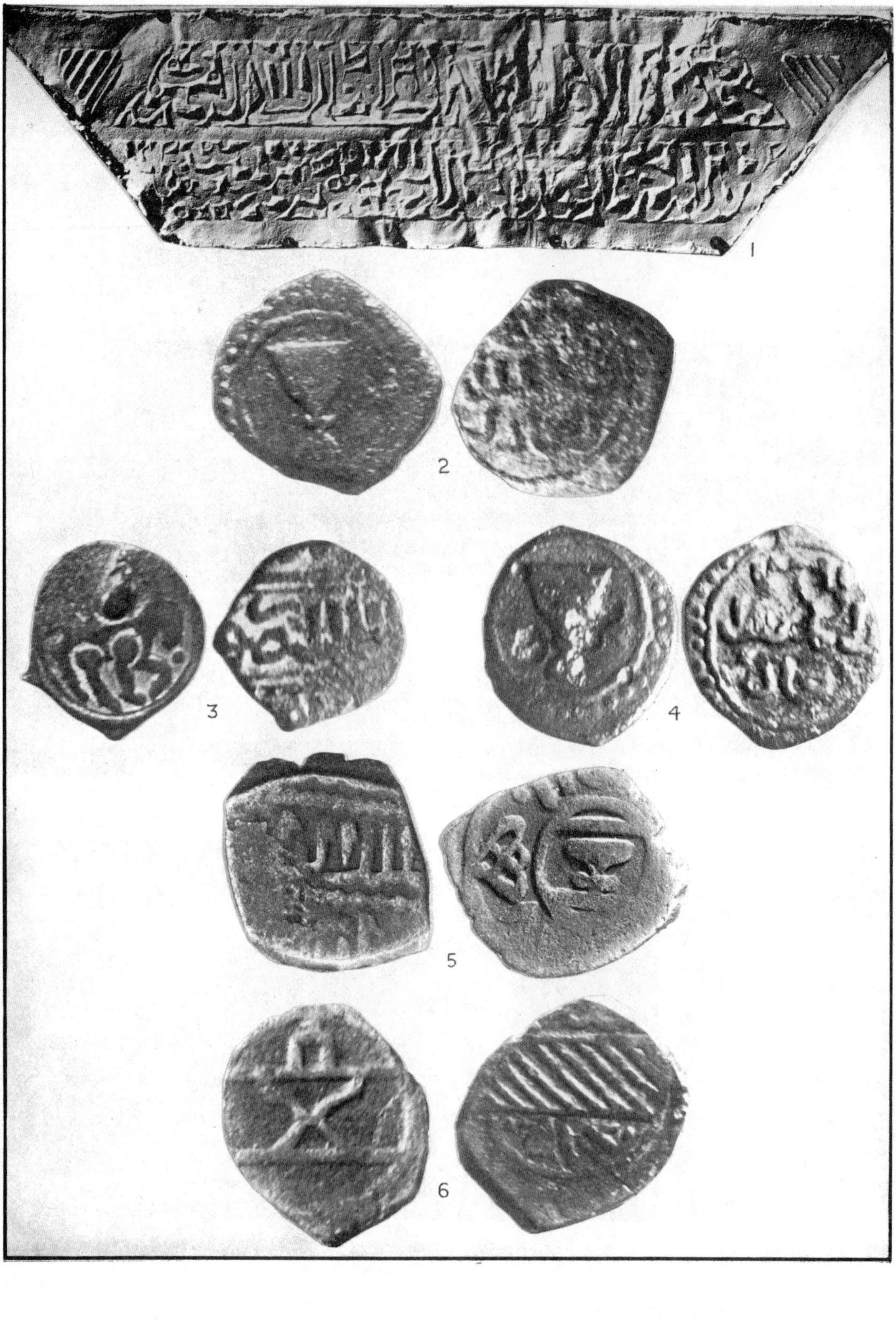

1

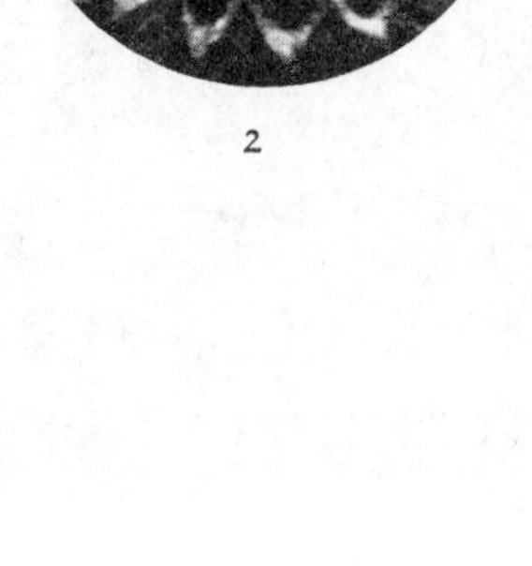

2

PLATE XXII

1

2

3

1

2

PLATE XXIV

1

2

3

4

1

2

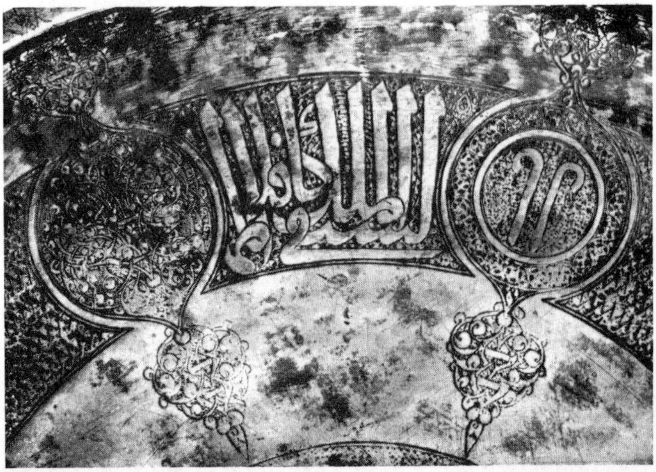

1

2

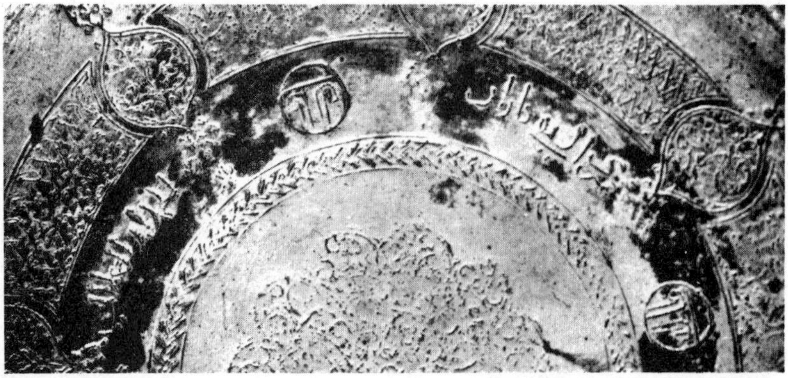

3

PLATE XXVII

1

2

3

4

PLATE XXVIII

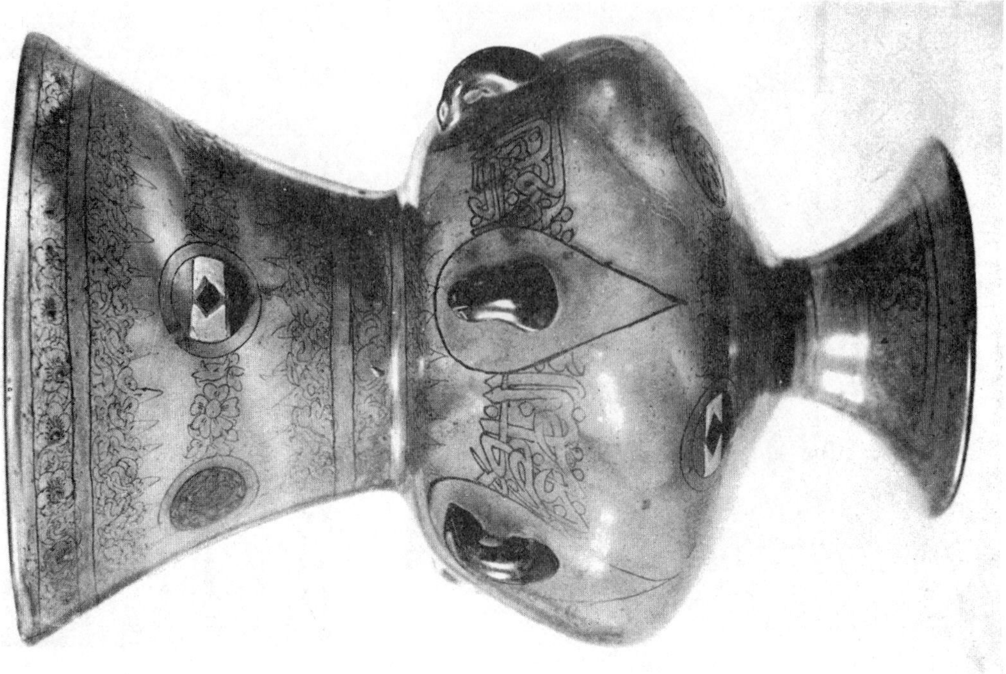

2

1

PLATE XXX

1

3

2

1

2

1
2
3
4
5
6

PLATE XXXIV

1

2

1

2

3

1

2

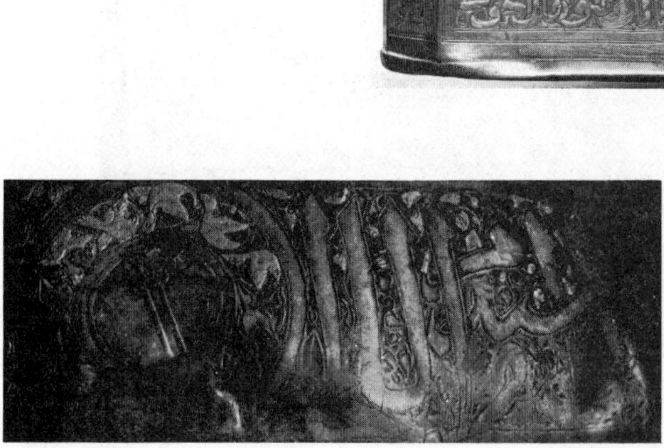

3

4

PLATE XXXVII

1

2

PLATE XXXVIII

Boîte ronde en cuivre.

Frise circulaire naskh mamel. caract. 8 cm

Paris Coll. Ch. gabeau.

مما عمل برسم المقر الاشرف العالى المولوى الامرى الكبيرى
السيفى برقوق عين مقدمين الالوف الملكى الاشرى ※ سنة

Dessus frise d'un ceau avec deux cartouches

C'est lui communiqué par Casanova, v. Corpus, palais mamâÿ

1

A côté, bloc cassé, c.à.d. linteau
d'une vieille porte disparue, bientôt
la porte de l'on pied entièrement disparu
qui contenait tous ce, tombe réunis
La moitié droite est cassée 3-e
in compl. à droite   à gauche cartouch

بعمارة المقر المرحوم (٤)
الد......ى كنجاك الخوارزجى

3 mots effacés   (2) [martèl l'mz] و   فص

فى ايام ...... وريق اجا

على رقا (3) ...

قم ......ملك شى ودسين و Salon

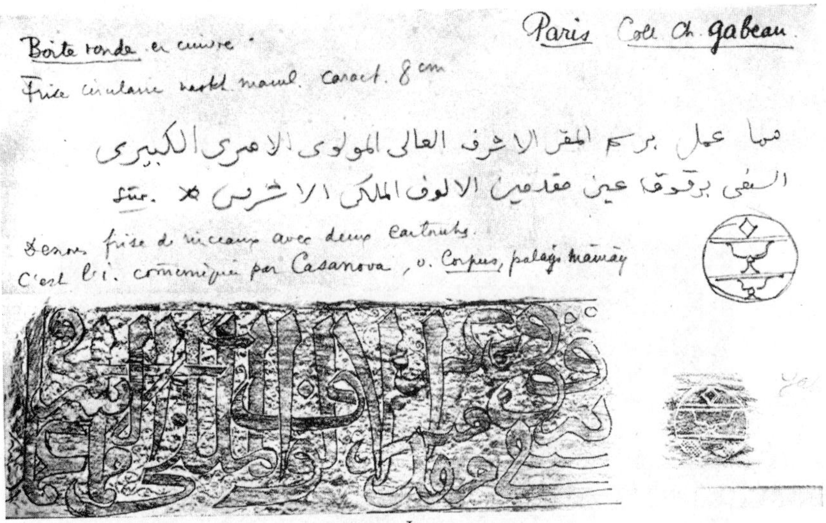

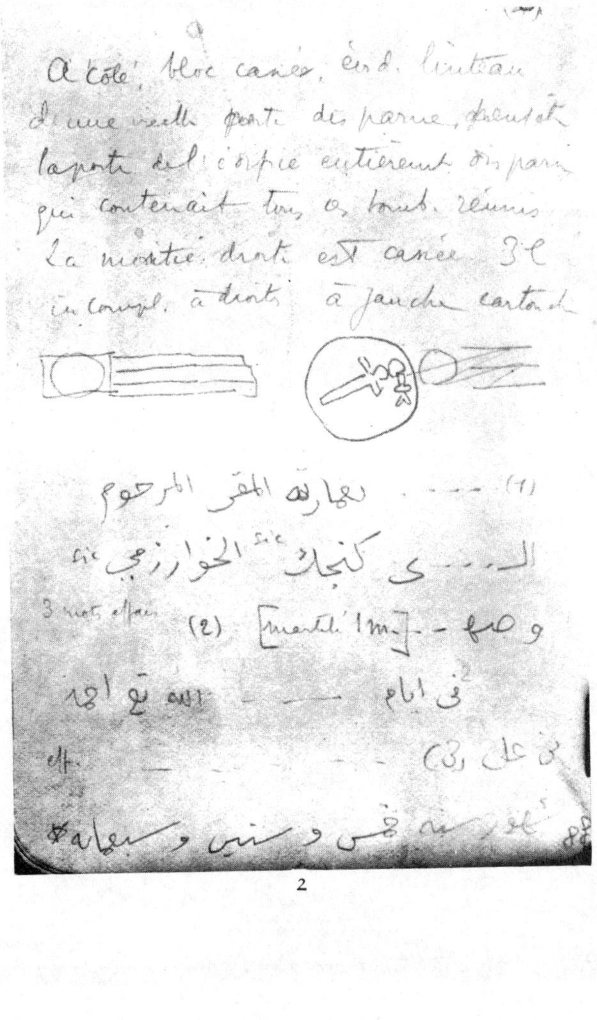

2

1

2

3

4

1

2

3

4

PLATE XLII

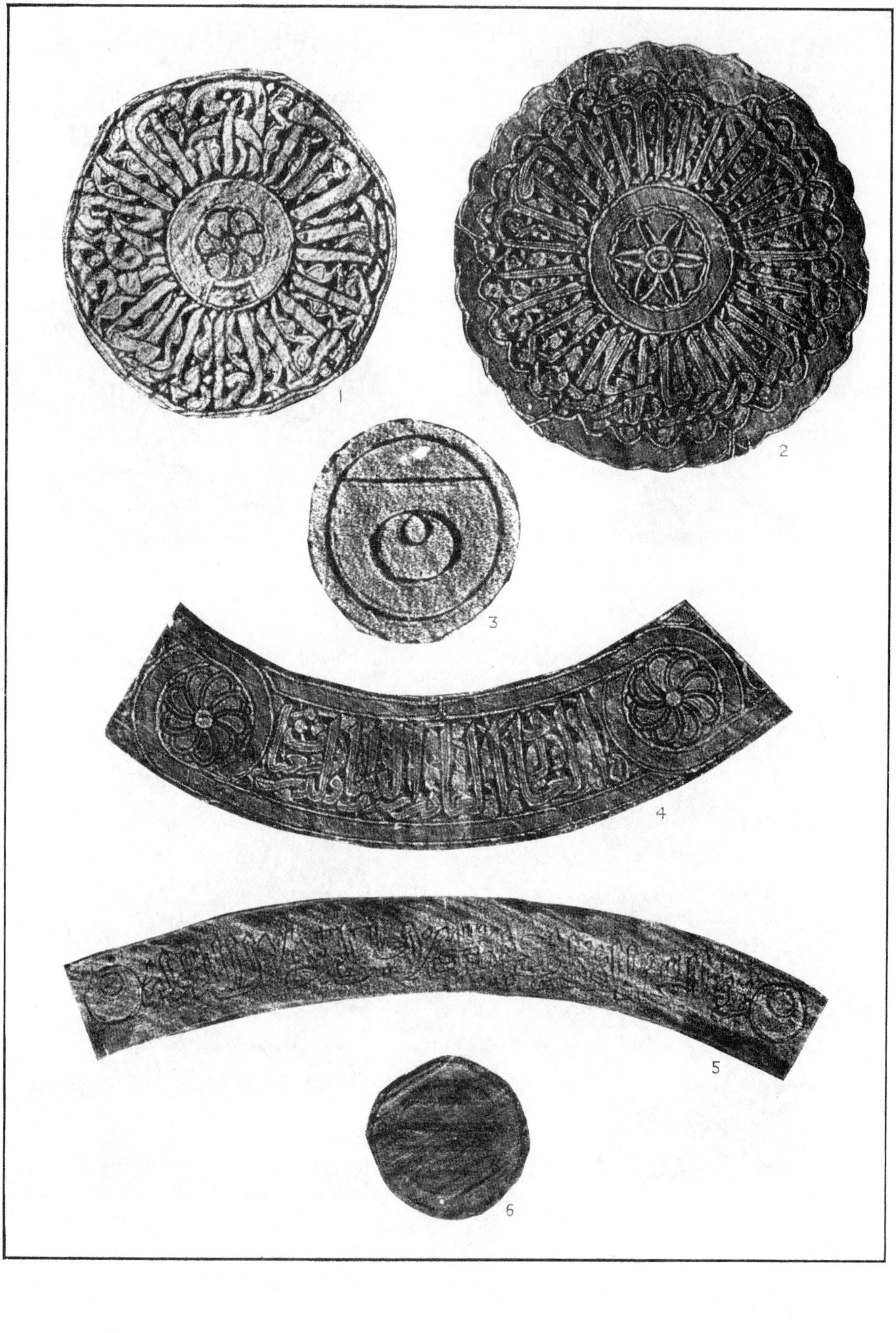

1

2

1

2

3

PLATE XLV

2

1

PLATE XLVI

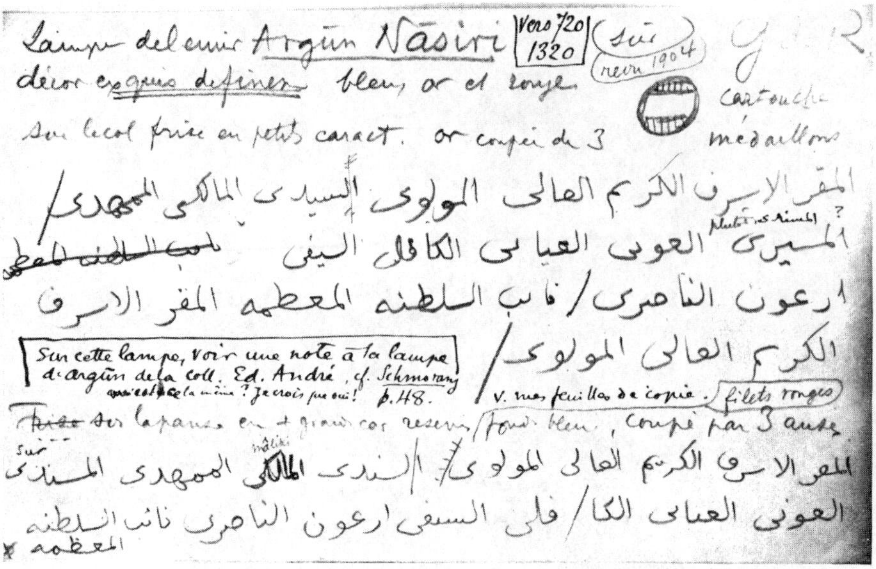

1

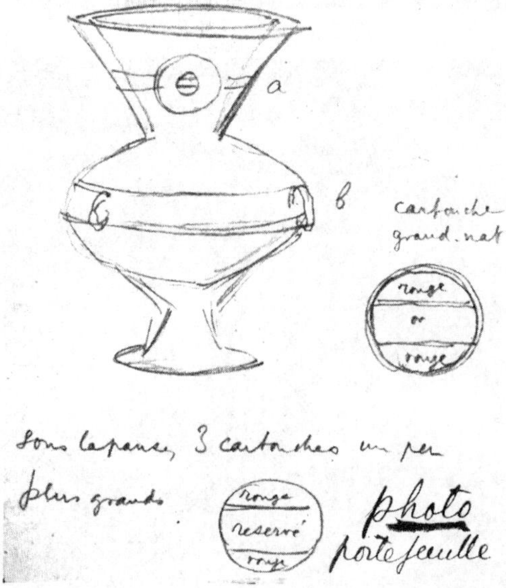

2

1

2

PLATE XLVIII

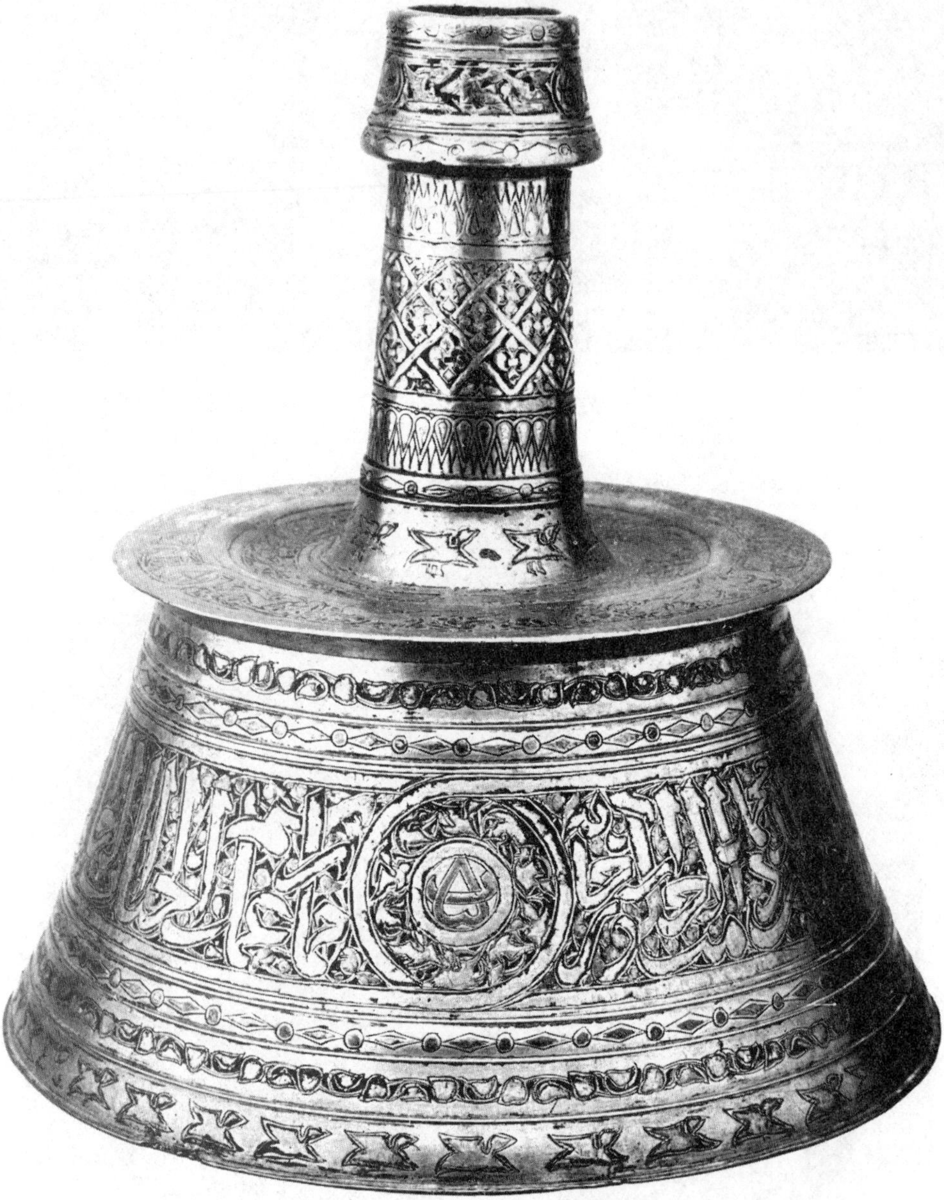

PLATE XLIX

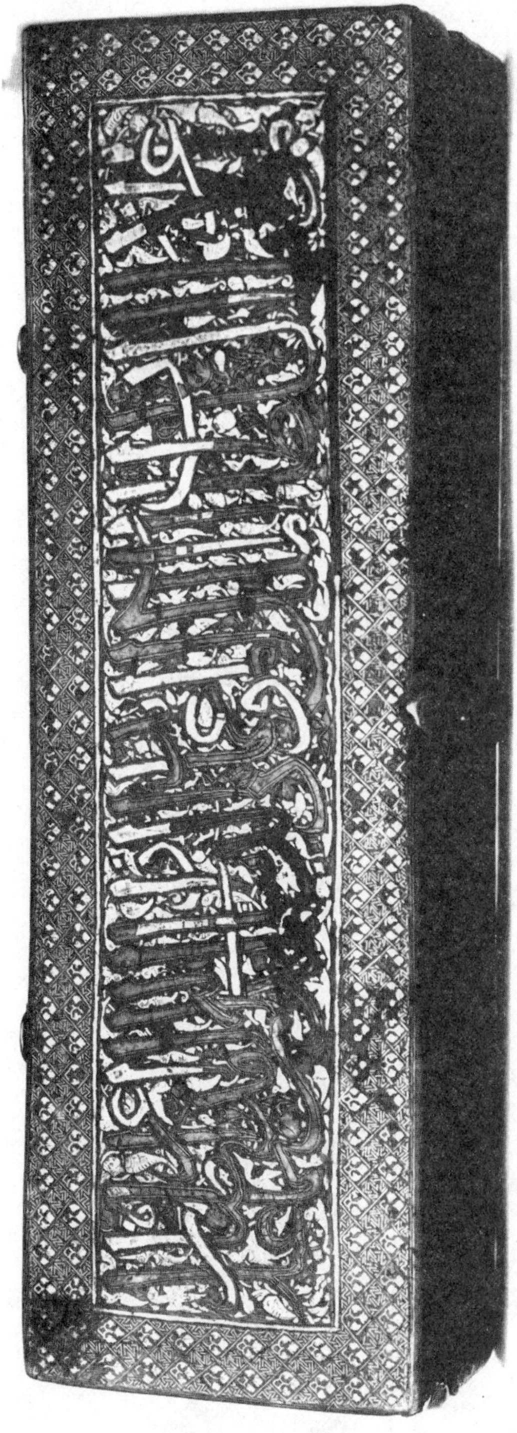

1

2

PLATE L

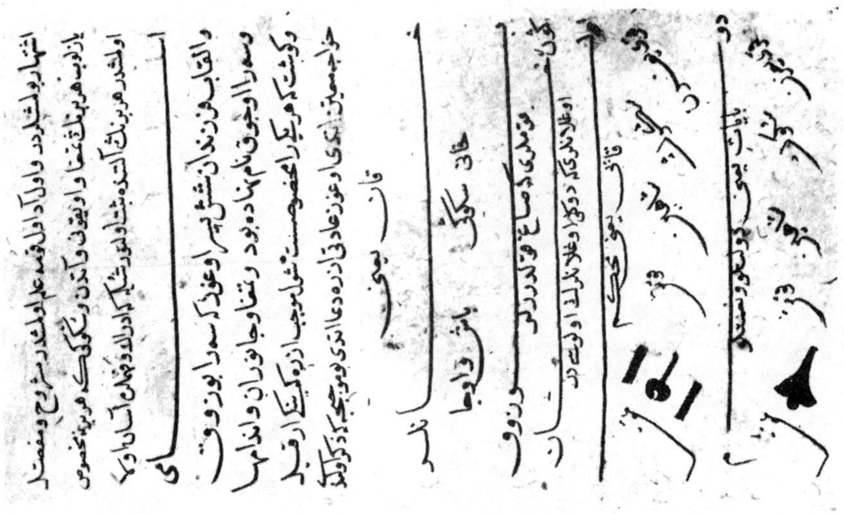

1

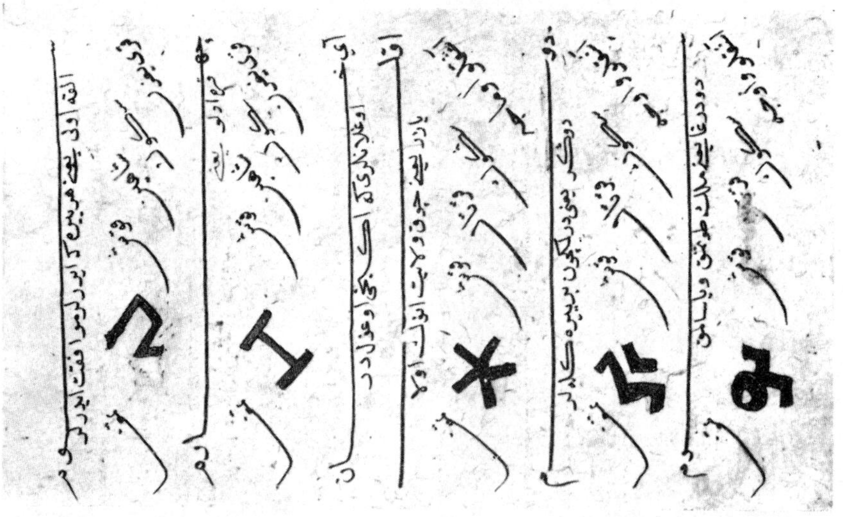

2

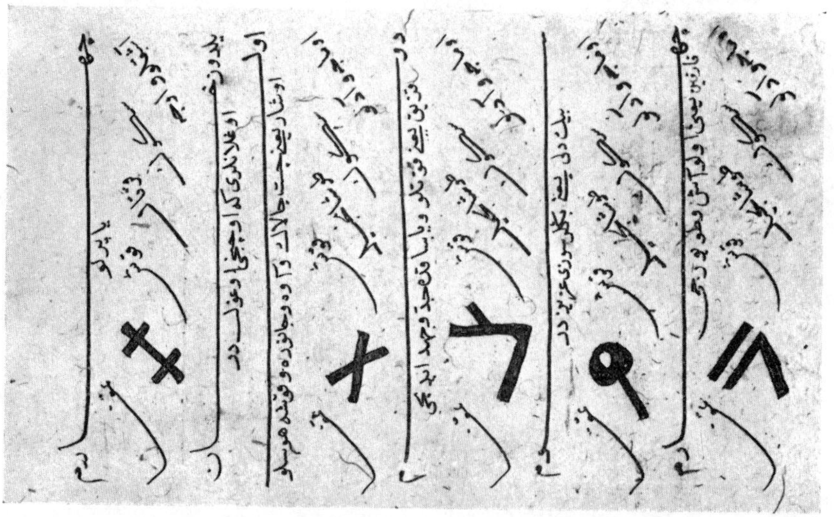

3

PLATE LI

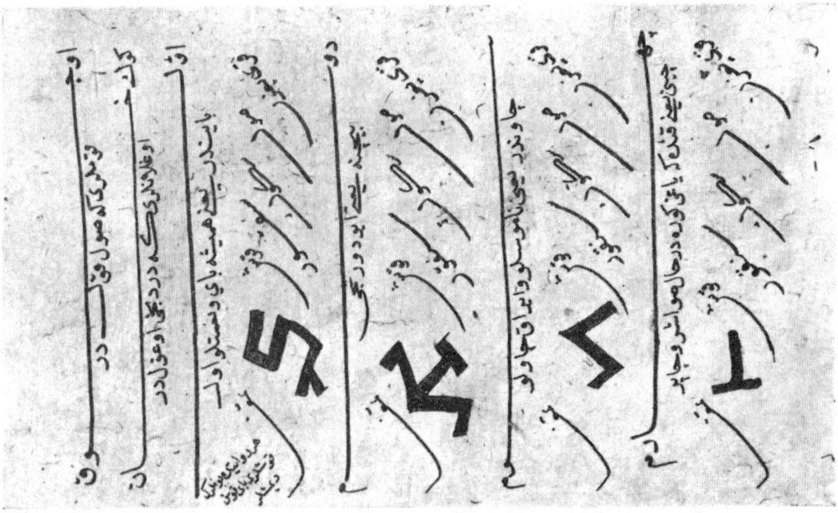

4

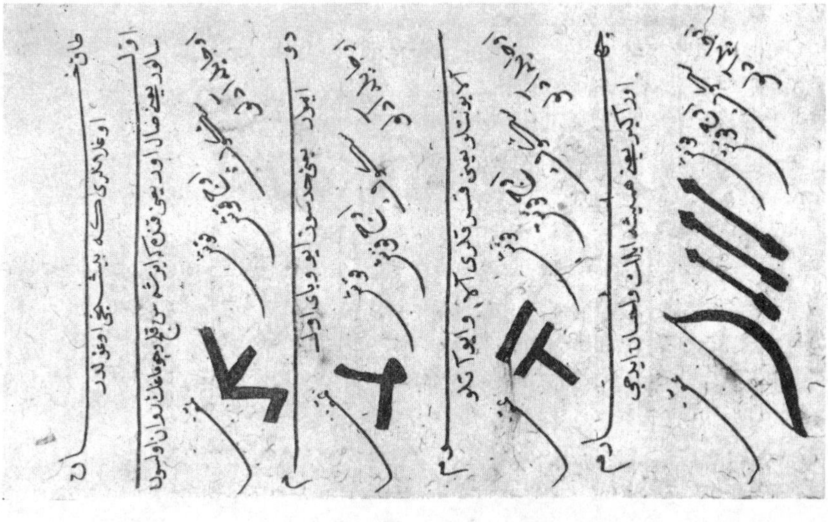

5

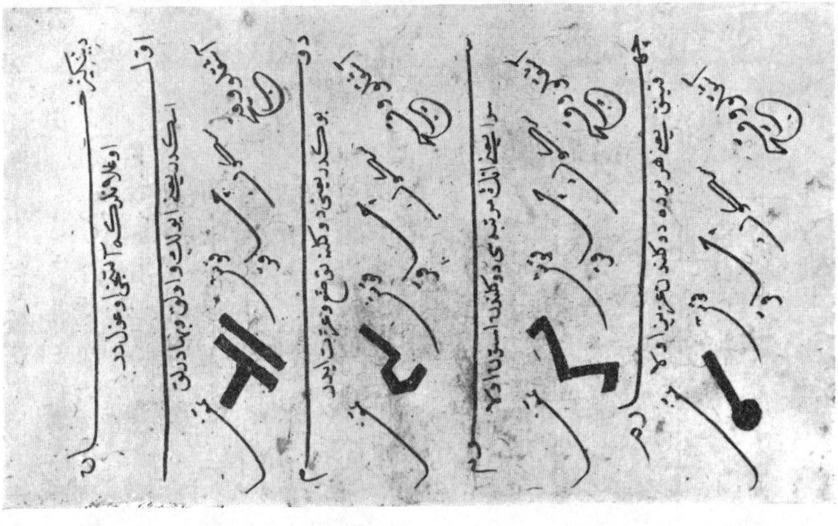

6

PLATE LII

1

2

1

2

PLATE LIV

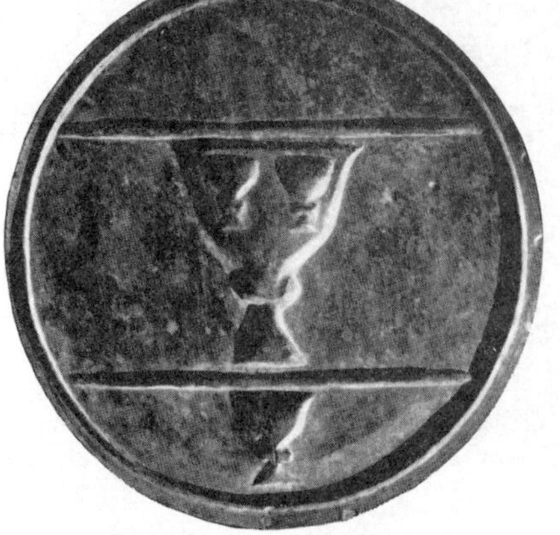

1

2

3

4

1

2

3

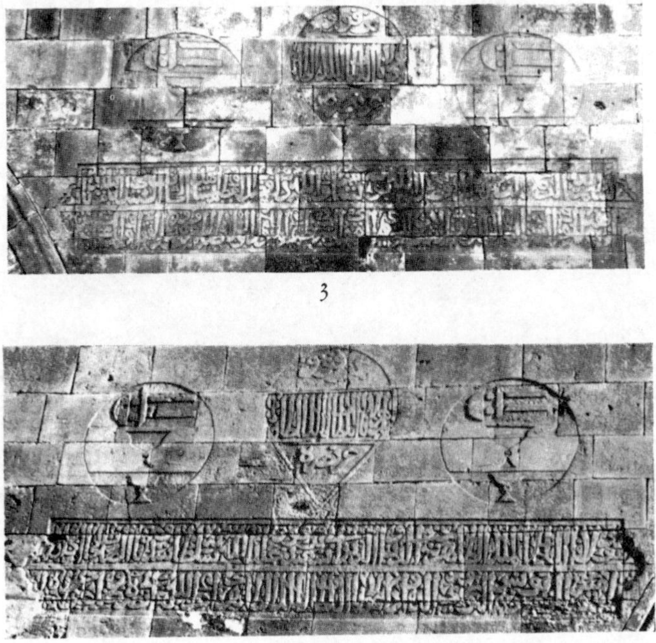

4

PLATE LVI

1

2

3

4

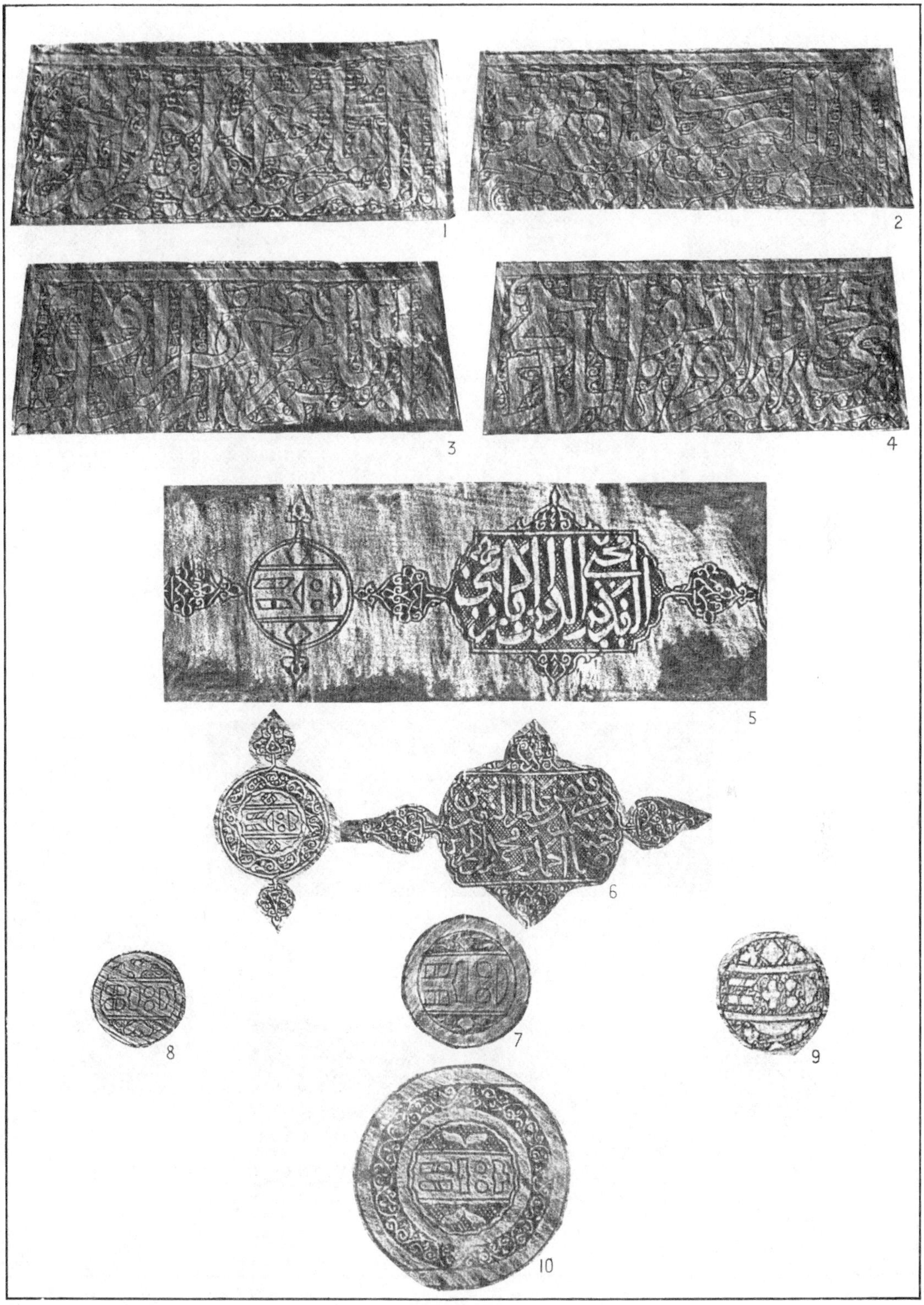
1
2
3
4
5
6
7
8
9
10

PLATE LVIII

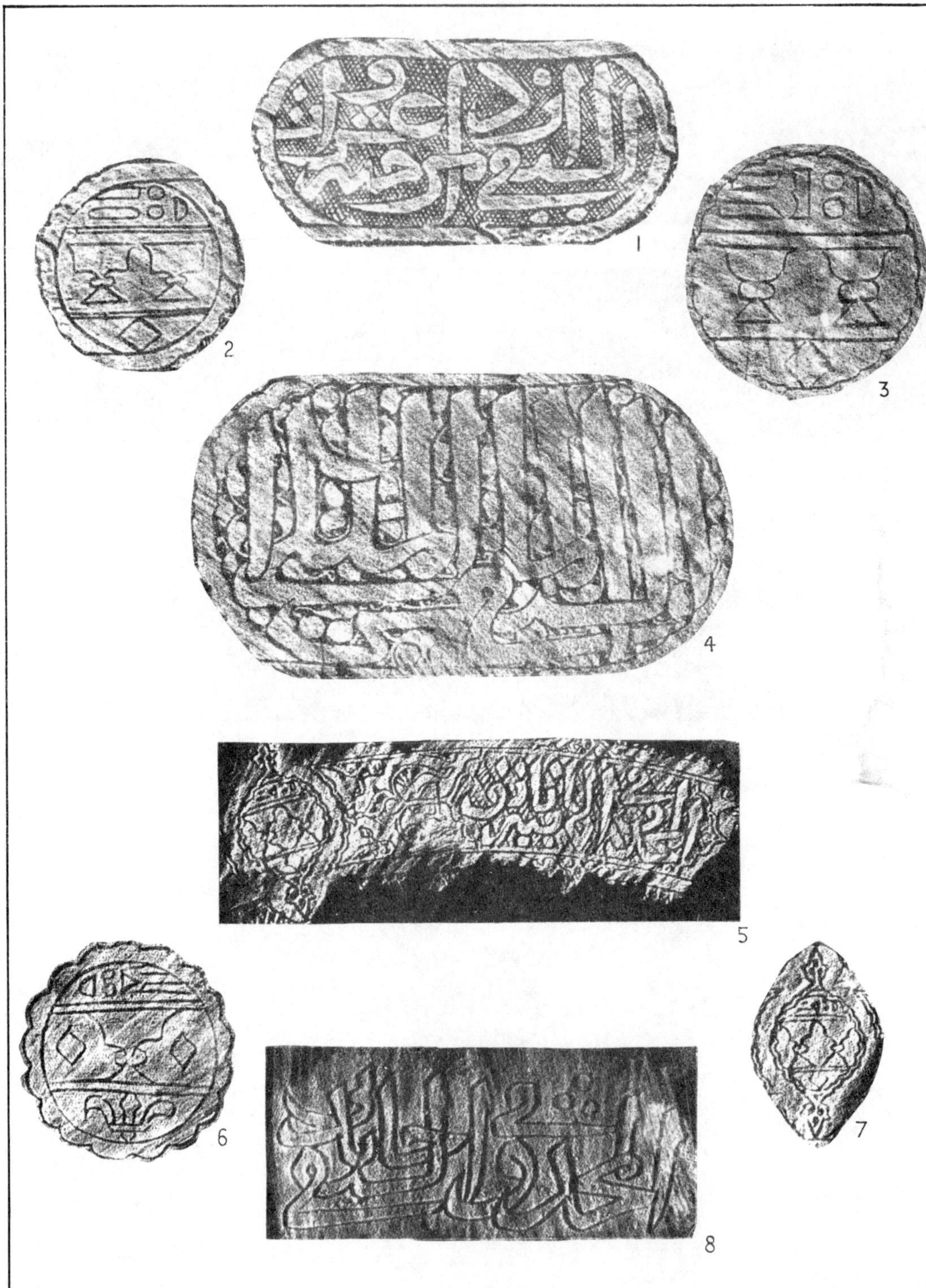

1

2

3

4

5

PLATE LX

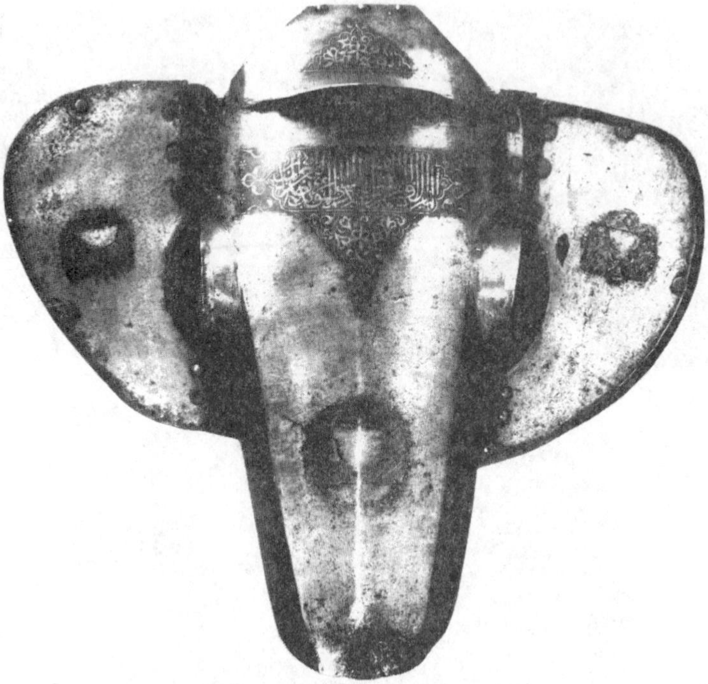

1

2

1

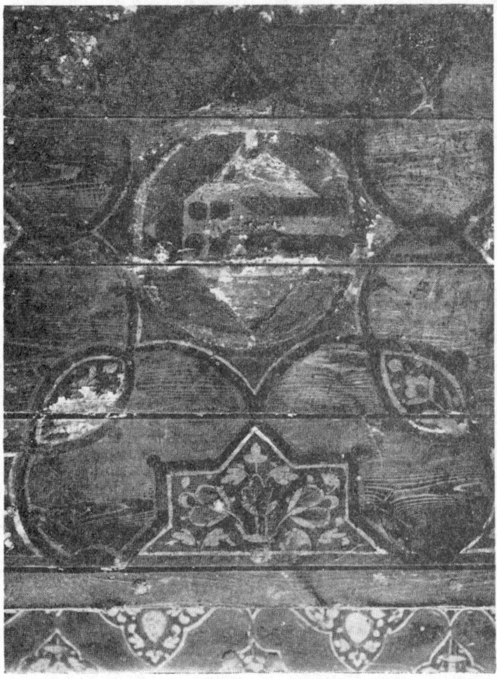

2

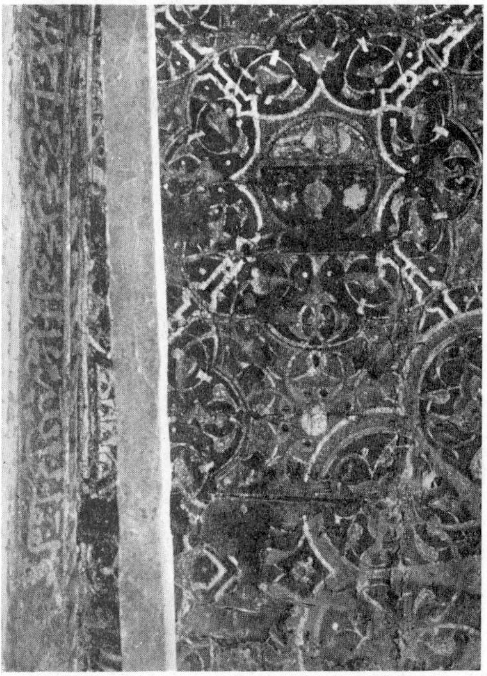

3

PLATE LXII

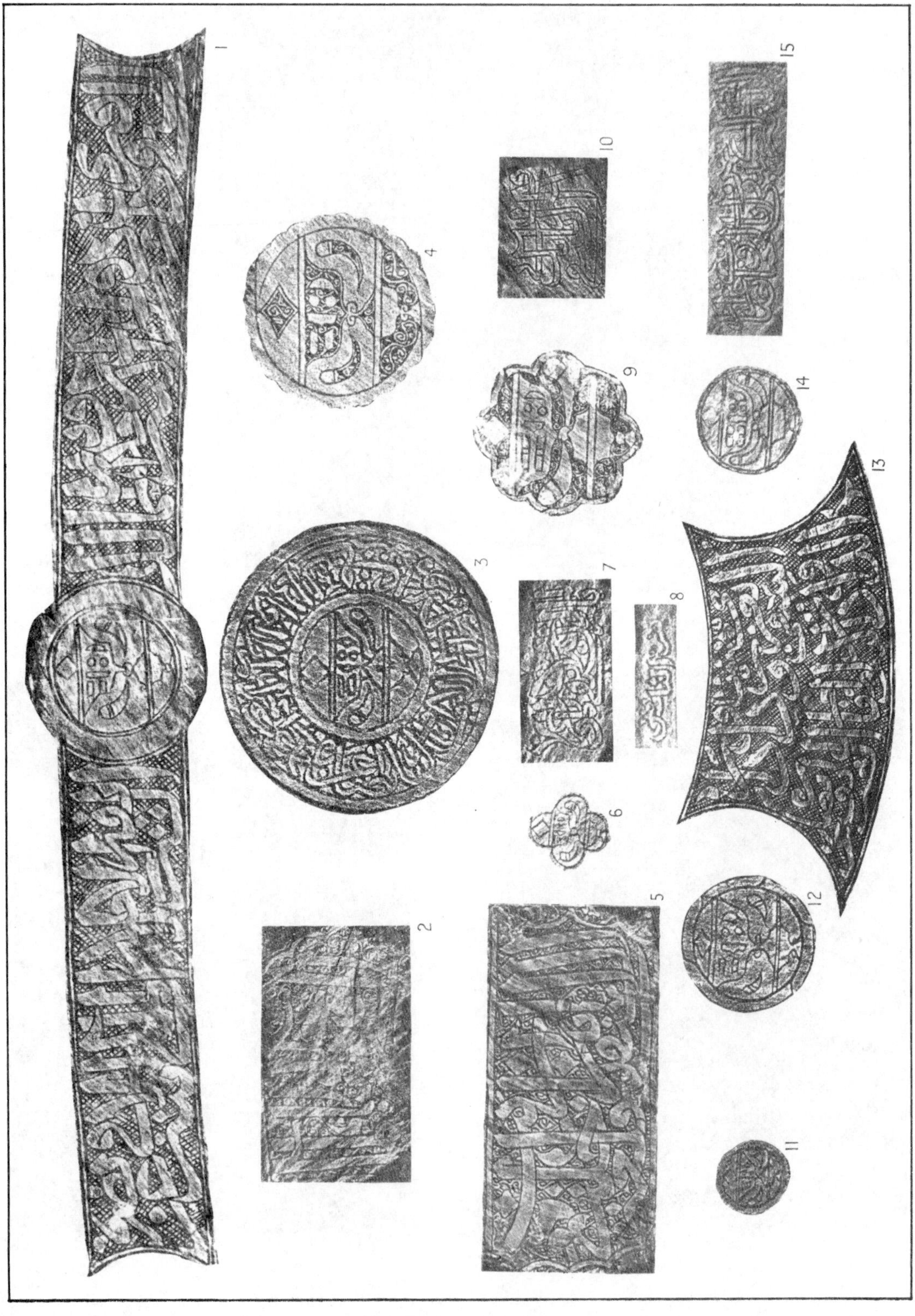

PLATE LXIV

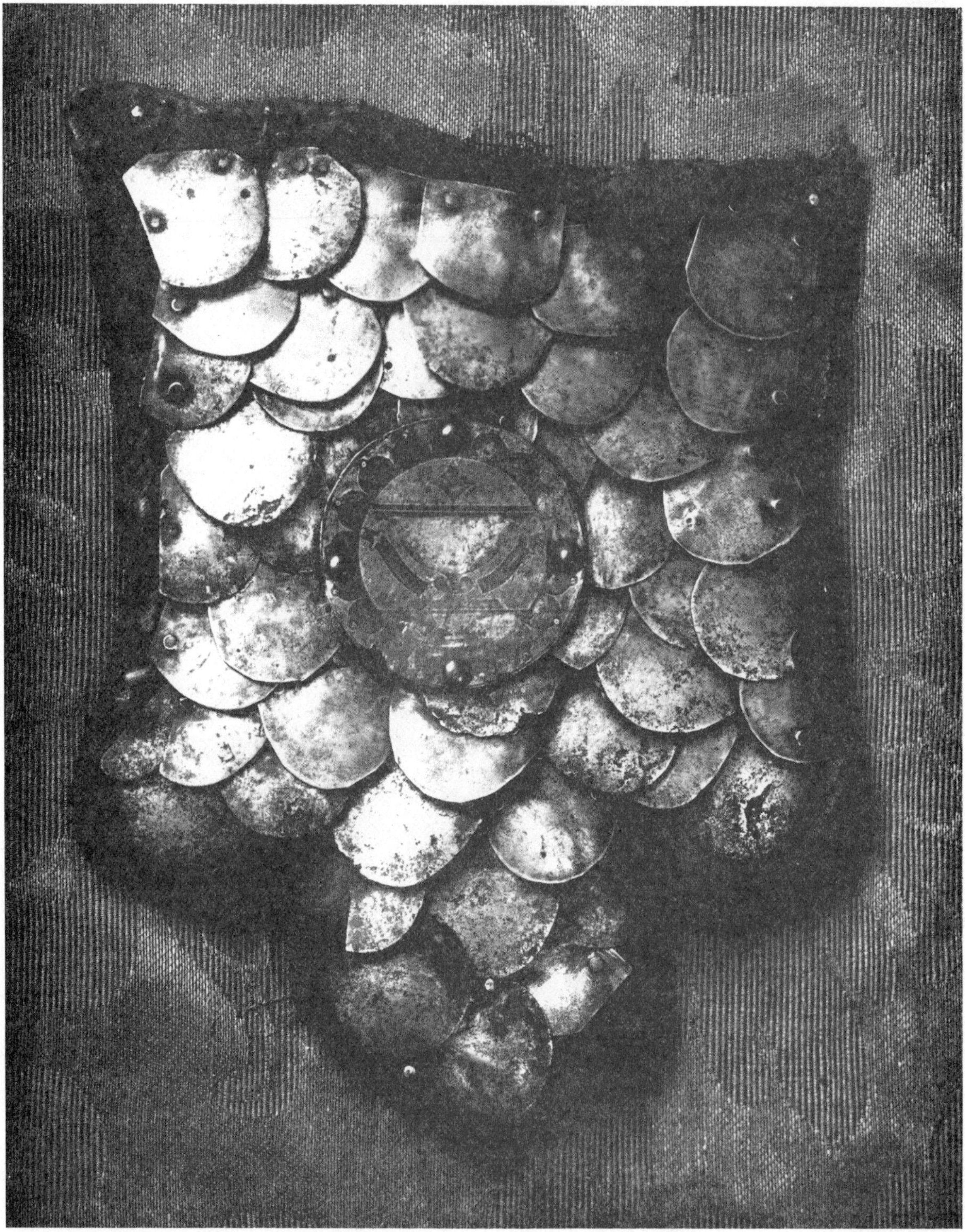

1

2

3

PLATE LXVI

1

2

3

4

1

2

3

PLATE LXVIII

1

2

3

4

5

6

7

8

9

10

1

2

PLATE LXX

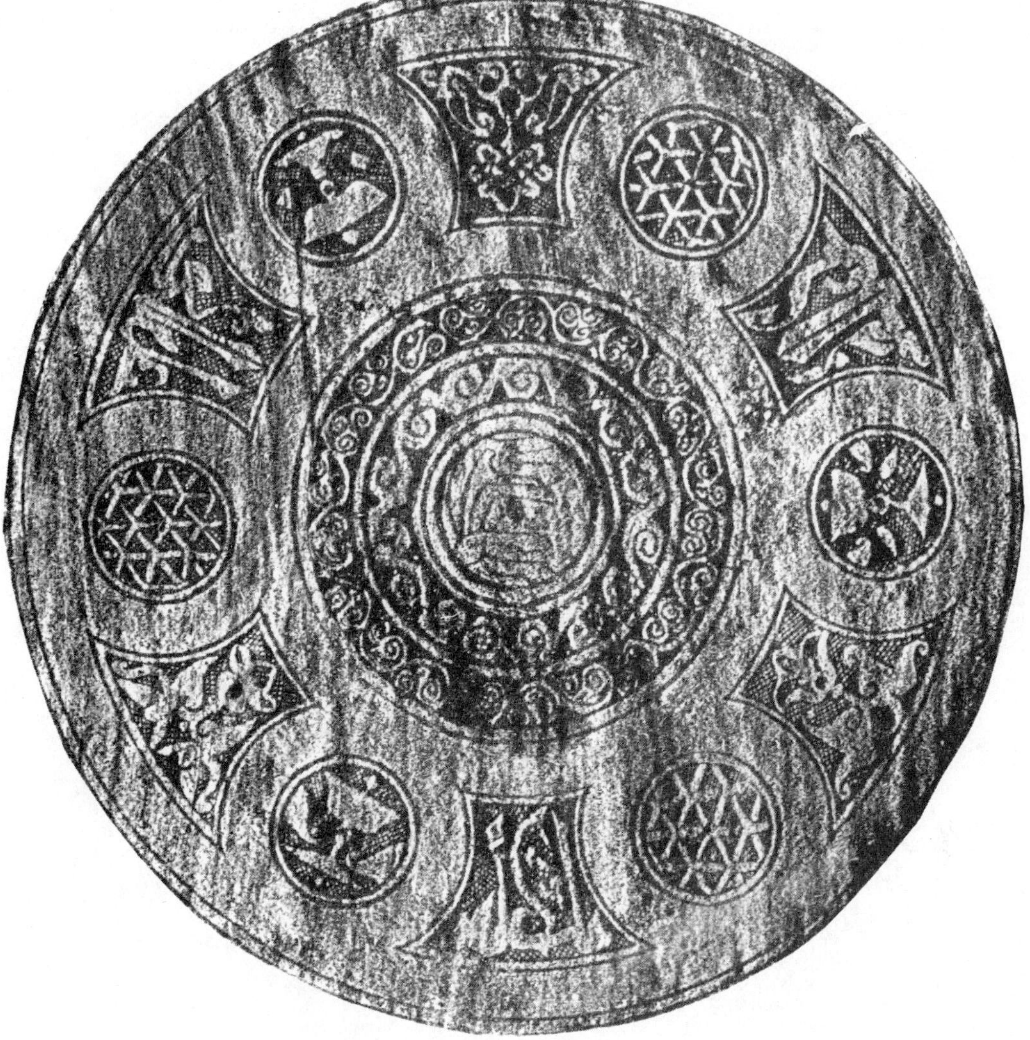

OTHER TITLES IN THIS HARDBACK REPRINT PROGRAMME FROM SANDPIPER BOOKS LTD (LONDON) AND POWELLS BOOKS (CHICAGO)

ISBN 0–19–	Author	Title
8143567	ALFÖLDI A.	The Conversion of Constantine and Pagan Rome
6286409	ANDERSON George K.	The Literature of the Anglo-Saxons
8228813	BARTLETT & MacKAY	Medieval Frontier Societies
8111010	BETHURUM Dorothy	Homilies of Wulfstan
8142765	BOLLING G. M.	External Evidence for Interpolation in Homer
9240132	BOYLAN Patrick	Thoth, the Hermes of Egypt
8114222	BROOKS Kenneth R.	Andreas and the Fates of the Apostles
8203543	BULL Marcus	Knightly Piety & Lay Response to the First Crusade
8216785	BUTLER Alfred J.	Arab Conquest of Egypt
8148046	CAMERON Alan	Circus Factions
8148054	CAMERON Alan	Porphyrius the Charioteer
8148348	CAMPBELL J.B.	The Emperor and the Roman Army 31 BC to 235
826643X	CHADWICK Henry	Priscillian of Avila
826447X	CHADWICK Henry	Boethius
8219393	COWDREY H.E.J.	The Age of Abbot Desiderius
8148992	DAVIES M.	Sophocles: Trachiniae
825301X	DOWNER L.	Leges Henrici Primi
814346X	DRONKE Peter	Medieval Latin and the Rise of European Love-Lyric
8142749	DUNBABIN T.J.	The Western Greeks
8154372	FAULKNER R.O.	The Ancient Egyptian Pyramid Texts
8221541	FLANAGAN Marie Therese	Irish Society, Anglo-Norman Settlers, Angevin Kingship
8143109	FRAENKEL Edward	Horace
8201540	GOLDBERG P.J.P.	Women, Work and Life Cycle in a Medieval Economy
8140215	GOTTSCHALK H.B.	Heraclides of Pontus
8266162	HANSON R.P.C.	Saint Patrick
8224354	HARRISS G.L.	King, Parliament and Public Finance in Medieval England to 1369
8581114	HEATH Sir Thomas	Aristarchus of Samos
8140444	HOLLIS A.S.	Callimachus: Hecale
8212968	HOLLISTER C. Warren	Anglo-Saxon Military Institutions
8223129	HURNARD Naomi	The King's Pardon for Homicide – before AD 1307
8140401	HUTCHINSON G.O.	Hellenistic Poetry
9240140	JOACHIM H.H.	Aristotle: On Coming-to-be and Passing-away
9240094	JONES A.H.M	Cities of the Eastern Roman Provinces
8142560	JONES A.H.M.	The Greek City
8218354	JONES Michael	Ducal Brittany 1364–1399
8271484	KNOX & PELCZYNSKI	Hegel's Political Writings
8225253	LE PATOUREL John	The Norman Empire
8212720	LENNARD Reginald	Rural England 1086–1135
8212321	LEVISON W.	England and the Continent in the 8th century
8148224	LIEBESCHUETZ J.H.W.G.	Continuity and Change in Roman Religion
8141378	LOBEL Edgar & PAGE Sir Denys	Poetarum Lesbiorum Fragmenta
9240159	LOEW E.A.	The Beneventan Script
8241445	LUKASIEWICZ, Jan	Aristotle's Syllogistic
8152442	MAAS P. & TRYPANIS C.A .	Sancti Romani Melodi Cantica
8142684	MARSDEN E.W.	Greek and Roman Artillery—Historical
8142692	MARSDEN E.W.	Greek and Roman Artillery—Technical
8148178	MATTHEWS John	Western Aristocracies and Imperial Court AD 364–425
8223447	McFARLANE K.B.	Lancastrian Kings and Lollard Knights
8226578	McFARLANE K.B.	The Nobility of Later Medieval England
8148100	MEIGGS Russell	Roman Ostia
8148402	MEIGGS Russell	Trees and Timber in the Ancient Mediterranean World
8142641	MILLER J. Innes	The Spice Trade of the Roman Empire
8147813	MOORHEAD John	Theoderic in Italy
8264259	MOORMAN John	A History of the Franciscan Order
8116020	OWEN A.L.	The Famous Druids
8131445	PALMER, L.R.	The Interpretation of Mycenaean Greek Texts
8143427	PFEIFFER R.	History of Classical Scholarship (vol 1)
8143648	PFEIFFER Rudolf	History of Classical Scholarship 1300–1850
8111649	PHEIFER J.D.	Old English Glosses in the Epinal-Erfurt Glossary
8142277	PICKARD–CAMBRIDGE A.W.	Dithyramb Tragedy and Comedy
8269765	PLATER & WHITE	Grammar of the Vulgate
8213891	PLUMMER Charles	Lives of Irish Saints (2 vols)
820695X	POWICKE Michael	Military Obligation in Medieval England
8269684	POWICKE Sir Maurice	Stephen Langton
821460X	POWICKE Sir Maurice	The Christian Life in the Middle Ages
8225369	PRAWER Joshua	Crusader Institutions
8225571	PRAWER Joshua	The History of The Jews in the Latin Kingdom of Jerusalem
8143249	RABY F.J.E.	A History of Christian Latin Poetry

8143257	RABY F.J.E.	A History of Secular Latin Poetry in the Middle Ages (2 vols)
8214316	RASHDALL & POWICKE	The Universities of Europe in the Middle Ages (3 vols)
8154488	REYMOND E.A.E & BARNS J.W.B.	Four Martyrdoms from the Pierpont Morgan Coptic Codices
8148380	RICKMAN Geoffrey	The Corn Supply of Ancient Rome
8141076	ROSS Sir David	Aristotle: Metaphysics (2 vols)
8141092	ROSS Sir David	Aristotle: Physics
8142307	ROSTOVTZEFF M.	Social and Economic History of the Hellenistic World, 3 vols.
8142315	ROSTOVTZEFF M.	Social and Economic History of the Roman Empire, 2 vols.
8264178	RUNCIMAN Sir Steven	The Eastern Schism
814833X	SALMON J.B.	Wealthy Corinth
8171587	SALZMAN L.F.	Building in England Down to 1540
8218362	SAYERS Jane E.	Papal Judges Delegate in the Province of Canterbury 1198–1254
8221657	SCHEIN Sylvia	Fideles Crucis
8148135	SHERWIN WHITE A.N.	The Roman Citizenship
9240167	SINGER Charles	Galen: On Anatomical Procedures
8113927	SISAM, Kenneth	Studies in the History of Old English Literature
8642040	SOUTER Alexander	A Glossary of Later Latin to 600 AD
8222254	SOUTHERN R.W.	Eadmer: Life of St. Anselm
8251408	SQUIBB G.	The High Court of Chivalry
8212011	STEVENSON & WHITELOCK	Asser's Life of King Alfred
8212011	SWEET Henry	A Second Anglo-Saxon Reader—Archaic and Dialectical
8148259	SYME Sir Ronald	History in Ovid
8143273	SYME Sir Ronald	Tacitus (2 vols)
8200951	THOMPSON Sally	Women Religious
8201745	WALKER Simon	The Lancastrian Affinity 1361–1399
8161115	WELLESZ Egon	A History of Byzantine Music and Hymnography
8140185	WEST M.L.	Greek Metre
8141696	WEST M.L.	Hesiod: Theogony
8148542	WEST M.L.	The Orphic Poems
8140053	WEST M.L.	Hesiod: Works & Days
8152663	WEST M.L.	Iambi et Elegi Graeci
822799X	WHITBY M. & M.	The History of Theophylact Simocatta
8206186	WILLIAMSON, E.W.	Letters of Osbert of Clare
8114877	WOOLF Rosemary	The English Religious Lyric in the Middle Ages
8119224	WRIGHT Joseph	Grammar of the Gothic Language